The Man Who Wrote *Aladdin*

Travellers in the Wider Levant
Hardinge Simpole Publishing

An Account of Japan, 1609
    Roderigo de Vivero
    9781843822240 2015

Barefoot Through Mauretania
    Odette du Puigaudeau
    9781843822011 2010

Embassy to Tamerlane, 1403-1406
    Ruy Gonzalez de Clavijo
    9781843821984 2009

Letters Written During a Ten Years' Residence
    at the Court of Tripoli, 1783-1795
    Miss Tully
    9781843821977 2008

The Curious and Amazing Adventures of Maria Ter Meetelen;
    Twelve Years a Slave (1731-43)
    Caroline Stone
    9781843822172 2010

The Story of My Life
    Fadhma Aith Mansour Amrouche
    9781843822165 2009

The Man Who Wrote *Aladdin*
The Life and Times of Hannā Diyāb

Translated by Paul Lunde

*with an Introduction and Notes
by Caroline Stone*

Hardinge Simpole

Published by:

Hardinge Simpole
An imprint of Zeticula Ltd
Unit 13
196 Rose Street
Edinburgh
EH2 4AT
Scotland
http://www.hardingesimpole.co.uk

First published in 2020

Text © Caroline E.M. Stone 2020
Cover design, adapted from an engraving by George Shaw
© Zeticula Ltd 2020

ISBN 978-1-84382-228-8 paperback

All rights reserved. No reproduction, copy or transmission of this publication may be made without prior written permission.

For Paul — with apologies:

et me post te vivere
mori sit assidue,
nec ad vitam anima
satis sit dimidia.

Foreword

When I first met Paul Lunde in the early 1970s, he was working on Arabic manuscripts in the Vatican Library, and especially on the Christian Arabic collection. One day he came home excited at having found a travel account by a Christian Arab, a priest from Mosul who visited the New World. Not long after, that document led him to the present work by the Aleppan Hannā Diyāb.

Originally, Paul's plan was to transcribe and edit the texts, and then to write in-depth on Christian Arabic vocabulary and usage, considering the ways in which it diverged from the standard Muslim Arabic of the region. He was also very interested in the Maronite community and in tracing the families of both these authors.

As Paul read passages to me and to his close friends, and saw that we found them fascinating and amusing, he decided to translate the two accounts. He also became determined — I would almost say obsessed — with tracking down every place and person mentioned, every unusual word or construction, and identifying every event in considerable detail.

Paul's project became a real treasure hunt and it gave us both great pleasure when he would come back from the Propaganda Fide, the Archivo General de Indias, or the University Library in Cambridge with another tessera to add to the mosaic. Unfortunately, though I listened entranced, I did not take careful note. All this took time, particularly against a background of earning a living, teaching, and writing commissioned articles and books, including translations of al-Mas'udi and Ibn Fadlan.

At a certain point, especially when the Vatican catalogues and manuscripts were being digitized, various friends, as well as myself, encouraged him to finish and publish, since it was obvious that sooner or later other scholars would come across the manuscripts and publish them. However — in spite of interest from more than one academic publisher — he continued to work in his own way, collecting the background details that fill dozens, probably close to a hundred, notebooks and files. Being, as he always was, extremely generous with his information and expertise, he happily shared his discoveries with anyone who was curious about his work.

I do not know why he decided not to publish — except, perhaps, that this research had come to feel like his own private garden, rather than a public space. I do not know whether he knew that "his" manuscripts had indeed been discovered and published. I imagine that he must have done, but he never mentioned it.

Paul Lunde died very suddenly in August, 2016 and there had been no occasion to discuss what he would like done with his books, papers or unfinished work. After a great deal of soul-searching, I have decided to publish his completed translations, beginning with Hannā Diyāb. I am not sure if it is what Paul would have wanted, but he was a fine scholar and an excellent translator, and the idea of the fruit of so much love and dedication ending up in the recycling bin seemed unbearable. On the other hand, it is hard to produce a very imperfect work on behalf of someone who was an absolute perfectionist.

I have not had the courage to go through his many notebooks to track down the numerous references (apart from the fact many of his notes are in Arabic) and reconstruct the story in detail — that task will fall to some future researcher. I have also not consulted anyone else's research on the subject, since I wanted this publication to reflect Paul's work as purely as possible.

What I have done is to annotate a few points, where I feel it would be useful or interesting, and I have tried to provide some orientation for the non-specialist reader in the introduction, in line with the other volumes in the *Travellers in the Wider Levant* series. The richness and breadth of learning — and humour — that Paul Lunde would have provided is, alas, impossible to emulate. I cannot stress enough that all errors in the following edition are mine, not his.

Finally, I would like to thank Donika Dimitrova, William Facey, Monika Kreile, Emma Loosely, Russell McGuirk and James Stone Lunde for their much appreciated help with specific problems.

Caroline Stone
Lucca, June 4th, 2019

Contents

Foreword	vii
Introduction	xiii
The Maronites	xiii
Consuls and the French Community in Aleppo	xvii
Hannā Diyāb as a Story-teller	xx
Paul Lucas (1664-1737)	xxiii
Clothing and Sumptuary Laws	xxv
Coinage and Numismatics	xxv
Mummia	xxvii
St George	xxix
Towers of Skulls	xxix
Slaves and Pirates	xxxi
Bombardment of Genoa — 1683	xxxii
The Clock at Lyons	xxxiv
The Sanctuary of Montenero	xxxv
Ambassadors	xxxv
The War of the Spanish Succession and *Le Grand Hiver*	xl
Antoine Galland and the Thousand and One Nights	xl
Melancholia	xlv
The Man Who Wrote Aladdin	**1**
Chapter I	3
Chapter II	17
My departure from Tripoli with Paul Lucas the Tourist in the month of February 1707	
Chapter III	23
My first sea voyage with M. Paul Lucas. May 1707	
Chapter IV	30
Our trip to Egypt, and what happened to us there. June 1707	
Chapter V	53
On our voyage to the Maghrib in the year 1708	
Chapter VI	94
Our voyage to France in 1708	

Chapter VII   131
    On Our Voyage to France
Chapter VIII   139
    On our trip from Provence through France, to the city of Paris
        Towards the End of 1708   193
        Antoine Galland   196
        The Story of Joseph the Jeweller   197
        Steven the Coffee Maker   201
        The Festival of St Michael   202
        The Story of Steven the Coffee Maker *Continued*   202
Chapter IX   219
    On Our Entry to the Lands of the East
        The Sights of Galata   226
        The Sublime Porte   226
        Arrival of the Venetian Ambassador   227
        Hannā enters the service of a Venetian merchant   229
        Launching five new warships   234
        Arrival of Eight French men warships   235
        A Swedish Prince arrives in Istanbul   236
        Departure from Istanbul   237

Notes   275
Appendix   292
Glossary   299
Hannā Diyāb Bibliography   302
Additional Bibliography (Caroline Stone)   306
Index   309

Illustrations

Beirut. From a print in *The Illustrated London News*	xiv
Wadi Qanoubine - Monks and pilgrims.	xiv
Frontispiece to *La Vie de Messire François Picquet, Consul de France à Alep*	xvi
Women in the harem.	xviii
The Citadel of Aleppo. From *Tour du Monde*	xviii
Frontispiece to Paul Lucas' *Travels*, Paris 1704	xix
Frontispiece to Vol. III of Galland's translation of *The Thousand and One Nights*, The Hague, 1706	xxi
Tripoli	xxi
English merchant, engraved from a painting	xxvi
Veiled Muslim women (Syrian left and European right).	xxvi
Copperplate print of Ottoman Costume	xxviii
Burj-Er-Roos - the Tower of Skulls	xxx
View of Tunis. Print published by P. van der Aa, Leyden	xxx
The Bombardment of Genoa by Duquesne.	xxxiii
Slave Market, engraving by Jan Luyken	xxxiii
Istanbul viewed from Pera	xxxvi
Great Avenue in the Tchartchi. Steel engraving	xxxvi
Istanbul. Drawing of Hagia Sophia, c.1876	xxxviii
Istanbul. View of the Hellespont	xxxviii
Le Grand Hiver. Contemporary woodblock print	xli
L'Anno Terribile 1709	xli
Portrait often said to be of Galland	xlii
Galland's diary. Page mentioning Paul Lucas	xliv
View of Afyonkarahisar (The Black Castle of Opium)	xlvi
The Church of St Sophia, Nicosia	xlvi
Taşköprü, the Great Bridge at Adana	274
The Tughra. or official signature, of Sultan Ahmed III	308

Introduction

Searching through Paul Lunde's (subsequently often PL) notes for the Introduction I knew he had written, I only succeeded in retrieving the first paragraph:

> Life at Versailles under Louis XIV was exhaustively — some might say, exhaustingly — chronicled by three remarkable memorialists. Best known of course are the inimitable memoirs of the duc de Saint Simon, one of the glories of French prose, filled with viciously satirical portraits of his fellow courtiers, most of whom he despised, as his social and intellectual inferiors. Saint Simon's compulsive readability has overshadowed the memoirs of two of his contemporaries, the marquis de Dangeau and the marquis de Sourches, whose sober, day by day, chronicles of court doings are much more reliable historical sources, devoid as they generally are of personal details or value judgements. They are, however, mind-bendingly boring.
>
> Not one of these three sources mentions the arrival of Paul Lucas, Hannā Diyāb, and their two jerboas at Versailles in the autumn of 1708, despite the sensation they caused.

What follows — not nearly as amusing as his would have been — is intended to clarify a few points that may be unfamiliar to the non-specialist reader, the sections arranged roughly in order of the topic's appearance in the text.

I have tried, insofar as possible, to retain Paul Lunde's transcription, reflecting Hannā Diyāb's (subsequently often Hannā) usage, rather than standard modern spelling.

The Maronites

The Syrian Maronite Church, centered in Lebanon, is in full communion with the Catholic Church, although self-governing and having a number of differences from the Church of Rome, since it follows the Antiochene rather than the Latin tradition. Historically, the Maronites spoke Aramaic — the language of Christ — and Syriac has remained the Maronite liturgical language.

The Maronite Church always had a strong tradition of monasticism for both men and women, going back to the 3rd century. St Maron is claimed as their founder, but there is

Beirut. From a print in *The Illustrated London News* 4.8.1860

Wadi Qanoubine - Monks and pilgrims. Anonymous hand-coloured print, mid-!9th c.

considerable debate about their origins. The ceaseless persecution, first by the Byzantines, on the grounds that they were heretical, then by the Arab invaders and later by the Druse, and in the 19th and early 20th centuries, by the Ottomans, who attempted genocide by famine, meant that the Maronite Monasteries tended to be heavily fortified, like the better known Greek Orthodox Monastery of St Catherine in Sinai.

They established themselves, both as hermits and in monastic communities, in the mountains of North Lebanon, especially the Qadisha Valley. Deir Qannoubine, where Hannā's story as we have it begins, is in the heart of the valley and was for centuries the seat of the Maronite Patriarch.

In part because of the founding of the Maronite College in Rome in 1584, the Maronites were, on the whole, receptive to the various waves of missionaries arriving from the Latin West, especially the Franciscans and the Jesuits. They were the Christian community in the Levant with the closest ties to Europe, above all Italy and France, Arabic speaking, yet Catholic; they made a natural bridge between East and West serving as an interface for merchants and other western travellers. Hence, it is not remarkable that Hannā should have known a number of Frenchmen, nor that he should have been in service with several of them before meeting Paul Lucas.

The Maronites, perhaps because of these contacts, also had a broader interest in education than some of the Oriental Churches. The first printing press in the Middle East was set up in 1610 at the Monastery of Qozhaya in the Qadisha Valkey, producing works in Arabic and Syriac. This, again, makes it unsurprising that Hannā should have been literate, although producing this kind of travel account, including so much autobiography, is very unusual in his culture.

About 1695, there was a major revival of Maronite monasticism initiated by a group of young men from Aleppo and it may be this movement which inspired Hannā (briefly) to become a monk. One of them, Germanus Farhat, may be the Prior Germanus mentioned by Hannā.

Frontispiece to *La Vie de Messire François Picquet, Consul de France à Alep*, by Charles-Léonce Anthelmy, Paris, 1732

Consuls and the French Community in Aleppo

The consular system was established by the republics of Venice and Genoa in the later Middle Ages and by Peter IV of Aragon from the 14th century, and it soon became a vital part of the Mediterranean trade network. The consuls dealt with both mercantile affairs and questions of navigation and, to a large extent, on-going diplomacy, since ambassadors were usually only sent to negotiate a specific issue and were not normally resident, except in Istanbul from the 16th century The consuls looked after merchants' interests, but also protected local Catholics and often intervened on behalf of minority groups who did not have a consulate of their own, for example the Sephardim.

The French consular network was originally organized by the Marseille Chamber of Commerce (1599). Subsequently, as its diplomatic potential came to be appreciated, it was increasingly taken over by the government, first by Colbert and then by Pontchartrain, as Hannā mentions. The consuls had a very wide, but legally undefined, brief. From 1681, however, they were given the right to judge cases relating to their co-nationals, as the scene at the lazzaretto of Livorno makes clear.

In 1715, the French had 56 consulates around the Mediterranean, the first having been founded at Tripoli in Syria. Consuls — not only the French — often had fine houses for reasons of national prestige, for example the Fondouk des Français in the medina of Tunis visited by Hannā, or Khan al-Banadiq — of the Venetians — and Souq Marcopoli of the hereditary Italian consuls in Aleppo. Not all countries were so generous, however, and a number of the British consuls, such as Mr. Tully at Tripoli in Libya, had reason to complain of their economic situation. This was particularly the case, since consuls were not supposed to engage in trade, something which may explain the secretiveness of certain of Paul Lucas' negotiations, in which his hosts were involved.

In general, however, consuls, like ambassadors, needed to show a certain level of wealth, since they were, in effect, showcasing their country's culture and products: clothing and arms, furniture and furnishings, textiles, luxury goods such as clocks, etc. The consuls

The Citadel of Aleppo. From *Tour du Monde*, an engraving by Edouard Charton, 1889

Women in the harem. From *The Natural History of Aleppo*, A and P Russell, 1794

VOYAGE
· DU SIEUR
PAUL LUCAS
AU LEVANT.

On y trouvera entr'autre une description de la haute Egypte, suivant le cours du Nil, depuis le Caire jusques aux Cataractes, avec une Carte exacte de ce fleuve, que personne n'avoit donnée.

PREMIER VOLUME.

A PARIS,
Chez GUILLAUME VANDIVE, Imprimeur
& Libraire ordinaire de Monseigneur le Dauphin,
ruë S. Jacques, au Dauphin couronné.

M. DCCIV.
Avec Privilege & Approbation.

Frontispiece to Paul Lucas' *Travels*, Paris 1704

themselves were originally from the country they represented, born and bred there, but as time went on, since language and local contacts were of the greatest importance, the post was often inherited, with consular dynasties, such as the Lemaire family mentioned by Hannā.

The consulates were not simply the residences of the consuls, but also often served as the place where merchants could store or deposit their goods. Some — such as Paul Lucas, who was travelling in an official capacity — were allowed to stay and in Hannā's account it is striking how they move largely from consulate to consulate, and how much more difficult their journey would have been without that option.

Although the European community in Aleppo was not large as a percentage of the total population, it was important financially and to some extent culturally, since the city was a major nexus in the trade between Europe and the Muslim world. At the beginning of the 18th century, families of consuls and merchants were generally not encouraged — although this was changing and there were exceptions, such as the Consul Lemaire at Tripoli, about whom Hannā tells the story of his little son Nicholas — with a result that the community was largely composed of adult men. The Maronites acted as a bridge, often providing interpreters, translators, guides and servants, as Hannā describes. It is not surprising, therefore, that he knew several and a good many are named in his account: MM. Bazan, Simon, Banfoy, Roux, Samatan, Ramuset, Chillon, Rimbaud, Duran, Sauron and others. Paul Lunde researched a number of them, but I have not been able to retrieve his notes; however some information may be found in Fournier (see Bibliography).

Hannā Diyāb as a Story-teller

Story-telling is a great Arab art form and it is unsurprising that Hannā Diyāb should not only have contributed to the canon of *The Thousand and One Nights*, but also shaped the narrative of his travels into a series of amusing and revealing anecdotes. This ability to set down events in striking and memorable form is found throughout Muslim Arabic writing from the *Hadith* or Traditions, relating to

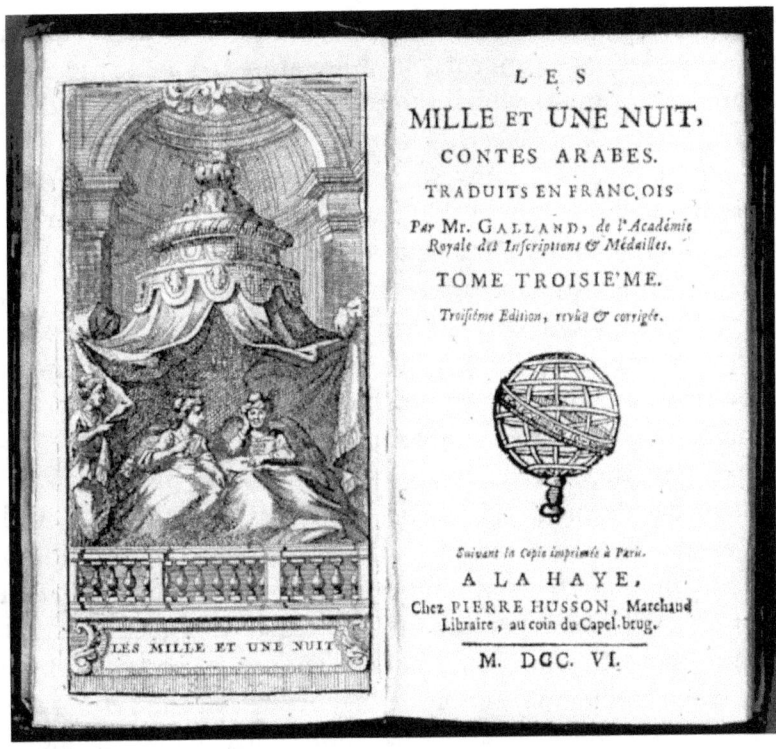

Frontispiece to Vol. III of Galland's translation of *The Thousand and One Nights*, The Hague, 1706

Tripoli

the life of the Prophet Muhammad, to the works of the historians, such as al-Mas'udi — and, of course, literature, including the telling of popular stories for which the professional *hakawātī* of Aleppo and Damascus were especially famous.

Many of Hannā Diyāb's stories are drawn from his personal experience and it is remarkable that set down fifty years later they should be so fresh and immediate — but, of course, there are other examples, even contemporary, such as the travels of Patrick Leigh-Fermor. Other tales have the form of traditional medieval legends: the Jew who bought the sun or the man who escaped hanging three times. The account of the founding of the great shrine of Montenero is told, almost unchanged, today.

Questions that inevitably spring to mind are why did Hannā suddenly decide, in old age, to write down his memoirs and why do they break off so very abruptly? The limited manuscript tradition and the unusual amount of personal information, particularly about his mother, suggest that the account was intended for family, possibly because some member was planning to travel to Europe. His sudden ending may simply be that he was old and getting tired — the last section feels somewhat more hurried and perfunctory than the earlier chapters.

Paul Lunde's translation was made from ms. Sbath 254, from the collection given by Paul Sbath to the Vatican Library in 1926, but he considered that the script was almost identical to that of ms. Sbath 109 and tried to see whether tracing scribes and authors would provide a clue to Hannā Diyāb's connections and possibly his intentions; however, no conclusions have come to light among his papers.

One endearing aspect of Hannā's anecdotes is the frankness with which he admits his indecision when confronted with a confusing and very alien world, and his timorousness. He often tells us that he was terrified or was about to faint with fear. Paul Lucas was, according to Hannā, even more cowardly, apt to run away and hide when faced with trouble. This is particularly amusing when compared with the braggadocio of his own account of events and, in all fairness, his decidedly adventurous past. "No man is a hero to his valet", as the saying goes, and while Hannā comments on this aspect of Lucas' character, as well as his temper and his dependence on wine, he clearly felt great respect for him and especially for his learning and medical skill, in which he believed absolutely uncritically, crediting him with almost miraculous powers.

It is fascinating to see Europe through the eyes of a foreigner and especially a Christian, who feels he should automatically approve of his co-religionaries, but often doesn't. On a number of occasions, Hannā finds that culture trumps religion, and he is, to a surprising degree, shocked by the cruelty and brutality he witnesses. Yet the Ottoman Empire was hardly gentle.

Many of his anecdotes set in Europe relate to these questions of cultural differences: the cleanliness of the inns in France — but the lack of lavatories; the art class drawing the crucifixion; the woman from the Levant afraid to go out unveiled, but languishing in deep depression in her home; the man who makes a fortune from the great novelty of the time: coffee. Then, there is the duplicity of Europeans, which he cannot work out, exactly paralleling the duplicity of the Levant, complained of by the Europeans. And, always, the terrible danger of travel, especially on the high seas, at the hands of both corsairs and a shifting range of political enemies.

Two aspects of Hannā's account that particularly interested Paul Lunde, and on which I am completely unable to comment, are the manuscript tradition, including tracing scribes within the Maronite community, and the peculiarities of Christian Arabic.

Paul Lucas (1664-1737)

Much of what is known of Paul Lucas and his travels comes from his various books. The picture he gives of himself is quite often at odds with the account by Hannā Diyāb, whom, by the way, Lucas never mentions. It is interesting to compare the occasions on which they describe the same incident: Lucas' version is much more dramatic and he is, of course, very much the hero. The incident at Livorno, related in his second volume of travels, is a case in point.

Paul Lucas originally set out for the Levant to trade in precious stones and in 1688 joined the Venetians and took part in the unsuccessful siege of Negroponte (Chalkis). He then captained a ship armed against the Turks. This is possibly where he met the corsair, Captain Bremond, and, perhaps, himself engaged in what was legalized piracy.

In 1696, he returned to France with a fine collection of coins and medals, as well as other antique pieces, which were acquired for the collection of Louis XIV — le Cabinet du Roi — and in 1699 made another buying trip to the Levant. In the following year, he set out on a very long journey, beginning with Egypt and then from Tripoli (Libya) by caravan to Baghdad, Baalbec, Damascus, Aleppo and, via Armenia, to Isfahan. As usual, he bought antiquities of various kinds, including many manuscripts, but they were pillaged by the Pasha of Baghdad's henchmen. He then headed back to Istanbul but, taking ship in 1702, was captured by Dutch corsairs and spent some time as a prisoner at Flushing.

Back in Paris in 1703, he published the first volume of his travels; and the next year the king appointed him his antiquary. In other words, he was licensed to travel and buy antiques for the royal collection, the consuls being required to advance funds and secure the shipping back to France, just as Hannā describes.

Lucas soon set off on another immensely long journey, in the course of which he met Hannā and took him with him to Paris. He set out on his third voyage in 1714 and it was probably then that he met up again with Hannā in Aleppo, although he also travelled to the Levant and Greece in 1723. In 1736, he decided to visit Spain in the hope of bringing back substantial quantities of Roman, Visigothic and Saracen antiquities. Philip V received him with enthusiasm and invited him to organize his collection. However, Lucas died at Madrid on May 12th, 1737.

Lucas' travel accounts were reprinted several times and translated into German. They were heavily "improved" by his editors, who added learned quotes and passages lifted from other sources — a common practice at the time and not seen as reprehensible. Antoine Galland had a low opinion of his work and stylistically it is undistinguished. Nevertheless, he includes an interesting account by M.Lemaire, the consul at Tripoli (Libya) mentioned by Hannā, based on original sources: *Mémoire pour server à l'histoire de Tunis depuis l'année 1684.* There is said to be an account of Lucas' last journey, still in manuscript.

See also the Appendix with notes on Paul Lucas by Charles de

Ferriol, the French ambassador to the Sublime Porte, with whom Hannā stayed briefly in Istanbul.

Clothing and Sumptuary Laws

From the very beginning, when Hannā decides not to become a monk, in part because he hates the habit, clothes are a major concern and often mentioned. Dress was very strictly regulated in the Ottoman Empire with different colours and materials for head-coverings, sashes, etc. being indicative of faith and rank. The type of turban permitted to a given individual was particularly accurately determined. The norms varied with time and place, but Jews were generally required to wear a yellow badge or sash (something re-imposed, incidentally, by the Taliban), while Christians wore blue, and so on. Hence a white sash (Muslim) would serve to disguise a Christian like Hannā in casual contact. Bright green was (and is) indication of a *Sharif*, or descendant of the Prophet Muhammad, and for a Christian to wear it (or certain luxury materials) would have given the gravest offence and could well have resulted in being lynched. Certain shapes and styles of headdress were also associated with particular ranks or professions. These sumptuary laws explain the problems of dress that Hannā was to encounter on his travels.

Conversely, Europe was fascinated by the exotic. Hence, Paul Lucas telling Hannā to bring his best clothes to wear at court — which was to make trouble of a different kind. Textiles were, as always, very major items of trade and Aleppo was an important center of silk production, so it is hardly surprising that Hannā was even more interested in them than most. Indeed, he went on to become a cloth merchant, trading in the broadcloth that was one of the major English exports to the Levant, being in standard use for everyday clothing and for the military.

Coinage and Numismatics

Hannā mentions a very large number of different coinages in the course of his narrative: *uthmānī, para, jadīd, fals, real, thaler, escudo, ducat, écu, dirham, jarq, sou, šahiyyāt*, etc. This is in itself interesting and shows the difficulties faced by merchants having to deal with multiple currencies with widely fluctuating values. Numismatics

English merchant, engraved from a painting by Jean Etienne Liotard, mid 18th c.

Veiled Muslim women (Syrian left and European right). The rather crude prints from an Italian Encyclopedia are apparently copying Cesare Vecellio's work *De gli habiti antichi et moderni di diversi parti del mondo*, 1590-99

being a complicated and technical field, very much one for the specialist, I have not attempted to give values to most of the coins. It is usually clear whether a large or small sum is intended.

Because coins had an actual bullion value, rather than being symbolic as today, they travelled widely and the preferred currency was often not that of the country. The Spanish *peso*, dollar, or piece of eight became an international currency from 1497, much in demand in China and elsewhere in the East, while the Maria Theresa *thaler*, always dated 1780, no matter when it was minted, was the preferred coin in the Gulf until the mid-20th century.

From his youth, Louis XIV had a passion for numismatics and had one of the most outstanding collections of all time. It was a fashion that swept Europe in the 17th century — Christina of Sweden was another avid collector. His original purchasing agent was Jean Foy-Vaillant (1632-1706) who, like Paul Lucas, travelled widely, not only in Europe, but also in Egypt and Persia, searching for coins and medals, and suffered even worse misadventures. As was so common for travellers at the time, he was captured and enslaved on his second voyage in 1674 and only freed at the request of the Dey of Algiers. Paul Lucas' first major collecting expedition was in 1696, when Foy-Vaillant had largely given up travelling.

Mummia

The widespread fashion for oriental exotica was relatively new, but the trade in mummies, as curiosities, and above all for the bitumen obtained from them and used as a drug, went back at least to the 9th century. and probably before. It was still very active at this period, although the medicinal efficacy of *mummia* was already much in question. The naturalist, Pierre Belon, in the first half of the 16th century, considered it valueless and probably dangerous, and thought its use was the result of misunderstanding Arab medical texts. Mummies were also sought after for the brown pigment obtained from them well into the 19th century. The export of mummies was banned by the Egyptian authorities in the 16th century, which, of course, led — as here — to a great deal of smuggling and fraud.

Ottoman Costume. Copperplate print from *Description de l'Univers* by Allain Manesson Mallet, Paris 1683

In 1717, a mummy (presumably a different one from Hannā's, as it was in an elaborate case), bought some years earlier for Louis XIV as a present to Charles XII of Sweden, who had a passion for archaeology, was arrested. The Ottoman authorities were under the impression that it was the body of the last Christian Emperor of Constantinople and that it was going to be used for magic against the Ottoman state. Lady Mary Wortley Montague, the wife of the English ambassador at the time, was more than scathing.

Eighty years later, the French diplomat, François Pouqueville was in the same prison as the mummy — still under arrest — and managed to steal the head.

St George

Although, he was shown the cave in Beirut where the monster lurked, rather surprisingly Hannā seems not to have been taken to the usual place where, according to tradition, St George slew the dragon. This may have been because the building was at the time a mosque — it changed affiliation repeatedly. Until recently, the actual spot was marked by a white marble column allegedly set up by the Empress Helena, who died in 327. St George was much venerated across the Levant, the Balkans, where he had great appeal as a warrior saint, Ethiopia, whose patron he is, and Kerala. His cult is thought to have reached England in the wake of the Crusades and he was made its patron by Edward III in 1350.

He was also revered by the Muslims, who identified him with al-Khidr, the Verdant One, mentioned in the Qur'an. His tomb was believed to be in the mosque of Nabi Jurjis (the Prophet George) at Mosul, which was restored by Timur in the 14th century, but destroyed in July 2014 by ISIS. The cult of St George is thought to have even deeper roots, perhaps going back to the classical legends of Adonis and, even into the 20th century, about his feast day — April 23rd — the women of various faiths would pick wild red anemones, known locally as Blood of Adonis, and throw them into the waters of the Dog River near Beirut, making petitions to the Saint.

Towers of Skulls

Borj er-Rous — the Tower of Skulls — was built from the bones of the troops killed in the disastrous battle of Djerba, where

Burj-Er-Roos - the Tower of Skulls - at Houmt Soukh, Djerba. Steel engraving by E. Benjamin from *The Shores and Islands of The Mediterranean*, by Sir Grenville Temple, London, 1840

View of Tunis. Print published by P. van der Aa, Leyden c.1725

a European coalition lost to the great Ottoman naval commander Turgut Reis (Dragut) in July 1560. The tower was c. 10m/34ft. at the base and contained the skulls of several thousand Christians. It was removed in 1848 and an obelisk to record the site was later built by the French. Towers of skulls were a Turco-Mongol custom — Timur built at least 28 of them according to an eye-witness — and one, again built by the Ottomans in 1809, survives at Niš in Serbia. It is interesting that Hannā was so horrified, as he was to be again by Christian brutalities in Europe.

Slaves and Pirates

Barbary pirates, often authorized by the Ottoman government, hence technically corsairs, raided for white slaves and harassed shipping for prizes and, again, slaves for sale or ransom. This created a major problem for all maritime travellers, fishermen and coastal communities, until the colonization of North Africa by the French in the early 19th century The danger was compounded by the corsairs from various European nations preying on the countries with which they were at war, again, very frequently, with a religious subtext: Protestant versus Catholic, etc. Christians captured by fellow Christians were not typically sold in the Muslim slave markets, but they frequently found themselves in the galleys in the conditions that so shocked Hannā.

The fear expressed at any sighting of an unidentified ship was completely rational. A number of accounts have survived both by slaves who ended, like Cervantes, in the *bagnios* of North Africa and were eventually ransomed — see the account of Maria ter Meetelen for an extensive bibliography — and by men condemned to the galleys. Those with specialist skills, or who caught the eye of an important man, as Hannā describes, had no chance of ever regaining their freedom, and those who were sent for sale to the slave markets of Istanbul were almost inevitably lost forever. And, of course, for boys and youths, there was the spectre of castration which, if they survived, would vastly enhance their value.

Piracy and slaving were largely economic ventures, as Paul Lucas' very dubious relationship with Captain Bremond makes clear. In the case of the Muslim corsairs, the fact that it could be considered a form of *jihad* and so was actively encouraged, was an added stimulus. At certain periods the Knights of Rhodes, and later of Malta, made the same claim — but their slaving was always on a very small scale compared to that of the Muslims. Nevertheless, one of the subjects that the first Ottoman ambassador to France wished to discuss was the liberation of a small number of his fellow janissaries, who had been captured by the Knights. The question of slaving, incidentally, was also a topic raised by the Moroccan ambassador, Abdallah ben Aisha, on his visit to Louis XIV in 1699.

Bombardment of Genoa — 1683 *(from PL)*

Louis XIV dispatched the French fleet against Genoa for having provisioned and fitted out four galleys for Spain, with whom, as usual, he was at war. Genoa was the port of entry for the Duchy of Milan, then under Spanish rule, and therefore also allied with the Hapsburgs in their wars against France. Not only had they provided military aid to an enemy of France, but the French ambassador in Genoa, François Pidou de Saint-Olon — previously ambassador to Morocco, on which he wrote a book — had been ill-treated and insulted by the doge. Although Hannā says the *cause de guerre* was the defilement of the ambassador's palace, and hence the Sun King's person, his account seems to be apocryphal, although far from unlikely. The Genoese had no reason to respect the French, who were their economic and maritime rivals.

The French retaliation, however, was out of all proportion to the offence. Between 17 and 22 May, 1683, the French admiral Abraham Duquesne, fresh from attacks on the corsairs of Tripoli and Algiers, bombarded the Arsenal and the city with some 14,000 cannon balls and the newly invented exploding mortar shells, which he had already employed against the North Africans, with devastating effect. More than half the city of Genoa was destroyed and thousands were killed.

These exploding shells were manufactured at foundries in Provence, which John Locke visited on his journey through France and enthusiastically described. The bombardments of Algiers and Genoa marked the beginning of modern naval warfare.

The Bombardment of Genoa by Duquesne. Print by Beaulieu le Donjon, 1884

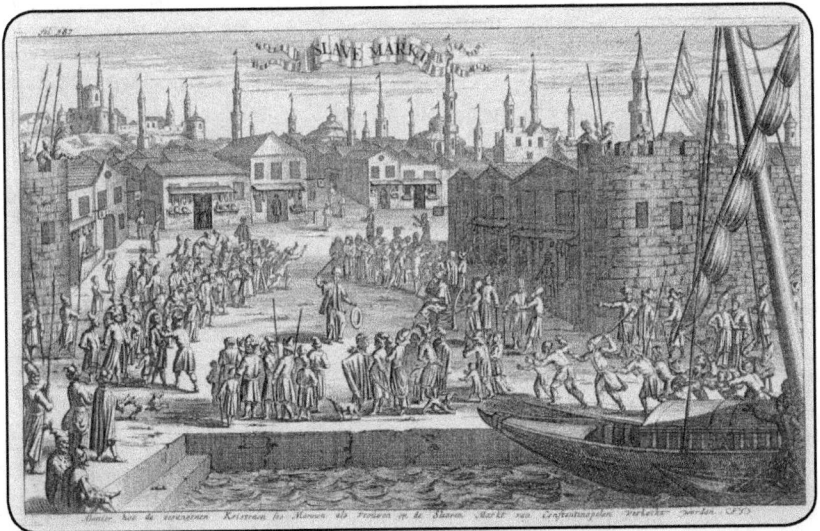

Slave Market, engraving by Jan Luyken. From Pierre Dan, *History van Barbayren*, Amsterdam, 1684

Genoa, like Venice, was a republican oligarchy, ruled by a doge and a senate composed of prominent citizens. The term of office of each doge was limited to two years, and during this period he was forbidden by law from leaving the city. The doge at the time of the French bombing was Luca Maria Invrea, but the humiliating task of journeying to Paris and abasing himself before the French king, as Louis XIV demanded, fell to his successor, Francesco Maria Lercari Imperiale.

Accompanied by senators Tomelin, Zaribardi, Durasso and Saluogo, the doge left Genoa in the Spring of 1685. The party reached Paris on April 18th, but were forced to wait in Paris almost a month before being received at Versailles. The king formally received them in the Hall of Mirrors on May 15th. The doge was forced to bow before the king and make a public apology, after which they were shown everything that might most impress them, were loaded with presents and allowed to return home on May 26th. Genoa was to remain within the French sphere of influence for more than a hundred years.

The Clock at Lyons

There has been an astronomical clock on the Cathedral since 1383, but this one dates essentially from 1661. The blinding of skilled craftsmen, so that they cannot repeat their masterpiece, is a common topos, generally urban legend.

Paul Lunde comments that John Locke, on 23 Dec., 1675, reports:

> "We saw St John's Church, the Cathedrall of the place, a very plain, ordinary building, & had noe thing in it very observable but the clock, which they say cost 200,000 livres. It hath many motions, but I had not time to observe them all accurately. There is a minute hand moves round in an hower, & the minutes are marked out in it in equall spaces on an oval, not a circle, & both ends of the hand keepe stil even with the inner line that describes the oval, shortening & lengthening stil as they approach the lesse or greater axis of the oval, & the end of every hower a cock that stands on top of all, claps his wings & crows. Then an angel comes out of a little door & visits the Virgin. She bows. A dove descends,

& the image of an old man, designed for the Father, shakes his hand. This is what is most looked at, but of least moment, there being other things far more considerable in it, as the place of the sun, the dominical letter, Epact, golden number, moveable feasts, etc, and other things of an almanac for almost an hundred years to come."

John Locke's Travels in France 1675-1679. New York & London: Garland Publishing, 1984. p. 6.

The Sanctuary of Montenero

The story of the founding of the Shrine of Our Lady of Grace at Montenero is told today in almost exactly the same words as Hannā reports it. The discovery of the ikon, the greatest treasure of the Sanctuary, in 1345, led to the almost immediate creation of the shrine. The monastery was greatly extended in the 18th century and so what Hannā would have seen would have been more modest than what is there today. The Sanctuary still has one of the largest known collections of votive offerings. It was not, unfortunately, possible to reproduce the one mentioned by Hannā, but very similar images of the same date relating to the sea are to be found — confusingly — in Montenegro and elsewhere.

Ambassadors

Hannā was, coincidentally, witness to a very important moment in the development of Ottoman-European diplomatic relations. The ambassador in whose house Hannā stayed briefly was Charles de Ferriol (1652-1722). (See Appendix for various notes on Ferriol and his comments on Paul Lucas.)

The Marquis de Ferriol was responsible for bringing the Flemish painter, Jean-Baptiste Vanmour, with him to Istanbul in 1699. Very little is known about Vanmour, but he appears to have lived there until his death in 1737. He painted hundreds of pictures, many of them commemorating ambassadors' audiences with the Sultan or the Grand Vizier. These include one of Ferriol's presentation to Sultan Mustafa II on his first arrival in the capital — although not, of course, the occasion described by Hannā on which he was refused admission, because of his insistence on wearing his sword. This led to his being recalled.

Istanbul viewed from Pera. Mid-late 19th century print

Great Avenue in the Tchartchi. Steel engraving by H.Griffiths after a picture by W.H.Bartlett, published in *The Bosphorus & the Danube*, 1850

In 1707, Ferriol commissioned Vanmour to paint a hundred pictures of the different officials and nationalities of the city, which he subsequently had engraved in a volume and published under the title: *Recueil de cent estampes représentant différentes nations du Levant (1712-13)*. The work was immediately translated into English, German, Spanish and Italian. It was an important source for a visual appreciation of the Ottoman world and, together with his paintings, give a very accurate picture of the people and scenes that Hannā describes.

Sometime before the period of Hannā's visit, Ferriol had bought a Circassian slave, Charlotte Aissé (1694-1773), as a child, for 1500 silver *livres*. Charlotte was raised by his sister-in-law and her romantic story, naturally, brought her much attention. Very beautiful, she was courted and resisted the attentions of Philip II, Duc d'Orléans. Her *Letters* were later edited by Voltaire.

A new ambassador to the Sublime Porte, into whose service Hannā Diyāb might well have entered if things had gone a little differently, was Jean-Louis d'Usson, Marquis de Bonnac, who held the post from 1716-24.

The Ottomans, secure in their sense of cultural superiority, up until this point had shown very little curiosity about the West, except as a military opponent and a source of certain desirable commodities, among them war materiel and expertise, and white slaves. However, the Battle of Vienna in 1683 and their subsequent loss of territory in Hungary and the Balkans caused them to review their opinion of the Christian West.

The Sublime Porte had always felt it beneath Ottoman dignity to send ambassadors to Christian lands, although envoys had been dispatched to negotiate practical matters on a number of occasions. As a result, when Ahmed III decided to send an ambassador to France, there was a great deal of speculation on both sides as to the reason.

On paper, he was to discuss repairs to the dome of the Church of the Holy Sepulchre and the raiding activities of the Knights of Malta, but probably his real mission was to try to learn how a society, always perceived as inferior, actually functioned and, above all, to find out as much as much as possible about the West's technology.

Istanbul. Drawing of Hagia Sophia, c.1876

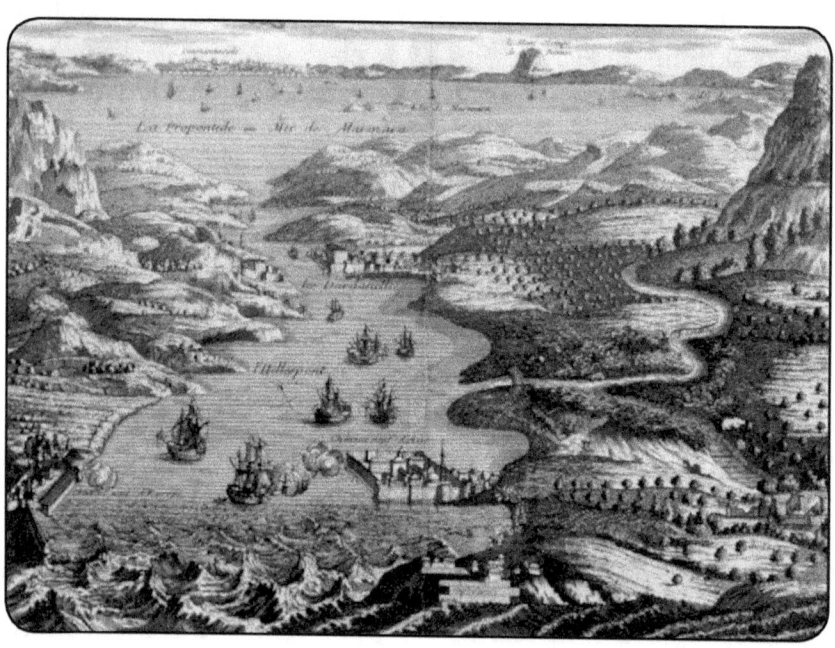

Istanbul. View of the Hellespont, Claude Duflos, 1747

The French government was unenthusiastic about the proposed visit of an Ottoman ambassador. The previous official visitor from the Sublime Porte in 1669, Süleyman Ağa, had turned out to be a low-ranking envoy, masquerading as an ambassador and his visit was generally disastrous — although it did give rise to some of the most famous scenes in Molière's comedy, *Le Bourgeois Gentilhomme*.

This time, in the first place, there was no pressing political need for him to come; secondly, it would be vastly expensive at a moment when the exchequer was empty and, thirdly, the plague was raging in the Marseille region, greatly complicating the ambassador's progress. There was, furthermore, the influence of Hannā's ambassador, the Conte de Ferriol, who had much resented being recalled from Istanbul and greatly wished to return. He suggested refusing the Ottoman proposal and sending instead a high profile French embassy, led by himself. This suggestion might well have been adopted, but before the French had come to any conclusion, the Ottoman ambassador, Mehmed Efendi, was on his way.

Mehmed Efendi, about 50 at the time of the embassy, had risen high in the ranks of the janissaries and had been entrusted with a number of diplomatic missions. Although shackled by protocol, he travelled with his son Sâi'd Efendi, who had much greater freedom to observe and report. In the course of time, he would go to Sweden as ambassador, following on Charles XII's period of exile in Istanbul, mentioned by Hannā, and be appointed Grand Vizier.

On Mehmed Efendi's return, he wrote an account of his travels. It was quite widely diffused thanks to the printing press, the first Muslim press in Ottoman lands, established with his son in 1727. Seventeen titles were published, including his account, before the 'Ulamā forced the closure of the press. His *Relation* was influential in creating a fashion for France in Istanbul, which paralleled the *orientaliste* taste that was developing in Western Europe at the same period. More importantly, it showed his great and active curiosity regarding Western science and technology (probably the real reason why he was sent). A tactfully edited version of his account was translated into French by the young Julien-Claude Galland in 1725 and was similarly well-received in the West.

The War of the Spanish Succession and *Le Grand Hiver*

Hannā Diyāb visited Paris at a particularly bad moment. Since 1701, the country had been embroiled in the War of the Spanish Succession, with the Bourbons of France and Spain against the Hapsburgs, the Protestant Netherlands, Britain and Prussia. Although France was not the worst affected, exhaustion and impoverishment were setting in and 1708 had not been a good year militarily. The battle of Malplaquet, on 11th September, 1709, was technically lost by the French, but there were many dead on both sides and during the period leading up to the battle, the war situation became increasingly complicated, with conflict also spreading to the colonies.

Hannā's description of what was known as *le Grand Hiver* is no exaggeration. It came at the tail end of the "Little Ice Age", its effect perhaps heightened by the eruptions of Fuji and Vesuvius, which propelled vast quantities of matter into the atmosphere. Numerous contemporary accounts support him, including that of the Duchess of Orléans, who speaks in a letter of 24,000 people dying of cold in Paris. The effect on the crops was disastrous and led to famine, which in turn resulted in high mortality from the plague that was just beginning to gather strength in Northern Europe. Hence the ships that Hannā mentions, which had been sent out to try and buy corn, wherever it could be found. An estimated 600,000 died across the country that winter from cold, hunger and disease, and the repercussions on agriculture would be felt for more than a decade, because of the loss of olive and fruit trees.

Antoine Galland and the Thousand and One Nights

Antoine Galland (1646-1715) is best known as the first translator of *The Thousand and One Nights*, on which there is an extensive bibliography. Having discovered and translated a manuscript of *Sindbad the Sailor* in Istanbul during the 1690s, which had a certain success, he went on to translate more stories from a 14th century Syrian ms. of the work. Hannā was introduced to him during his time in Paris, as Galland relates in his diary and Hannā in his autobiography, and told him a further 14 stories, several of which

Le Grand Hiver. Contemporary woodblock print, anonymous c. 1709

L'Anno Terribile 1709 Contemporary engraving by Giuseppe Maria Mitelli.

Portrait often said to be of Galland - of whom no reliable likeness is known - but probably of the famous traveller and scholar Jean de Thévenot, nephew of Melchisédech Thévenot, mentioned by Hannā. Philippe de Champagne c.1660-3

he used, including — apparently — some of the most famous, such as *Aladdin* and *Ali Baba and the Forty Thieves*. Hannā's sources for these are unknown. Were they simply part of the local oral tradition, told him by his mother or his nurse? Or did he hear them from the professional story tellers — *hakawātī* — that were so much a feature of Middle Eastern popular culture and still existed in Syria until the present war? Their mss. were working copies, often dirty and worn, and these particular stories might not have made their way into more elegant compilations and hence survived only at street level. Did he and/or Galland make them up? Hannā Diyāb was a good story-teller, but that seems unlikely. It remains a mystery. Paul Lunde did not resolve it, although he produced the following chronology from Galland's diaries:

25 October 1708 — Meets Hannā for first time(?)
17 March 1709 — Comments that Hannā is *fort cultivé*
25 March — Galland says Hannā tells good stories and promises to write them down
4 May — Hannā begins *Aladdin*
5 May — Hannā finishes *Aladdin*
6 May — *Qamr al-Din* and *Badr al-Budur* (from this day on Galland takes notes)
10 May — Hannā begins the *Adventures of Harun al-Rachid*, cycle composed of three stories, *The Blind Baba Abdalla*, *Sidi Nu'man* and *Cogia Hassan Alhabbal*. Cycle completed 29 May (sic).
13 May — *The Enchanted Horse*
15 May — *The City of Gold*
25 May — *Two Jealous Sisters* [The date must be wrong!]
22 May — *Prince Ahmad and the Fairy*
23 May — *Sultan of Samarkand*
27 May — *The Ten Wazirs* and *Ali Baba*
28 May — *Ali Cogia Merchant of Baghdad*
31 May — *Hassan, seller of Ptisane*

Galland was not simply the translator of the *The Thousand and One Nights*. He was an important scholar, whose work added a great deal to the West's knowledge and understanding of the Islamic world. He made several prolonged trips to the Levant, in the course of which he added Arabic, Turkish and Persian to

Galland's diary. Page mentioning Paul Lucas, March 17th, 1709

Greek, which he had learned earlier. In 1679, he was commissioned to travel and acquire antiquities, especially coins, for Colbert and when that contract ended, he was appointed antiquary to Louis XIV and continued to collect on the king's behalf. On his return to France, he worked with Melchisédech Thévenot, scientist, cartographer and collector of travel accounts, who was also the Keeper of the Royal Library. His career set a pattern for men, such as Paul Lucas, who hoped for remunerative commissions travelling for the king, followed by an appointment of the kind described in Hannā Diyāb's account.

Melancholia

Accounts of mental illness in the past are interesting and clearly Hannā's mother was suffering from severe depression. As Paul Lunde points out, Paul Lucas' cure is strictly in line with what was recommended at the time. Richard Burton and the Sevillian physician, Nicolás Monardes, for example, were convinced of the value of certain stones worn as remedies for disease, mental as well as physical. This adds an extra dimension to Lucas' collecting. Burton tells us in his very popular work, *The Anatomy of Melancholy*:

> "Granatus a pretious stone so called, because it is like the kernels of a pomegranate, an unperfect kind of Ruby, it comes from Calicut, if hung about the neck, or taken in drinke, it much resisteth sorrow, and recreats (sic) the heart. The same properties I find ascribed to the Jacinth and Topaze, they allay anger, griefe, diminish madnesse, much delight and exhilarate the minde."
> [p. 219, Part 2.Section 2]

Again, he mentions "Chalcidonye" — probably the stone the name of which Hannā transliterates from the Italian:
> "There is a kinde of Onyx called a Chalcidonye, which hath the same qualities, avails much against phantasticke illusions which proceed from melancholy, preserves the vigour and good estate of the whole body." [p. 220, ibid]

Caroline Stone,
Bath, August 9th, 2019

View of Afyonkarahisar (The Black Castle of Opium). From a 19th c. postcard

The Church of St Sophia, Nicosia (13th c.) from *Through Cyprus* by Agnes Smith *(Lewis)*, 1887; now the Selemiya Mosque

The Man Who Wrote *Aladdin*

Chapter I

[The first nine pages of the manuscript are lost. They presumably dealt with Hannā's family and life in Aleppo before he made the decision to join the monastery of Qannoubine [1] in the Lebanese mountains.]

We passed the night in the guest house until dawn. After mass, the prior summoned us to his cell. When we had kissed his hands, he welcomed us and bade us sit. Then he asked us if we intended to become monks. We told him that this had been our wish since long before our departure from Aleppo. Then he said to us: "May God bless you and bless your intention! You have now been in our monastery for four days, and are familiar with our way of life and our rule. Now you must go on retreat for three days, and each of you must examine his conscience and prepare to make a full confession and receive the Holy Sacraments. Then at last you may don the habit of the novice and follow the rule for monks set out in this pamphlet." He gave each of us a pamphlet and told us to study it, then summoned the director of the monastery, Yūsuf al-Mabūdī, and told him to give each of us a cell. Then he blessed us and consigned us to Yūsuf's care, who gave us each a key to his locker and his cell and a prayer book.

We spent three days in retreat. The prior appointed a priest to guide us and instruct us in spiritual matters. When the three days were up, we each made a full confession and received the Holy Sacraments, that is, the Eucharist. The director of the monastery then took us to the monk's wardroom. First of all, he handed me a shirt and underclothes and a thick rough gown, a robe of black wool, a padded belt, a turban cap and two turban lengths of brown wool and black Tarīsī sandals.

Then the director said to me: "Strip, O my brother, and we will dress you in the angelic habit of the monk!" So I took off my fine clothes and put on that thick rough shirt and the other things. Over them I donned the heavy coarse robe and girded on the belt. I looked like a lemon vendor, with my breast pockets stuffed with my wares. I took off my turban sash and *kavuk* [2] and put on the black cap and wrapped the brown woollen sash around it and put on the sandals. Then I regarded myself, and decided I looked absolutely frightful.

From that moment, I rejected the monastic life in my heart and regretted what I had done. Pride, however, prevented me from showing my feelings. Then my companion dressed just as I had done. The director let us go at last, and we departed. All the monks and novices came and blessed us and rejoiced on our acceptance to the novitiate.

We then retired to our cells until the bell announcing lunch was rung and we went to the refectory. The prior and the monks showed us where to stand. Then he came in and sat at the head of the table and the priests followed him, each seating himself in his place. Then the monks entered and took their seats. The novices remained standing. After a little while, the prior gave permission for them to come forward. So we did so, and each of us took his place, that is, the older sat above the younger. They brought three courses to table. The first was a stew of lentils and wheat mixed with other kinds of grain and similar dishes made of grain and vegetables. The second was cheese and the third figs preserved in honey. Between every two monks stood a jar of wine and a mug, and everyone drank as much as he liked and was able to hold.

Stacked on shelves above the table were the skulls of former monks. Each skull had the name of its owner written on it. At a high place at the end of the table sat a monk, who read aloud the lives of the martyrs and the horrible, unbearable tortures they endured, as everyone knows. When I saw and heard these things I was horrified, and lost my appetite for food and drink.

The prior finally noticed that everyone had stopped eating and rose from his place. Everyone rose with him and recited grace and left the table. Then the cook and the monk who had been reading sat down and ate. The prior and all the monks then passed through the gate of the monastery to a place like a cloister. Some sat down, others walked about, conversing of holy things. They stayed there for half an hour. Then everyone went to the task assigned him by the prior, that is, the tailor to his sewing, the shoemaker to his shoes, the scribe to his scriptorium, the gardener to his garden, and the various similar tasks required by the monastery. You never saw anyone idle in that monastery.

In the evening after vespers the dinner bell was rung. After dinner they gathered once more in the previously mentioned cloister and strolled about as was the custom. Afterwards, everyone entered the church to pray privately. Finally, the prior entered his cell. One by one, everyone went in to confess his thoughts. This was not a confession, but a kind of guidance, so that the prior could judge whether our thoughts proceeded from Satan or from the promptings of the Holy Spirit or were inspired by one of the angels. Then he would guide him and lay bare the artifices of the cunning Devil. And if he found evidence of sin, he would order him to confess fully before sleeping. So in this way the monk and the novice could sleep in complete comfort and security. After everyone had gone in to the prior and come out again, they kept silence, no one speaking to his companion until early the next day.

Finally, whoever wished could go to their cell, while those who preferred to stroll in the monastery could do so. Then everyone returned to their cells to sleep. At exactly midnight the sexton made the rounds of the cells carrying a bell to summon the monks and novices to the midnight prayer. All the monks and novices and the prior gathered in the church to perform the midnight prayers, which lasted an hour or a little less. Then they returned to their cells and slept until daybreak, when a big bell was struck to announce the dawn prayer. After the prayer was over, masses began. Everyone attended mass and then went to his appointed task without eating until sext, an hour before noon, when a bell was rung to announce lunch, as we have said.

Every monk and novice was required to confess and take communion every week. Among the novices was a striking, venerable individual, tall, mustachioed, with a white beard. I asked one of the monks about this man, what his age was, and how someone so old could have entered the monastic life and still be only a novice.

The monk said to me:

"If you ask about this man, O my brother, he was once the owner of an estate and a dispenser of bread. Every night he welcomed twenty guests or more to his table. He has seven married sons and married daughters as well. Then he and his wife decided to reject the world and pass the remainder of their lives in monastic orders. With joy, his wife entered a convent, and three years ago he came to this monastery. He went to our father, the prior Germanus, and asked him if he could become a monk. When the prior heard these words, he was astonished and said: "O my brother, you have given the flower of your life to the world and now, towards the end of your life, you wish to give your old age to the monastic life?"

Our prior said this in order to test his determination. The remarkable old man replied, "Perhaps God will accept me, even in the eleventh hour, father!" And he continued to insist and beseech the prior until he took pity on him and said: "My brother, I cannot let you enter the monastery and enroll you with the monks until I have tested your determination." The old man said to him: "Do with me as you wish!" Then the prior said to him: "You must remain outside the monastery and not associate with the monks for as long as our Lord wills."

The old man agreed, saying, "You have commanded me, my father, and I will obey your orders!" When the prior saw his determination, he ordered him to stay within the gate of the lower monastery as gatekeeper. "I hear and I obey", replied the old man. Outside the gate was a little house, like a hut. He spent three years in that little house, enduring the cold of winter and the heat of summer patiently and without complaint, content with a few scraps of food left over from the monastery table. When the monks and priests saw the patience and steadfastness of this man, they beseeched our father the prior to let him enter the monastery and join the novices. He accepted their petition and allowed him to enter and clothed him in the garb of a novice. He has now spent three months in the novitiate. So this is his story and the explanation for his presence.

When I heard the story of this man from the monk, I was astonished, and filled with misgivings and unsettling emotions. One day we entered the refectory to eat as usual and after the prior and the monks had come to the table and everyone had taken their seats, the prior gave permission to the novices to enter, and we did so. When that remarkable man tried to come in too, however, the prior reprimanded him and forbade him to enter. So he went outside and stood with his hands folded and his head bent. He remained in that posture until the monks had finished eating.

The prior then got up from the table and drew near him, frowning and angry. The old man prostrated himself on the ground at his feet. The prior began to upbraid and curse him, saying "You foolish, shameless old man!" Then he began to mock him. And watch out when a poet decides to mock somebody! After he had spattered him with detestable words, he kicked him and said, "Get up, you scoundrel, and eat with the cook!" He immediately got up and kissed the prior's hand, begging his pardon and forgiveness in front of all the monks and novices. Then he went to the table to eat with the cook.

We went out to the usual place to promenade. As for me, when I saw this terrible thing, I was appalled, and said to myself: "If the prior behaves with such severity to a venerable old man like this, what will happen to me if I commit a fault? What harshness will he use against me?" I continued to think about this until evening and was very downcast. When the time came to reveal our thoughts, I went in to do so, as was customary. The first thing I said to the prior was: "I have been thinking of you all day, father, and the harshness with which you treated that venerable man. I have blamed you in my thoughts".

He smiled, and said to me: "O my brother, the truth is that I have never seen any sin whatsoever in this man. But my position requires me to act this way with the novices until I have brought them to humility and the destruction of the self, so they will grow in virtue. Now I love this man well, because he is saintly. I did what I did to rebuke some of the proud, so that they might profit from his humility and patience and obedience, for everyone knows that I rebuked him without reason." He continued to exhort me and question me until my heart grew cold. I left him, feeling sick and depressed. It was then that I realized what "the revealing of thoughts" actually meant.

Another day, we left the table after lunch and went outside the gate of the monastery to relax, as was the custom, as we have said.

The prior summoned a monk named Musa. This monk busied himself with the requirements of the monastery. The prior used to send him to Tripoli on errands for the monastery, and to other places as well. When he came before him, the prior ordered him to take brother Arsaniyus with him, and when he came to the town of Bsharra [3], to mount him on the mule and take him on to the town of Sayyida Zghrata [4] and deliver him into the hands of the village curate, then return the way he had come. He gave him a letter for the village curate, in which he offered advice and guidance.

He then sent one of the monks to summon the aforementioned brother, I mean Arsaniyus. But he was ill, and didn't have the strength even to walk in the monastery, except with difficulty. When he came before the prior, he prostrated himself and kissed his hand. Then the prior began to speak with him in this manner, saying to him, "I command you, O my brother, with an order that must be obeyed, to go with our brother Musa to the curate of Sayyida Zghrata and place yourself under his authority in everything that he might ask you to do. If he orders you to eat your fingernails, you must eat your fingernails. You must take the medicine he gives you without inquiring into its composition".

When the prior finished speaking with him, he rose up, kissed his hand and went out and sank down on the stairs. The prior scolded him and summoned him back. When he returned, he bowed low before the prior and said to him: "Forgive me, O our father", and kissed the ground. The prior began to rebuke him, saying: "O man of little understanding and discernment! If you are capable of walking, in accordance with our rule, then walk from here to the town of Zgharta, if you have the strength! But pride conquered you, O scoundrel! Get up and listen to what is said to you and don't contradict!" The submissive brother got up, and bowed to the ground, saying: "Pardon me, O our father!" Then he said to him: "When you get to Bsharra, mount the mule, and don't walk!" And he ordered one of the brothers to bring him his prayer book, his staff and his robe. Then he gave them to the aforementioned brother Musa and blessed him and he set out.

Then the prior turned to us and sighed, saying: "I could have wished, O my children, that the blind obedience of this brother could be found in all of you! Did you see how he did not seek to excuse himself to me by saying 'O my father, I don't have the strength to walk?' No; he immediately set out, obedient to my words, without misgivings that he could not walk." And the prior spent the half hour of our recess exhorting us on that theme.

I saw many things in that holy company. Some monks behaved like angels. I have mentioned this, but they were the few among the many. No, I have only mentioned it through shame and to put others on guard, lest they seek to become monks without being prepared for this holy step. And especially, above everything else, he should spend a long time asking God to show him his vocation, and seek guidance from a wise and intelligent preceptor. Only then can he be sure he has a vocation.

Shortly after beginning my novitiate, I fell seriously ill for the space of two months, and then spent another month convalescing. During that month, the prior absolved me from the monastic rule, and began to send me out of the monastery with the monks who went out on monastery business. I would go with them to keep them company.

One day, two of the monks went to the mill to grind the wheat for the monastery. The prior ordered them to take me with them to the mill so that I might have a walk. I accompanied them to a place called Ra's al-Nahr [5], where the mill was located. When we arrived and unloaded the wheat from the backs of the asses, they realized that they would not get a turn at the mill, because so many people had arrived before them to grind their corn. So they decided to sleep there until their turn came.

Then the monks said to me: "Brother, get up and go back to the monastery, and take the she-ass with you and tell the prior why we have slept at the mill, so he won't worry". So I rose up and drove the she-ass before me and went on until I reached the river and we began our descent from that height. The ass went in front of me, and as it descended I saw it was on the point of falling to the bottom. I grabbed hold of its tail to stop it falling and it dragged me along with it, still clinging to its tail. At last it slipped away from me and ran off. I fell the whole way from top to bottom, cracked my ribs, and fainted.

After a little while I came out of my faint and took in my state. I couldn't see the ass. At that moment I said to myself that one of the Hamidīyya [6] had taken it and gone off with it. What was I going to say to the prior? I was very worried and began to wander about the valley looking for the ass or its tracks. I was sad and at a loss, upset at not retrieving it. I headed back to the monastery, walking very slowly.

I finally arrived on the very day all the novices from Aleppo, had decided, in a great state of commotion, to ask to leave the monastery. This went very hard for the prior, who feared that the resolution of the other novices would be weakened. He began to summon them one by one and inquire whether it were true or not. Finally he sent for me, and the monks told him "Our brother went with the monks to the mill as you ordered". He replied: "When he returns from the mill, send him to me!"

At that very moment I arrived at the monastery. When I ascended the stairs to the monastery, red-faced and terrified because of having lost the ass, the monks said to me: "Go to the prior, for he has summoned you!" When I heard these words, I was sure the prior had learned of the loss of the ass, and my fear increased.

When I stood before him, and had kissed his hand, he bade me be seated. Then he said to me with a frown "O my brother, do you know why I have summoned you?" I said to him "No, father". Then he told me that several of the novices had asked to leave the monastery, but because they could influence the other novices, he had begun to examine them one by one, in order to find out if it were true or not, because every time one left, it tempted another to do the same. At last, after a long speech, he said "Tell me if you are firmly committed or not!" "No, father", I answered immediately, "I must go to be cured in Aleppo, and when I am perfectly healthy, I will return to the monastery."

Then he thrust his face close to mine and began to gently exhort me, saying "Don't be conquered by temptation, O my brother, and return, defeated, to the world, O my son!" He continued to speak kindly and affectionately to me until I said to him, "Father, let me think about it today and I will see what God advises me". The prior blessed me and then dismissed me so that I could go and reflect.

When I left his presence, I saw some of the monks waiting for me in order to plead with me not to abandon my resolution to lead the monastic life. I asked them about the ass, and whether they had found her or not. They were surprised at my words, and asked, "What is this ass you are talking about?" So I told them how the outing had finished. Then they began to smile, and told me "The she-ass which the monks hired in Bsharra did not run away, it just returned to the village. Don't worry, brother, it didn't go astray. Asses usually return to their place, at least those that were with you do".

So my heart was comforted, and I went to my cell to think over what I had done. I remained sunk in thought all day and all night, until dawn broke. After we had taken communion, the prior gathered us together and asked if we were still resolved upon leaving the monastery. "Yes", we told him. Then he ordered our personal effects to be brought to us and they removed our novice robes and we put on our own clothes. There were four of us: myself, Dā'ūd ibn Jabūr al-Kuwais, Yūsuf ibn Shāhīn Jalabī, and Mīkhāyīl ibn Tūmā Hawwā. After we had put on our clothes, the prior and, the monks bade us goodbye and we left the monastery.

At that moment, the superior of the order, the priest 'Abd Allah ibn Qara'alī, arrived at the monastery. When he saw we were leaving, he was saddened that we were abandoning the monastery. He prayed over us, then called me to his side and spoke to me privately, saying "I believe, O my son, that of all the novices who have left, I could not bring myself to take back one, but if you decided to return, I would accept you". Then he blessed me, and said "Go in peace!"

We all set off, and didn't stop until we got to Tripoli. There we found a caravan just about to leave for Aleppo, so we hired a place in it and went to Aleppo and each of us returned to his home. I passed the day at home in order to rest, and the next went to pay my respects to M. Remuset [7]. When he saw me, he reprimanded me, and reminded me of what he had told me before. He was very upset, and refused to hire me back.

So I spent three months at loose ends, with no job and no hope. The world seemed to close in on me, yet I had no inclination to return to the monastery. I bore it all patiently, until a caravan was organized, bound for Tripoli. I went to hire a mount from the leader of the caravan, telling him that one of my friends wanted to go with him. I did this so no one would know I was leaving Aleppo, lest they try to prevent me. The next day I woke early and took some things I would need, like undergarments and shirts and so forth. I packed everything in a satchel which I had had with me since my first journey. I left the house and headed for the Khan al-Zayt [8], where the caravan leader was lodging.

When I got there, I asked for the caravan leader, but they told me he had gone off to deliver something to a certain Frank who was lodging in the house of M. Sauron, my brother's employer, with whom I was acquainted. This Frank was a traveler, one of the travelers of the Sultan [9] of France. He had come from the country of Armenia, having travelled in that country in the guise of a wandering physician. From Aleppo, he intended to travel to the lands of the East, that is, of the Arabs. His name was Paul Lucas.

I slung my satchel on the horse. Quite a few Aleppans were travelling with the caravan, and I said them, "Mount up, let's ride about until the caravan leader arrives". So we mounted our horses and rode until we came to the shrine and the pillar [10]. The caravan leader didn't come, so we sat down to wait for him. Meanwhile, I disguised myself, wrapped my white sash around my waist [11], put on boots and packed the things I was going to carry with me, as was required. Now I was in my travelling costume.

The conductor of the caravan arrived a little later, and after him, the above-mentioned Frank, accompanied by five merchants, all of whom knew me. I quickly mounted and rode off alone and got out of sight before they came up to us. At last they bade him farewell and went back and our caravan set off. The pack-animals had preceded us by a day, to Kaftīn [12]. We rode on, through the rain, until we reached Kaftīn, almost drowning from the downpour. We entered the house of our caravan conductor, and he immediately lit a fire for us in the stove. We took off our wet clothes and began to dry them. The Frank alighted there too, along with his servant, a man from the land of Armenia, and a Catholic, on his way to Jerusalem.

A little while later, I heard the Frank and the conductor of the caravan arguing, but neither understood the other. Then the conductor remembered that I knew French, and said to me, "By your life, ask the gentleman what he wants, and what he is demanding". So I asked him in French what he wanted. He told me, "I left some things with him in Aleppo, and now I can't find them!" When I had told the caravan leader, he said "I have them right here, packed in my saddle bags". Then the Frenchman relaxed, and thanked me. He asked me if I were a Christian, and I said "Yes, by the goodness of Almighty God!" "It didn't occur to me", he said, "because I noticed that you were wearing a white sash, so I thought you were a Muslim."

Then he asked me to sit down and eat with him, but I refused. Finally, he prevailed upon me to sit, and I did so. He ordered his servant to bring dinner, for he had brought abundant provisions with him from Aleppo and good wine. He and I dined, and when we were finished, drank coffee. The boy brought us smoking utensils and we sat there chatting. "What sect do you belong to?" he asked. "I am a Maronite" I replied, "and I heard of you when you were in Aleppo and staying in the house of M. Sauron, the Frenchman. My brother was working for him as his accountant." "His accountant was your brother?" he said. "Yes!" I replied. He wondered at it, and asked, "Why are you travelling with us?" Then I told him that my brother knew nothing of my departure from Aleppo. "Why doesn't he know?" he asked. "If he knew, he wouldn't let me go" I replied. Then he asked, "Where are you going?" I was shy of telling him my story, so I said, "I am going to travel the world to see the sights".

I said this only to mislead him. He was astonished that I was going to tour, and thus does God provide! He said to me, "If you wish to travel, you couldn't do better than come with me!" He told me that he had been sent by the Sultan of France to travel through countries and write down what he saw, and to seek out old historical manuscripts, medallions and coins struck by ancient kings, as well as medicinal herbs that grew in these countries.

Then he asked, "Do you read Arabic?" "Yes", I told him, "as well as French!" If you come with me", he said, "I will find you a post in the library of Arabic books and obtain a stipend for you from the king, and you will live all your life under royal protection. I have been authorized by the chief minister to take with me a man from this country who knows how to read Arabic. This could be a great opportunity for you. Would you like to travel with me?" "Yes!" I said. Then he asked, "Can you give me a definite decision that you will come with me to Paris?" "I can't give you a decision until we reach Tripoli", I replied. And, I added to myself, not until I had checked his story and found out whether or not he was telling the truth.

Finally, he said, "Then let's not discuss this anymore until we reach Tripoli". He wanted me to translate for him, because those who were travelling with him did not understand Arabic. They only knew a little Italian. I answered him, "Upon my head and eye!" and excused myself and rejoined my friends.

We spent the night there, and the next morning when we awoke the conductor of the caravan said that he wanted to spend the day in his village, as was the custom. When the *khoja* [13] heard that the caravan was going to spend the day in the village, he began to ask the people if any ancient buildings from the days of the Christian kings were to be found in the vicinity. They pointed out a nearby mountain, an hour's ride away, and told him that there he would find Christian structures, a monastery and a church, but that they were in ruins. They said some of the stones were inscribed with Frankish characters.

When he heard this, he called the conductor of the caravan and told him that he wanted to go to the mountain and take a look. He answered that the place was a hide-out for thieves and Bedouin, and that he was afraid he might be robbed. "That is not your affair", he answered, "Just bring me some mounts so that I may ride". So he hired a mount in the village, because his own animals were tired and he wanted them to rest so they could travel the next day.

When the mounts arrived, we provided ourselves with food and drink and hired four stout guards to accompany us, for fear of the brigands. So off we went, and ascended that mountain. We walked about a bit, until we found the ruins the villagers had told us about.

The *khoja* began to walk around that place, copying the inscriptions on the stones. When he had finished, we went to a place and found a tomb covered by a piece of stone the size of a mountain. He circled the tomb, searching for a place by which to enter, but all he found was a narrow passageway leading into it. He wanted one of the guards to enter it, but none of them would. They told him, "This could be the lair of a wild beast, a hyena or tiger or some other wild animal which would attack me when I entered".

We were still talking when a tough-looking shepherd passed by. One of the guards called him over and told him to go into the tomb. He said, "How much will you give me if I do?" The *khoja* gave him a third of a Dutch *thaler* [14], and when he saw it in his palm, he threw off his cloak and went down into that place. The depth of the tomb was the height of a man, plus his upraised arm. Then the *khoja* called down to the shepherd, "Walk about in the tomb, and hand me everything you find". So the shepherd searched the tomb and found a human skull and handed it up to us. It looked like a piece of plaster. The *khoja* said to us, "This is the skull of man!" Then he handed us another skull, smaller than the first, and the *khoja* said, "This is the skull of a woman!" The *khoja* surmised that this was the tomb of a governor of those lands and country.

Then he threw him a trowel and said to him "See what you can find in the earth of the tomb, and hand it up to me". He found a number of things and passed them up to us. Among them was a large, flat seal ring. The *khoja* examined it, and saw that it was Egyptian, but the inscription was not clear to him and he couldn't tell if it was made of silver, gold or some other metal entirely. He kept it, and then said to the shepherd, "Feel around the wall of the tomb!" He did so, and found a niche in which was a lamp like an oil lamp. He couldn't tell of what metal it was made, but he took it too.

When the shepherd could find nothing more, he climbed out of the tomb and went his way, while we returned safely to the village. The next day we journeyed on from Kaftīn to Jasr al-Shughl [15], and from there continued traveling until we arrived safely in Tripoli. The *khoja* lodged at the house of M. Balan, the Frenchman. I stayed at the Khan al-Ghamīdā [16], at the house of the Aleppan monks, that is, the monks of St Yash'.¹⁷ The key to the house was always deposited in the room of the *odabashi*, that is, the concierge of the *khan*. I got the key from him and put away my baggage. The concierge knew me from the time my companions and I withdrew from the monastery, and stayed in the *khan*.

I spent the day there, and the next went to pay my respects to M. Ruman, to whom I had brought a letter of recommendation from my employer, M. Ramuset, the first time I came to Tripoli, so that I would be made welcome. After greeting him, I told him of Paul Lucas' offer, and asked him if it were true that he had been sent on behalf of the Sultan of France in order to travel about. "Yes, it's quite true", he said. Then I asked his advice about going with him to Paris. "It could be to your advantage. Go, don't worry, he is a good man."

Then I took my leave, and went to Father Elias, the Carmelite. I used to know the Father when I was in the monastery of St Yash'. I greeted him, and told him the whole story, I mean, about Paul Lucas. When the Father heard what I had to say, he said "I have made enquiries about this man, and have learned that he is travelling on behalf of the Sultan of France. If you wish to go with him, I can see no objection. Go, do not fear. I advise you to do so."

In the light of this, I decided to go, so I went to Paul Lucas and told him of my firm decision to go with him. When I had told him what I had decided, he asked me if I had anything other than the clothes I was wearing. "No", I said, "but I have others in Aleppo, very fine." Then he said to me, "If you have some fine clothes, write to your brother to send them to you at the city of Sidon, for if we arrive safely in Paris, I want you to come with me to be presented to the Sultan of France, and it would please him if you were dressed in the style of your country." I took his advice, and wrote a letter to my brother, telling him my story and requesting him to send me my clothes at once with someone going to Tripoli, and from there to forward them to Sidon with one of the Sidon merchants. I also asked him to send that same merchant some travelling expenses for me. By a stroke of luck, a courier was leaving that very day for Aleppo, so I sent the letter with him, and told Paul Lucas that I had done as he advised and sent to Aleppo.

Chapter II

My departure from Tripoli with Paul Lucas the Tourist [in the month of February 1707] [18]

A few days later we left the city of Tripoli in the company of a nobleman from the al-Khāzin clan called cavalier Hannā. He had met the *khoja* in the house of the French consul, and they had become great friends. When we came to Mt Kisruwān [19], to a place called Zūq Mīkāyīl [20], where the cavalier's house was located, the *khoja* wanted to go to his house and breakfast with him, while we — I mean myself and the servant who accompanied us — dismounted in the market square, tethered our horses and collected our baggage and clothing and stood around waiting for breakfast to be sent by the cavalier, who had promised to do so.

When we realized that no food was forthcoming, and because we were suffering from hunger, for we had travelled all night, we took out some fried fish, bread and wine and sat down to eat. We had hardly started when a crowd of people gathered around and began asking us, "Are you Christians?" "Yes, we are", we replied. "Then why are you eating before the time?" they asked. We said, "We are travelers, we have journeyed all night, and are not fasting". For it was the beginning of Lent, and some of the people of that town fasted till noon, and others to the ninth hour, and no one could eat before the appointed time. The same thing happened to our *khoja*, for the cavalier sought to distract him until mealtime, and when food was withheld from him, he left and came to us. He saw we were preparing to eat, and sat down to join us, without the cavalier.

At that moment, cavalier Hannā appeared, and asked pardon for the delay of his breakfast, urging him to return with him, and saying that they would eat immediately. So he excused himself and went off with him. Then he sent us a tray on which was a dish of honey, oil and two loaves of bread. We took a couple of bites and sent it back.

We spent the rest of the day, until the next morning, in the market. Then we said goodbye to the cavalier and travelled through the mountains from place to place, town to town, while the *khoja* looked for herbs in the mountains. At last we arrived at the city of Beirut, where we lodged at the monastery of the Capuchin fathers. They welcomed us, and gave our *khoja* a furnished room, I mean, one with a bed, carpets and chairs and so on. The same day one of our friends from Aleppo came to the monastery. He was named Yūsuf ibn al-Mukāhil, and had been my companion in Aleppo. When he saw me, he greeted me with great affection, and asked me the reason why I had come to Beirut. I told him all about it, explained my situation and how I had become involved with this traveler.

Then I asked him to walk about the city of Beirut with me, so that I could enjoy myself before we set off again. "Willingly!" he said, "Get up, and come with me. I will show you the whole city, place by place." I wanted to take off my white turban sash and put on a blue one, but he prevented me from changing it, saying, "Even if you wanted to wear a green turban sash in this town, there are no restrictions on the way Christians dress."[21] In the end, I didn't even wear my blue sash. I went out with him to walk about the city, and we continued to do so until we reached a place like a small palace. It had an imposing entrance and sitting in it were three or four *aghas*[22] dressed like Ottoman Turks.

Their heads were bound with sashes with embroidered ends, and over their shoulders were cloaks of angora wool. They carried jewel-encrusted daggers. In front of them were ten or fifteen youths with red turbans — and some were green! — with silver knives and steel swords. When I saw them, I stopped dead and retraced my steps. But that youth — Yūsuf al-Halabī — said to me, "What's the matter? Don't you know who these gentlemen are?" "No, I don't", I said, "but I think they are the governors of the city." "Yes", he replied, "they are the governors of the country, that is, Kisruwān, and this place is the customs house, of which they are the officers. They are Maronites from the clan of al-Khāzin, and they are employed by the ruler of the country." From there he took me and showed me the harbour and the cave where St George killed the dragon. Then we returned to the monastery.

We did not travel the next day, because the *khoja* wished to remain a few days in Beirut to look about, for I had told him what I had seen that first day. When we left the monastery, he said to me, "From now on, if anyone asks you about me, tell them that I am a physician". He was dressed in the clothes of our country, and wore a *qalpaq* [23] on his head. So we went out to tour the city, from place to place. He was looking for old coins, I mean, medallions of ancient kings. That day we bought forty or fifty pieces and then returned to the monastery. The next day we again went down into the city, and visited the jewelry market. He began to look at stones and engraved rings and we found quite a few, as well as a number of coins.

Then, while we were on our way back to the monastery, a *mu'as irāni* [24] Muslim called out to us, and said to me, "I have some coins to sell". "Bring them and show them to us!" I told him. He went into his shop and brought out forty coins for us, each the size of a third of a piastre, but thicker, and placed them before us. When the *khoja* saw that they were all corroded and their inscriptions illegible, he refused to take them, but said to me in French, "Buy them from him!" Then he left us and went off. When he had gone, I started to leave too, and the man said to me, "What's the matter with you, why don't you buy them?" "Because they are so corroded", I replied, "and the inscriptions are worn away. They are worthless." Then he said "Take them for whatever you want". "The doctor doesn't want them", I answered, "but I'll do you a favour, and buy them. How much do you want for them?" "One Egyptian piastre for the lot". I handed him half a piastre, but he wouldn't take it, so I departed and went my way. He followed me, yelling, and showed me a stone engraved with a Solomon's seal, with a beautiful portrait head depicted on it. Under it were letters, in a language I didn't know.

When I saw it, I went back for the *khoja*, and when he saw the seal ring, he tossed it down and went off again, telling me in French, "Buy it for what he asks!" So I said to the man, "I will buy the lot, the stone and the coins". After hard bargaining, I got him to agree to a price of one piastre. "No more!" I told him. So he gave me the coins and the seal stone and I gave him the piaster, took my purchase and departed. The *khoja* was standing in the street, waiting impatiently for me. When I came up to him, he said "Did you buy them?" "Yes, I did", I told him, "but he wouldn't give them to me for less than a piastre." "Don't worry; let's go back to the monastery."

When we arrived, he said "Bring me a bowl with a little vinegar". He put the coins in the vinegar and began inspecting the stone and the inscription. He was obviously pleased. Then he said to me, "Truly, if that man had asked a price of one hundred piastres for this alone, I would have given it to him, for this stone possesses great virtues". But he didn't want to tell me what they were. Instead, he told me that the engraved image was the portrait of one of the kings of ancient times, and that he would find out his name from the histories.

Early the next day, I went in to him and found him working to remove the corrosion from the coins. I saw that they were all pure silver, and that their inscriptions were perfectly legible. The *khoja* told me that these were the portraits of the king whose image I had seen on the seal which we bought from the *muʿas irānī* Muslim. The proof was that we had asked that man where he had come upon the coins and the stone, and he had told us that he had found most of them in the foundation of an old wall when it fell down. He was setting about to repair it, and found them buried in the earth.

That day too we went out to walk about the city and look for old coins. This time, the news that the *khoja* was a physician had spread, and people began to lead us from place to place, where he treated some of them and prescribed for others. As the price for his treatment, he asked for old coins. We collected quite a number of these, and found that some of them were silver and copper, and more than one was of gold, and we bought them by weight.

A few days later we left Beirut and went to Jabal Druze [25]. We travelled around those places, also searching for coins. The *khoja* practiced medicine, and to pay for the treatment, they would search for coins for him. We came across quite a few, as well as some medicinal herbs we found growing in those mountains.

From there we went to the city of Sidon, where we lodged at the house of the consul, which was inside the *khan*, where the French merchants also stayed. The *khoja* was made thoroughly welcome by the consul and the French merchants. At this time a number of monks from Scotland arrived, on their way to Jerusalem. The *khoja* wanted to travel with them, for he had promised his manservant that he would take him to Jerusalem, so he decided to take him along, and travel with the monks and leave me in the consul's house. I was unlucky enough not to go with them.

So I stayed there, till one day while I was sitting at the gate of the *khan*, one of the merchants staying there called out to me, asking my name. I told him my name, and sect. He said to me, "A letter from Aleppo has arrived for you". He took me to his storehouse and took out the letter and handed it to me. I opened it up and read it. It was from my brother, and he reprimanded me severely for having left Aleppo without telling him. He said I must return immediately, with the first caravan heading back. He told me that I should stay with the *khoja* until he sent someone to Tripoli, and that I should travel with them without fail, and must not disobey him.

When I finished reading the letter, a great sadness came over me, because he had not sent the things I had asked for. Then that gentleman turned to me and said, "I have also received a letter from your master, M. Ramuset, telling me to send you to Aleppo, whether you want to go or not". I told him, "I am not now under the orders of *khoja* Ramuset, and you can't make me go! I am a free man, and am now serving M. Paul Lucas, a traveler for the king of France. When he returns from Jerusalem, he will answer for me."

Finally, after a great deal of argument, backwards and forwards, he handed me a second letter from my brother, in which he said, "If you really don't want to return, may God smooth your path! I have sent you by the hand of this gentleman a bundle of clothing which you asked me for, so take it from him, plus whatever you need in the way of travelling expenses. Send me a receipt for the clothing and whatever expense money you take from him. Goodbye."

When I read the second letter, I was delighted at the arrival of my clothing. Then he took out and handed me the bundle of clothing and asked me how much I needed in the way of travelling expenses. I took from him a certain amount of piastres, and gave him a receipt for everything in my own hand. Then I returned to the house of the consul, as pleased as could be.

I stayed in Sidon, walking about and looking at everything. It was Easter, and among the Maronites the custom is, that no one may confess or partake of the Eucharist except in church and from a priest, for certain reasons. A friend invited me to his house on the night of the festival, so that we could go early and confess to the priest and hear mass and take communion. After we had performed our obligations, he again took me to his house and entertained me most hospitably.

I stayed in Sidon until my master returned from Jerusalem. I told him about the arrival of my things and the letter from my brother, and how he had written to that gentleman, telling him that he should make me return to Aleppo, either by kind words or by force. Then I told him, "But now I am firmer than ever in my decision to remain with you". And he replied, "And I am too, and will fulfill my promise to you and take you safely to Paris". The manservant whom he had taken with him to Jerusalem didn't return with him, but stayed there until he returned to his own country. So I alone remained in his service. A little while later, we decided to sail to the island of Cyprus.

Chapter III

My first sea voyage with M. Paul Lucas, May [1707] [26]

On May 5th we departed from Sidon early in the morning on board an Italian settee [27], making for Cyprus. The ship set sail from the harbour of Sidon at the second hour of the night. From the moment I boarded I felt seasick, and slept beside the mast. We caught a good breeze, and before dawn broke arrived at the harbour of Larnaca on the island of Cyprus. When I awoke, still seasick, and saw the sails and the people in the harbour, I could hardly believe we had already arrived in Cyprus, and that our passage could have been so swift and easy, and that in one night we had sailed from Sidon to Cyprus.

We disembarked at the jetty, and there collected our baggage and went to the house of the French consul. When we entered, and he saw us, he warmly welcomed my master and prepared a furnished room for him, I mean, with a bed and bed clothes and chairs and the other things necessary for a bedroom. They also carried our baggage to my bedroom.

The next day we went out to look around. The French merchants resident in that place began to invite us to visit them. All of their servants were Greeks, and none of them spoke anything but Greek. Among them, I was like a deaf man at a wedding party. I didn't understand their language, and they didn't understand mine. When I spoke to them in French, they understood me, but replied in Greek, mocking me, because they despise Catholics as heretics, and there I was, in their midst.

Several days later, my master wanted to visit a city which is a little less than fourteen hours journey from Larnaca. This city is called Nicosia, and is the principal city on the island of Cyprus. The Franciscan Fathers dwell there. When we had decided to go there, the consul gave us a letter of recommendation, so they would put us up in their monastery. We hired a guide, and travelled all day until evening, when we arrived at the guide's house, where we stayed the night. An hour later, I heard a great crashing about and uproar outside, so I went out to see what was happening. I saw herds of pigs returning from pasture, and one herd of them came to the guide's house where we were staying. Outside the house was a sty, and they put the pigs in it. We were unable to sleep that night because of the oinking of those pigs.

When dawn broke, we journeyed on. It was as if we were travelling through a garden. There were many trees and flowing water and all the land was green, even the ruins buried in the earth were all of beautiful stone, white and dark blue, of noble form. Don't even ask about the vineyards, found so plentifully in these hills. They have no equal. Now I knew that what I had heard of the island was true, that it was indeed 'The Green Isle'.

Towards evening we came to the city, and put up at the monastery of the Fathers I mentioned before. They received us warmly, and gave us keys to our cells in the monastery, and told us, "Go wherever you wish!" We stayed there that night, and the next morning heard mass.

A short while later a messenger arrived for the Father from his superior, who lived in Larnaca. He asked him to come to him immediately, as soon as he received the letter, without delay. So the Father made his excuses to my master, and showed him the letter, telling him that he must go, for the orders of the superior must be obeyed. But he gave us a key to the cellar, and told us that everything we needed was to be found there, ghee, olive oil, old and new wine, salt pork and ham, olives, cheese, and such-like things, but no bread. The bread of Cyprus is unparalleled in taste and texture. We used to buy it fresh every day. Finally, he bade us goodbye, and set off to see his superior.

We spent that day in the monastery, because we had found no one who knew the roads. Finally, a Frenchman who lived in the city heard of our plight. His name was Kālīmīra [28]. He came to us and greeted my master and welcomed him. My master was delighted the man had come to him, for he was a native of the country and knew the roads. They sat and talked together far into the night. Then my master asked, "Could you very kindly trouble to take me with you so that I can see the city?" "Willingly", he replied, "Upon my head and eye!"

My master then prevailed upon him to dine with us, so he stayed and we all had dinner. After dinner, my master asked him his profession. "I am a doctor", he replied. My master went on to ask, "Are medicinal herbs to be found in your mountains?" And he showed him a book in which were depicted some of the plants for which he was always searching in the mountains. The Frenchman answered that that they were to be found on a certain mountain, a day's journey distant, and that there were also ancient buildings, like churches, monasteries and towns, but that they were all in ruins. "If you want to go to those places, I will go with you", he added. My master very much wanted to go, and asked him if he could hire a muleteer that very night so that they could leave early in the morning.

The next day he sent out to buy the necessary provisions. They took a native of the town with them as a servant, and asked me to remain in the monastery, because the Father had entrusted it to our care when he went off. For this reason, it was not permissible for us to leave the monastery empty, lest something harmful happen to the Father. So it was decided that I should remain alone in the monastery, while they went off.

I went out to walk about and see the sights of the city, but didn't go far lest I get lost. Then I returned to the monastery, where there was an old man who was paralyzed. The Father had told me about him, and asked me to feed him at lunchtime and dinner. He lived in a small house in the courtyard of the monastery. I had given him lunch, and filled a jug with water for him, then forgotten him. He began to talk to me in Greek, and when he saw that I didn't understand, he spoke to me in Turkish, and asked me where I was from, and of what stock.

I told him that I was from Aleppo, and a Maronite. He replied to me in Arabic, and said, "Peace upon a son of my own community!" I said to him, "Are you a Maronite?" "Yes", he replied, "I am the remnant of the descendants of the Maronites [29] who dwelt in the island when it was a Venetian possession. There used to be more than 500 families. Some of them are to be found to this day, but concealed, for fear of the heretic Greeks. I have sought refuge with the Father, who gives me morsels to eat because I spent my life in the service of the monastery, but now I no longer have the strength to serve". I comforted him, and remained with him talking until evening fell.

Then I left him, and cooked myself something to eat. After I had eaten, and fed him, I filled my pipe and went to stroll in the courtyard of the monastery. I noticed a stone stairway leading to the roof. I saw a curtain, and was curious about what lay behind it. I saw a courtyard, in which was a harem, and a man who looked as if he were the owner. When he saw me, he started to curse me in Greek and Turkish. As soon as I saw the harem, I turned and ran. The man kept yelling and cursing. I went back down the staircase to the courtyard of the monastery and began pacing about in it. I didn't see anybody, and then someone began to beat on the door of the monastery with a stone. I went to the door, and said "Who's knocking?" He answered in Turkish, "Open up, dog, open up!" He began cursing and threatening me, "If you don't open up, I'll go and bring you a little bad news from the pasha, and find out what kind of man you are, peering into peoples' harems!"

When I heard these words, I grew very worried, and began to plead with him, "O sir, don't blame me, I am a stranger, and didn't know there was a harem behind the curtain". The only result was that the more I tried to sooth him and calm him down, the more he cursed and threatened, beating the stone on the door. At that moment, a Greek passed by. He was a Catholic Christian, whom God had sent to save me from that ruffian. He began to talk to the ruffian in Greek, and calm him down. He didn't stop soothing him until he had led him away from the door. When he finally left, the Greek began to address me in Italian, saying "Open up, don't be afraid. I am a friend. I got rid of that character, and he is gone". I was still afraid to open the door, and he repeated his words, and said "Open the door. Have no fear. I am a Catholic Christian like you".

As soon as I heard these words, I opened the door so that he could come in. Then I quickly locked the door for fear that ruffian might return. He told me never to go up to the roof again or anywhere near the curtain. "If you do it a second time", he added, "he will shoot you and kill you, as he swore to me he would. And don't think for a moment that it is because of his sense of honour. No, it is because of his hatred for this Father and the monastery, which he hates with a devilish hatred. All the energy of these Greeks goes into closing the monastery, for fear their children will take to the Roman Catholic faith. They always say, 'Better Muslim than Roman!' Not one of their houses is without a Muslim or two, or sometimes three, for they marry their daughters to the soldiery, so that they will be a protection for them against the government, and so forth. For they have no honour, and no religion".

When I saw how friendly and kind he was, I asked if he would visit me every day, until my master returned. "Gladly", he said, and wished me good evening and left. My thoughts continued to be troubled, fearing that scoundrel would fall upon me during the night and kill me. I went to my cell and barred the door and locked it. I worried all night, and couldn't sleep for fear.

When day broke, the young man came to visit me, calmed my fears and made me forget them. When I saw how kind he was, I asked him if he would take the trouble to show me the city before I journeyed on. He acceded to my request, and we left the monastery together. We began to walk about in the streets of the city, but most of the buildings were in ruins. We passed through a wide open place, and I saw a lofty, spacious mosque with a tall minaret and a large dome. The base of the dome is decorated with marble statues of angels, and the entrance with white and black marble in intricate patterns. It is flanked by statues of St Peter and St Paul, also in white marble. When I saw this beautiful building, I was amazed, and asked that youth, "What is this place?" "A mosque", he told me. "How can it be a mosque?" I replied "when it is decorated with statues of angels and two saints? This is forbidden to Muslims!" He answered that inside were many other statues, built into the walls. all of them incorporated into the fabric of the building. If they tried to remove them, they would have to completely destroy the church. This is the reason they left them, rather than destroy the building.[30]

Then he took me on a walk through the town. In the narrow strects I saw women selling wine. Each of them had a skin full of wine in front of her, crying out that it was good and old. They cost a single *para*, and a cup could be had for a single *uthmānī*. Some of them were selling swine's flesh, and some of them carried casks of wine on donkey back and went about selling it house to house. All of their faces were uncovered, and without veils.

When I saw this shameless sight, I said to my companion, "Now where is the talk of that man who reprimanded me for having looked at his harem? Now I find their wives with uncovered faces, sitting in the alleys in full view of the passers-by, without modesty or shame!" "You're right", he said, "but I told you before that what that ruffian did was not because you looked at his womenfolk, but because of his hatred of the Father and the monastery".

I then asked him how the Muslims living in the city could sanction the selling of wine and pork in the streets and alleys. He replied that they were permitted to do so by the authorities for a single reason: the taxes that were levied upon them. For the taxes dated from the time when this country was first populated. Now it is ruined, but they still make them pay the same old taxes, and this is what has made so many people flee the great oppression visited upon them.

We finally finished the tour and returned to the monastery. I stayed there that night, and the next day my master returned, along with the doctor who had accompanied him. They brought with them the plants which were depicted in the book I have mentioned. I told the *khoja* what I had suffered at the hands of that ruffian during his absence. When my master heard my story, he grew very angry, and immediately wrote a letter to the consul describing the episode, and asking him to immediately send a dragoman so that he could swear out a complaint against that man to the pasha, and obtain satisfaction from him, so that he would learn to control his temper and not try again to harm the monastery or the Father. He paid the man who had guided them to take the letter and deliver it to the consul in Larnaca.

At that moment, the doctor appeared, and, learning the *khoja's* intention, began to dissuade him from carrying out the matter as he intended, because it would result in harm to the Father, the monastery, and to the Greeks living in that city. For the Father could only live among them through flattery and kindness and bribes. Otherwise, he couldn't live in that monastery even a single day. When the *khoja* heard these words, he changed his mind and took back the letter.

We stayed in the monastery until the Father returned. Then we handed over his monastery to him and bade him goodbye and set off for Larnaca, to the house of the consul, where we stayed until the arrival of a French ship bound for Alexandria. We bought passage on it and set sail on that ship, intending to voyage to the land of Egypt.

Chapter IV

Our trip to Egypt, and what happened to us there. June 1707 [31]

We left the harbour at Larnaca and a day later came to the port of Paphos which is on the island of Cyprus, where the ship anchored. The captain intended to take on a cargo of bitumen and tar, for in the mountains are found seeps from which the bitumen is collected. The mountain people collect it and sell it to the authorities. When we docked, we noticed that all the houses were in ruins, and no inhabitants were to be found, except for the Ottoman *agha* and his entourage, and a few peasants who collected the bitumen and the tar.

The sailors went hunting in the mountains until evening, and returned to the boat with three head of goats and a cow, all killed by shooting. I began to scold them for what they had done, considering it lawful to take the property of another, something that is not to be permitted. Then one of the sailors assured me that the goats and the cow had no owners, because their owners had all fled from the oppression and abandoned their flocks in the mountains, and many goats, cows and pigs had been left there. You could see their vines, with the grapes remaining on them year after year, with no one to pick them. All this had befallen them because of the little love they bore one another.[32]

After the captain had taken on his cargo of bitumen, we set sail for Limassol. When we arrived and had anchored the ship, we went into town. It is inhabited, I mean, there were people there, buying and selling, but the only thing they had to sell was wine. A quintal of wine sells for five piastres. The wine was contained in barrels, each holding 20 quintals or more. This is because vines are so plentiful in those mountains. The captain bought fifty casks of that wine to sell in Alexandria, and each cask contained an Aleppan quintal. As we have mentioned, a cask sold for five piastres. It is taken from Alexandria to Cairo.

After the buying and stowing away was finished, the captain got ready to sail with the first suitable breeze. That night, about two hours after sunset, while we were pacing the deck, we saw a man swimming in the sea. He came up to the side of the ship. He had wrapped his shirt around his head. He put on his shirt and covered himself, then climbed aboard. He asked to see the captain. The captain came out and asked him, "Who are you? What do you want?" The man flung himself at the captain's feet, and begged him to take him with him to Alexandria. The captain asked him, "Do you have a permit from the *agha*?" "No, sir" he said, "I am running away from him!" "Don't you know", the captain replied, "that there is an absolutely binding rule that no one can come on board ship without a government permit?" "Yes, I do" he said. Then the captain told him, "Given that you know this, how can I possibly take you on my ship?" Then he ordered the sailors to put him in the dinghy and row him to shore. The man began to weep, and beg us to intercede for him to the captain. My master's heart went out to him, and he asked the captain to take him with us. So the captain agreed to take him for my master's sake, but imposed a condition on him: that he shave his chin and put on seaman's clothes, and wear a wig and a hat, so that no one would know he was a Greek.

The man happily agreed to those conditions. They immediately shaved his chin and moustaches, and the sailors gave him some old clothes and a wig and hat, and he stayed aboard with the sailors as their servant.

Two days later a favourable wind rose and we set sail, bound for Alexandria. We arrived twenty-four hours later. Just as we were about to enter the harbour, a storm wind from landwards drove us back out to sea. There we stayed, beating back and forth in the sea for twelve days, until finally a favorable sea breeze rose and we safely entered the harbour.

We disembarked and went to the house of the consul, who warmly welcomed my master, and ordered the servants to go to the ship and bring our baggage. Furnished rooms were prepared for us, and they brought all our belongings, without any of them having been examined by the customs officials.

We stayed in the consul's house, treated with every attention and respect. Various French merchants invited us to their houses, showing great honour to my master. A few days later, they took him outside the city and showed him a tall column, the height of a minaret, near the sea.[33] Engraved upon it were the shapes of birds, insects, gazelles and similar creatures. In my master's opinion, the column was forged of metal, because it was impossible that it should be of stone, for there are no mountains in that country and no stone at all. Secondly, the weight of the column and its size, made it impossible that it could be transported in a vehicle or raised, or that anyone could move it. The part buried in the earth was equal to that above ground and for this reason, my master was certain that it was forged of metal on the spot.

My master then stood by the column and transcribed all those pictures engraved upon it. When they asked him why he copied them, and what they meant, he said the pictures represented letters and words. They had secret meanings, known to the Greek philosophers of those times.

Next to the column was a cave, called 'The Cave of the Slave'.[34] It is hollowed out of the rock, and the sea pours into it, the surge of the water making a terrific noise. Very few swimmers are able to enter it. Those that have, report that it is a wide cave whose depths no one can penetrate because of its great size and the pounding of the waves.

Then we went to a place where there were forty wells which supplied drinking water to the people of the city when their springs became spoiled because of the influence of the stars, according to the opinion of some astrologers who lived in that age. They said that those who drank the corrupted water went mad. This is the reason they dug these wells. The astrologers watched out for the appearance of certain stars, and then turned to these wells, from which they drew their water until the influence of the stars waned. This is what we were told about the digging of the wells, but God knows best.

Then we visited a great many places and ancient buildings, because the city of Alexandria is one of the greatest cities which existed in ancient times, according to the histories. At last, we returned to our quarters. We stayed in the city a few days, treated with great honour and kindness. I used to go every day to the port to look at the fish which were caught in that sea, where it mixes with the waters of the

Nile. They surpass description. From the point of view of taste, I have never seen, or tasted, fish to compare with them, in all the countries through which I have travelled. They have placed traps in this part of the sea to catch fish. They create a disturbance in the water in order to drive the fish into the traps, and they are unable to get out. Then they can capture them with no trouble. You see them piled up on the jetties in great heaps. They remove the roe, salt it, cut it in strips and dry it. They export great quantities to other countries. The main article of their diet is that fish. Their other product is Asyūtī linen.[35]

My master then prepared to go to Cairo to see the sights. We rented a *ma'āsh* [36], that is, a type of large boat they sail on the Nile. We left the house of the consul at the time of the dawn prayer and boarded the boat and sailed the salt sea until we reached the strait that leads to the Nile. Here there are always pilots available to guide the boats through the strait, and show them which side they should enter, because the sand continually accumulates at the mouth of the strait and creates a barrier across the entrance.

Now I saw something wonderful. The fresh water was flowing into the salt sea without mixing with it. I saw a marked division between the waters of the Nile and the salt sea, as if the Nile forged a path through it. This is something I noticed sailing the salt sea too. When the sea was calm, I saw white streaks in the depths of the sea. I asked what they were, and was assured that they were the fresh water rivers which flowed into the sea without mixing with the salt.

According to what some said, the clouds drank from these rivers. I witnessed this too, during the winter, when the clouds descend in a column to the sea and create a great fissure, I mean, they cleave the sea in order to reach the rivers and drink fresh water from them. The proof of this, is that in the Encircling Sea, I mean, the Indian Ocean, when the ship's water is exhausted, they lower a copper bucket to an undersea river which flows in a certain place and it fills with fresh water.[37] The bucket has a hinged cover, and when it is full, the cover closes over the top so tightly no water can enter. Thus they obtain fresh water, as we heard from those who had sailed in the aforementioned Encircling Sea.

Now we will return to our subject. We entered the Nile on board the aforementioned *ma'āsh* and sailed all day long until we arrived at the port of Rosetta, which is one of the ports of Cairo. The other is Damietta. When we came to the port, we disembarked and went to the home of a French merchant named M. Duran. When we entered his house, we climbed a wide staircase and at the top came to a spacious terrace, paved with stone. At the end of the terrace was a loggia, with a view of the Nile and marvellously green rice paddies, like emeralds. It was a sight to ravish the mind.

Then M. Duran came to greet us, welcoming my master very warmly. He ordered the servant to bring our baggage, and prepared a room for my master, furnished with everything needful. We stayed there all that day, until evening. After they had dined, and I had also eaten, with all the servants, I stayed chatting with the servants until bed time. Then one of the servants called me, to show me a room which they had prepared for me. But I refused, and said to him, "I am going to sleep on the terrace. No one could sleep inside a room during the summer, when it is so hot!" He tried to dissuade me, once and then twice, but I wouldn't listen to him. He finally left me and went off. I remained alone on that terrace, strolling about. Finally, I spread out the carpet I had brought and lay down to sleep. I don't know how I survived that night.

I heard a tremendous buzzing, and covered my face. It was mosquitoes, I mean, the insects that live in the water of the rice paddies. When I covered my face, these mosquitoes got under the bedclothes like madmen. I tried to keep them away from my face, legs and feet for some time, but I couldn't get rid of them until I lit my pipe and smoked. As long as I was smoking tobacco, they left me alone and went off. I walked about on the terrace with the pipe in my mouth. I was finally so tired that sleep overcame me, and I returned to the bed to sleep. There what had afflicted me before afflicted me again. So I got up once more and walked about and smoked tobacco so that the mosquitoes wouldn't come near me.

I spent the night like that, almost until the dawn prayer. Then it occurred to me that the servant had told me that he had prepared a mosquito net for me in my room. So I went and examined the doors one by one until I came to the door of a room, opened it, and entered. I saw a bed with a mosquito net, that is, a thin curtain, and inside, a bed covered with two linen sheets, as nice as could be. I knew then that the bed was mine, and that I was not mistaken. I immediately lay down on that soft bed and slept until they came to wake me up for breakfast.

When I woke up and put on my clothes, I felt dizzy, and had no inclination for food. I told the man who had come to wake me that I had changed my mind. Then I stood up and found that I could barely open my eyelids. I saw a mirror hanging on one wall of the room, and when I looked at my face in that mirror I saw that it had become so ugly I didn't recognize myself. My face, my cheeks and my eyelids were all so puffed up they almost met, my lips were thick and I was in a disgusting state. All this was from the bites of the mosquitoes.

I stayed in the room until evening without eating, embarrassed to be seen by anyone. My master missed me at last and inquired about me. They told him, "He is hiding in his room and doesn't want to come out!" He supposed that I was ill, and came to see me. When he saw the state I was in, he asked me what the matter was. I told him what had happened to me that night from the mosquitoes, and how I had not taken that servant's advice. He said to me, "Don't worry". He immediately brought me a salve, and rubbed it on my face. The swelling went down and my face returned to its former state that very day. And here let me give some advice to anyone who goes to Rosetta: Don't sleep without a mosquito net.

The next day, my master and I went out to tour the town and see the sights, the streets and the *khans*. We saw a *khan* in which Jews lived with their families. Their women were sitting in the arcades of the *khan*, working without veils or head coverings, not paying attention to anyone, as if they were in the land of the Franks. I saw this in no other place in Egypt.

Their coffee houses are on the banks of the Nile, and are always open, night and day. It is perfectly alright for anyone to walk about at night without anyone interfering with him, either the authorities or anyone else — unlike other places in Egypt. In short, it is a town completely open and safe as could be. I found no faults in it at all, except the mosquitoes.

Because we enjoyed this town so much, we stayed there twelve days, and they seemed like only one. Then we hired a *ma'āsh* and sailed up the Nile to Cairo until we reached Bulaq, the port for Cairo. We consigned our baggage to the donkey man, and rode those 'ambling' donkeys into the city. The donkey man advised us that we should head for the Muski [38] quarter, which is where the French merchants live, and where the French consul's house is located. When we entered that quarter, he went to inform the consul of our arrival. The consul sent his servants, and they took us to his house.

When the consul saw my master, he embraced him, and welcomed him with great warmth and generosity, for he had heard of his arrival in Alexandria, and that he had been sent for the purpose of sight-seeing by the king of France. This was why he honoured him so greatly. He prepared a beautiful room for him — the best — and, unlike other consuls, ordered the servants to wait upon him.

We stayed in the consul's house for three days, until my master had finished greeting the French merchants. After three days, he asked the consul's permission to go out and look about the city of Cairo. So the consul ordered one of the Ghuzz [39] Turks who was at his door to go with us and show us the city. Every day that man took us to one of the squares of Cairo and showed us the sights, I mean, the Palace of Pharoah [40], the Citadel, the Ramla, the houses of the *sanjaq*s [41] and other, similar sights. We continued to tour with the Ghuzz guide for three days, and he taught us about the main streets, side streets and alleys.

Then my master wanted us to walk around on our own, without the Ghuzz, because he wanted to search for the things he was always collecting, in every country he visited, such as ancient medallions, old books of history and precious stones, like diamonds, sapphires, emeralds, chrysolite [42] and other precious gems. Some stones have special virtues, which are unknown in the East, except by a few. My master had a deep knowledge of precious stones and 'lost mines', unknown in our countries. We will mention some of their properties and virtues in the appropriate place.

According to what I saw of the man — I mean, my master — he was versed in every science. I mean, he was skilled to the last degree in the science of medicine, for by looking at a man's face, he could tell what his ailment was, without having to ask him. He was also versed in the science of astronomy, as well as the sciences of engineering, philosophy, the natural sciences and physiognomy. He knew all the properties of herbs and plants, different sorts of drugs and similar things in the science of medicine. He gave many proofs of this, which we will mention in their place.

After our tour with the aforementioned Ghuzz, my master resolved to visit the house of Our Lady [43], the Virgin Mary, which is in Old Cairo. It is three miles distant from New Cairo, more or less. When we arrived, we stayed at a monastery of holy monks, and a Father took us to the House of the Virgin. It is now inside a Coptic church. We entered that noble place, where the Virgin and St Joseph and the child Jesus dwelt for seven years, as the Noble Gospels relate. Afterwards, we attended mass, performed by the Father in the Chapel of the Virgin, which is inside the above-mentioned House.

After mass, the Father invited us to his house to have lunch with him in the monastery. After we had eaten, he took us to show us the ancient ruined sites. Among these were the granaries [44] for wheat built by Joseph the Good, as mentioned in the Holy Book. The remains of four granaries are visible, not counting those which have been entirely destroyed, and of which no trace remains.

After our tour, we returned to our quarters in the house of the consul. From then on, we went out touring on our own, without a guide. We went to the markets and coffee houses, and sat with the shop-keepers, so that word would get out that my master was a doctor. Many men sought us for treatment, and he treated them all for nothing, he only asked them to find medallions, I mean, ancient coins, for him. They brought him quite a few.

One day a Copt brought us a Torah written on parchment. Its commentary was in the Estrangelo [45] tongue, derived from Syriac. He told us it was written in the days of the Children of Israel, when they dwelt in the city of Cairo at the time of the Pharoahs, and that in those days, paper did not exist, so they used to write on parchment. When he saw it, my master wanted to buy it from him, on the condition that he be allowed to examine it for several days. The man agreed, and gave it to us. We took it, and fixed its price at forty 'royal' piastres, if it turned out to be an authentic Torah.

My master took it, and showed it to the father, so they could determine whether it was a Torah or not. After investigating its authenticity, they confirmed that it was, indeed, a Torah. It contained the Book of Genesis, according to people versed in this language. Finally convinced that this was an authentic Torah, my master gave its price to that man, as we have said — 40 reals. Then my master said to me, "This Torah will be worth 4000 piastres to me". He was extremely pleased at its acquisition.

We bought books of ancient history in other languages in this country, and also elsewhere. Afterwards, we went out and walked about through the streets of Cairo, and entered the jewelry market. My master bought many different kinds of precious stones, especially a great many chrysolite stones. Because we bought so many by weight, the price was low. In the land of the Franks, this stone is sold at the price of emeralds.

The next day, a Jew came and asked me if we wanted to buy a precious stone. "Yes", I said. "Then come with me", he replied. We walked with him until we came to his storehouse, I mean, the *khan* of the Qaysariyya.[46] We climbed up to the top floor, and he took us into a room and locked the door behind us. Then he opened a French, iron-bound chest and began to take out precious stones for us, like diamonds and sapphires and emeralds and similar valuable gems. My master selected a number, and after he agreed on a price for them, said to him, "Come with me to the house of the consul, so that I may give you the money". He bore an order from the government to all the consuls in the countries of the East, to the effect that, whatever money Paul Lucas demanded, they must give it to him.

Just as we were about to leave, the Jew said to us, "I want to show you something, but only on the condition that you promise me that you will not reveal the secret". My master agreed that he would keep the secret, and not to worry. Then he took out a belt for us, all bejeweled, worth a treasury. He told us the belt had belonged to one of the kings of the Turks. When my master examined it, he saw that it was very valuable. He did not want to buy it, but he said to him, "If you cut some of the stones from this belt, I will buy them". The Jew refused to do that.

Then he took from the chest a purse, in which was black diamond weighing twenty-five carats, absolutely unique. My master's heart longed for that stone, but he proceeded to tell the Jew that it was not natural, but dyed. They argued about it for a good hour, the Jew asserting that it was genuine. Now, my master intended to buy that stone, but was afraid lest he make the Jew greedy, and not succeed in striking a bargain with him. He pretended to him that he was ignorant of its value, and did not know whether or not it was a real diamond. So he said to him, "Come with me to the house of the consul, and there we will put it to the test, and I will give you a price for it".

The Jew refused, fearing that news of the stone would get out, and that one of the *sanjaq*s would take it from him by force. We were at last able to reassure him that we would let no one know about it, and that he had nothing to fear on that count. With great effort, we finally got him to go with us to the house of the consul. The consul, the dragoman and my master went into the consul's room and remained closeted together for a good three hours. Then the Jew came out and went his way. I did not succeed in learning how much my master paid for it. The transaction remained a secret between them.

It also chanced that one of the French merchants bought an engraved gem stone from a peasant for one hundred *para*s. He showed it to my master, who wanted to buy it, but the man wouldn't sell. He had made the man greedy about the price, and wasn't able to buy it. Finally, he offered him two hundred and fifty piastres, but the man still didn't want to sell. My master complained to the consul, asking him to insist the man sell it, telling him that all the gems he bought, along with the other things, belonged to the treasury of the King of France. So the consul summoned that gentleman and insisted that he sell the stone. He could not refuse. He gave him the stone and received the price we just mentioned.

39

During this time, a peasant from the countryside came to the Muski, I mean, the quarter where the French merchants lived. He told a secret to one of the consul's servants: he had found a mummy, and feared that the authorities would hear about it and confiscate it and send it to the sultan, because there was an absolute prohibition against buying a mummy.[47] For that reason, when the peasants found one, they hid it until they could sell it to the merchants for a high price. The mummies are found near the *Marāmāt* [48], I mean, the tombs of the ancient kings of Egypt, the Pharaohs, but it is rare to find one, because the tombs are buried beneath hills of sand. After hundreds of years, it sometimes happens that a storm wind blows the sand away from those areas, exposing the tombs. The peasants who work in the fields go out to look, and occasionally find a tomb in which is a preserved body. When they find one, they hide it, and after a time they sell it to the merchants.

When my master learned about that mummy from the servant, he immediately told the consul, who had the peasant secretly brought to him. He tried to learn the truth of the matter from him, that is, whether he was actually in possession of the embalmed corpse. The peasant answered that it was true, and that he had it. They agreed on a price of two hundred and fifty piastres for it, on condition that it was delivered in secret, so no one should know of it. So they reached agreement, and the peasant went on his way. A few days later he returned, with a few bales of straw, and put them in the consul's stables, so the consul's groom could pay for them. He asked a higher price than usual for fear that otherwise the groom might inspect them and find the embalmed body. The peasant left the bales in the stable and went to find the servant with whom he had first spoken of the mummy. He told him to inform the consul of his arrival.

When the consul heard that he had arrived, he sent for him and had him brought into his presence and asked if he had brought what he sought. He denied it, and said, "Those who told me they had it, now deny it, and disclaim all knowledge of it. When my expectations were dashed, I loaded a few bales of straw and brought them to your stable to sell to your groom, but he questioned their price. Please come and order him to buy them from me for the stated price". Then he drew near the consul and kissed his hand, so that he would order the groom to purchase them at that price. At the same time, he gave a sign to the consul that the mummy was to be found inside that straw. As proof, he slipped him a piece of the sack cloth in which the mummy had been wrapped.

The consul understood perfectly what the peasant meant. He said to him, "Go, I will order the groom to buy the straw from you, and give you its full value". So the peasant went to the stable and sat down beside the straw. At the same time, the consul summoned the groom, and dispatched him as a messenger to Rosetta, ordering him first to give the peasant the price of the straw. They intended to unload the straw during the absence of the groom. The groom carried out the consul's orders, and gave the peasant the price of the straw. Then he ordered his assistant to help unload the straw during his absence, and departed for Rosetta.

As soon as he had left, the consul sent for one of his servants and ordered him to lock the stable doors and bring him the key, and not to unload the straw until the groom returned. The servant did just as the consul ordered, and brought him the key. The peasant promised to come the next day to collect the sacks in which the straw was packed. The consul waited till midnight, when all the servants were asleep. Then he and my master went down to the stable alone and opened the sack the peasant had indicated. There they found the body, wrapped in pieces of Egyptian linen. They carried it up to the consul's rooms and locked the door and the consul took the key.

All of this occurred without my knowing a thing about it until after our departure from Cairo. Then my master told me everything I have related of the particulars of the mummy, and how they concealed it so that no one should know of it, not even the servants who knew the peasant's story.

Several days later, the consul sent for a carpenter and gave him the measurements for a chest, its length and breadth. He asked him to divide the interior of the chest with two strong shelves, so there would be a hidden chamber. This was so that only the visible portion would be searched. The next day, the carpenter delivered the chest made to the consul's specifications, as good as could be wished. Then he placed the mummy in the middle chamber of the chest, and on top of it the best and most costly textiles, I mean, bed coverings, sashes, linen, and other such precious luxuries, until the top layer was filled. Then he nailed on the top. He then turned the chest over, and filled the bottom portion with textiles, and nailed the cover over it as well, as he had done with the other side.

The consul did this so that if the customs inspectors opened the chest from either side, all they would see were the aforementioned textiles. That chest, together with all our purchases in the lands of Egypt, coins, gems and books and many other items, were left with the consul for him to send later to Marseille, the port of France. My master obtained from the consul a bill of lading and list of all the things he had deposited with him and had it certified in the chancery, I mean the 'law court', of the consul in the city of Cairo, as was the custom. He did the same thing with all the consulates in the countries we visited, so that when we arrived in Marseille we would find all the purchases we had made in those countries and regions.

Afterwards, we walked about the entire city of Cairo, looking at all the sights. We visited the khans, the markets, the houses of the *sanjaq*s, the citadel, the Janissaries' Gate and the Western Gate, and similar things. The reason we were able to enter all these places was the medical treatments my master gave free of charge to anyone. This was why he was accepted by everyone, and we were able to see everything.

My master now wanted to visit Mt Sinai, and obtain blessings for visiting that Holy Mountain. When the consul heard this plan, he was uneasy about it, and began to speak of the difficulty of the journey to that mountain, and the dangers of the road. He told him that he would have to ride Bedouin racing camels, and because of their speed, the rider must be lashed in place, lest he fall from the camel's back and be killed. No drinking water or food is to be found along the way. Instead, they take their supplies of food and water with them, enough to last four or five days, according to the speed of the camels. They can cover seven or eight days' distance in just one day. "And for this reason" he said, "you should not make this journey. I advise you against it". When my master heard what the consul had to say, he changed his mind about facing death to travel to that Holy Mountain.

He then decided to visit Upper Egypt and go to the source of the Nile and to the countries of Abyssinia and the Sudan. He sought advice from people who had been to these lands. They dissuaded him from that journey as well. They said to him, "O *khoja*, you cannot go to those lands. The inhabitants are thieves and sorcerers. They are savage by nature, and the way to that country is fraught with danger. It is not certain you will return safely. We have found this out for ourselves. If you really wish to learn about those lands, you should go to the city of Fayoum, and there seek information about them and their rivers without running any danger yourself".

So he firmly decided on going to Fayoum. Again, he asked the consul's advice. He was pleased, and told him that a certain Father Hannā was to be found there, adding, "And I will give you a recommendation, so that you can stay with him in his monastery, and you will be safe. He is a wise man, and in the good graces of the *sanjaq* who is the governor of the region'. So we prepared for the journey and boarded a *ma'āsh* sailing to Fayoum. This was during the time when the Nile flood was at its height.

When we left Old Cairo in the river boat, we discovered that the river was overflowing its banks, flooding the countryside and reaching its outer limits. The area is four days' journey in length and breadth. All of the villages were surrounded with water, as if they were floating. They weren't submerged, because the water was only a span deep. When the villagers saw us passing by, the boys and girls, completely naked, swam out to us to beg us to throw them a piece of bread or biscuit. The oarsmen in our boat were four robust men, because we were moving against the current. The captain repeatedly strayed from the course, running aground. It took great effort to get the boat back to the middle of the flow.

At night, they moored beside the bank and everyone disembarked and camped there till dawn, when we continued our voyage. We went on for four days. On the fifth, we arrived at the canal [49] of Joseph the Good. When he brought his father, Jacob, to Egypt during the days of his sultanate, he built the city of Fayoum for him as a dwelling place, as is set down in the Holy Book. He built a canal for him, so the waters of the Nile could flow through and irrigate the land. Because of this, it is called 'Joseph's Canal'. His history is inscribed in stone. When we arrived, they moored the boat to the land and transferred the cargo to another, on the other side of the canal. We spent the day there, until the transfer was completed.

We ate fish caught by people fishing from the top of the embankment. The fishermen lower their nets without having to set foot into the water flowing from that canal, because the force of the water falling from the canal carries the fish, which fall into the nets. Thus they catch and sell them, three or four little fish for half a silver coin, I mean for a *para*. There are people sitting about with grills, who grill them for a *jadīd*, that is, a *fals* [50], each. The next day we boarded the new boat on the other side of the canal embankment, and sailed till evening, when we reached Fayoum.

We asked directions to the hospice of Father Hannā, and when we arrived, my master gave him the consul's letter, requesting that he let my master lodge with him, and remain in his care, and that he should show him the city. When the Father had read the letter, and understood its contents, he welcomed my master warmly and prepared a place for him to sleep, insofar as he was able, for his house was very small and narrow.

We stayed there that night, and in the morning attended matins and drank coffee. Then the Father advised us not to leave the house until he had introduced us to His Excellency the *sanjaq*, who was the governor of that country and its dependencies — the villages, farms and lands, up to the border of the Sa'īd, or Upper Egypt.

This Father was very much in the good graces of the *sanjaq*, and was his physician. If it were not for him, the Father would have been unable to live in that city, because the people are scoundrels and wild, some of them Copts and some country folk. Their dress consists of a long shirt [51], and they go barefoot. Their faces are concave and ugly, and it is impossible to distinguish the Copt from the country folk. Their women spin linen, and the men weave Asyūtī cloth and plain Samānī [52] mats and other similar work.

Now let us return to our subject. When the Father went to the *sanjaq* and told him that "A wise, clever man, versed in all the arts and sciences, has come to me. Would Your Excellency like me to introduce him to you?" The *sanjaq* answered, "Bring him immediately, so that I can meet him!" "On my head and eye!" replied the Father. "Tomorrow morning I will bring him with me to Your Excellency so you may meet him. Now it is time for you to go to Government House, but tomorrow morning I will bring him."

Then the Father left and returned to his house, where he told my master of their conversation. The next day, we accompanied the Father to the *sanjaq*'s palace. We entered a reception room between the women's quarters and the government palace. We waited a while, until the *sanjaq* came out of the palace which housed his womenfolk. We rose to our feet, and kissed his hands, and he commanded us to sit beside him. He gave orders to his servants to bring us dates and coffee, and afterwards they began to talk, the Father translating. They talked together for almost two hours. Finally, we asked leave to go. At that, the *sanjaq* turned to the Father and told him to make my master visit him every morning for coffee, without exception. 'I hear and I obey!' he replied.

The reason for this was that the *sanjaq* was learned in astronomy and geometry, and when he asked my master about these subjects, he responded with highly satisfactory answers. This was why he was delighted with him. So early every morning my master and I went to him and drank coffee, and he and the *sanjaq* sat conversing, while I translated between them, until the time came for him to go to the Government House.

When we left him, we were able to stroll about the city without fear or worry. We looked for old coins, and saw a great many. We also bought figurines, some of silver, some of bronze, as well as books written on parchment in Hebrew, and some in Estrangelo, from the days of the children of Israel.

Walking along one day, we saw a man sitting beside the road with a rug spread out in front of him. Placed on it were bits of iron and nails, coloured pearls, some seal stones, some of carnelian and some of coloured glass, and similar junk. My master looked at the rug and told me in French to buy the entire contents. I thought he had lost his mind, and said to him, "What possible use is all this stuff, except to make people mock us?" But he insisted I buy them, and walked off. When he was gone, I decided to go ahead and buy them. I agreed on a price with that man — thirty pieces of silver [53] — spread out my handkerchief, took them and followed my master to the house of the Father. He asked me, "Did you buy the contents of the rug?" "Yes" I replied. "For how much?" he asked, "For thirty *para*s." He laughed, and said "You paid dearly!" Then he took the handkerchief and went into his room.

A little while later, he came out and gave me back the handkerchief and its contents and said, "Take it and throw it away outside!" I was amazed at this, but he knew what was on that rug, and it included a piece of unworked gem-stone worth quite a bit of money. I didn't afterwards get a look at that stone, but he described it in his diary under the corresponding date [54], and gave the name of the stone, which was of a rare gem, not frequently found. This man could recognize precious stones even uncut, and sometimes he would buy a stone unknown to others. I knew nothing about them, and on our journey never had a chance to examine them closely.

The most unusual thing was that he knew their properties. One time I told him about my mother, how she had suffered from depressive melancholy for twenty years. In the jewellers' market, he bought a stone like a carnelian for two *para*s. It was pierced. He gave it to me and told me to hang it around my mother's neck, so that it touched her breast. When I returned to Aleppo and hung that stone around my mother's neck, she immediately recovered from that old ailment, after not having been able to sleep or talk or eat normally. When I put the stone on her breast, she returned to the way she had been before she had fallen ill, and was completely cured. This was after we had spent a great deal on doctors and prescriptions, to no avail whatever. The only thing that worked was that stone which he bought for two *para*s.

Now let us return to the subject in hand. We continued visiting the *sanjaq* every day, so they could talk together. Then one day he said to me, "Tell your master that tonight he must come and dine with me". When I told my master what His Excellency had said, he hesitated, and did not want to reply. Then the *sanjaq* said to him, "What's the matter, Sir, don't you want to eat our food?" Then my master said to me, "Tell His Excellency that this is a great compliment to me, but that we are unable to eat without something to drink". When I translated these words to the *sanjaq*, he said to me, "Don't worry. Tell him I have what he wants!" For the *sanjaq* drank. Then they both laughed, and agreed to eat together.

Afterwards, the *sanjaq* entered the Government House, and we returned to our lodging until evening, when he sent two of his retainers to escort us to his palace. We accompanied them, and entered the palace and sat in that place between the harem and the Government House. We waited there until the *sanjaq* arrived. Then we rose to our feet to do him honour. He gave us leave to enter the palace of the harem, and we went in. It was like a reception room, with beautiful carpets. Facing it was a garden, full of citron, lemon, bitter oranges and other fruit trees everywhere the eye reached. The sight was something to refresh the mind.

He asked us to be seated, and when we had sat down, a beautiful boy came out of the harem with a cup of coffee in his hand. He gave it to the *sanjaq*, then gave a cup to my master, then a cup to me. Then he brought us tobacco pipes with *qāqūn* [55] wood. They chatted together like old friends for about an hour. Then the *sanjaq* told the boy to prepare the table. The boy laid the table, bringing a silver tray inlaid with gold, and laid out hand towels around it and many loaves of thin bread. Then he brought us an excellent wine in golden cups, and then began bringing plates of food from the harem, lining them up. There were twenty different dishes, and this is no exaggeration. Now he presented plate after plate of delicious food to us. The *sanjaq* said, 'In the Name of God!' and stretched out his hand and took two mouthfuls from that plate, and then my master did the same, and so did I. Each of us took two mouthfuls. Then the boy removed the dish and brought another. We continued like this, taking two bites from each dish and the boy then removing them and bringing another.

Then he produced a dish of chicken, the delicious aroma of which would break your heart. It is a famous dish, called *qaz'an kebab* [56] in Turkish. My master tried it and found it wonderful. The boy came to take it away, and bring another, as was their custom, but my master grabbed the dish and reproved him in French, because this was contrary to Frankish custom. The sight made me break out in laughter, to the point where I couldn't speak. The *sanjaq* asked me, "What's the matter with you?" I kissed the hem of his garment, and said to him, "My Lord, please excuse my bad manners. I must tell you, My Lord, that the custom of these Franks is to put all the food on the table and everyone eats from the plate he likes. This man really liked the chicken dish, so he grabbed it, and prevented the boy from removing it".

The *sanjaq* laughed, and ordered the boy not to take the plates from the table until they were finished. So we continued eating and drinking that excellent wine until we had finished all the dishes. They ate sweetmeats and fruits that have no peer elsewhere in Egypt. Then they drank coffee, and went down into the garden. There we greatly enjoyed the meadows and running water in those channels and pools. We stayed there until evening fell and the time to leave had come. We left the garden, and went back to the room in which we had dined. Then the *sanjaq* ordered two of his retainers to take us back to the Father's house. My master thanked him effusively for his generosity, and then we returned to our lodgings escorted by the two retainers.

We continued to visit the *sanjaq* every day, until everyone knew that he kept an eye on us, and no one in that town harassed us in any way. It happened one day that a certain peasant told us that about an hour away from Fayoum a tall, thick, black pillar was to be found.[57] It was covered with pictures, and no one knew why it should be found in a sandy place without a single stone. When my master heard what the man had to say about the pillar, which was exactly his sort of thing, he immediately decided to go see it. Without informing the Father, he told me to rent mules so we could go examine the pillar, without considering the danger that might be involved in going to those places. On the contrary, he was convinced that because of his reception by the *sanjaq*, no one would dare lay a finger on him.

After having gathered provisions, I mean, food and drink and other things we needed, we mounted and rode the mules until we came to that pillar. We dismounted there, and saw an imposing, lofty, thick column, like the one we had seen outside Alexandria, but even thicker and taller. Engraved upon it were birds and animals, I mean, gazelles, leopards, dogs and other kinds of wild beasts. These were all riddles, with hidden meanings, according to my master, although there were history books which explained their meaning. After we had rested a little and had breakfast, he set about copying the inscriptions on the column. We were completely unaware that we had suddenly been surrounded by at least two hundred men from the fields. They were barefoot, their heads uncovered, a horrid sight.

They stared at us, and said to each other, "There used to be two columns here, in the days of our grandfathers, and they told our fathers that one day a Greek came to this place and muttered a spell over one of the columns. It fell down, and he took the gold that was hidden at its base and vanished. Before this one does the same, and takes the gold, let's kill him and take the gold that is under the pillar". Others said, "Let's take the gold from him first, then kill him!" One after another they drew near, threateningly, saying to my master, "Give us the gold under the pillar! If you don't, we're going to kill you!"

My master couldn't understand what they were saying, so I stepped forward and told him. I was terrified, almost fainting from fear of those scoundrels, or rather, wild, savage beasts. When my master heard what I told him, he was sure he was going to die. "What can we do?" he asked me, "Where can we flee? What is going to happen to us?" "Let me talk to them", I said. I told them, "Be patient, wait until he gets the gold, then he will give it to all of you, and I will take my share too. But first let him find the gold, then we will take whatever we want". These words temporarily calmed their boiling fury.

Then, at that moment, in that very village, God brought us deliverance. In the distance appeared a cloud of dust, from which a horseman mounted on a fine horse emerged, heading right for us. When those men saw that horseman, they all fled, like bees from smoke. You couldn't see a single one left behind. In a short time, the horseman came up to us. When he saw us, he dismounted and greeted my master, whom he had met before, in the *sanjaq*'s palace. "What were you doing with those rascals?" he asked, "I trust they didn't annoy you?"

Then we told him what had passed at the hands of those wild men, and how they threatened to kill us. "If God, May He Be Praised, had not sent you to us, they would certainly have slaughtered us." Then he comforted us, and told us the reason he came to us. He was in the village of which he was governor, sitting in a high place that looked out over the site of the pillar. "I saw a dense crowd of people crowded around the pillar", he said, "and was puzzled at what they were doing, so I jumped on my horse, rode here, and saw you. Now you are safe, and need fear no one."

So our minds were put at rest, and our fear and terror calmed. My master continued copying the inscriptions on that column and the soldier waited until he had finished. Then we all rode together until we came close to the village. The soldier invited us to come into the village with him, and we entered his house. We climbed up to the top, and it was all furnished, with windows that looked out over the countryside on all four sides. He ordered a servant to prepare lunch for us, and we were served boiled eggs and cheese. For our part, we took out what we had of food and wine.

After lunch, we drank coffee and rose to leave. The soldier dissuaded us, and said to us, "Wait here until it grows cooler, and I will go with you". So we stayed until an hour before evening fell. Then we rode with the soldier until we came to the Father's hospice, and he went his way. We thanked Almighty God for saving us from those savages. Now my master changed his mind about going to Upper Egypt, where they had warned him not to go because the inhabitants were so dangerous, as we have mentioned previously.

So we stayed on with the Father without taking a single step outside the city. Instead, we explored the city itself. This city is like a paradise, with its gardens and abundant water and delicious fruits and refreshing breezes. But the inhabitants are like wild beasts, as we have said, and fleas abound there like worms. I used to see them swarming over the walls. I have never seen so many anywhere else. They were as plentiful as ants, and the Father's hospice was beyond description, so infested I used to have to change my shirt three or four times a day. From the moment we entered, I was never free of them, everything was infested with them.

One day I said to my master, "Let's get out of this place, the fleas are eating me alive". Then he said to me, "Have you ever seen a single flea on me?" "That is very surprising," I answered, "why do the fleas avoid you, and eat me and crawl all over my body?" "Now I will free you of them," he said. He immediately opened his chest, and took out something wrapped in linen I didn't recognize, and tied a cord on it. Then he told me, "Hang this around your neck, inside your shirt, touching the flesh, and you'll never see a flea again". I did as he said, and didn't see another flea the entire time I travelled with him.

The Father with whom we were staying was outwardly healing bodies, but secretly healing souls. Many men and women and children came to him, some Copts, others peasants and he taught them the way of faith. He used to treat their ailments with a strange treatment. He would heat a small iron instrument in a stove and brand the patient, some on their forehead, some their neck, and some upon their breast or thigh. One day I said to him, "O Father, how do you have the heart to brand these people with a hot iron?" "My son", he answered, "The nature of these people you see here is the nature of wild beasts. If it doesn't cause them pain, they believe it is no remedy, so I decided to treat them with this kind of cure, which is used on animals". [58]

This is what I saw in the city of Fayoum. I have only written about a few of the many things I saw, for fear of prolixity and of boring the reader. A little while later, we decided to return to Cairo. After saying farewell to the *sanjaq* and the Father, we embarked on the *ma'āsh*. We sailed till we came to Joseph's Canal, and transferred from that boat to another, which was moored in the Nile, on the other side of the canal. We set sail on the Nile, and our trip was much easier than before, because we were sailing with the current. Before we knew it, we had arrived in Cairo.

We loaded our baggage onto the donkey and entered the city, making for the Muski quarter, and the consul's house, where we stayed. A few days later we took a boat to the port of Rosetta, and from Rosetta returned to Alexandria, where we lodged at the consul's house where we had stayed before.

We waited a few days in Alexandria while they prepared a ship bound for the city of Tripoli in the Maghrib. The ship was French, and one of the soldiers from the garrison in Alexandria had hired it and loaded it with a cargo of coffee and Egyptian textiles and other goods that sold well in that country, filling the hold to bursting with things that would sell there. Then he caulked the hatch so that no water would enter.

The ship was known in French as a *pinque*[59] that is, a small settee with a single hold. The soldier had sold deck space to pilgrims returning from the Hajj, and heading for Tripoli in the Maghrib. There were two Maghribi women with their husbands. In all, we numbered forty passengers, not counting crew. The *khoja* — that is, my master — wanted to voyage on that ship, but the consul and merchants tried to dissuade him, saying "The ship is small, the passengers many, and the deck narrow. The passengers are all Berbers, and their company will be very rough for a man like you". My master answered them, saying "These are the days of the *kūn*[60], and there are many corsairs on the sea. If I voyage with this settee in the company of these Muslims, we will have nothing to fear from English corsairs. Secondly, this ship can hug the coast, and none of the corsairs will be able to spot it". Then they told him, "Do whatever you like".

Chapter V

On our voyage to the Maghrib in the year 1708

We boarded the ship bound for the city of Tripoli in Barbary in the month of February.[sic!] [61] We went by sea, but in the greatest discomfort, in the company of those Berbers, until we reached a place called 'The Gulf of Sidre'.[62] It was a tongue of the sea which extended inland for some two hundred miles and was also two hundred miles wide. This is called a *dil* [63] in Turkish. Because our ship could not leave the sight of land, it entered this gulf.

The next night, about two hours after nightfall, when half the sailors were asleep and the other half awake to keep watch, as is their custom, the *yāzijī* [64] and I were strolling on the deck when what did I see, but something flying out of the water like birds! Some fell onto the deck, and the *yāzijī* and I and the sailors ran forward and grabbed some of them. I saw they were fish, with wings like birds! I was astonished at this strange creature.

The sound of our voices woke the master and the captain and everybody else in the ship. When the master, who is in charge of the ship, an old man with long experience in nautical matters, saw the fish, he immediately ordered the crew to strike the mainsail and lower the foresail, which is called the *trinchetta* [65]. They tightened the ropes holding the sails and performed the other tasks required for battening down ships on the sea. When I saw them doing so, with nothing to justify this precaution, for the weather was clear, the sea calm and the breeze mild, I asked the *yāzijī* the reason for striking the sails and tightening the ropes and reinforcing the anchor cables. They had even lashed down the ship's boat, carried on board the ship, with strong ropes, yet the weather was fine and the sea calm.

The *yāzijī* answered that this man, the master, had spent many years at sea, and knew its ways, and that he said "These fish portend a great storm. Because the sea is heaving and waves are surging up from the depths, these fish flee from the turbulence and take flight. This is the reason". When I heard these words, I decided the master was feeble-minded and paid no heed to what he said. Instead, I went to sleep in the ship's life boat. There I slept until around midnight, when I woke up and saw that the sea was rough and waves were piling up on each other. Some of them broke against the ship, so that water was flowing onto the deck to the depth of half a cubit. The scuppers [66] couldn't expel all the water, and the sailors began to bail with scoops until dawn broke. Now things were worse than ever. You could see the waves towering like deep-rooted mountains, and lifting the ship to the summit. Then it would suddenly plunge to the bottom of the sea.

Every one of us crouched down and held on to a rope or the masts or the anchor chains, fearing lest the power of the wind and breakers cast us into the sea. Everything was made much worse for us by the heavy rain and thunder and lightning bolts and the thick fog that surrounded us.

We endured that perilous plight two days and two nights, staring at death and drowning, without food or drink or sleep. We begged Almighty God to save us from drowning and destruction. On the third day we sighted a thick column of dense cloud fall into the sea. As it fell, the sea parted, leaving a great trough in the middle. These were the clouds that drank from the rivers flowing in the depths of the sea, as mentioned previously. I couldn't believe I was seeing it with my own eyes! When the master and the captain saw it, they started back, overcome with fear, for they knew that if the ship fell into that gap it would certainly sink, because when the cloud lifted back up into the sky, the sea would close up over it once again, and the ship would plunge to the bottom of the sea, with no hope of escaping drowning.

Then, despairing of salvation, the captain ordered the *yāzijī* to pray to the Virgin and all the Saints. When the sailors prayed, all those Maghribis on board knew they were going to drown. They all prayed too, and began to weep and cry out loudly. They bade one another farewell, and everyone asked his companion to swear that if he survived, he would look after his children and family. I, too, was staring death in the face. Seeing the sailors, some holding on to barrels, others clutching the rudder and other things, preparing for the worst, I fainted dead away.

At the time, I was crouched in the ship's boat in which I had been sitting. When I came to, I heard the sound of a small child crying. I was puzzled by that, and was sure that child came out of the sea and had fallen from the clouds. Then I fainted away again, as if I were in a heavy swoon.

I didn't recover until the hoped-for cry resounded in my ears. It was the lookout lad, giving the good news that he had sighted land. I immediately came to myself and called out in my turn, waking up all the Maghribi passengers. We were all filled with joy at the news.

This good news came about because the captain, when he saw the clouds, and the trough in the sea, and despaired of salvation, ordered the helmsman to turn the rudder and make for land. He said to himself, "Let the ship run aground, rather than sink in the sea". That was an inspiration from God, and it saved us from drowning. When the ship drew near land, the captain sent the boy to the masthead, to look out for it. The ship was about a mile off shore. It was just sunset, and the sea was calmer than before. The boy sighted land, and immediately came down from the mast and gave the good news to the captain and the passengers.

At hearing the good news, we came to life, filled with joy. We gave thanks to Almighty God for all the good he had done us. Half an hour later, we saw land for ourselves. A short time later, they dropped anchor and the ship came to a halt. The passengers disembarked like the dead rising from their tombs. You would have seen them looking as if they were issuing forth from a sewer, their clothes covered with filth and urine, for during the past three days they performed their natural functions in their trousers and shirts. They were absolutely filthy.

Finally, they washed and changed into clean clothes. We were so hungry and thirsty that we could barely speak to one another, for our saliva had dried up. Everyone began to search for something to eat, but they found the biscuit spoiled with sea water, along with the rice and ghee and everything else. The sea had entered everything, and nothing could be eaten because of the bitterness of salt water. We remained without anything to eat or drink until morning.

When dawn broke, we saw that the sailors had thrown everything on deck into the sea, including the water barrels, the stove, firewood and all of the provisions for the sailors and the captain, as well as what we had brought with us. Then the passengers beseeched the captain to give them something to eat, if he had anything left. The captain took pity on them, and took from his cabin a sack containing biscuit, in which were four or five *ratl* [67] of biscuit for his breakfast, and half a barrel of good drinking water. When the soldier who had chartered the ship saw that the sack of biscuit and half barrel of water was all the provision there was, he ordered one of his servants to draw his sword and stand in front of the barrel to protect it, lest they drink it all at once. Then he issued every one of us half a biscuit just to keep us alive and a small glass of water to wet the throat. When the passengers saw these measures, they despaired of their lives. Having prayed God to save us from drowning, we were now going to die from hunger and thirst.

No one had any idea what to do because the land we had discovered was desert. No one lived there, and there was not a single living thing, not even a bird, because of the scarcity of water and food. It was a sea of sand. Eventually, one of the passengers, an elderly man, told us, "There are people to be found in this land because of the date harvest. They dry them, pack them in baskets and sell them in the lands of the Blacks." [68]

So we had a consultation, and decided to send out a search party and see if they could perhaps find someone who would sell us provisions. The captain and the passengers agreed to the proposal, and they launched the ship's boat into the sea. The *yāzijī* and I and a few of the passengers got in and were taken to the mainland. We walked until we saw palm trees. Now we were sure there were people in that wasteland. When we drew near the palms, we saw some tents, like those of the Bedouin. We were overjoyed, and in our happiness walked faster. We walked for about half an hour through the sand, until we were completely exhausted and out of breath, because our feet sank into the sand up to our ankles.

Finally, in the last stages of exhaustion, we reached the tents. I and the *yāzijī* and a Maghribi man went into one of the tents. I saw a man sitting there. He looked like Satan himself. His eyes were like those of a monkey, his head wrapped in a black cloth. He was black too, and looked terrifying. We asked him if he had any bread to sell. He answered, saying, "What is bread, you unfortunate?" We replied, "Well, what do you eat?" "We eat", he replied, "*basīsa* and dates". We asked the Maghribi who was with us, "What is *basīsa*?" "*Basīsa* is made of barley flour," he answered. "When they come to these lands to harvest the dates, each one of them brings with him a leather bag of barley flour and some ghee. In the palm of their hand, they take a little of the flour and ghee, knead them together, and eat it. This is their food, along with dates."

Then we consulted each other, and agreed to buy some pressed dates from them. We finally agreed on a price of one piastre for two baskets of those dates. We loaded them onto a camel and sent them to the ship along with one of our companions. We told him, "Load the camel on the return journey with two barrels, so we can fill them with the water found here". They refused to allow that, and told us, 'We don't have enough water for both you and us'. They showed us a hole they had dug in the sand. At the bottom was a little water. When we drank from it, we found it was salty, very little different to sea water.

At last, with great reluctance, they gave us permission to fill one barrel for a piastre. In the other barrel they put a little sand, so that it weighed the same as the one with water. Then they loaded them on the camel and we went back to the ship. When we arrived, we loaded the barrels into the boat, got in with them, and rowed to the ship. We began to eat the dates and drink the salty water. We spent three days anchored in that place until the sea grew calm. At last we raised the anchor, opened the sails and voyaged on.

The first two days the storm wind was still blowing, so the captain once more gave the order to make for land, lest we suffer the same disaster we did the first time. When we drew near land, we found that the water was very shallow, so they decided to anchor three miles off-shore. They dropped anchor, and there we spent the night. When dawn broke, we saw that the ship was anchored and sunk in the sand. We were all astonished at the sight of this new disaster. We asked the master, "Why is the ship stuck in the sand and why have the waters of the sea receded almost a mile behind us?" "In this place", he answered, "there is an ebb and flow of the sea. Sailors know that this is a natural thing, and not to be feared".

The upshot was that we spent the day and night with our ship anchored in the sand. At daybreak, we saw the sea returning as it was, but the ship remained fixed in its place. The master and the captain were perplexed at that as well. They immediately ordered the sailors to get in the water and dig under the ship to see what the trouble was. They found that it was stuck on a reef. They began to try to push it into deep water with all their strength and power, but couldn't move it an inch from where it was grounded.

While we were in these dire straits, God sent the remedy. Another ship passed in front of us, and we began to call out for them to come to our aid. When they drew near, the captain and the crew beseeched the captain to ask his sailors to get into the sea and help ours push our ship into deep water. The sailors jumped in the water and worked with ours to push the ship into deep water, but they couldn't budge it. They spent all day battling with it, to no avail. They said, "Take care, lest the ship be smashed!"

So again we were downcast and frightened and despaired for our lives. But by the mercy and care of Almighty God, they advised the master that we should all transfer to their ship, to lighten ours so it would float off the reef. They ordered us down into the skiff, one by one, and took us to their ship. We were finally all on board, except the womenfolk, who were all still in the captain's cabin.

When they saw us all leaving, they were frightened and began to weep and beg us to take them with us. At that moment I heard a child crying. Then I remembered hearing the cry of a child in the depths of that terrible storm. I was deeply astonished at the time, and could not believe that a woman would give birth in such conditions. But Almighty God saved her, and the child survived. I saw it in one of the quarters of Tripoli, being carried by its father. They nicknamed it *Gharīq*, 'Drowned'.

Now let us return to our story. After we were all back on board our ship, our sailors worked to pull it into deep water. We aided them with prayers and supplications for almost an hour, until at last our ship was delivered from danger and floated upon the water, completely undamaged. We gave thanks to Almighty God for His goodness to us. Then they unfurled the sails and we voyaged on. Two days later, the master sighted an old harbour and made for it. He dropped anchor there, thinking that perhaps we could find something to eat and drink.

We encountered no one when we entered, for it was an ancient harbour and in ruins. The inhabitants had migrated many years before. We spent the day there, eating dates and drinking that salty water that dried out our throats and sapped our strength. The sailors had reached the point of eating the ship's cats. If we hadn't had those dates we would have been forced to eat each other. And don't even ask about the effects on us of eating those dates, as we patiently bore the judgments of Almighty God upon us, until He brought us relief.

We passed the night in that harbour and everyone slept, except for a few sailors who took turns keeping watch. Around midnight we were roused by loud cries. It was the captain of the ship, who had awoken and found that the ship had drifted near the shore and was on the point of being smashed to pieces. When the captain saw the situation, and found that all the sailors were sleeping, he almost lost his mind. He grabbed his staff and began beating the sailors without mercy, screaming at them to move quickly, the ship was about to be wrecked. The sailors all jumped up like madmen and started to drag at the anchor rope and pull the ship back into deep water. They found that the rope had slipped from the stern anchor, and there was no way they could pull the ship back into deep water.

Every ship or boat anchors when it is about half a mile from the harbour. The ship drifts, but the rope prevents it from entering the harbour until they loosen it. When they want to enter, they pull up the anchor, so that it no longer holds the ship in position. The ship stays in place, because the stern anchor holds it in position, and it cannot advance a single foot. When they want to sail, they pull on the rope to the stern anchor, until the ship is directly above it. The place is marked by a buoy made of a barrel tied to the anchor rope and floating above the anchor, marking its position for the sailors. They pull it up by the rope until it is beside the starboard side of the ship, and lash it firmly down. When they enter the harbour they drop anchor about half a mile from shore, as we have said. This was the reason our ship was so close to land, because the anchor cable had snapped, cut by reefs on the sea bottom.

Let us return to what we were saying. The master ordered the sailors to get in the ship's boat, and fasten a tow rope from the boat to the ship, man the oars, and pull the ship into deep water. They did as he said, and with the aid of Almighty God, towed us into deep water. Then they unfurled the sails and sailed away, until they were twenty miles from the harbour. They had saved themselves from destruction.

At dawn, our ship returned to the place where the barrel was floating on the surface of the water, as we have explained. They raised the anchor from the depths of the sea and lashed it to the side of the boat. Then we set sail. The wind was fair and the sea smooth, so much so, that we made eight hours sail in one, and the master assured us that we would reach the port of Tripoli in North Africa, which we have already mentioned, that very night. We were overcome with happiness and joy. We congratulated one another on our deliverance, and forgot all the dangers we had undergone, the hunger and privations. Our ship had flown over the surface of the water like a bird.

We continued sailing all day, and that night till midnight. It was a bright night, because the moon was full. We asked the master if we were close to the port, as he had told us. But he was now perplexed at how wrong his estimated time of arrival had been, and he began to sound the depth in that place. When he measured it, he realized it was not the bay of Tripoli as he had thought. He immediately ordered the sailors to furl the mainsail, and set the foresail at half-mast until dawn, so he could see where we were.

Our ship advanced little by little, like the steps of a little child, until dawn broke. We saw land far off, and a high mountain. Then the Maghribi passengers who were with us said to the master that this was the land of Old Tripoli [69], which is sixty miles from New Tripoli. Then the master was certain we had missed the harbour of Tripoli because of the force of the wind we had run before, which had driven our ship eight hours voyage in just one. Finally, he turned the ship about, so the wind that had been with us was now against us, so that now the ship took eight hours to make one hour's headway. We continued like this for three days and three nights and finally reached the harbour of Tripoli. Just as we were about to enter, a storm wind blew off the land, preventing us from entering despite all our efforts. Then two skiffs came out and towed the ship into the harbour. The sailors dropped anchor and furled the sails as was their custom.

All of us were dying to disembark. At that moment, another skiff approached, bearing food, I mean, fruit and a round wooden tray laden with loaves of fine wheaten bread. The captain bought the entire tray and gave it to the sailors to eat. I took a loaf of bread and ate a mouthful, but couldn't swallow it. The bread tasted like ashes. I threw down the loaf and cursed the country that had baked inedible bread.

When the *khoja* saw what I had done, he asked, "What's the matter with you?" I said to him, "After all these trials and tribulations, we get here safely and find that the bread of this country is inedible and tastes like dust!" When he heard these words, he laughed at me and said, "The bread is excellent, but your taste has changed, because it is so long since you have eaten bread".

We finally loaded our baggage into the skiff and went to shore. We headed for the house of the French consul who dwelt in that city. His name was M. Lemaire [70], and he had a fine house. When we entered, we found him at table, eating lunch. When he saw my master, he jumped to his feet and warmly welcomed him. He invited him to lunch with him, but he refused, telling him what we had undergone from the moment we departed from Alexandria until our arrival in Tripoli, and how we had had nothing to eat for fifteen days, and ten days of eating nothing but dates and drinking salty water. When the Consul heard what my master said, he immediately ordered the cook to pluck four fat chickens and make chicken broth. He told my master to eat nothing but chicken broth for several days, until our throats and stomachs were eased. For eight days we ate that broth and drank vintage Cypriot wine, seven years old, until we recovered our strength and our throats returned to normal.

We began to go out and walk around the city of Tripoli, without being harassed at all by anyone, because the consul was very much in the good graces of the Bey [71] who ruled those lands and cities. The consul was like a brother to him. The reason was that the Bey had been taken captive in Malta when he was a young man, and a French cavalier had bought him and taken him to Marseille. He spent a number of days with him, serving him, but was suddenly taken very ill. His owner sent him to the hospital.

One day, Consul Lemaire decided to visit the hospital, in order to comfort the patients, as was their praiseworthy custom. He chanced upon that captive, who was lying in his bed. He sat down beside him and began encouraging and comforting him, urging him to be patient in his adversity, and the patient received great solace and comfort from his words. At last, he asked him his country and religion, and he answered that he was from the Maghrib, from the city of Tripoli, and that he was native to the country and his people were powerful there.

Then M. Lemaire's heart was melted, and he instructed the director of the hospital to put him in a chair and have him carried to his house. He ordered his servants to prepare a room for him and change his clothes and serve him and attend his every need. He immediately sent for a doctor to give him the appropriate treatment, and told him not to stint on the best medicine available. That man remained under the care of the servants and the doctor until his health returned and he recovered from his dreadful malady. He was at last able to get out of bed; as good as he had been before his illness. Then he thanked his benefactor for his generosity, and asked permission to return to his master.

In the end, M. Lemaire added to his kindness by purchasing him from his master and putting him aboard a ship bound for Tripoli. He paid the captain for his passage and food, recommending him to his good graces. Then he bid him farewell and departed. The ship set sail and arrived safely at its destination. He spent a number of years in the service of the reigning Bey, who favoured him because of his faithful service, and he obtained a high position.

He was, in fact, the administrator of the country. He continued to administer it wisely and well, and the people were pleased with him and loved him very much. Now it happened that the reigning

Bey fell gravely ill and a few days later, died. The government and people chose him to be his successor, and rendered obedience to him, in accordance with their ancient custom.[72]

At that very time, M. Lemaire was chosen consul of Tripoli, in complete ignorance of the fact that the captive whom he had purchased from his master and sent back to his country had now become Bey and was governing the country. A few days after M. Lemaire's arrival in Tripoli, he went to present his credentials to the Bey, as is the practice of consuls. When he entered, and the Bey saw him and recognized him, he rose to his feet and embraced him, welcoming him most warmly, saying to the assembled notables, "This man saved me from captivity and death. He who honours him, honours me!" When M. Lemaire left his palace, he sent with him all those who were stationed at his gate, along with his servants. This was the greatest honour ever shown a consul, more than that accorded any of his predecessors. He always called him 'my brother', because of the love he bore him. This is what we heard from trustworthy people of the story of the Bey and the consul.

What I myself witnessed of this blessed consul is something wonderful. What beautiful manners and comportment, what love for the poor and for the captives found in that city! Beside the entrance to his house was a room especially set aside to distribute alms to the poor and unfortunate, and one of his servants was always stationed there to distribute bread and biscuit, which he never neglected to do. He was very pious, and every night before bedtime he would gather his three small boys and his daughter and all the servants in his chapel. He would turn to face them, making sure they were all present, then lead the prayers and vows to the Virgin. When the prayers were ended, everyone went to bed, and he would follow, last of all. In the morning, he would lead everyone to mass. He spent all his energy in purchasing captives and sending them back to their countries, because alms to do so were sent to him from Christian lands for the purpose of ransoming captives. In short, his entire life was spent in good works.

Now it happened one day when we were in Tripoli that some Bedouin of the country brought news that a large Venetian ship had run aground three days' ride from Tripoli. Because Venice was always at war with the North Africans, the Bey sent five hundred soldiers and ordered them to impound the ship and everything of value in its cargo and bring everyone on board captive to Tripoli. After dispatching them, he summoned his brother, Consul Lemaire, and asked him to send one of the ships in the port to transport the booty and the cannons and other things found in its hold. The consul answered, "I hear and obey!"

He immediately left the presence of the Bey and summoned one of the captains of the ships at anchor in the port, and ordered him to go to that shore and load everything found aboard — money, cannon and men — ostensibly to bring them back to the port of Tripoli, but secretly, only God would know where they went. The ship sailed off, looking for the place, but before they reached it, the Bey's soldiers had arrived and the sailors had removed everything from the ship but what was in the hold, which was full of wheat, which they had taken on at al-Adāt.[73] When they had finished loading it, they had headed for Venice, but as they were sailing along, the ship began to founder. So much water entered it, that it was in danger of sinking. So the captain headed for land, for the ship was off the coast of North Africa. Fearing the ship would sink and drown everyone on board, he ran it aground on the sand. They unloaded what they could, and left the ship foundering in the sea, along with the cargo of wheat.

At that moment the Bey's troops arrived, led by one of his officers. They wanted to take the Venetians captive, but they would not surrender. Instead, they immediately fired their cannon and muskets at them, dispersing them and causing them to flee out of range of the guns. They stood them off until the ship sent from Tripoli by the consul arrived. When it had anchored, the captain disembarked and met with the commander of the Venetian soldiers, and understood that they did not want to surrender.

So the French captain consulted with the captain of the Venetian ship and said, "I have been sent on behalf of the French consul, who at the moment is in the city of Tripoli. He ordered me to load everything on your ship, cargo and men, and bring them to Tripoli, on the orders of the Bey and the consul". "We will never give ourselves up and become captives", they replied, "We would rather die on this shore than surrender."

When the captain saw that the Bey's army could do nothing against them, and he couldn't either, because the ship's soldiers numbered two hundred men, not counting the sailors and passengers, he said to them, "Do what I say and I will rescue you from these people and take you safely back to Venice, on the condition that you give me your word in writing that if we arrive safely in Venice, you will protect me from the French, lest they send to take me and punish me. Secondly, you must grant me a pension until my death". They agreed on the spot, and wrote out a document for him, granting what he had asked.

On board that ship, which was a warship, were some distinguished people, among whom was a knight, that is, a *sipāhī* [74], and military officers and high-ranking figures from among the leading men of the Venetian state. When agreement had been reached, the captain went to the commander of the army that had been sent by the Bey, and reassured him, saying that the ship's complement and all the soldiers would obey, for there was no place to which they could flee. Then the commander and all the soldiers who accompanied him returned to the shore, and the commander ordered them to transfer everything that had been on the Venetian ship to the French captain's vessel. When the cargo had been transferred, he ordered the captain and all the ship's complement on board, with the exception of the two hundred soldiers.

The captain did what the commander told him. Then the commander ordered the five hundred soldiers who were with him to escort the two hundred captive Venetian soldiers, and drive them before them to Tripoli and present them to His Excellency the Bey. After he had dispatched them, he wanted to board the French ship, but the captain prevented him, saying, "Let me go to the ship first, and stow everything in the hold, lest it impede us on our voyage. Then I will send the ship's boat to collect you and your servants, because I first want to prepare a place for you worthy of your status". This flattered the commander, and he allowed the captain go to his ship.

The French captain did this because he didn't want the Bey to blame the consul if he took the commander and his retinue captive, for as soon as he reached the ship, he ordered the sailors to raise the forward anchor, and when the ship was positioned over the stern anchor, to raise it as well. Then they unfurled the sails and sailed away.

When the commander saw the ship sailing off, he realized the deception, and immediately decided to rejoin his troops and return to Tripoli. Meanwhile, the French ship made for Venice with its passengers and saved them from captivity.

A few days later the commander and his troops reached Tripoli, along with the two hundred Venetian soldiers they had taken captive. Their entry caused a great sensation. The captives were bound with rope, and he led them before His Excellency the Bey, who ordered them all to be thrown into prison.

Then he summoned the consul, and told him what he had heard from the commander he had sent on his behalf, and how the captain had stranded him ashore and sailed off, and as yet he hadn't learned the reason for his departure for their country and for rescuing them. "But you may be certain that if the affair turns out as I suspect, I will kill every one of those two hundred soldiers. If it were not for the love I bear you, I would impound all the French ships in the harbour, until that ship is returned to me."

When the consul heard these words from the Bey, he replied that he too was enraged at what had happened, if indeed it turned out to be true. He began to soothe the Bey and calm his anger. He promised that if the story were true, the ship would be returned, and that he would write to the Sultan of France that he was sending an envoy on his behalf demanding the return of the ship. Then he asked, by the love he bore him, to release the prisoners unharmed, for they were guiltless. The guilt lay with those who forced the captain to flee. And this was because of the commander's lack of judgment, who had given permission for everyone to board the ship, so they were able to overpower the captain and his men and take possession of it. When the Bey heard what the consul had to say, he said, "You're right, my brother, the whole fault lies with the commander, and I will punish him for it". He immediately ordered the two hundred imprisoned soldiers to be freed, "Out of respect to my brother, the consul". The captives were brought before him, and when they were in his presence, he told them, "I am releasing you at the request of the consul, so kiss his hands, and go in peace!" When all was over, the consul rose and thanked the Bey for his generosity, and returned to his house. I was an eyewitness to all this from the beginning.

They told me another story of the love of that Bey for the consul.

It happened that the corsair ships of the Bey of Tripoli were cruising the seas as was their custom [75], when they came across a Genoese ship, pursued it and finally overcame it. They boarded it and captured it and brought it to Tripoli. After anchoring in the harbour, they informed the Bey of their prize. The Bey ordered them to bring the men found on the ship before him. When they were gathered before him, I mean the captain, the soldiers, the sailors and the passengers, they numbered just under two hundred souls. The Bey examined them closely, and noticed a boy among them, very young, with handsome features and looks, which shone with marks of nobility and grace, dressed in fine clothing. The youth was the son of a Roman prince, whose father had sent him to visit his aunt in Messina, and enjoy the voyage there. The Bey was captivated. He was so smitten that he drew near him and caressed him. He ordered the dragoman to calm his fear and terror, and tell him, "Don't be afraid, His Excellency the Bey loves you, and wants you to be his son, and his heart's love!" But the youth was inconsolable, and began to weep. When the Bey saw that the boy would not be consoled, and kept weeping, he was unable to bear the heart-rending sight, and sent him to his womenfolk to be comforted. Then he chose two of the prisoners, both very young, and ordered them to serve that youth and befriend him. He sent the other men into captivity.

As for the youth, he tried, day after day, to win his affection. He began to leave the harem and stand before the Bey, modestly and politely, and love for him grew in the heart of the Bey. He would frequently clasp him to his breast and kiss him. Everyone in the palace honoured that youth for the sake of the Bey. Time passed, and he was admired by everyone. Then one day a French ship came into the harbour. The captain disembarked and went to the consul and gave him a letter, sent by one of the dukes of France. A passage in it read, "A youth has fallen captive there in Tripoli. His name is such-and-such. His father sent us a letter asking us to write and urge you to do your utmost to redeem his son from captivity. No matter what it costs, we will send it to you. He sends, in the custody of the captain who is delivering this letter, two chests of valuable gifts. If they won't free him for money, you could present these gifts to the Bey who reigns over that city. If he wants money on top of these gifts, give him whatever he wants, you have free rein in this matter. In sum, the only answer we expect from you is sending us the boy. That is all. Peace."

When the consul had read the letter, he had no idea what to do, because he knew of the great love of the Bey for the boy, and that he would never free him. Finally, he went to the Bey, as was his custom, to make another request entirely. When he came into his presence, the Bey invited him to sit down, and after they had chatted away like the old friends they were, the consul asked the Bey to give him his word that he would grant his request. Otherwise, he would not make it.

The Bey, never imagining that he would make a request regarding the boy, answered immediately, saying, "Speak, my brother, I will grant your request, whatever you ask". The consul still hesitated to make his request, and the Bey once again said, "Speak, my brother, whatever you want, you know any request you make of me won't be refused, if it lies in my power".

So then the consul told the Bey about the letter which he had received from the duke, and that "He wanted me to ask you to return that boy to his father and mother, and they have sent to Your Excellency gifts suitable to one of your rank". Then he sent for the gifts and presented them. But the Bey refused to look at them. Marks of anger appeared on his face. The consul did not say another word, and neither did the Bey. He rose and left the consul alone and went angrily into his harem.

This matter went hard with him for two reasons. First, he had given his word that he would not refuse a request. Second, he couldn't bear being separated from the boy. When the consul saw that his wish would not be granted, and that his hopes were dashed, he returned to his house, very downcast and depressed. As for the Bey, he feared losing the love and respect of the consul for not granting his request.

The next day he summoned him to his presence to put his mind at rest, and when the messenger came to deliver the invitation to visit the Bey, he thought of a subterfuge to free the boy. The consul had a little son named Nicolas, whom the Bey loved very much, like a father. Whenever he accompanied his father to visit the Bey, the Bey would hug him and kiss him and give him whatever he wanted, and never refused his requests. This little boy was extremely clever. His father the consul told him, "When the time comes to return from visiting the Bey, grab the boy and hold on tightly, and don't let him go. When they try to take your hands off him, cry, and appeal to the Bey to let him go with you". They strolled about together for the rest of the day until evening. Then he warned him, saying to him, "Make sure you don't let his hand go, even if I order you to do so, don't release him!"

After he had warned him, and told him what to do, they went to visit the Bey. When the consul stood before the Bey, the Bey welcomed him and eased his fears, saying to him, "I have been concerned that you may be annoyed with me for not acceding to your request. If I had known you were going to request the boy, I would not have given you my word that I would grant any request you made. But the fault was not yours". When the Bey inspected the gifts the consul had brought from the boy's grief-stricken father and mother, his annoyance vanished. Then the consul and the Bey began to chat as they used to.

When they had had drinks and coffee, an hour passed, and the son of the consul played with the boy, the way children do. At last the consul rose and asked the Bey's permission to return to his house. Then Nicolas grabbed the boy's hand, and wanted to take him with them. The servants tried with soothing words to convince him to release the boy's hand, but no one could make him do so. He began to cry, and begged the Bey to let him take the boy with him, as his father had instructed him. The Bey was unaware of the subterfuge, and tried to soothe Nicolas. He sent for a little mare he could ride, and go with his father, but he wouldn't go unless the boy went with him. Then his father the consul scolded him, ordering him to release the boy, but he cried even more and implored the Bey.

When the Bey saw how determined the child was, he didn't want to anger him, out of respect for his father and his love for him, so he gave his consent to taking Nicolas and gave him leave to stay as long as he liked. Nicolas was filled with joy, and ran to kiss the hand of the Bey, and the Bey embraced him and kissed him and let him go, giving permission for the boy to go with him as his wished. The two boys went together to the consul's house, happy and joyful.

The boy spent several days in the consul's house, but the Bey did not enquire after him. It was as if he had forgotten him. When the consul realized that the Bey was not going to ask about him, he understood that he had given him to his son Nicolas. The consul immediately sent for the captain of the ship which had brought the gifts, and ordered him to ready his vessel to sail. At midnight he sent the boy to the ship. As soon as he was on board, the ship set sail with the boy.

Sometime later, letters arrived from the duke and the prince, the father of the boy, thanking him for his generosity and kindness, and that of his son Nicolas, who had freed his son from captivity. Inside one of the letters was a legal document, like a *hujja* [76]. This document stated, "I grant to Nicolas, the son of Consul Lemaire, the Frenchman, an endowment in perpetuity of the annual revenues of my properties to the amount of one thousand piastres annually, and let no one may oppose this grant to him and his descendants forever. It is signed by my hand in witness of what I have stated. Peace!" His agent in Rome sent one thousand piastres every year, and still does to this day.

This is the story of the love of the Bey for the consul, as it was told to me at the time by the consul's dragoman. He was present during the events, and what he told me is true, for I heard the same story from others.

We stayed in the consul's house in great comfort and pleasure until one day the Jesuits living in this city celebrated a festival.[77] I wanted to go and attend mass with them, to receive absolution. I dressed in my finest clothes, the ones I had sent for from Aleppo. Then it occurred to me to wear the turban sash and the *kavuk* [78] that are the costume of our country. When the consul saw the way I was dressed, he admired me, for my costume amazed him. Then I went to the Jesuit monastery and attended mass.

After mass, I left the monastery and headed back to the consul's house. As I was walking along, four janissaries chanced upon me. When they saw me, they stopped and stared at me and began to shake their heads and curse me in their language. They came towards me as if they intended to kill me. I feared for my life. Then one of them left the others and ran at me as if he were going to kill me, tore the turban from my head and went off with his companions. I was left trembling with fear and terror, almost fainting. When I saw that they were now quite far away, I pulled myself together and walked on, glancing behind me to make sure they weren't following me.

I came to the consul's house, my head uncovered and still trembling. Nicolas, the son of the consul, was standing at the door with his sister Margarita. When they saw the state I was in, they ran and told their father, the consul. When the consul and my master heard what had happened to me, they both came downstairs to see how I was. The consul was horrified, and asked what had happened to me, and who had stolen my turban. I told him everything that had happened to me.

When the consul heard my story, he was furious, and immediately told me to bring the dragoman into his presence. When the dragoman arrived, the consul ordered him to discover who had stolen the sash and *kavuk* from the head of one of his guests, and to bring them back without fail. The dragoman left his presence and sent someone to summon me, and ask me where the incident had occurred. I told him it happened near the Jesuit monastery. Then he left me and went off.

An hour later the dragoman summoned me again and said to me, "Why did you don the turban sash and *kavuk*? In this country, no one is allowed to wear such a sash and *kavuk* but a pasha sent from Istanbul by the Sultan as an ambassador! No one else may do so! Now there is no way those who stole your sash are going to return it. I fear this matter is going to lead to trouble, and you are the cause of it. Therefore, if the consul asks you about the sash, tell him they sent it back, and let's extinguish this fire. The soldiers of this country are hard, troublesome men, and each unit protects all the others. They do not fear the Bey when they are out to make trouble".

When I heard these words from him, I swallowed my misgivings and promised him that I would tell the consul that my sash and *kavuk* had been returned, and that if he asked me to put them on, I would excuse myself by telling him that "In this country it was embarrassing to dress in sash and *kavuk*, and that is why I ask you to kindly excuse me from wearing them, lest harm befall me".

So I agreed to do as the dragoman said and wore only my *qalpaq* when we went down for lunch with the consul. When he saw me, he asked if they had sent back my sash. "Yes, they brought it", I replied. "Then why aren't you wearing it?" he asked. I answered him, giving the reasons told me by the dragoman. "Go put it on", he said, "You have nothing to fear from anyone in my house."

These were his words, and then he went in to lunch with my master. When I didn't appear, he sent one of his servants and summoned me to his presence. He was seated at the table, "What's the matter with you, why aren't you wearing your turban?" "I'll wear it tomorrow" I replied. "I want you to put it on right now!" he said, and my master told me to go do the same.

I didn't know what to do. If I told him that it hadn't been returned to me, I feared being the cause of strife. If I told him it had been sent back, he would ask me why I wasn't wearing it. I decided to tell my master in secret that it had not been sent back, while the consul sat waiting for me to return. When my master saw that the consul wanted to know whether my turban had been returned or not, he decided to tell him the whole story. When the consul heard that the dragoman had not brought back the turban, he sent for him.

Now this dragoman had formerly been a captive. He converted to Islam, and the consul brought him into his household in order to bring him back to the Faith. When the dragoman stood before him, he began to scold and curse him. Finally, he ordered him to go to the Bey, "And tell him on my behalf to arrest that janissary and give him two hundred lashes, take the turban cloth and send it to me immediately!"

The dragoman left his presence, with no idea what to do. If he went to the Bey, he knew from his knowledge of the man, that he would not refuse a request from his brother the consul, and would arrest the janissary and lash him, in which case the garrison would revolt, and no good would come of it.[79]

So he didn't do what the consul had asked. Instead, he went to the officers of the janissary's company [80] and told them what had happened. When they heard what he had to say, they ordered the commanding officer of that company to immediately send the *shāsh* and the *kavuk*. He obeyed their orders and sent both to them. They gave them to the dragoman, and told him to deliver them to His Excellency the Consul on their behalf, and tell him, "The officers of the garrison dissuaded me from complaining to His Excellency the Bey about something so trivial. He can set his mind at rest; we will punish the wrong done to him".

The dragoman returned to the consul, bringing with him the turban cloth and *kavuk*, and told him everything that had happened, and that the officers of the garrison did not want him to lodge a complaint with the Bey for something that did not merit such a serious step. He sent him greetings on behalf of the corps, and promised him that disciplinary measures would be taken against the soldier, as he asked. Then the consul asked me to don the turban cloth, and I did as he requested, and put it on in his presence. In my heart, however, I was still terrified that those soldiers might encounter me wearing that *shāsh,* and attack me again. Now whenever I left the consul's house, I would remove the *shāsh* and don my *qalpaq.*

When I returned to Aleppo from my travels, I discovered that M. Lemaire was now consul there, and his children were with him. I went to say hello to him and to his son Nicolas. He welcomed me warmly, and paid me every honour. He told the merchants all about me and our time together in Tripoli, and the things that had happened when I was his guest along with my master, Paul Lucas.

Now let us return to our story. I stayed in Tripoli in the house of Consul Lemaire for thirty days, eating and drinking and enjoying life all that time. We went out to look at many things, but I will not go into detail about them, for the sake of brevity. At the end of our stay, my master wanted to go overland to the city of Tunis, in order to visit places and see the lie of the land.

When he informed the consul of his plan, the consul went to the Bey and obtained a *firmān,* or *berat* [81], recommending my master to all the governors found along our route that lay in his territory and under his authority. Then he supplied us with abundant provisions and summoned a good and trustworthy caravan conductor, instructing him to take us wherever we wished to go, and not oppose our wishes, whatever we wanted to do. This country is so safe it is possible to carry gold and travel without fear.

Finally, we bade the consul farewell and set off from Tripoli, heading for the city of Tunis. We journeyed for five days along the desert route, but we went at our own pace. Every time we came to a village, we visited it, and observed the peasants, their occupations and fields and so forth. At last we came to Jerba.[82]

When we entered the city, all the inhabitants came to look us over, because they saw we were strangely dressed. They asked our guide about us, and he told them, "This man is a doctor. He was with the Bey of Tripoli, and is now on his way to Tunis, to practice medicine there". We asked them where the palace of the governor was, and they showed us the way.

When we came to the palace, we asked permission to enter and meet His Excellency the Governor. They granted us permission to enter his presence, and my master handed him the *berāt* the Bey had issued him. When he had read it, and understood its contents, he smiled at us and welcomed my master. I translated between them. The Bey asked me about my master, who he was, and what was his nation? I answered that he was a doctor, and a Frank, of French origin. Then he asked me for what reason he had come to this country. I said to him, "My lord, this man travels about, searching for medicinal herbs that are found growing in these lands".

So he gave us permission to be seated, and ordered the servants to bring refreshments and dates and coffee, as was the custom of their country. Then he asked my master to treat his very severe abdominal cramps, which prevented him from eating. If he ate even a little, he felt pain. When I told my master what the governor had said, my master told him, "Be consoled; I will prepare medication, which if you take for three days will strengthen your insides and you will be able to eat five times a day without feeling full".

When the governor heard this, he was very pleased, hoping

for relief. He immediately ordered us to be given fully furnished quarters, food and drink, and dismissed us. We entered our quarters, and my master immediately began to prepare the medication. It was a compound of parsley water, thickened with sugar, to which he added four *mithqāl* [83] of ground pearls and some drugs. He poured it into a Chinese cup and sent it to him. He took it that day and the next, and his stomach relaxed and he began to eat even better than he had before he fell ill.

When he saw that he had recovered, he summoned us to his presence and thanked my master profusely, treating him with great honour because he had cured his stomach ache. He had begun to eat just as he had formerly. He asked my master to fill a large Martaban [84] jar with that medication, so he could use it whenever he needed. My master answered, "With pleasure, upon my head and eye! However, I will need fifty drams [85] of pearls, either ground or whole". He immediately sent for that amount of pearls and had them brought to our quarters, where we prepared the compound.

Then we went out to walk about and look at the sights of the city. One day when we were strolling along, we passed by a square in which were three high towers the shape of sugar cones [86], built of human skulls. We were horrified at the fearful sight. An elderly man was passing by, and we asked him, "What is this horrible spectacle, why are these skulls built into these towers?" [87]

He answered, "When this city was in the hands of the Spanish Christians, and the Ismā'īlī [88] of the Maghrib went to war with them, they conquered the whole island. When they came to this city, it resisted them, and they besieged it for three months. The only way they could take it was by starving them out. The commander of the army swore that when he took the city, he would kill all the inhabitants, men, women and children, to the last man. When he captured the city, he ordered the soldiers to kill them all, sparing no one. They built these towers of skulls as a memorial for the ages. The dead lie inside and their skulls reinforce the structures, solidly built into as they are with plaster, so they will never crumble, and will last for centuries". When we heard this sad story, we were saddened at the fate of the people of that country, which is called

Africa [89], once the home of eighteen bishoprics, and their story is well-known in the history books.

After we had seen the sights in that city, we went to the governor to seek his permission to travel on and to bid him farewell. He gave us a letter of recommendation to the governor of Sfax. We took the letter and journeyed on through those lands. On our way we passed towns and villages, many of them in ruins. We continued until we came to Sfax. It is a populous city with strong walls and gardens, streams and orchards.

They showed us the way to the governor's palace, and after asking permission, we entered and presented him with the Bey's letter and the letter from the governor of Jerba. When he had read them, he welcomed us and gave us permission to be seated. They brought us refreshments and coffee, as is the custom and he began to question my master about that medicine which we had given to the governor of Jerba, asking if we had any left. My master had a little in his chest, so he said, "Yes, I do" and promised to send him a small Martaban jar of it. At that, he ordered them to give us a place to stay, and there we took our ease for the rest of the day.

The next day we left the house and went to the governor and gave him the medication. He was very pleased, and ordered his servants to make us welcome and attend to our needs. We thanked him for his kindness and went to tour the city and visit the ancient sites. These were the remains of buildings from the time when Christians dwelt there, churches, monasteries and schools. All were in ruins. My master copied historical inscriptions from the stones which identify those places.

We bought many ancient medallions, of silver and copper, which were used as money in those places, as well as other old things, like books of stories and histories of the Circassians [90], some in Arabic, others in Latin. All of this was by means of practicing medicine, for my master would treat patients and ask them to search for these things, and then pay well for them.

We stayed in that city for seven days, then went to the governor to say goodbye and ask for a letter of recommendation to the governors we would encounter along our way. The governor answered, saying,

"When you are a day's ride from here, you will enter the territory of the Bey of Tunis, and my letter won't help you at all. But fear not, the way is safe". Finally, we said goodbye and went to our place and got provisions for the road. We travelled with the guide who had brought us from Tripoli.

We travelled for eight days. Along the way we passed many ruined buildings. Among them was a land in which there were vestiges of habitations, and we saw olive trees of stone, bearing stone olives. We also found stone watermelons and a cheese [91] of stone. We broke one of them open and saw yellow stone seeds. We found a dry riverbed, and among the rocks a stone fish. There were flat pieces of stone on which were the forms of fish. We wondered at the sight.

We asked the guide about these things we saw. He told us, "This place was built and inhabited by men, but God became angry with them and sent a powerful storm wind, so strong that it heaped up sand and completely covered the town that had been in this place. They were all buried beneath the sand for many years, and because of this the trees and plants were changed to stone. Finally, Almighty God sent a great wind which blew away that sand, and it became the high dune you see right in front of you".

We took the olive and the watermelon and the stone imprinted with the image of a fish and travelled on until we came to the city of Sousse. When we arrived, our guide forbade us to enter, saying to us, "The people of this town are heretic scoundrels. They will not befriend Sunni Muslims, Christians, or Jews, in fact, no one of any other faith, because of the extent of their fanaticism and hatred for others". So we decided to alight outside the walls of the town, and there spent the night.

When dawn broke, we prepared to travel, and sent the guide to the town to buy enough food and meat for the road. After he had purchased everything we needed, he rented a pack animal from one of the inhabitants of the town to take with us. He already had two animals with him, but he always rented a pack animal in every town we visited, along with its owner, who travelled with us. Once he had rented the animal, he loaded it with all our things, as he had always done. My master and I rode our animals unencumbered, but he used the rented animal to carry our baggage.

When he had finished loading the man's animal, the owner was upset that his animal should carry everything, while his own animal was unburdened. The guide responded by saying, "I didn't rent your animal in order to carry everything myself!" They began to quarrel and fight with one another. Then that man went up to his animal and tossed everything to the ground. Amongst the baggage was a crate containing twenty-four bottles of excellent wine, supplied to us by the consul of Tripoli, because we would find no wine along our route. My master was unable to drink water unmixed with wine.

When he saw that man dump the animal's load to the ground, including the wine box, he was sure he had broken all the bottles and he would be out of wine. He went out of his mind, and screamed in a loud voice and cursed that man in Turkish and Arabic and French, for he knew the Turkish word *kabak* and the Arabic word *kalb* meant 'dog'. He went up to him and pushed him, as if he wanted to throw him down on his face[92]. And what did we see, but the man suddenly running towards the gate of the town, yelling "Help! Come and save me! They cursed me and tried to kill me!"

Everyone swarmed out of the gate like hungry locusts and headed towards us. When the guide saw the crowd issuing forth from the gate, he feared for us, and said to my master, "Flee! Save yourself, or they will kill you!" My master fled, and took refuge in a corner of one of the watchtowers on the wall. Meanwhile, the crowd descended on us, and the only one they saw was me. They grabbed me and started to strangle me, but the man stopped them, saying, "He is not the one who cursed me!" and gave me a hard push that released me from their grasp. I entreated that man and the others to calm down, but they ran off searching for my master.

As for him, he had found a crevice and taken refuge in it, hiding himself from sight with straw that he found there, which concealed him and they couldn't find him. Meanwhile, the guide and I went to that man and I promised him that I wouldn't load his animal with anything, I would just ride it unburdened. I also won his allegiance by promising him two gold pieces on top of his hire. When he heard about the two gold pieces, he recovered himself. He got the men to go back, by telling them, "I will lodge a complaint against him with the Bey when I get to Tunis, and he will know how to deal with him".

They finally all went off and we went back to loading our baggage on the guide's mount. I inspected the wine box and found that not a single bottle had been broken. They were all in good order, and none of the wine had leaked. After we had finished loading up, we walked along the walls looking for the *khoja*, but saw no one. We stood wondering what to do, when he spotted us from underneath the straw and climbed out of the hole and joined us. He was terrified, and his face was pale. I tried to encourage him by saying, "Don't worry, those people aren't going to come back, we have nothing to worry about. And the box of wine is fine, not a drop has been spilled".

I told him everything that had happened during his absence, and how I had only been saved from their hands with great difficulty, saying "If it had not been for that man getting them to go back, they would have killed me without doubt, and if they had been able to find you, they would have killed you too. Let us thank Almighty God for His goodness and aid, which saved us from the hands of those ruffians, those savage beasts".

At last we mounted and rode until we were some two hours from the town. We dismounted in a green meadow with a spring of water. We unloaded our things from the animals and had lunch and rested a while. After lunch and a rest, we rode on through desert until evening, without finding a single village or human, not even a bird. We spent that night out in the open, without a covering.

At dawn we rode on, travelling through the day until evening, when we reached a valley called *Wādī al-Sibāʿ*, 'The Valley of the Wild Beasts'. We saw a group of people camped there, so we camped alongside them. That valley can only be traversed by a group of at least twenty or thirty, in order to cross it without fear of the beasts.[93]

We spent the night there, and at dawn rode down into the valley. There were fifteen of us, most from neighbouring villages and farms. We rode all that day until evening, when we came to a large open plain. All around it fires burned night and day, because every caravan that entered the place cut down the trees and set them afire, lest the wild beasts enter and attack the men and animals. We spent the night on this plain, and all night long could hear the snarling of the beasts and the drubbing of their tails on the ground and the whinnying of the horses, because they could see the beasts in the darkness.

When dawn broke we journeyed on through the valley until around midday we rode out of the valley, and continued on our way. Towards evening we came to a salt flat, stretching as far as the eye could reach. The salt was white as snow. We spent the night beside it, and entered it the next day, because there was no other route. We covered our faces with blue handkerchiefs or *bawāšī* to protect our eyes from the glare. We rode over that salt flat for a little more than three hours, until we came out of it and continued until we came to a town called Hammamet.

Hammamet is populous and its inhabitants are seafarers. We entered it and stayed there that night. The next day we went out to look around and see the sights, and met some people from Tunis and befriended them when we told them that we were on our way to Tunis to stay with the consul. We told them about the man from whom we had rented the horse in Sousse, who was still with us, and how he had roused the people against us and how they wanted to kill us. When they heard this, they rose up against him and wanted to kill him on the spot, saying, "You heretic! You deserve to die!" Finally, my master intervened for him and gave him the hire for his horse and we got rid of him. He didn't even stay to insist on the two gold coins I had promised him.

We spent the rest of the day there, and the next set out for the city of Tunis. When we came to a caravansary three hours from Tunis the caravan halted. The merchants in the caravan didn't want to enter the city in the light of day, because they wanted to smuggle some goods past the customs' officials. So we stayed in the caravansary.

Nearby was a hot spring [94], I mean hot water issuing forth from the ground, and I went to see it. I entered the place where the spring was, and saw a large pool, some one hundred feet long and wide. Rising above it was a high, wide dome, protecting the pool. All around it were people taking the waters, some standing knee-deep, others up to their bellies, and others up to their chests. The hot vapour rising from the water reached the top of the dome. There were people guarding the clothes, and when a man stepped out of the water, he gave the man who kept an eye on his clothing an *'uthmānī*. So I took off my clothes and left them with one of the guardians, then tested the water with one foot.

When I discovered how hot it was, I immediately withdrew it, certain that it had been scalded by that very hot water. The man beckoned me to his side and said, "Why are you going off? Sit down and I will show you how to take the waters". So I sat down beside him and he told me, "Put one foot in, slowly, slowly, to test. Now put in the other foot, slowly, slowly". So I did as he advised, and found that my feet rested on a step, and the water reached my ankles. I stayed that way until my feet grew accustomed to the heat of that water, and I could no longer feel them burning. Then the man told me, "Now place your feet on the second step" so I did as I had done the first time. And then I reached the third step, until the water reached my chest. In the end, I stayed in the water about half an hour, and no longer felt the heat. I could feel the moist humours accumulated in my limbs dispersing because of that sulfurous water, for it has great beneficial effects on ailments and diseases, and many of the people who suffer from *asqām* [95] and leprosy and other ailments seek these waters. That pool is always brimming with water, night and day. I got out of the water at last and put on my clothes and returned to my master. I told him about those waters and the pool that had such benefits.

When he heard the story from me, he wanted to go take the waters too. So we went there and entered and he saw the water boiling and said to me, "How on earth could you get in that?" So I told him the method of gradually immersing oneself, as I and others there had done. He stuck his hand in the water to test the temperature, and found it too hot to bear, and refused to go in. So we went back to our place. He was amazed that people could get in water that was so hot without being scalded.

We stayed in the caravansary until close on midnight. Then the merchants and the guide arose and loaded up their goods and left the caravansary and we accompanied them. As we travelled through the desert, my master studied the stars and saw that it was midnight. He didn't want to continue following the caravan, so we remained there in that wilderness. Our guide had preceded us with the caravan and the pack horse loaded with our belongings. He was unaware that we had lagged behind and been separated from the main body of the caravan.

We stayed in the desert until dawn, then mounted our horses and rode towards the city. Unfortunately, we went the wrong way and strayed from the track. When the guide and the caravan reached the city and he realized we were missing, he turned back to search for us. We, however, were on a different track, and came upon a peasant heading towards his village. We asked him if we were near Tunis and he said, "You've missed Tunis, the city is to the north of you. Turn back until you find a wide path and follow it until you get to the city". Then we asked him to come with us and show us the way and that we would recompense him. So we went back with him until he pointed out the way.

We followed the road for about an hour, and met our guide and two North Africans from Tunis. The reason they were with him was that the guide had sent our belongings to the consul, and when the consul asked where we were, he told him that we had fallen behind, and not entered the city with the caravan. When the consul heard that we were delayed, he sent two of his men with the guide to bring us back to his place. When they reached the outskirts of the city, they knew we must be nearby, but saw no one. They rode on swiftly, and came to the place where we had spent the night, but saw no sign of us. The guide was worried, and feared something had happened to us. They turned back, and then sighted us in the distance. The guide called out to us, and we turned and rode back to them. They asked the reason for our delay, and we told them what had happened to us, and how we had strayed from the track.

Then we all rode together until we reached the city, and from there went to the consul's house. It was a large *khan*. The French merchants all stayed there. We climbed a staircase, and entered the consul's quarters. He came forward to meet us and welcomed my master, and they greeted each other. The consul had received a letter from the consul of Tripoli, informing him of our arrival, and telling him that my master was one of the King of France's travelers. He received him with great honour and gave him a furnished room to sleep in. They gave me a room too. All our belongings were moved to our rooms, and a little while later all the merchants dwelling in the consul's house came to greet my master and congratulate him on his safe arrival.

We spent the day there, meeting the merchants, and the following day my master went to return their visits, as is their custom. After three days, the consul asked my master to go with him pay his respects to the Bey, who is the sultan of Tunis. My master was delighted to do so. They readied a coach and my master and the consul rode side by side. Some of the merchants and servants accompanied them on horseback, I among them.

We went together to the Bey's palace, which they call the Bardo [96], about an hour and a half from the city. When we reached that place, I saw something beyond description. There were gardens and greenery and springs of flowing water. In the middle I saw a beautifully constructed palace, with lofty pavilions splendidly decorated, with glass windows on all sides. We entered the main entrance of the palace through an *iwān* [97] and a pool brimming with water and splendid architecture. Then we passed through a second gate to the Bey's palace, bigger than the first, its buildings nobler and even more elaborate. We then climbed a wide marble staircase, with an easy ascent. Finally, we reached a courtyard, paved with white marble, with a pavilion in each corner dedicated to one of the four seasons.

The Bey was seated in the pavilion dedicated to the season of spring. They informed the Bey of the arrival of the consul, and he granted permission for him to enter. So we all entered the pavilion and stood before the Bey. The consul and his retinue bowed to the Bey, and he welcomed them and invited them to be seated. After we were seated, they brought us refreshments and coffee, as is the custom. Finally, the consul told the Bey of the arrival in his country of my master in the course of his travels, adding "And now he has accompanied us in order to meet you".

Then my master arose from his seat and bowed to His Excellency the Bey. The Bey greeted him and made him welcome. He began to ask him about some of the things he had seen on his travels, and the cities he had passed through. My master answered all his questions. The consul's dragoman was expert at translating what he said clearly and the Bey understood everything perfectly.

The Bey was pleased at my master's responses to his questions, especially his praise for his country and its beauty, and the good order and beautiful craftsmanship he had observed in his palace. He told him that he had seen its like nowhere else in Ottoman lands. Then the Bey asked him, "So you approve of my palace?" "I do", he answered, "but the greatest pleasure is your radiant face and kindly nature, and the beauty of your gracious speech", and he made other similar polite compliments to His Excellency the Bey.

Finally, after extended courtesies, the consul arose and requested permission from the Bey to depart. The Bey granted his request, but told the dragoman to tell my master that he must continue to visit him throughout his stay in Tunis, until his departure. "I hear and I obey!" replied my master, "This is a great honour for me." Then the Bey told them to bring him one of the best horses to ride when he came to visit his palace. My master thanked him profusely, and we left his presence and headed back to Tunis to the consul's house.

The next day we left the consul's in the company of one of his servants to look at the city. We saw that its buildings and good order were without parallel. We walked through the streets and markets, where the merchants sat before their shops as if they were princes, judging by the beauty of their clothes and their gentle speech and the honourable reception they gave to customers. Several of them invited us to sit with them, to see if they could be of service to us in case there was anything we required, or wanted, that they could supply, with similar expressions of courtesy and thoughtfulness. The fact is, we found the people of Tunis completely unlike those of other countries in North Africa.

On our excursions I told anyone who asked that my master was a doctor. The news that a French doctor had come to town spread throughout Tunis. They began taking us from place to place to treat patients. My master diagnosed them and wrote out prescriptions. Many people were cured of dire ailments.

We came to a *khan*, which was the *khan* of the captives. We entered, and found many men there. Each had his own job. In the *khan* was a church for the captives, and Capuchin monks who celebrated mass there. There were three other *khan*s for captives. Each had its own church and monks from one of the four monastic orders.[98] We visited those *khan*s as well, to see what they were like, and I saw that the life of those captives was extremely easy, unlike the lot of captives in other countries. This is all because of the wise policy of the Bey.[99]

They also took us to the houses of the great men, to diagnose their sick. We visited many other places as well, until there was no a single place we hadn't seen. I found the markets and layout of this city similar to Aleppo, except that it is smaller.

We visited the Bey frequently, and when we arrived at the palace, he would send people to conduct us to his pavilion, because from there he could see us leaving the gate of the city. My master would sit and chat with him while I translated.

One day the Bey asked my master if he knew anything about jewels and precious stones. He admitted that he knew something about them. Then we entered the treasury of the old king and they brought out gemstones and jewels. My master knew about such things, and was able to value those rubies and emeralds and diamonds and similar gems. There were stones unfamiliar to the Bey, who didn't know their names. He began to give them their correct names, and describe their special properties and values. The Bey was very pleased with him and impressed by his knowledge. They sat in the treasury until evening.

The Bey and my master left at last and went up to the pavilion. The Bey noticed through the window that the Father was just leaving the city gate. He said to the captives standing in his presence, "Go greet your Father!" One of the Fathers would come every night to the Bey's palace and sleep in the room of the captives in the Bey's service. The next day he would celebrate mass for them. This was with the Bey's permission. They would all spend the day with the Father, and return early the next day to their posts with the Bey. My master was astonished at the kindness of that Bey. His wisdom was unbelievable. This is what I witnessed of that gracious, refined, and noble Bey. I don't know how to describe him, but whoever reads this account can see how his deeds describe him well. At last we asked permission to depart from His Excellency the Bey and returned to our place.

Another day, one of the merchants summoned us to his house because there was a sick person in his household. We went to the merchant's house and he greeted us with honour. After my master had examined the patient, the merchant invited us to breakfast. After breakfast and coffee, the man showed us through his palace.

In the reception room was a cage, and in it I saw some small wild animals. My master examined them and was struck by their strange appearance. They were charming to look at. Their bodies were really odd, and their form was like this: one of them was the size of a small rabbit, about two feet tall, with small hands under its chin, with palms and five fingers like a human, to eat with. It tail was long, like a wild beast, and curled over its back. The lower third of its tail was tufted with white, and speckled with black. Its eyes were like those of a gazelle. Its nose was like that of a pig, and its fur like that of a deer. There were four or five animals in the cage.[100]

When my master saw them, he was astonished at their strange form. The merchant asked him if he had ever in his life seen the like on his travels through the world. Finally, my master asked him to sell them to him. The merchant answered, that the animals had been sent to him by a friend from Upper Egypt. "If you like" he added, "I will write to the man to send me a few, and when they arrive, I will give them to you without fail. If he doesn't send them, I will give you these."

Then my master asked him if many were found in that country, and he answered that they were, but they were very difficult to catch. "For this beast cannot be caught by dogs, falcons or horses, because it moves so quickly, swifter than a bird. So they catch it by a ruse. The hunters know the location of its burrows, and when it leaves its nest to forage, the hunter reaches into the burrow up to his elbow and blocks it on the inside. When the animal returns to its burrow, he stretches out his hand and grabs it. This is how they capture them." The merchant then promised my master that he would write to his friend to send him several of those animals. My master thanked him for his generosity, and we returned to our place.

During that period, two Jesuit Fathers arrived and lodged with the consul. These monks came once every year to ransom captives with alms donated by Christians. One of them was a preacher, a master of the art. One day the consul requested that preacher to preach a sermon that would bring comfort to our souls. "Willingly," he replied, "on condition that my sermon lasts two hours for seven days." [101] The consul was pleased at that, because he was a God-fearing Christian and loved the good and virtuous.

The Father began to preach his first sermon two hours after the end of mass, that is, at ten o'clock in the morning. He entered the church and locked the door, closed the windows and the skylights and extinguished the candles, so that we were in total darkness. After making the sign of the cross, he opened his sermon with this mental exercise: that we should close our eyes and walk with him in spirit through all the parts of his sermon, and reach every place he entered in spirit. He began the first part of his sermon by recounting the creation of the world, the sun, moon and stars and the angels, the waters of the sea and everything God created on the face of the earth. The second part was devoted to the creation of Adam and Eve, and placing them in Paradise, Adam's Fall and his Expulsion from Paradise. Then he recounted the life of our Lord Jesus the Messiah, and similar stories from the Holy Gospels. Finally, he described for us the four last things of mankind, I mean Death, the Last Judgment, Hellfire, and Grace. We followed him through them all in spirit, until we all accompanied him to Hell. At every level and place in Hell, he asked the souls what their sin had been, until they came to that place of Hell where they are punished without mercy, cut off forever from hope until the end of time.

At last we ascended with him to the Kingdom of Heaven, and here he asked the saints how they came to be saved, and they described this eternal happiness in words that stirred the soul. This was how the sermon ended on the seventh day. We finished those devotions like men who were drunk and almost comatose, each of us certain he was sunk in sin.

One day I was kneeling in prayer in church after mass, so worried that I lost consciousness, and remained in a trance until lunchtime. They came looking for me to come to lunch, and found me praying in the church, without my even being aware of it. They woke me from that trance and then we all confessed and received the Holy Sacraments.

Meanwhile, my master fell very ill. He was on the point of death. All hope seemed to be lost. I spent that night sleeping beside his bed, terribly sad at the thought of this man's impending death. I was in despair about what would happen to me after his death. What could I do, with no protection from anyone, far from my homeland? Half the night passed, when I suddenly heard the rap of his staff on wood, for he had completely lost the ability to speak. We had decided to put his staff beside his pillow, and a board on the floor beneath it, so that if he wanted something, he could strike the end of the staff on the board and we would run to him to see what he wanted.

When I heard him strike the board, I quickly ran to him. He asked me to bring his medicine chest close to the bed, so I brought it and placed it on a chair beside him. Then he asked me to reach under his pillow and get out his purse and take out the key to the chest. I did what he said and opened the chest. In the middle was a smaller chest of ebony bound with strips of brass. It was locked, but looked like a single block of wood, with no place to insert a key. He showed me the mechanism, which was worked by one of the nails, which looked like all the others on the box. When I pressed it with my thumb, the box opened. Inside was another little box, inside which was a crystal jar with a brass stopper. Then he asked me to bring him a glass containing two fingers of wine. When I brought the glass of wine, he said to me, "Twist the stopper in the mouth of the jar". I did as he said, and opened the jar, and saw a second stopper, covered with beeswax. I removed it all, and he said, "Now put your thumb over the mouth of the pot, and pour out three drops of the liquid inside, no more". Lastly, he told me to put everything back in its place and lock the chest and put the key back in the cloth purse. After I had finished doing all this, he took the glass I had been holding from my hand and drank it. He then poured in a little of the wine and drank it, and lay back and went to sleep, while I returned to my own bed and slept till dawn.

He woke me with more taps of his staff. I jumped up and went to his side and asked him what he wanted. "Bring me some clothes, so I can change", he said. I brought him the clothes, and he got out of bed himself, with no help from me. I was astonished at how he was able to get up, how his strength was returning. I began to help strip him, and found that his clothes were soaking with sweat, so that it was difficult to remove his shirt. After dressing him in clean clothes he took my hand and rose up from his bed and sat on the chair. Then I asked him, "What would you like?" "Change the linen", he said, "and turn over the bed, because it is damp with sweat." I did as he asked, and he got back in bed and slept for around two hours.

Then he awoke and asked me to bring him a bowl of broth, so I went to the kitchen and got the broth, a napkin and a spoon and went back to feed him the broth. I found him pacing the room. I was overjoyed, but amazed that he had risen from his bed after the previous night being on the verge of death. I didn't realize that the three drops he had taken were the cause of his recovery from the terrible illness to which he had succumbed, until he himself told me that he was cured by drinking those three drops. When I heard these words from him, I said to him, "Why didn't you drink them when you first fell ill, and spare yourself and us all this pain and worry?"

He laughed, and said to me, "Mark my words, if I had not known that I was about to die, I would not have taken them. I have been travelling through this world for twenty-four years, searching for a unique herb, the elixir that releases mankind from sickness and disease. I came across the story of a certain traveler, preserved in the annals of the monastery of St Francis in Paris. On the festival of that saint, they grant a general pardon to those that confess, and they receive the Holy Sacraments.

It happened that one of the monks was sitting in his confessional, listening to confessions. A handsome youth came and sat in the confessional and asked to be confessed. He blessed him, and said, "Confess, my boy, how long has it been since you did so?" The youth answered, "O Father, I haven't confessed in sixty years". The priest was astounded by what he said, and replied, "What is this levity, do you not know that there is no place for jokes or lies in confession?" The youth answered, "Why do you say this, Father? Do I look stupid or mad, that I should lie to you, and before Almighty God Himself?" The priest replied, "You speak truly, my son, but how can I believe that you have gone sixty years without confession, when you are clearly not more than twenty years old? Go confess to someone else. I cannot confess you until you tell me the truth. If you do, I will confess you". "Rise up", replied the youth, "let's go into the monastery, and there I will tell you my story." The priest agreed, and they went together to his cell, and he invited the youth to enter. [They sat down and] the priest said to the youth, "Now tell me the truth".

> If you ask about me, Father, I am a native of this country. When I was forty years old, I went out to see the world, and spent sixty years travelling in far away countries, searching for the herbs and simples depicted in ancient books. I found the herb I was seeking, the elixir of life, called in the works of the Greek philosophers *bīrū fīlūsūfa*, that is, 'The Philosopher's Stone'. From this herb I made a potion, and when I had finished, I tested it, and found its properties exactly like those described in those books. If a man takes a single dose, it immunizes him against sickness and disease for ten years, and he will be as healthy as in the days of his youth. I took a tablet every ten years, and have become, as you can see, a youth. This is what made me ignore and forget about death, and I thought nothing of the salvation of my soul. Now God has taken mercy upon me, and has knocked on my heart with His blessings and I have awakened from that evil dream, and know that I am inevitably going to die, because God, may His Name be Exalted, prescribed death for man. Those philosophers who used this herb

are all dead. This is the reason I have returned to my country and sought confession and repentance before death."

When the priest heard the youth's words, he was astonished, and said to him, "Do you have any of the elixir you mentioned with you now?" "Yes", answered the youth, "I have some with me." "Would you give me a little, so that I can test it, and substantiate your story, and see whether it is true or not?" "Of course", he answered, and took from his inner pocket a silver box and gave to the priest ten tablets and told him, "If you take one every ten years you will live for one hundred years, whatever age you are now". The priest took them from him, and he made a full confession, and the priest gave him absolution, prescribed penances and sent him on his way.

Then the priest began to think how he could test the tablets. It occurred to him that in the monastery was a very old dog, no longer strong enough to walk. He used to bring it a bowl with a little broth for it to lap where it lay. So the priest took one of the tablets and soaked it in the broth and placed it in front of the dog. The dog lapped it up as usual and the priest left him and went to his cell to perform his devotions. When he had finished his prayers, he went to look at the dog. He found him running about the courtyard of the monastery, for he had regained his former strength. At that moment the priest knew that what the youth had told him was true. He wrote an account of the whole affair on parchment, and at the end wrote, "If you don't believe me, go look at the decrepit dog, how he has recovered his former strength". Then he left that parchment on his desk and went off and no one has ever found a trace of him.

When the monks couldn't find him, they asked permission from the prior and broke the lock on his door, went in, and found the parchment on his desk. When they had read it, they were astonished, and ran to look at the dog, and found that he was exactly as he said. Then news of all this spread throughout Paris, and people flocked to the monastery to see the dog. Then they inscribed this story in the annals of the monastery. A proof of its veracity is that my master was more than sixty years old, but you would think that he was a youth of thirty.[102]

Let us return to our narrative. My master recovered from that deadly malady, and his health returned to normal. We would wander through the streets of the city as usual, and sometimes go with the Father to visit the Bey. We delighted in those water meadows and gardens, and His Excellency the Bey continued to treat my master with great honour and affection, until my master decided to leave Tunis. He went to the Bey to bid him farewell, and was received most graciously.

We returned to our lodgings at the consul's house, but on the way we encountered the merchant who had promised to send my master those animals we had seen in his house. After greeting my master, he gave him the good news of the arrival of the animals, and that there were five of them. My master was delighted they had arrived, and we went with him to his house and saw them. They were in a cage made of palm branches. My master wanted to pay the cost of transporting them, but he wouldn't take a thing. Not only that, but he ordered one of his servants to carry them to our lodgings. My master thanked him for his generosity, and we went to the consul's house and found the boy already there, holding the cage and waiting for us. My master gave him a tip of ten piastres and dismissed him.

He immediately sent for a carpenter and showed him the kind of cage he wanted, with rooms and sleeping places for each one, so that they would be separated from one another. We put them in the cage, and immediately each one entered his bedchamber and hid.[103] We gave them a little food, like almonds and hazelnuts and other nuts. They ate everything we gave them except meat. When they finished eating, they swept the bottom of the cage with their tails, and pushed the detritus and their waste out of the cage. Their appearance, behaviour, and cleanliness when eating were a wonder to behold. They would eat standing up, pick up the nuts with their hands and place them in their mouths just like humans. When they were finished eating, they would each retire to their bedchamber and hide. We put loose wool in their cage, and they would fluff it up and clean it and cover themselves with it to keep warm, because the country they come from is very hot. The merchant had warned us not to let them get cold, and we had given them that wool to keep them warm.

Finally, after we had arranged their cage, my master put the cage and the animals in my charge, to watch over very carefully, lest they die of cold. "If we arrive in Paris, and they are well, you will greatly benefit, for by their means you will be received in places no one else has entered." I suggested to him that we embellish their cage with a broadcloth covering, which we did.

A number of days later, a small English ship arrived in the port of Tunis with a cargo of wheat to sell in Livorno. When the consul heard the news, he advised my master to sail with it, saying to him, "English corsairs won't attack you, and you will have no trouble with French corsairs, given that you are French and an agent of the Sultan of France". My master took his advice, and bought passage to Livorno from that English captain. A few days later, the captain advised us to send our baggage to the port, which is located at the city of Carthage, once famous for its size and power. The sea swept over it and destroyed it. When that country was taken by the Circassians [104], they set to work to build the city of Tunis. It is three or four miles distant from the port. Finally, we carried our belongings to the port. The consul had prepared ample provisions for us, wine, chickens, a sheep's head and similar things needed for a sea voyage.

Chapter VI

Our voyage to France in 1708

We left Tunis at the beginning of June [105] and boarded the ship we have just mentioned. We left the next day, and sailed until we reached the island of Corsica, which belongs to Italy. When the ship had dropped anchor in the harbour, the captain asked the people of the island whether they had any news of a French corsair in the nearby waters. "Yes", they replied, "there's a French corsair ship raiding near here, and they are keeping watch for it, because it is a large ship, manned by two hundred soldiers, not counting the sailors, and carrying twenty guns."

When the captain heard this news, he decided to stay at that island until he had news that it had left that area. We stayed the night in the port, and talked to the people of the island from on board our ship. Travelling on our ship were eighty captives, ransomed by the aforementioned Fathers. One of them was elderly, and was from this island. He had been a captive for twenty years. This man began asking about his wife, and whether his children were well. So they brought them, and when they stood before him on the dock, and he had seen that his wife and children were well, he began to weep with happiness. His wife and children too began to weep. They begged him to disembark, and serve out his quarantine in his village, I mean, enter a place where arrivals from both east and west must stay for forty days. After that period, they are released and allowed to enter the city. But he didn't want to disembark! He told them, "I am going to Livorno to take care of some business, and will come back to you soon". His family continued to implore us to convince him to disembark, but he wouldn't listen to anyone, and stayed aboard ship, only to suffer further ill-fate.

We spent all day until sunset in the harbour. Then a land breeze good for sailing began to blow. When the captain felt the breeze, he said to himself, "There are only sixty miles between here and Livorno. If I set sail, I can reach Livorno this very night, and escape that corsair ship". He decided to put the thought into action. He ordered the sailors to raise the anchor, unfurl the sails and set sail. They did as he asked, and the ship sailed with the land breeze for thirty miles. At that point, the wind dropped and the sea became completely calm. There was no wind for the sails, and our ship sat there as if it were at anchor in a harbour.

When the captain saw the disaster that had befallen, he feared the worst, and was terrified. He ordered the crew to pray, and beseech God to send them a little wind so they could traverse the short distance that remained. God did not answer his prayers because He had other intentions. We spent that night on the motionless ship, until dawn broke. Then the captain ordered one of the sailors to climb the mainmast and look out for a ship. The sailor climbed up and announced that he could see a black shape to the west, and they guessed that it might be mountains on the Italian coast.

The captain didn't agree, and sent the *yāzijī* to the top of the mast to ascertain the truth, whether the black shape was a mountain or a ship. The *yāzijī* climbed to the top of the mast just as dawn broke. He looked out, and said to the captain that he saw a large ship, and that it was heading towards them. The ship had sighted us before we spotted it. Then the captain took the telescope and climbed up and saw the ship coming towards us swiftly, because it was propelled by oars, for it had thirty-six *körek* that is, oars, manned by two hundred young men.

The captain then decided to use oars too, and six were found. He implored those on board to row, and turned the ship in the direction of the island which we had left that night. We all pitched in to help and did what we could to flee the oncoming ship, but the enemy redoubled its efforts to reach us. In a short time they came up to us, and when the captain saw how close they were, he ordered the sailors to lower the ship's boat into the sea. They tied the boat to the prow of the ship and the *yāzijī* lowered himself into it, along with four sailors to row and pull the boat forward. But the captain's intention was something else. He had with him four chests of coral which he had purchased in the places where it was harvested, that is, in the sea where it is formed, for it grows rooted in the sand like a tree. He also had a number of Spanish *reals*.

While we were all busy trying to make headway and escape, he lowered those four chests of coral and that sum of *reals* into the boat without anyone noticing. In a short time the corsair ship drew near and fired a cannon. The ball passed over the mainmast. When they saw we did not surrender and were still intent on flight, they fired a second cannon and the ball struck the middle of the mast. We still didn't surrender, and the captain encouraged us and urged us on. Then they fired a third time, and the ball passed right over our heads and we all fell flat on our faces, terrified at the sound the ball made. If it had hit us, not one of us would have survived. Then we all jumped up and surrounded the captain and urged him to surrender, and some of our number ran and lowered the flag. This was a signal to stop firing.

When we lowered the flag, the corsairs hailed us through a trumpet, saying, '*Amenez a la France, amenez!*' that is, 'Surrender to France! Surrender!' Then we struck the sails, and when the *yāzijī* in the ship's boat saw the surrender, and that there was no hope of salvation, he cut the rope mooring the boat and fled towards that island. God saved him, and he escaped.

The corsair ship paid no attention to the ship's boat, but instead launched a large boat into the sea holding fifty armed men to come and capture our ship. I was standing on the side of the ship watching. Next to me was standing the captive I have mentioned, the one from Corsica whose family had seen him there after twenty years, but who had refused to disembark and go with them, as we have explained. I saw that he was holding a money belt stuffed with coins and was about to throw it into the sea. I tore the belt from his hands and said to him, "Why are you going to throw it into the sea?" "Let me throw it in", he answered, "I'm not going to let those people take what I have worked and sweated for over twenty years." "Give it to me", I said, "Perhaps God, May He be praised and exalted, will save it from the hands of those men."

I went and hid it in the pack holding the cooking implements, like a pan, a pot, some plates and spoons and similar items for cooking which I took with us when we were on the road. At the same time, the rest of the captives gave my master purses and bundles so he could hide them in his chest, for they knew he was French and that the corsairs wouldn't rob him.

At that point the boat sent from the corsair ship drew alongside, and the soldiers immediately boarded and attacked like ravening wolves. They rounded us all up and put us in the boat, while the soldiers who had been in the boat stayed on board our ship. The sailors took us to the corsair ship, and when we climbed aboard, my master saw the captain of that ship and recognized him. They embraced, and greeted each other lovingly. The captain asked my master, "Where are you coming from, and how did you come to be on board that ship?" My master answered, "I was in the city of Tunis, and the consul suggested I take passage in that ship, for fear lest English pirates rob me". The captain said, "You did the right thing". Then he said to my master, "I will send for your belongings on that ship, lest you should lose something". My master accepted, and thanked him for his generosity. Then he ordered me to go with the boat back to the ship, and collect all of our belongings and put them in the boat.

When I got into the boat, the captain ordered the sailors to bring all our belongings, as well as those of the captives, and not to leave anything behind. They did what he told them, and we went to the ship, and first I carried all our belongings onto the boat, then those of the captives. We went back to the corsair ship, and they took on board all our baggage and that of the captives and put them in the captain's cabin. Then they took all the sailors and imprisoned them in the hold.

The corsair ship stayed in that place till the next day, which was Corpus Domini. [106] There was a Father on board, and he celebrated mass for us on that holy day. After mass we had breakfast and then the captain ordered all our belongings and those of the captives to be brought before him. He opened all their chests and bags and wrote down everything found in them. Then he began taking whatever he wanted of our possessions. We had with us a rifle with four barrels and a single lock, a brace of pistols, also each with four barrels and a lock, a two-barrelled rifle with its lock and a very valuable sword from Eski Sham [107], and a number of other things, like a poignard and a fine French fencing foil. He took them all. He opened my things and took whatever he wanted, among them my sash with the mulberry fringes, saying to me, "You won't need a sash, you're going to the land of the Franks". He saw the purses filled with *dirhams* in my master's chest, along with a number of Tunisian *tarbushes*, and deduced from them that the purses and *tarbushes* belonged to the captives, so he took them.

Then my master exploded with anger, and turning to the captain said, "Are you going to rob me and take my things? Don't you realize that I am on a mission for the Sultan of France?" He took out and showed him the *firmān* which the king had given him, recommending him to all the consuls dwelling in the Levant. The captain answered, saying, "Here in my ship, I am the sultan! Since I found you on an enemy ship, why shouldn't I rob you? Go throw your *firmān* in the sea, and drink the water!" This was witnessed by the other captain and the ship's officers. None of them objected to the captain's words and they all kept silent.

My master left him to do whatever he wanted until we arrived in Livorno. We stayed there all that day, and on the next, early in the morning, entered the port of Livorno. We anchored in the harbour, and a little while later the ship's boat, which had fled from Bremond [108] the corsair's ship with the chests of coral and *real*s entered the harbour, and he soon got the news of how they had fled with the most valuable things in the ship. When he realized what had happened, it went very hard with him, but what could he do? The bird had flown from his hands.

Then he gave orders that the English captain and his crew be sent ashore in the ship's boat and be taken to the quarantine. After they had been deposited there, the boat returned to the ship and the captain loaded it with our things, except for what he had stolen, and my master and I got in too and went into quarantine. There they gave us a room. It was a barren, flat place, surrounded by a wide canal filled with sea water. It was like an island. We stayed there that day, and early the next my master wrote a letter [and sent it] to the French consul in Livorno. This man is like an ambassador, sent on behalf of the Sultan of France. When the letter arrived, he asked the people in his palace, "Who is this man?"

Captain Bremond had anticipated this, and told the consul's retainers, "This man is one of those braggarts who travel about the world. If he complains to the consul, don't listen to him, because he is a liar. He has a *firmān*, which he showed me. It's a forgery". So they told the consul what they had heard from the captain, and the consul believed them, and didn't answer the letter. My master waited patiently all day, but no answer came from the consul. The next day he wrote another letter and sent it to the consul, but the consul didn't reply to that one either. We waited all day long, but no answer came.

That day I went for a walk near the place we were staying and saw at a distance that captive from whom I had grabbed the money belt. He was walking along too. I suddenly remembered that belt, and went and reached my hand into the bag where I had stashed it. I found it among the pans and plates and took it out and went outside. I showed it to him from a distance and called to him to come to me, but when he saw the belt, he fell to the ground on his face. He was so happy he was unable to get up! I went over to him and took him by the hand and he stood up and began kissing my hands and thanking me. I said to him, "My brother, thank Almighty God, who prevented them from noticing your belt. Didn't you see how they searched our luggage? But they didn't search the sack the belt was hidden in. This was a sign from Our Lord of the goodness of your family. In the end, he wanted to open the belt to give me part of the money, but I refused to accept any and sent him away.

The day passed at last, but still no answer came to my master's letter, and he became extremely angry, and said, "Tomorrow afternoon you are going to see what happens to the captain and his crew!" Early on the third day, he wrote a letter and sent it to the consul, ordering him, by the power invested in him by the Sultan of France, to come to the lazaretto and hear his complaint against Captain Bremond. He included some secret signs that proved he was an emissary of the king. Only an hour passed before we saw a large crowd coming out of the gate of the city. It was the consul riding in his carriage, surrounded by his retainers, and accompanied by all the French merchants. They all entered the lazaretto, crossing the canal. The captain of the lazaretto went out to meet them, bringing a chair for the consul. Chairs were also provided for the merchants and they also sat down beside him, while all the servants stood, doffing their caps out of respect.

Then His Excellency the Consul ordered the captain of the lazaretto to summon *khoja* Paul Lucas the Frenchman who at that time was in the lazaretto. So the captain ordered the official in charge of the people who had been on the ship of Captain Bremond and *khoja* Paul Lucas to come into the presence of His Excellency the Consul. My master rose and put on his fur coat and took the *firmān* with him and told me to follow him. So we went together to meet the consul. When he came before him, his first words were, "There was no need for you to trouble yourself coming here to see me in person, it would have been sufficient to have sent the most lowly of your servants to deal with the quarrel between me and Captain Bremond. His offence against the king — May God Preserve him! — which impugns his sovereignty, which is something you must deal with directly with him".

"What is your complaint? What are you charging Captain Bremond with?" asked the consul. "First", he replied, "he robbed me, and took my possessions, and I am a Frenchman. When I told him that I was on a mission for the Sultan of France, and had a *firmān* from him, he answered by saying, 'On my ship, I am the sultan! As for the *firmān* you have with you, I don't believe it. Go soak it in water, then drink it!' The witnesses to this are the ship's officers. Then he took the *firmān* from his breast pocket and showed it to the consul. The consul ordered them to take the *firmān* so he could read it. So they plucked a cane growing nearby, split the end, and fixed the *firmān* in the slot of the split cane and fumigated the *firmān*, then handed it to the consul.[109]

When he had read it, he immediately rose from his chair and doffed his hat to my master, and began to reassure him, saying "Don't reprove me. Rumours about you reached me, which are clearly unfounded". Then he gave orders to his followers to go to the jetty and bring the captain and his crew to the lazaretto. So they went and ordered the captain on behalf of the consul to come to the lazaretto with his crew. When they arrived and he and his crew stood before the consul, the consul asked him whether he had said the words Paul Lucas claimed he had, but he denied it. Then my master turned to the witnesses, and they couldn't deny them because they were said in the presence of the ship's company. They then bore witness to what the captain had said, word by word. After they had testified and the truth had been established, the consul ordered the captain to be imprisoned in the lazaretto and sent the crew back to their ship. The investigation was then put off till the next day. He bade my master goodbye and returned to his house, while we returned to our quarters.

The next day the consul returned, in the company of his retainers and the merchants as before, and they held a council. The consul sent for the captain to be brought before him and ordered them to bring from the ship to the lazaretto everything that had been stolen from my master and place it before him. When it had all been brought, he invited my master to come and take back the things the captain had taken from him on the ship. When my master stood before the consul and the others, the consul and the rest rose to their feet. Then the consul said to my master, "See if any of your possessions are missing". So my master told me, "Go through our possessions!" I went through everything, bundle by bundle. My master said, "I am missing four purses of coins and a red purse inside of which were two hundred and twenty medallions, that is, ancient coins, and also inside the purse was a silver ring with a seal of Solomon. There were also six dozen Tunisian *tarbushes*".

The consul ordered the captain to go to his ship and bring the purses he had taken from my master's chest and the *tarbushes* too. The captain insisted that he didn't have the purses, and that in fact they were the purses of the captives. The consul responded by saying, "Are they among the captives' things?" "I saw them in Paul Lucas' chest", answered the captain. The consul rebuked him and said, "It's none of your business to know to whom they belong, if you took them from this man's chest. Go, quickly, and bring them here!" The captain went off to his ship and brought back the purses and the *tarbushes*, but not the purse full of medallions. So my master asked him for it. The captain answered, "This is what I took from your chest, I only saw these purses". My master turned and said to the consul, "Those medallions were registered in the chancery of Tunis and were especially for His Highness the King, because in all my travels I have never seen their like. And I want, nay, implore, the captain to take all my possessions, but return the aforementioned purse to me".

This was a trick on the part of my master, because of the spite of the captain. For the purse which he mentioned was safe, and in it was the ring, but he had left the medallions with the consul in Tunis, along with the rest of the things we had collected in North Africa during his travels. He did this in every city in which there was a consul with whom he could leave medallions, books, engraved stones and precious gems and similar things, and have them listed in the chancery and take a receipt from the consul, so that he could send them to Marseille, where he could collect them and take them to Paris.

When the consul heard about the loss of this purse from my master, he ordered the captain to go back a second time to the ship and search for the purse. The captain answered him, saying, 'I would like to ask you to please order some of your own people to go with me to search the ship, place by place. Perhaps they will find it, because I didn't see it and have no knowledge of it. Then the consul gave permission to my master to go to the ship, and he sent the chancellor with him, plus two of his retainers, in order to search the captain's cabin and his chest and the chests of the crew, in case they might find it. So my master went to the ship with the above company and they searched the captain's cabin and found the purse with the ring inside. They returned before the consul with the purse in their hands. When the consul saw it, he turned to the captain and said to him, "The purse with his seal has been found. Where did you hide the medallions which belong to the King of France? How can you deny it?" The captain began to curse and swear they could kill him, but he knew nothing and had seen no trace of those medallions.

The consul was confused by the investigation and didn't know what to do. The merchants advised him to send for all the ship's company and examine them, and perhaps find evidence of the medallions. The consul agreed with their suggestion and sent for the entire ship's company, including the sailors. When they came before the consul, he began to question them, one by one, asking them if they knew anything about those medallions, but they all denied it.

The consul grew angry, and ordered them all to be imprisoned and those closest to the captain's cabin to be tortured if the medallions turned up. When the sailors realized they were being sent to prison, they started saying, "Not one of us is guilty! The fault lies with the sentinel, that is, the guard responsible for the captain's cabin and the powder magazine. He allowed his friends to steal from the possessions of the captives". When they heard these words, they informed the consul of what the sailors had said. He summoned them before him and asked them what happened. The treachery of the sentinel outside the captain's cabin was evident. [The sentinel was summoned] before him, but swore he had stolen nothing. Then the sailors testified against him, and the consul ordered him to be hanged if he didn't return the medallions. He gave orders to seize him, shackle him, and take him to be hanged.

When my master saw that his trick could lead to a killing, and that the man was innocent, he feared lest the consul turn on him next, and demand his blood. So he said to the consul, "Don't rush to judgment. Put the man in prison while we investigate and question the rest of the ship's company. Perhaps we will get information from them. In any case, do what seems best to you". So he sent him to prison, and this was because the consul feared censure and rebuke by the minister of state. He gave orders to imprison all of them, and sent to the harbour master and ordered him to remove the rudder from the ship, and to hold on to it until he received an order from him to release it. Then he took the purse with the ring in the presence of everyone and said to my master that he was sending the purse and a copy of the charges to the minister, and whatever the minister ordered would be done. So the ship's company and the captain remained in the lazaretto. The consul and his retainers and the merchants left, and we returned to our place. This is how the case ended up.[110]

We stayed in the lazaretto until twenty days had passed. Then the chief physician visited the lazaretto. Each of us was summoned before him, and he examined us all one by one to see if we displayed any signs of disease. After examining us all, he ordered us all to be stamped on the wrist and on the lower belly. Then we were all fumigated and at last let go.

We entered the city, and as we walked through the gate, the governor's men searched out luggage, lest [we were smuggling tobacco], salt or spirits, because duty had to be paid on these three items. Any one [caught smuggling] was sent to the galleys, without exception, and they sequestered the tobacco, [salt and spirits]. I had with me forty packages of very fine tobacco from Tunis. The night before they had told me that tobacco smugglers were sent to the oars. Those who carry it openly must pay an import duty of four piastres on every Aleppan *ratl* and this was so heavy a tax that no one tried to take tobacco with them to that country. Instead, the government itself imports tobacco from other countries. There is a profit of one piastre on every three or four *ratls*, and they sell each *ratl* for four piastres, and salt for the like.

When I heard about this, I had no idea what to do. I thought to myself, "How can I smuggle that tobacco I have with me?" without considering the danger I was running. I plucked out the thread of our mattress and scooped out the woolen stuffing. I cut the fastenings on the tobacco, and placed it in the mattress, stuffing the wool under and atop it. Finally, I sewed up the mattress and redid the fastenings as before. Five packages of tobacco were left. It didn't occur to me to give any to the watchman who had been in our service at that time. Then I had an idea, and opened a chest that contained wine bottles. I took the bottles out of the chest, and the wool that was under the bottles. I broke open those parcels, and placed them under the wool, then put back the bottles as they were and locked the chest. When the customs officials came to inspect our luggage, the mattress was wrapped in a rug and tied with a rope. They cut the rope, removed the rug, and found a mattress and a little pillow, but saw nothing else. [Then they asked me] to open the chest, and I opened it for them and they saw the bottles [and nothing else]. They looked through the rest of our things and our packs and found nothing. So they allowed us to pick up our belongings and go.

We gave everything to the porters, and went to the house of a Frenchman, married in Livorno. He was a friend of my master. When we entered his house, he welcomed us very warmly, and immediately ordered his servants to move our things to the upper floor. He had prepared a room for my master, furnished with handsome bed and chairs and similar things which a well-furnished room must have. They also gave me a room, and put my things inside. Then the man's wife came and welcomed us, and congratulated my master on having safely arrived in the land of the Christians. After they had finished greeting each other, my master came in and changed out of his traveling clothes into other clothes, not customary in our country.

Afterwards, a barber appeared. He shaved my master, who asked him to shave me too. I sat down on a chair, and after he had shaved my face and chin, he took the razor and passed it over my chin, and in doing so, the razor sliced off half my moustache. When I realized he had cut off half my moustache, I screamed at him so loudly he was terrified and stood there stupefied. "What's the matter with you, I didn't cut you!" he said. "Would that you had cut me, rather than my moustache!" I replied. "Didn't you know that the children of the East never cut their moustaches, the way you do?" In the end, all I could do was let him trim the other side as well. For in this country, they shave their beards and moustaches, even the priests, not excepting the Capuchin Fathers.

We spent that day in the house of that man in the greatest ease and comfort. Some of the merchants came to visit my master, to welcome him and greet him. Among them [were friends] of Captain Bremond, whom they urged him to forgive, and not let the charges against him [reach] the minister. He told them, "The charges are not in my hands. They were made in your presence and that of the consul. Now matters are in the hands of the minister and under his authority. This affair will not be settled in this country". They kept on about it for three days, coming every day about the same thing. Finally, after three days and great efforts, he gave them his word that he would pardon him. They thanked him for his generosity, and went to the consul and told him that *khoja* Paul Lucas had forgiven the captain, and that he would inform the minister.

Then the consul prepared a banquet and sent his secretary to invite my master. The following day my master went to the consul's house and lunched with him and my master was pleased. The next day the consul again sent his secretary to invite my master to come with him. He went with him to the consul's palace, and when they all came face to face, they greeted each other. Then the consul asked my master if he wished to release the captain and his crew from prison. My master answered, "In accordance with your wishes and those of the merchants, I will take full responsibility for this. Free them, and let them go where they wish".

The consul thanked him for his generosity, and immediately summoned the captain and his officers. He said to the captain, "Give thanks for the generosity of this gentleman! If he hadn't pardoned you, you and your men would have stayed in prison until an answer had been received from His Excellency the Minister, and you would have been sent to him and your ship impounded to be used by someone else, for you showed no respect for the Sultan's *firmān* or the man who carried it. You treated them vilely, and this extended to the author of the *firmān*, I mean, His Highness the King. Then the captain bowed to my master, embraced him and apologized and they made peace. At last they all sat down at the table together and drank to each other's happiness with joy and contentment. Then everyone went their way.

After that day, I went out to walk through the streets of the city. I was astonished by the sight of something I had never seen before. This was the first city I had ever been in the land of the Christians. When I saw women in the shops, buying and selling just like men, and walking through the streets with uncovered faces, without a veil, it was as if I were dreaming. As I was walking along one of the streets, I heard someone calling out to me in Arabic. I turned and saw a man in a coffee shop. I went up to him and he said to me, "Welcome to a son of my country! Come in so that I may breathe the scent of my native land!" When I had entered, he wished me peace in Arabic, and I returned his greeting, and asked him, "Who are you, O brother, and what country are you from?" "I am from Aleppo" he answered, "and a Maronite." "I, too, am from Aleppo',

I told him, and he embraced me and shook hands. He asked me to sit down with him, and after welcoming me, he gave me coffee and brought me a water pipe. We sat and talked with each other, and friendship grew between us. I visited him every day and asked him about the customs of that country and he would tell me about all their peculiarities. Another day I was walking by the sea shore and came across a man wearing the costume of our country. He stopped and stared and asked me where I was from. I told him that I was from Aleppo, and he welcomed me very warmly. I said to him, "Perhaps you recognize me?" "Truly", he answered, "I don't know who you are, but you are a son of our country, and so I feel affection for you".

Then he said,

> Come with me, O brother. We will walk together, and I will tell you what happened to me and the disaster that befell me. If you ask who I am, why I am a man from Damascus in Syria, and belong to the sect of the Syrians, but am Catholic in faith, a son of the Church. The heretical Syrians [111] oppressed me until they had robbed me of half my capital. When I saw that is was simply not possible for me to remain in Syria, I hit upon a stratagem. I liquidated the assets I still held and paid my debts without anyone becoming aware of what I was doing. I entrusted my house and its furnishings to one of my kin, and let it be known that I was going to take my family on pilgrimage to Jerusalem. My family consisted of my wife, two daughters, and a son. I set off with a group of pilgrims, and visited Jerusalem. I returned by sea, taking a ship to Sidon. I waited in Sidon a number of days for a ship bound for Christian lands. I intended to go and live in Rome with my family.
>
> During the days I was there, a French ship arrived, bound for Smyrna. I said to myself, "I'll take this ship and shop in Smyrna for the sort of things that are exported to Christian lands", for I was carrying a quantity of *dirhams*. I decided on this course of action, and took passage on that ship. In a few days we reached Smyrna. A few days after our arrival, I went to ask about the kind of goods in demand in the lands of the Franks. I encountered a man, a sailor, who suggested I buy Persian products, like Indian printed fabrics from Isfahan, rhubarb, and *kharīsāna* [112] and similar things which

were in demand in those lands. After I had finished shopping, I bought some woolen carpets of *kharīsān* workmanship, extremely expensive, as well as some honey-coloured wax to take to Rome for the churches. The cost of all this was more than five thousand piastres. I was left with one thousand piastres in Venetian gold ducats for travelling expenses. I stayed in Smyrna several days, while they fitted out a ship bound for Marseille.

It was a large ship, crammed with Smyrna merchants. I bought passage on it, and loaded all the goods I had bought in Smyrna. A few days later, the ship sailed, bound for Marseille harbour. When we were just off Malta, the captain sighted a ship in the distance. Fearing that it might be an English corsair, he put into Malta harbour, and we stayed there at anchor for ten days, for fear of the corsair. Then our captain received news that that ship had sailed for eastern lands, and that the sea was clear of corsairs, and he decided to continue the voyage.

We left Malta by night, and the wind was with us. When dawn broke, we sighted a ship coming towards us. It was a forty-gun warship, and our ship mounted only twenty. Then the two ships prepared for battle. They began to fire at each other. My family and I went down to the hold. We were absolutely terrified, especially my wife and children. I regretted that a wife should be exposed to war like this. We despaired of life, the mother wept for her children, the children wept for their mother. I was like someone who had lost all hope and feeling.

Finally, our captain saw the ship could not be saved. A shot hit our ship and killed and wounded many men. The mainmast was shattered and about to collapse and we could not oppose that ship in any way. So he surrendered to that warship. They captured us and took us to Livorno. There they put us into quarantine at the lazaretto and laid hold of all our possessions, except for my wife's chest. They didn't open it because it was a woman's chest and they had mercy on her and gave it back to her. In the chest there was a purse with her travelling money, inside which were one hundred piastres and her jewels, which were worth five hundred piastres. This was all that remained of our money, and now all we had to live on. I got jobs for the children, and my wife has sat in the house for three months now, without going into the city, because she couldn't go out without a covering and veil.

I implore you, since you are a son of our country, to kindly have a word with her. Perhaps she will listen to you, and come out and breathe the fresh air, and cast off her depression.

"Willingly", I answered, "what time would you like me to come to you?" "Tomorrow afternoon", he said. "It is Sunday, and I will wait for you in the church, and we can go together to the house and perhaps take her for a walk outside the city, to refresh her a little." So we agreed to meet the next day.

After attending divine service, I went with him to his house. When I entered, I saw that part of it had been curtained off, and she was inside. I greeted her, and she returned my greeting from behind the curtain. She didn't want to come out and see me. "What is this madness?", I said, "Come out and look! All the women are going about unveiled! No one stares at them. This is a Christian country. They think the *hijāb* is stupid."

After much palaver, I was unable to get her to come out without a veil. Finally I asked her, 'Do you have a thin piece of cloth that covers the head and face?" "Yes", she replied. "Then put it on and come with us!" She listened to me, and took out of her chest a nice dress and pretty head covering. She donned the dress, wrapped herself in the shawl, and she and the children came out with us. We passed through the city gate, and at that time of day there were many people, men and women, going out to promenade in the outskirts of the city. When they saw a veiled woman, they all came over, quickening their pace in order to glimpse her face, and asking us why she was veiled.

We didn't know what to say to these people, especially to the women. We became very distressed by both the men and the women, because we were quite unable to walk along that road. We had no option but to deviate from the road and seek refuge in a cave in the mountain near the sea. When we got to that place, no one could see us. Then I turned to that woman and said to her, "If you want me to walk with you, remove the veil, and walk along dressed like the other women, and no one will notice you!" But she refused, and would not take off her veil. When I realized that she was determined not to, I left them and returned to the city. I don't know what happened to them. It was clear to me that the women of our country were unable to follow the path of the women of this one, for they were raised in concealment.

Another time, when I was sitting with my friend, the Aleppan coffee-shop owner, a good-looking youth, tall and handsome, with the marks of good breeding, came in. After drinking a cup of coffee, he left and went his way. His great beauty and dignity had greatly pleased me, and I asked the owner of the coffee shop who he was. He said, "He is the 'Son of the Dead Woman', and his story is a strange one. And he began to tell it to me.

> "The father of this youth was a merchant, and very rich. He married the daughter of a fellow merchant. During the ceremony, he gave her a diamond ring worth five hundred piastres, for it is the custom during the marriage ceremony that the man gives the woman a ring, and the woman gives a ring to the man. After the ceremony was finished, she went with a number of her relations to the house of her groom. She lived with him some time, and every day became fatter and fatter, until she became very fat indeed.
>
> One day the man looked at her hand and saw that the ring had been entirely obscured by her fat. He wanted to remove it from her finger, lest it do her harm, but he was unable to get it off. He sent for a jeweler to come to the house, and ordered him to cut the ring and remove it from her finger. When she heard that the jeweler had come to cut the ring and take it from her finger, she refused to let him. She went to her husband and beseeched him not to let the jeweler remove the ring from her finger, telling him that the ring did not hurt her and that she was fine with the way it was. Her husband tried to tell her that he had asked the jeweler to simply remove the ring to enlarge it, but she said, 'If you love me, don't remove the ring from my finger, even when I'm dead'. Her husband loved her very much, and didn't want to upset her, so he sent the jeweler away, and the ring remained on her finger.
>
> One day while she was sitting, she suddenly fainted. Two hours later she was dead. At that time, such sudden deaths were common in the town. When they were sure she was dead, they held the

burial service, stripped off her clothes, and wanted to remove the ring from her finger, but were unable to do so. Then they suggested to her husband that they cut off her finger, and remove the ring. Then he remembered her saying, 'Don't remove the ring from my finger, even when I'm dead'. So he prevented them from removing it, and it remained on her hand. Finally, they buried her, placing her in a coffin, and put the coffin in the crypt as is their custom, and departed.

One of those present at her funeral noticed that the ring was still on her finger, so that night he hid in the graveyard enclosure. At midnight he opened the door of the crypt and lowered himself into it. He had a candle, a flint and steel. He lit the candle and stuck it in the earth, then opened the lid of the coffin. He reached in and took her right hand, on which was the ring. He already knew the ring wouldn't slip off, so he drew his knife and cut off her ring-finger. Blood flowed, and the dead woman started up from her swoon, and screamed in a loud voice, "Where am I?" Hearing her voice, the man was terrified she would recognize him, so he snuffed the candle, put away his knife and fled.

When the woman had come to herself, she saw that she was in a sarcophagus inside a coffin inside a crypt, surrounded with the dead. She began to scream and yell, until she woke the sacristan. He hurried to the crypt to see who was screaming and yelling and saw the lid of the crypt was ajar, and inside was a spent candle. The sacristan was terrified at the sight, and at the sounds coming from among the dead, and ran to tell the prior and the monks what he had seen and heard in the crypt.

They all ran to see what was going on in that place, and saw just what the sacristan had told them. They were all frightened by this terrible event, and tried to urge one another to enter the crypt and discover the truth, but no one but the sacristan had the courage to enter. He said to the prior, 'Pray for me, father, I will enter'. The prior blessed him, and they fastened a rope around him and lowered him to the bottom of the crypt. When he reached the bottom, he saw the snuffed candle beside the tomb of the woman who had risen from the dead. She was still screaming and weeping. He approached the sarcophagus, shaking with fear. Then he pulled himself together and said, 'Who are you, O corpse?' The woman answered him, from inside the sarcophagus, "I am so-and-so, wife of so-and-so, for the love of God get me out of here, I am on the point of death!"

Then he drew near her and helped her from the sarcophagus, the blood streaming from her hand, the knife beside the tomb. He was filled with wonder, not understanding what had happened to the woman. They finally got her out of the crypt, and saw that she was the person who had been buried the day before. They asked, "Who was it who wounded your hand?" "I don't know", she answered, "all I know is that I woke from my swoon and found myself in a sarcophagus, and that my hand was cut and bleeding." When they examined her hand, they saw that her ring-finger had been half cut off, and the ring was hanging from a shred of skin. Then they realized that she hadn't died, but fainted because blood wasn't reaching her heart, but when her finger was cut, the blood that had been withheld from her heart began to flow, and she woke from her swoon. The reason she survived was the ring. Then they sent to inform her husband and family, and they came and took her home. The most wonderful thing is that after this incredible event, she bore three children, two boys and a girl. The young man that I saw was one of the three.

Another day when I was walking through the streets of the city I saw soldiers all prepared for a campaign, each of them armed to the teeth.[113] They were formed into companies, each company marching separately, with drum and fife and a captain. I asked someone, "What is this army?" "At the beginning of every month", he answered, "the militia gathers in a certain square. It is a wide, open space, used to drill the soldiers in case of war."

So I went to that place to watch. I found a vantage point, where there were many people gathered. At the end of the training ground was a high platform where a distinguished looking man dressed in fine, expensive clothing was seated. He was the commander-in-chief and all the companies passed before him. If he saw a soldier whose tack was not clean or who was missing equipment, he ordered him punished, that is, he was given a hundred lashes [114] in his presence, to make an example of him to the others.

After the companies had paraded before him, they fell in behind each other, until the ranks were full. You could see that not a single foot was out of line. There were twelve ranks, divided into two halves, each divided into six others by a short space. Then the drums of the six companies in front rolled, and then, at a single drumbeat, they presented arms, holding the rifle in the right hand and raising it. Then the drumbeat changed, and each soldier shouldered his weapon as if aiming at a target. You would have seen all of them raising their rifles in a single manoeuvre. They all moved as one man. If you looked down the line, you would see their feet exactly lined up, not even the space of a barley stalk between them. The drum rolled again, and they all turned to the right. The beat changed, and they turned to the left. Then they faced forward again, presenting arms as if about to fire. Finally, a trumpet sounded, and all the drums rolled and they all stood down their muskets in the style and good order we have mentioned.

Then the drum beat changed, and the company captain shouted an order, and what did I see, but the six companies in the front exchanging places with the six companies behind them, and in the blink of an eye those who had been in front of the formation were now at the rear, and those who had been at the rear were in front, like the first. Those now in the front line knelt to load their muskets, until those behind them had fired theirs. But telling all this is not the same as seeing it. I couldn't begin to describe and record the manoeuvres I saw during this exercise. It is something completely unknown and unheard of in the countries of the East.

Another day I saw marching as before, and followed the soldiers until they reached the parade ground, and lined up on all four sides. In the center was a man kneeling, with his arms bound in front of him and holding his cap in his hands. The executioner was standing over his head, and in his hand was a document. It was the sentence which had been passed on that man. When the companies were finished lining up, the executioner began to read out the sentence. It said that the man had betrayed his commanding officer and fled, and deserved hanging. Nevertheless, mercy had been shown him because of his contrition, and he was sentenced to the galleys for three years. Yet it was known to all that the law sentenced the traitor to have his nose slit and his forehead branded with the sultan's seal with a hot iron. After the reading of the sentence, his nose was slit and his forehead and temples branded with a hot iron seal. Then the entire company marched past him. They then discharged him and handed him over to a captain of a galley. The soldiers broke formation and everyone went their way.

Another day, I climbed up to the fortress with a friend who was one of the guards, who showed me everything, place by place. He showed me the cannons, notable for their great size. Placed on every borehole was a thin lead plate, fastened to the cannon, with a seal on the knot. The wheels and pulleys moved easily, so that even a small child could run out the guns with the greatest ease.

Then my friend took me to the armoury, which occupied four stoutly built halls. Each hall was lined on both sides with various kinds of military equipment, hung on wooden hooks from floor to ceiling, including muskets, pistols, two-edged swords, rapiers, lances and other weapons. One hall was devoted to armour and steel helmets, as well as steel shields. I even saw armour specially made for women. They say that in former times, in the days of idolatry, women used to go to war.

He showed me in that place twelve men who wiped the arms with oil lest they be damaged by rust. As soon as they finished one side of the room, they began on the other, until they had finished oiling them all. Then they started all over again from the beginning. These twelve men were salaried, and permanently resident. When one of them died, he was replaced by another.

Then I thought of the fortress of Aleppo. There is not its equal in any city in the world. Yet its cannons are mostly half-buried in the earth, the gun carriages broken, everything covered with rust. If you enter the armoury tower, your find the dust so thick your feet sink into it. All the equipment and weaponry is rusty, and thrown on top of each other. Centuries have passed since anything has been cleaned or oiled, and everything is completely ruined and useless. All of this is the result of the lack of care. What I say is not a criticism of the fortress or the armoury, it is a criticism of those whose job it is to look after the royal treasury.

Finally, my friend took me up to the walls of the city. I saw built into the fabric of the walls towers constructed of stone, each with an opening through which one could shoot towards the land or the sea. The towers were built every hundred paces. I asked the man, "What are these towers?" "These are watchtowers", he explained, "Each company of guards based in the city sends a sentry every night, and they keep watch in the towers for four hours. When the time is up, they return to their barracks and another takes their place. This goes on till dawn. Hanging in each watchtower is a bell, and every hour the sentry in the first tower strikes his bell. When the sentry in the next tower hears the bell, he strikes his, the third does the same, and so on, all around the wall. This racket warns the soldiers not to fall asleep. If their commanding officer finds one of them asleep, he wakes him up and whips him several times with the whip he carries. This precaution is taken because of the fear that the enemy might hide during the night, and when the gate of the city is opened in the morning, charge and enter and take possession of the city."

One night, I and my friend, the Syrian I have mentioned, were walking along the seashore outside the city gate. We stayed out till sunset. The man suddenly said, "Get going! Hurry, before they shut the city gate!" We rushed back and arrived outside the gate. I saw about fifty armed soldiers, carrying their muskets come out of the gate, as if about to attack. When I saw them, I was frightened and turned back, trembling. The man said, "What's the matter with you? Go on back and go in, don't worry, I'll explain the reason for all this." We went in, making our way through the soldiers, to the city. Then I asked him why the soldiers were standing there, all holding their muskets. He told me, "This is an old custom of theirs. When the gates of the city are opened or closed, the soldiers stand guard, as you saw, fearing lest the enemy is lying in ambush. This is the reason".

During this time, news came of a very strange and remarkable event.

> A Jewish man, one of the Jewish notables living in Livorno, had learned that the Grand Duke, called the duke of Tuscany, who is the ruler of that country, and who lives in the city of Florence, needed a loan in order to pay the wages of the army and other expenses. He had no option but to borrow a sum of money from one of the great

men of his country. When he consulted the officers of his kingdom about who might be able to loan him money, they answered, "There is a very rich man in the city of Livorno. Send and have him brought before you". When the man came into his presence, he welcomed him with honour and allowed him to be seated. After chatting in a friendly way, he said to him, "I need eighty purses of coin. I want you to lend them to me until the time I have collected the taxes from my kingdom, when I will repay you". That clever scoundrel answered, saying, "I hear and I obey! What the servant possesses belongs to his lord, the custodian of his well-being!"

The duke thanked him, and ordered the clerk to write out a promissory note for the sum. Then the Jew arose, and bowed before the duke, saying "What is this, my lord? Does the servant take from his master a promissory note for his own money? I am your servant!" The duke answered, "I don't want to cause harm to any of my subjects. If you will not accept the promissory note, I do not wish to become indebted to you. Go in peace!"

Then the Jew thought of a devilish trick, never before heard of. He answered, saying, "I know, my lord, that masters do not share the same desires as their servants. For this reason, I want your lordship to sell me something that is in your power to sell for this sum". Then the duke agreed, and asked him, "What is this thing you want?" The Jew answered, saying, "Sell me the sun for this sum, and every year I will give you eighty purses. Write me a contract certifying what I have said, and that I am obligated to pay this sum".

The duke was astounded. He thought the man was mad, and had taken leave of his senses. He said to him, "O you of little wit, how can you want me to sell you something I don't own? Can the sun be bought and sold?" "You are right in what you say, my lord", answered the Jew, "but grant this to your servant, and let the people laugh at me." Then the officials who were present said to the duke, "Give him what he wants, Your Highness, and let him sequester the sun!"

When the duke heard what the officials said, he was pleased, and anxious to see an end to the whole strange affair. He ordered the secretary of the council to write a *firmān* for that Jew, selling him the sun, as well as a document saying he was constrained to pay the sum of eighty purses of *dirhams*, amounting to forty thousand *escudos*, that is, piastres. So he wrote out the *firmān* for him and composed the document we have mentioned and then dismissed him. The duke and the officials of the palace were unaware of the wickedness of that Jew. On the contrary, they thought him stupid and held him in contempt.

So the Jew returned to his city, that is, to Livorno. As soon as he arrived, he went to the town hall and registered his *firmān*. Three days later he summoned the landowners who grew wheat and other grains and read them the *firmān* issued to him by His Excellency the Duke, selling him the sun. He told them, "Your crops only grow because of the sun, so I want you to pay me every year such and such a tax. If you don't accept this, then I will sow your lands myself and pay the tax to His Excellency the Duke".

These men were completely at a loss at what to do. In the end, they decided to write out a promissory note for the sum he had asked them for. Then he summoned and had brought before him the market gardeners, came to an agreement with them, and wrote out a promissory note for them and dismissed them. Then he sent for the fullers and goldsmiths and everyone else who made use of the sun and wrote out a contract for each of them.

The news of what the Jew had done in the name of the *firmān* from the hand of the duke spread in the city. Then the rich and powerful men of the city summoned the judges and bishops and clergy. They all agreed that the matter was impossible, because God, May He Be Praised, made the sun shine on good and bad alike, and no one could sell or give the sun to one of His worshippers. They all agreed on this opinion. They wrote out a petition and everyone signed it with their own hand, saying they refused to accept the order of His Excellency the Duke.

They chose a number of the leading men of the city and sent them to the duke. When they arrived and stood before him, they gave the customary bow, then handed him the petition, which bore more than two hundred signatures, of bishops, priests and heads of households. They said to him, "Your Excellency, our lord and author of our well-being, has been fooled by a Jewish man, and an enemy of our faith. In this matter he has pocketed much more than three hundred purses". They told him everything that had happened, how he had made everyone whose job depended on the sun pay tax of a certain amount.

When the duke read the petition, he grew very angry, and realized his mistake, how he had granted that trickster a sword with which to assault his subjects. Immediately, one of the captains of the guard was sent to bring that treacherous Jew. He rode off, and in a short time brought him back. When he appeared before the duke, the duke said to him, "So this is how you fooled me and led me into error, betraying both God and the ruler". He took the *firmān* and all the documents which he had written to his subjects from him and ordered him to be hanged and his property impounded. The executioner cried out, "This is the fate of those who con their kings!"

Another strange thing involving a Jewish man happened about the same time. This man, when he was quite young, asked to become a Christian and was baptized. After spending three years as a novice, they examined him carefully, and found that he was firm in his decision, and had never wavered. Then the bishop ordered the priest to baptize him, confess him, and give him the Holy Sacraments. The man afterwards stayed true to his faith. Every day his devotion grew stronger, until he decided to become a monk, and spent a number of years in devotion and leading a godly life. Then they were sure of his faith, and he donned the holy habit of a monk.

A little later, he entered the priesthood, and everyone bore witness to the goodness of his life. For a number of years he was the most exemplary, god-fearing priest you could want. One night, the watchmen were making their rounds in the streets of the city. They passed beneath the windows of the monastery in which that priest of Jewish origin we have been talking about was staying. They noticed smoke and flames billowing forth from some of the windows, and they thought one of the cells was burning. One of them ran and knocked loudly on the portal of the monastery, until he woke a servant, who ran to open the door. The soldiers said to him, "Hurry, put out the fire that is burning one of the cells of the monastery! We have come to warn you!" The servant ran and told the prior and the monks about the fire in the cell.

They went from cell to cell until they came to the one occupied by the Jewish priest. The saw smoke issuing forth from cracks in the door, and were afraid the cell and the monk would burn together. The prior ordered them to break down the door, and quickly enter, lest the monk be consumed by the flames. They did as he said, and entered the cell and found that wretched monk had emptied the straw and dried herbs they use to fill mattresses from his mattress, and set it alight. He had tossed the cross into the fire so that it would burn, but the fire didn't harm it, and it was completely unharmed. They pulled the cross from the flames and rescued it. Then they turned to that man of unhappy fate and asked him why he had done such a thing. Foaming with rage, he answered, saying, 'I wanted to burn the cross which you worship because I am a Jew, and an enemy of the cross.'

The prior and the rest of the monks were bewildered by the daring of this wicked, ill-fated man. Then the prior ordered them to apprehend him and put him in prison. The next day, he informed the bishop, who ordered him to be brought before him. His Excellency the Bishop asked him whether he had done this thing in full possession of his senses, or had he been temporarily insane? He said this seeking to comprehend his motive. The cursed one answered that he was a Jew, enemy of the cross, and that is why he wanted to burn it. Then the bishop sent him to the governor of the city, informing him of what he had done.

When he stood before the governor, and the charges were read out, they sent him to the law courts, I mean, the courthouse. When they had investigated the affair, they decreed that he should be burned alive for what he had done. After the sentence of burning had been passed, they took him to the governor for it to be carried out, as ordained by law.

When the governor saw that he had been condemned to be burned, he did not want him to die this ghastly death, for he had a soft heart. He could not go against the law, however, for fear of public opinion. So he sent him to the city of Florence, to the Grand Duke, to do with him what he wanted. He freed his conscience by this means. When the prisoner appeared before the Grand Duke, and he read the sentence that had been passed upon him, he immediately ordered him burnt. So his body was burned in this world, and worst of all, his soul still burns in Hell.

One Saturday morning, I saw men and women from our neighbourhood preparing to visit the church of Mary the Virgin on Montenero.[115] This mountain is close to the city, about three miles away. They had told me of the nobility of this church, founded in the name of the Virgin Mary, and the numerous wonders to be found in it. I very much wanted to visit this church, so I asked permission of my master to go and visit the church, and he gave me permission to do so.

Then the lady of the house where I was staying sent one of her servants with me to accompany me on the way. She gave me a hat of plaited palm fronds the size of a winnowing basket. Despite its size, it weighed less than an ounce. She told me, "Wear it when you climb the mountain, to protect yourself from the heat of the sun", for the weather was hot, as it was towards the end of August.

That youth and I walked until we came to the foothills of the mountain. I saw many people, men and women, climbing, many of them barefoot, on those black stones, which were sharper than knives. Some of them went up on their knees, in great agony. They were fulfilling vows made to the Virgin, worker of miracles. Others, their heads bowed, sought her intercession. Eventually, we reached the summit of what was called 'Montenero'. At the base of the mountain was the sea, the waves dashing the mountainside. I saw an imposing church, beautifully built. Beside it was a large monastery. We entered the church, just as they were beginning to say mass at the altar of the Virgin, below her icon. The icon has three beautiful veils. A third of the way through the mass they drew aside the first of the veils. During the second third they drew aside the second veil. In the final third they drew aside the third veil. Then the image of the Virgin was revealed, and the congregation knelt. This is done every Sabbath throughout the year.

After we had celebrated mass, we sought blessings from that chapel. Then the young man took me all around the church, showing me the miracles the Virgin Mary had performed for those who sought her aid in times of adversity and danger. There was a picture of every miracle, with a caption beneath it, made by the donor.

> Among them was a passenger on a ship that was wrecked, who sought the aid of the Virgin who dwelt on Montenero. He was saved from drowning by a fish called a 'dolphin', which carried him to land. He presented a little silver ship to the church, with a little silver fish under it.

Among them was a man who fell from a very high ladder and cried out to the Virgin and she saved him in mid-air. He hanged a silver ladder in the church, and underneath it wrote an account of the miracle wrought by the Virgin Mary, and so forth, for the miracles commemorated in that church were beyond counting. Even if I had spent three days, I couldn't have counted all the illustrations of miracles displayed in that church.

Among them was one performed in Austria. A band of soldiers and their commanding officer were stationed in one of the castles of Austria to keep watch. Two of the soldiers made a pact with each other to flee at night from the castle without the permission of their commander. They fled, and the next day the news reached the commander. He was furious, and swore an oath that when they were caught, he would hang them both. He sent several soldiers to search for them and do their utmost to find them, wherever they might be hidden. The soldiers went out searching and inquiring about them and two days later found them and arrested them. They took them before the commander, and when he saw them he exploded with fury, and ordered them both to be hanged.

One of them implored him, saying "Have mercy upon me, O my lord, I am not at fault, my companion led me on". The other soldier began to speak, telling the commander that he was not guilty as the first man had charged. The commander had no way of knowing which of them deserved hanging. He said to them, "I am going to cast lots, and the loser will be hanged". He cast the lots, and one of them was the loser. The commander ordered him to be imprisoned until the next day, because evening had already fallen. So they threw him in prison. He sat down and wept, lamenting his fate. He was sitting there sadly when the companion with whom he had fled entered, consumed with remorse at his fate. In the prison was an image of the Virgin Mary hanging on the wall. He began to speak, saying, 'Do not fear, my brother, take refuge in the Virgin Mary, who dwells on Montenero, and she will save you. No one has ever sought her aid and been refused. Then the man prostrated himself before the image of the Mother of Mercy, weeping hot tears, and all night long implored her aid, until dawn broke.

Then the commander ordered the man to be brought before him, and told the executioner to hang him immediately. He was handed over to the executioner, who led him to the gallows. He put the rope around his neck and made him climb up the ladder fixed in the ground beside the gallows. Then he pushed him from the top of the ladder, and the man shouted in a loud voice as he fell: "O Mary the Virgin, who dwells on Montenero, help me!" The rope immediately broke, and he fell to earth, still alive.

The commander ordered another, stronger rope to be brought. It was put around his neck, and they made him climb back up the ladder. The executioner kicked him off the top as he had done the first time. That man of great faith in the Virgin Mary, who had saved him the first time, shouted again in a loud voice, "O Mary the Virgin who dwells on Montenero, save me!" And the rope broke once more, and he fell unharmed to the earth.

The commander was furious, and ordered them to bring a very strong, flaxen rope. When that had been done, the stupid fool, with little faith in the Virgin Mary said, "If you somehow break this rope too, I still won't believe the Virgin Mary performed this miracle, twice breaking the rope!"

They made him climb the ladder a third time, his faith in the Mother of Mercy still unwavering. The executioner kicked him off and he cried out at the top of his voice, imploring the Mother of Miracles, who dwells on Montenero, and the rope this time shredded into little pieces.

When the spectators saw this wonder, they cried out with one voice, "Stop, commander! Renounce your error, and believe in the miracles of the Virgin Mary, worked before your very eyes!" Then the commander finally believed the miracle and repented his evil action and small faith. He summoned the soldier and clasped him to his breast and asked his forgiveness. He raised him in rank and said, "From now and henceforth, you are relieved of your military duties, and will serve me in a high position". But the man replied, "Let me go and serve for what remains of my life, the one who saved me three times from death, and performed this magnificent miracle".

When the commander heard what he had to say, he responded, "Do as you wish", and he gave him generous travelling expenses and supplies of food as well, and let him go. The man went to Montenero and thanked the Virgin Mary for her generosity, became a monk, and entered her monastery, where he spent the rest of his life in fasting and prayer and worship of Our Lady.

Now it happened that after my return to Aleppo, I told a group of Christians the story of the miracles of Our Lady of Montenero, explaining to them that the supplications of no one who took refuge in the Virgin Mary of Montenero, went unanswered. I told them of her miracles, which I had seen depicted in her church, as I have explained.

Not long afterwards, one of the men who had been present when I spoke of the miracles of the Virgin Mary, came to me and said, "My brother, I heard you speak of the miracles of the Virgin Mary who dwells on Montenero. For a number of years, I have been afflicted with great misfortune, from which I could not free myself. When I did what you said, and took refuge in her, as you said, and made a vow to her, I was suddenly released from all my afflictions. And now I give you an offering". And he took out and gave me twelve Venetian ducats [116] to send to her church.

I took the gold pieces from him and said, "Follow me!" I took him to a French merchant named M. Chillon, who traded with Livorno. I asked him to send the offering to his partner, to donate to the church of the Virgin of Montenero. The man agreed, and wrapped the gold pieces in paper and wrote upon it, 'Offering for the Virgin Mary of Montenero'. We thanked him profusely, and went our way. A little while later, another man came, with ten Venetian ducats, also an offering to that church. Our Lady had come to his aid and saved him from a baseless accusation that could have ruined him.

And I, the writer of this account, after the fifty years that have passed, lost something in the order of 1100 piastres. After having gone missing for forty days, I lost all hope of recovering them, and was sure I was ruined. Then one day it occurred to me to seek the aid of Mary the Virgin of Montenero. That very night the one that had robbed me went to confess what he had done to a certain priest. The priest got in touch with a close friend of mine, and he informed me that what I had lost had been found, without my knowing who had taken it. The next day he brought it to me, and not a single coin was missing. I thanked the goodness of the Virgin Mary, Mistress of Miracles.

And now we will tell of what I heard from trustworthy people about the discovery of this noble icon and the founding of the church.

A shepherd was pasturing his sheep on that mountain. One day, in a certain place on the mountainside, he found an icon of the Virgin Mary among the stones. When the shepherd examined it, he saw that it was surpassingly beautiful. He lifted it up from the rocks and hung it in a tree that was growing there. When the time came to leave the mountain, he said to himself, "I will take the icon with me to town and give it to the bishop. Perhaps he will give me something for it". When evening came, he took the icon, went to the bishop, and gave it to him. When the bishop examined it, he realized that it was unique, the work of a great master. The bishop asked him where this beautiful icon came from, and he answered, "I found it on Montenero, thrown on the rocks, and I brought it to Your Excellency". The bishop thanked him, and gave him a tip and dismissed him. So the shepherd went off.

The next day he drove his sheep before him and went to the mountain to pasture them as usual. When he passed by that place, he saw the same icon, cast among the stones, just as he had found it the first time. He was astonished, and went and picked it up and took it to the bishop. When the bishop saw it in his hand, he was amazed, and asked, "Where did you find that icon?" "I found it," he answered, "in the same place I saw it yesterday, among the stones." The bishop was full of wonder, and sent one of the novices to look in his cell to see if the icon were still there, where he had hung it. The novice returned, and said there was nothing there. His astonishment increased, and he gave the shepherd a tip and sent him on his way. Then he hung the icon in his cell, where it had been before.

On the third day, the shepherd went to that place and saw the icon exactly where he had first found it. He was amazed, and thought to himself, how stupid it would be for someone to steal something from the bishop, and then throw it there. So he picked it up once again and took it to the bishop, and said, "I think, my lord, that one of your servants must have taken it and thrown it in that place". At that, the bishop arose and went to his cell and found that the icon was no longer there.

He realized that this was a miracle, worked by the Virgin Mary, and that she wanted a sanctuary on that mountain. He immediately sent orders for the curates, priests and priors of monasteries, and all the clergy, to gather in the bishop's palace. They were dressed in their priestly robes, the deacons carrying candles and censors. They went there in a magnificent procession.

The next day everyone assembled as the bishop had ordered and went on procession through the city. When they returned, the bishop raised the icon with great care and respect about his head, and they all processed to the mountain. They fetched the shepherd and asked him where he had found it. He showed them the place, and the bishop gave the joyful news that they would build a church on the site. They brought architects and masons and with joy began to build the church. They created a special chapel for the icon of the Virgin Mary, and from that time till now this image of the Mother of Mercy has not ceased to work wondrous miracles, and anyone who seeks her aid in good faith will attain his wish.

This is what I saw and heard of Our Lady who dwells on Montenero. Her story is famed throughout the Christian world, so much so, that every ship that passes beneath her shrine, no matter what their faith, demonstrates their devotion and obedience to Our Lady by firing a salute. If they refrain from doing so, they will certainly be wrecked and perish. This is known from experience. If you don't believe me, ask the truth of this matter from people who have actually been there.

After this I fell ill, with chills and fever, and remained so for two weeks. During that time, news reached us from Genoa that three galleys had arrived there belonging to the Sultan of France. They had come from Messina, and were bringing the princesses who had gone to Messina to attend the marriage of one of their number to a daughter of the kings of France. When my master heard this news, he rejoiced, and immediately prepared to go to Genoa to join the galleys and go with them to Marseille, without running the risk of corsairs. After he had all his things prepared to leave, he said to me, "You are ill, and unable to go with me. Stay here in this place until you recover, and I will wait for you in Marseille".

When I heard these words I was very downcast. I was all alone, and ill. Then I beseeched the Mother of Mercy, Mary the Virgin, and at that very moment a distinguished gentleman, a philosopher, visited us to say goodbye to my master. When he saw the condition I was in — and he knew me because I used to visit him with my master — he asked me, "What's the matter with you? What's happened to you?" I told him about my sickness, and that my master wanted to travel and abandon me here. "Don't worry, if God wills, you will be able to travel with your master. Come to my house this afternoon at 4:00." Then he left.

I waited until 4:00, and went to his house. He was expecting me. He asked me when I suffered chills, and I said, "They attack me at 9:00 A.M., and last till afternoon. Then I get feverish until sunset, and after that I am able to rest". Then he took a glass vial from his chest and poured about thirty drams of distilled liquid, into a smaller vial and handed it to me. "Drink a third of it when you go to sleep, then the second third when you get chills and the last third before you sleep again. It will cure you of getting chills for the rest of your life." I did what he said, and never suffered the chills again, and I am now seventy-five years old! I obtained this blessing from the Virgin Mary, because I sought her aid when I fell ill.

A day later we left Livorno in a small boat, never losing sight of land, for fear of corsairs. When we arrived in the port of Genoa, we disembarked and took our baggage and entered the city. We found an inn, and tried to enter, but the innkeeper wouldn't let us do so until we had brought a permit from the governor's palace. This procedure is on the governor's orders. No one can lodge a foreigner without a permit from the governor. This is so the governor will know how many foreigners there are in the city, for fear that enemies might enter the city and conceal themselves.

The result was that I and my master went to the governor's palace. When we entered, I saw a man sitting in a room. He was the official entrusted with these matters. He asked us, "Where are you from?" and my master told him that he was French, and that I was a Levantine. Then he asked, "What is the purpose of your visit to this country, and where are you going?" My master told him why we had come, and that we were on our way to France. So he wrote out a permit for us, dated it, and gave it to us.

We went back to the inn and gave the permit to the patron. Then they brought in our luggage and gave us a room. We stayed there waiting for the galleys, so we could sail with them. Three days after our arrival, the innkeeper came to us again and told us that we had to go and renew our permits with the same man who had first issued them. So we had to go back, and he gave us new permits, with the current date.

We stayed in Genoa for fifteen days. During that time I went out to tour the city, especially the fine buildings and palaces, all solidly constructed of white marble, and visited the splendid churches. One day I was walking through the narrow streets of the city and I saw some houses in ruins, reduced to heaps of rubble. I was surprised to see such strong, beautifully made houses all ruined. I asked the reason for their destruction.

> They told me, in answer to my question, that the Sultan of France once had an ambassador in this city, who represented his authority. It is the custom of kings to send representatives to principalities on their behalf, in order to forge alliances against common enemies. Unfortunately, the people of this principality were tyrants, and it was called 'The Tyranny of Genoa' [117]. They scorned that ambassador and the gifts he brought, and did not treat him with the honour that was his due. The ambassador bore these slights patiently, because he was a God-fearing man, and didn't want to be the cause of dissension or hatred.
>
> But deeds have consequences. It happened one day that the servants of the ambassador found filth spread on the door of the palace, and on the insignia of the Sultan of France hung above the door. They went and told His Excellency the Ambassador what they had found. When the ambassador heard, he went to see for himself. He was overcome by the dishonour shown to his sovereign, the Sultan of France, and to himself, by the vile actions of the people of Genoa. He decided to protect himself by leaving the country. The next day he took what he needed for the journey and embarked on a galley and went to Marseille.

No one knew the reason for his return to France. When he arrived in Marseille, he immediately took a carriage, along with two of his advisors, and travelled until he arrived in the city of Paris. When the Prime Minister received him, he told him what had happened, and was taken to His Highness, King Louis XIV. When he stood before His Highness the King, he presented a full written account of what had happened to him in the city of Genoa, and of that vileness which had been done by the people of the city, and of how little respect they had for His Highness, the Sultan of France.

When the king read that report, he exploded with anger. He immediately summoned the commander of the army before him. He gave him an order to take forty galleys and ships loaded with soldiers, go to the city of Genoa and rain bombs and cannon volleys upon them and pulverize the city, leaving no stone upon another, even if it meant killing all the inhabitants.

The commander went and carried out His Majesty's order. When he arrived before Genoa, he ordered the captains of the ships to anchor some distance from the port, and the galleys to anchor close to the city on the other side, out of range of the cannons in the city's fort. All this happened without the people of Genoa knowing why they had come. It never occurred to them that they wanted to destroy their city. They had no time to react. Bombs suddenly fell upon them like burning coals from the sky, striking those places and reducing them to rubble.[118] The people were in complete panic, terrified lest their family and friends should be crushed in the ruins.

Then the duke and the leading men of the city, the bishop and priests, took boats to the commander of the army and begged him to stop the bombing, lest everybody be killed. The commander answered them, saying "My Lord the Sultan of France ordered me: 'Destroy this city and don't leave a stone standing. If they fear for the lives of the people of the city and their families, they should order them to evacuate, lest they all be killed.' I cannot disobey an order from My Lord, who is the Sultan of France. I am going to reduce this city to rubble." Then they begged him to grant them a cease fire, while they went to the king to see if perhaps he would pardon them. The commander accepted their proposal and ordered a ceasefire until new orders came from His Majesty the King, and told them, "We will await your return".

Then the duke chose twenty men from among the leading men and nobles of Genoa and sent them with gifts to the Sultan of France in the city of Paris. When they arrived, they were received by the Prime Minister, and begged him to grant them permission to enter the king's presence. The Prime Minister granted their request, and gave them permission to enter. When they came into the presence of His Majesty the King they immediately threw themselves at his feet, humbly imploring him to pardon their city and its people, who were in dire straits because of his anger towards them.

The king took pity upon them, pardoned their crime and gave them his protection. He ordered the Prime Minister to look after them and treat them with honour. He did as he had been ordered and prepared a magnificent banquet for them. He showed them all the sights and *divertissements* in the palace, which has no peer in the rest of the world.

After they had seen everything and feasted, and prepared to return, the Prime Minister asked them, speaking on behalf of His Majesty the King, "Were you surprised at the good order and beauty of My Lord the King's palace? Were you glad and pleased with what you saw?" "Yes, My Lord", they answered, "Everything was in perfect order and incredibly beautiful, with the exception of one thing. That was the sight of the great men of Genoa falling at the feet of the Sultan of France."

This was because of their great tyranny and pride. Even death would have been preferable to them. The humiliation and indignity which they underwent was bitter for them. The Prime Minister rebuked them for these words, filled as they were with presumption and pride, and praised the reasonableness and mercy of the king. Then he dismissed them, shamed and regretting what they had said. They left Paris, and continued travelling until they reached the city of Genoa.

They gave the commander the order which they had been given by His Majesty the King lifting the siege, and then returned to the city. But because of the words they had spoken, the Prime Minister sent a messenger overland with a letter for the commander: "Don't leave until they have reimbursed you for outfitting the ships and galleys and the expense of supplying the troops and similar costs." Then the commander sent to the duke, demanding the cost of outfitting the ships, as we have said, which reached a sizable sum. And he didn't leave until his bill had been paid in full. Then he returned to France, and reported everything he had done to His Majesty the King.

Chapter VII

On Our Voyage to France

Several days later we left with the French galleys bound for Marseille. They gave us passage on the flagship, the *capitana*, which was the ship carrying the princesses we have already mentioned. This great honour was done for my master because he was known to the Sultaness.[119]

When I boarded the galley, I saw things I had never seen before. It was over one hundred cubits long.[120] In the stern was a high structure housing the captain's quarters. Outside his room, was something like a council chamber, with windows looking out on the sea. Tables lined both sides of the room, and they were beautifully varnished. Above the captain's quarters was a ceiling with above it a large cupola of clear glass, the height of a man. Beneath the captain's quarters were mounted long, heavy cannons, each with its gun port. I entered the captain's quarters, and it was like a royal palace. The ceiling was mirrored, and it was furnished with four tables laid with princely utensils, gleaming like silver. All the surfaces shone with silver and gold, stunning the viewer.

Mounted in the stern were two huge cannon with gun ports giving out on the sea, and above that was a large deck the width of the galley, where the soldiers assembled. Beneath it was the kitchen and an iron stove and a small iron oven for baking fresh bread every day. Around the captain's quarters and the council chamber were planters to grow various herbs for making salad. In the hold were chickens and doves and pullets and sheep for providing fresh meat every day. In short, everything was in as good order as could possibly be wished.

When I looked into the hull of the galley, I saw that there were twelve benches on each side. Between each bench was a space of about two cubits. On each bench, on both sides, were six naked criminals manning the oars. On the gangway which separated the benches were soldiers, each with a bull whip in his hand. When they spotted one of the six oarsmen collapsing from fatigue or slacking off, the soldier holding the whip would lash all six on the back, until you could see black bruises from the power of the blows. The sight of them was pitiful, as if they were in hell and the devils were skinning them and torturing them.

When I saw this terrible sight, I turned to the ship's chaplain who was standing there beside me and said to him, "Father, how can Christians be so cruel as to permit this?" The chaplain answered me, saying "Don't trouble yourself with this. You are a foreigner, and don't understand these matters. If you ask me about these people, my son, I would have to answer that each of them deserved death for what he did, but the law took pity upon them for certain reasons, and instead sentenced each of them, depending on his crime, some to three years, some to five and some until they die. This will be a warning to others not to commit these detestable crimes". When I heard these words from the chaplain I was at a loss for words. It seemed as if I were in heaven, looking down at the others in hell. May God preserve us from such a fate!

A few days later we entered the port of Marseille. As we entered, the cannons in the two castles that guard the entrance fired a salute, because ships pass through a strait between two impregnable castles. When a ship arrives in the strait, it must furl its sails and launch a skiff to tow it through the strait to reach the dock and tie up, because this port is right inside the city. It is an extremely ample harbour, and all the ships and galleys enter it. The two fortresses that guard the strait are linked by a thick iron chain, and when the sun sets, they pull up the chain with a mechanism until it is level with the surface of the sea, so that even a small boat cannot enter or leave that strait. At dawn, they lower the chain into the sea again, so that ships can enter and leave.

I witnessed dredging operations going on in order to cleanse the harbour. I saw a large boat, very wide, and mounted on it was a large, wide wheel inside which were two condemned men, turning the wheel by stepping from one stair to another inside, while they remained in the same place. When the wheel turned, two iron scoops appeared; one descended and scooped up mud, brought it up and dumped the rubbish and mud in another boat. Then the other scoop is lowered, scoops up mud, and is raised and emptied into the boat. They have a mechanism by which, when the scoop is raised, it is emptied without anyone touching it. And so on, all year long.

After the princesses had disembarked from the galley, a grand reception was held for them. They were escorted into the palace of the *commandant*, that is, the governor of the city, in a great procession, doing them exceptional honour, since they were daughters of kings. The festival lasted for eight days, and there was not a single thing worth seeing that was not brought before them.

Among these was a young man from the galleys, son of one of the royal princes. He had done something that earned him a sentence of death according to the law. Despite the entreaties of princes, friends of his father, they were unable to obtain a pardon. Instead, he was sentenced to life in the galleys, with no remission. This young man was handsome, and very skilled at dancing, unique in France in that art.

The governor of the city decided to bring him to dance before the princesses, so he sent a squadron of soldiers to the captain of the galley where he was to be found, and ordered him to be released from his bonds and sent to him. When the youth stood before the princesses, he paid them the respects that were their due. I was right there at the reception when he came in. Then the governor commanded him to dance before them, and demonstrate his talent in the art of dancing.

The young man began to dance to the sound of musical instruments. All the spectators were enthralled. After he had finished, and ended his dance, he approached those princesses and asked them, with hot tears streaming down his face, that they order his release, for they were princesses, and had the authority to do so. One of them — the eldest — answered him, saying "Ask whatever you wish, young man, anything, and it shall be yours, anything, except your freedom. The law has found you guilty, and there is nothing we can do to revoke it. Go in peace". His hopes dashed, his spirit broken, he departed, weeping and heartbroken. All those present were saddened at his plight.

Now let us return to our narrative. When we entered Marscille, we went to an inn called *Le Petit Paris*, which means 'Little Paris'. The hostess welcomed us warmly and prepared two furnished rooms, that is, supplied with everything necessary to a stay. Two hours later, I needed to perform a natural function. I went downstairs to look for the lavatory. One of the servant girls said to me, "What are you looking for?" and I told her what I was searching for. "Go upstairs and you will find it" she replied. So I went upstairs again and began looking, opening doors, but couldn't find what I wanted.

I went back downstairs and asked the servant girl to show me the place, for I was running out of patience. She said to me, "What you want is in your room, under the bed!" So I climbed upstairs yet again, went into the room, and lifted the bedclothes from on top of the bed, and found a large pot. It was then clear to me that they didn't have latrines. I had no option but to leave the inn and ask someone how I could get out of the city. They pointed out the way, and I walked into the gardens and finding a secluded place, performed my natural function, and returned to the inn.

I later sought information about this strange matter from a fellow Aleppan whom I met there. He told me that this city didn't have latrines, because the water table under the city was so high. For this reason, they couldn't dig deeply into the ground. So everyone performed their natural functions in their rooms, as I had seen from the pot. At night, they empty them out of the windows into the street, and the night soil collectors come and remove the filth. Yet each quarter of the city has a channel of running water, which runs down from a high elevation, and everyone could use the water to clean the filth from in front of their door.

In the center of the city is an open space between the Rome Gate and the Paris Gate called *Le Cours*. Both sides are planted with trees, and between each tree and the next is a stone bench. Beneath them a channel of water flows night and day. The walkway through the middle is long and wide, and the grandees of the city and many ordinary people stroll along it. It is an open space, like a garden. The trees protect it from the sun's rays.

Another sight is called 'The House of the City' — *Hôtel de Ville* — it is a large, high building. All the merchants and agents gather there to make deals and to buy and sell, from ten in the morning till noon, and from two in the afternoon almost to sunset. Just beyond is the house of the consul, and there he deals with complaints by the merchants, just like a *shahbandar*.[121]

Another place is called the 'House of the Merchants', which handles matters regarding merchants who trade with India and the Levant. This institution has authority over everyone who trades with those places. No one can engage in trade and become a merchant, except with the permission of the officials of this place. They make enquiries about him and if other powerful merchants will guarantee him for a certain sum of money, they give him permission to trade with whatever country he chooses. The agents of the port act as guarantors as well. They purchase this office for three thousand piastres, because all the dealings of the merchants go through their hands, and they give them their money because they are trusted. The merchants employ them in all their sales and purchases as if they were the possessors of the money; no one opposes them in the slightest thing. This is what I learned of the way they organize trade in France and have here written it down.[122]

I used to walk around Marseille sightseeing and visiting churches and monasteries, day after day. They showed me the cave of Mary Magdalene, where she and her brother Lazarus dwelt when the Jews exiled them from the city of Jerusalem. They put them in a skiff without sails or rudder and set it adrift. Our Lord saved them from drowning, and guided the boat to Marseille. The people in those days were idol-worshippers, and when they entered the city, they took refuge in a cave and began to recover their strength and appetite. They performed a number of miracles, until the people of the city came to believe, because of the number of miracles they worked. Finally, apostles came to that city and baptized all its inhabitants. The stories about them are endless.

I went to visit that sacred cave [123], which is on the other side of the port. Near it are the warehouses of the *marlūs*.[124] Anyone who has been to the city knows the place. I also visited the church of the Virgin who protects Marseille. It is built on the top of a mountain, and is called in French, *Madame de la Garde* and is associated with some miracles. When I ascended the mountain, with a crowd of people from Marseille, on their way to worship the Virgin, I saw a house built at the base of the mountain. It had a window, and inside was Jesus, on his knees, praying in the Garden of Olives. He was made in the form of a real man, sweating and afraid, as it says in the Holy Gospels. Looking at him was saddening. This was made especially to make us rest our hopes in the Mother of Jesus. As I went on up, I found another house, inside which was Jesus tied to the pillar, with the guards holding whips as if they were whipping him. Higher up still was another house. Inside, it showed the guards, placing the crown of thorns on Jesus. Above that was yet another, showing them forcing Jesus to carry the wooden cross. Beyond that was the last of them, showing the Messiah stretched out upon the wooden cross and the executioners beside his hands and feet holding the nails in their hands, as if about to pound the thick nails into the extremities of the Messiah. In front of the soldier was a little boy holding a basket of nails.

All this was done with such perfect art that the onlooker saw it as if he were present at the scene at which these barbarous tortures were inflicted. When people encounter these five painful scenes on their way to visit the church, they are filled with bitter remorse and pity.[125]

At last I reached the church. It is in lofty position, on the summit of the mountain, looking out over the sea for three miles. From there, they can observe ships entering the harbour, so watchmen are always stationed here to watch the sea, in case the enemy approaches.

I entered the church, and heard a noble mass, then started back to the inn. On the way I chanced upon one of the Marseille merchants. I saw him stop and stare at me. He asked me, "Aren't you Hannā Diyāb, from the city of Aleppo?" "Yes, I am", I answered. "Don't you recognize me?" he said. I looked at him closely and recognized him. I had worked for him in the days of my youth.

His name was M. Rambaut.[126] We exchanged greetings, and he asked me how I came to be in Marseille. I told him what had passed with me, from beginning to end, and all about my master, with whom I was going to Paris. When he heard this, he became concerned about me, and asked me to accompany him to his house. I entered and he told the servant girl, 'Bring me breakfast!' When we had finished our breakfast, I asked his permission to return to the inn. He wouldn't let me go, saying "Stay here with me, in my house. It bothers me to send you off with a man unknown to me". I answered him, "Then I suggest you please find out about him, because I have a great desire to go with him to Paris, especially since he promised to obtain a position for me there".

He listened to what I said, and sent one of his staff to invite Paul Lucas to come and lunch with him. When my master arrived and they were face to face, M. Rambaut said to him, "Did you know that I raised this lad, when I was in the city of Aleppo? Now that I see he is here, I want him to stay with me forever". My master responded by telling him that he was one of the Sultan of France's travelers, and that he was under the orders of Pontchartrain, the Minister for Eastern Affairs, to bring back with him a man from the lands of the East who could read Arabic, so that he can take charge of the Arabic manuscripts in the King's possession, "This lad will thus obtain an important position". When M. Rambaut heard what he had to say, he was reassured, and pleased that I was going with him.

After we had lunched, and my master had departed, M. Rambaut said to me, "Go with him, but if it turns out that he doesn't keep his promise to you, I will give you a letter to one of my friends in Paris to keep an eye on you, in case you should need anything, and he will send you to me". I thanked him warmly for his kindness, and went my way.

After this, every one of the Aleppo merchants who had known me invited me to visit them, treating me with great kindness. The first of them to do so was M. Bazan, and then M. Simon, M. Banfay, M. Roux and then M. Samatant, who was the most powerful of my acquaintances in Aleppo. They entertained me in their gardens and welcomed me to their homes, treating me with kindness and affection.

We spent ten days in Marseille and my master collected from the 'House of the Merchants' all the items he had sent from the East at the hands of the consuls, as we have mentioned. They consisted of seven sealed chests, so they could not be charged customs duties by customs officials along the way. He obtained a certificate from the customs in Marseille stating that they were duty free, and they put the king's seal in lead on each. When the collection of the chests was completed, they were sent along with other sealed items to the coachman who was travelling to Paris, so that he could deposit them in the customs house there. For the coachmen in that country carry packages on the top of long coaches, stacked on top. The coaches are drawn by six stout horses. We consigned those chests and our luggage to them, and took with us only what we were wearing and the cage with the animals. Only two remained alive, for three had died along the way.

Chapter VIII

On our trip from Provence through France, to the city of Paris

We left Marseille in the month of March, 1709 [*recte* July,1708]. The first city we entered was Aix, a city of beautiful buildings. One of the kings of France gave it to His Holiness the Pope, one of the former popes who visited the ruler of France. It is still under the jurisdiction of whoever occupies the Apostolic See. This city specializes in law, and all the judges and lawyers resort to it to resolve legal questions.

We left that city the next day and followed the road, passing through various cities and towns. We lunched in inns along the way and dined and slept in others, and were always treated with the greatest respect and courtesy. We continued on our way until we came to the city of Lyon, and lodged in one of the inns.

We stayed there five days. During that time, I toured the city and saw the sights. The city is populous and large, with high, solidly built walls, handsome houses and palaces. It possesses splendid churches, and a wide river runs through the city. Every sort of craft may be found there. It specializes in silk weaving and fine luxury textiles, especially silk brocade made with gold and silver thread, a cubit of which sells for sixteen piasters, as well as other luxury textiles. Here they cast the templates for drawing gilded silver thread. They have many other crafts not found elsewhere.

This is a large city, about the size of Aleppo in extent. There is a large church, called the Cathedral of Saint John, which I visited. After looking at the chapels, I ended up in a place within the church and found a tall, tempered steel clock, the height of a man plus his outstretched arm, on top of which was a brass dome. On top of the dome is a bronze cockerel and below it are angels, each standing in front of a bell and each bell rings. It has four faces. The first is oval, that is, long and narrow. It has an iron hand that revolves once every hour, indicating the minutes. As it moves, it lengthens as the oval does. When it reaches the middle, it stops automatically as the oval narrows. And it is a single piece of iron, in such a way that the beholder is astonished at this movement. The hand on the second face revolves once every twenty-four hours, while that on the third face revolves once a year. There it gives you the calendar of that year, marking festival days and fasts as well as eclipses of the sun and moon and other celestial events. The hand on the fourth face revolves once every hundred years and gives notice of things known to scholars learned in astronomical matters. Under each day, is listed the name of the saint it commemorates.

When the hour strikes, the cockerel on top of the dome flaps its wings and crows three times, exactly like a real cockerel. After crowing three times, the angels below the dome begin to strike the bells before them, like a musical performance. When that is finished, the Virgin Mary appears and bows and the angel Gabriel appears before her and salutes her. At that moment, the Holy Spirit appears above them in the guise of a white dove, flying above their heads. When all these movements are completed, the clock chimes the hour. Everything we have described happens every hour, night and day, and it never loses a minute, without anyone ever having to wind it. Travelers say its like cannot be found in any other part of the world. For this reason they blinded those who made it so they would never be able to work for anyone else, so it would remain unique in the world. And this is what I saw and witnessed of this wondrous clock.[127]

I observed many other things in this city, which I will pass over in the interests of brevity. When the five days were up, we travelled on, passing through villages and fortresses and visiting inns along the way. We slept in an inn every night with the greatest courtesy and comfort. Everything we wanted was at our service and our lodging the best there could be.[128]

We continued on until we came to a high bridge of wondrous construction, called the 'Bridge of the Holy Spirit'. It has two gates, each manned by a sergeant appointed by the government to monitor arrivals and departures. This is the main route to the interior of France. After the check, we crossed the bridge.

Near it is a large, populous village. We lodged there in an inn for the night, along with twelve other travelers. The mistress of the inn asked us if we all wished to sit together at the same table, and everyone said they did. Then the mistress of the inn asked "What would you like for dinner?" One of our companions replied "Feed us well". "Willingly", she replied.

She went off and immediately sent us a serving girl with a jug of wine, and she served us all, one after another. We all drank, and afterwards the table was prepared, laid with a table cloth, clean napkins, silver forks and spoons and fresh bread of the finest flour. Afterwards, she presented us with a large platter of roast turkey and twelve roast chickens on a large spit and two platters of fricasseed pullet's wings and a joint of meat and two bowls of salad. We sat down at table to eat, and two serving girls bearing cups poured excellent wine for us all evening, until we had finished dinner. They removed the plates from the table and brought us a piece of French cheese, sixty olives and sixty apples for fruit. Then they washed our hands, cleared the table and brought a large European porcelain bowl filled with water and around it, in the water, six cups and two coolers of wine. Anyone who wanted a drink could simply stretch out his hand and drink whenever he liked.

Finally, when the time came to retire, they politely invited each of us to retire to his bed. At that moment, the mistress of the inn appeared and opened a large chest filled with clean white bedding, more than two hundred sheets. She ordered the serving girls to give each of us two sheets for his bed, one to put under, the other over, with the blanket on top of all. When they had finished doing what she had told them, they retired to their quarters. Then we lay down in our beds under the soft bedding. Beside each bed was a *priedieu* facing an icon, so that anyone who wanted to pray could do so, kneeling on a thick white linen cushion. At last we all went to sleep, utterly content.

When dawn broke, we all got up and went to mass, then returned to the inn. They then brought us a breakfast of cheese, fine white bread and a jug of wine. After breakfast, the owner of the inn asked us four piasters for the price of our room and board, which worked out to a third of a piaster each. They thought it too much, and offered her three, which she was pleased to accept. She thanked us and we took to the road and travelled on.

If someone should ask me if we ever found in our journey any place as inexpensive as this, I would have to say no, for Provence is cheap in comparison to France, and poverty is widespread, especially in the countryside and villages.

From here we entered Bourgogne, where fruit and vines abound. According to what I was told, it is four days long and four days wide, all planted with grape vines. They call it the 'source of wine' and it has no rival in the land of France. It is similar to the *Jurudī*[129] wine of the Lebanon.

In any case, we continued travelling until we came to the city of Paris. We arrived in this great city about the middle of the evening and when we looked out over this city I saw before me a great plain, extending as far as I could see. And that plain was glittering with light as if it were on fire. Then I asked my master "What are those lights and those flames?" He answered, "This is the city of Paris, and it has no walls to impede the view".

We entered the city and passed through its alleys and thoroughfares. I noticed that they were flanked with shops on both sides, and each was lit by two or three torches. Suspended every twenty or thirty steps were glass lanterns with a long candle burning inside. The huge extent of Paris and number of its houses is something impossible to describe.

Beside the door of every house is a shop belonging to the owner, and inside the shop is a workshop producing every sort of craft. From it you can go upstairs to the apartment of the owner on the first floor, for their houses are built with five floors. Each floor is five or six steps higher than the next. When you reach the second floor you see a landing and a door. If you go through the door you see a space divided into a room, a kitchen and a bedroom. The main room has large windows that look out on the streets. If you go up to the third, fourth and fifth floors, you will find them exactly as we have described.

As for the street lights, they are maintained by the public purse, which distributes candles to the inhabitants of each quarter to illuminate their neighbourhood. Each lantern has a supply of candles in a lockbox fastened to the wall, and every native of the quarter must tend the lamp for an entire month.[130] Also, the governor has issued an order that every householder is responsible for sweeping the street in front of the door of his house early every morning. One hour after sunrise, the sergeant, entrusted on behalf of the governor to patrol, fines any householder who neglects to sweep one piastre, which is levied on the man employed to sweep, or upon the householder himself. As for the garbage piled in the street, there are men who collect it and dump it in a container carried on a cart and it is discarded outside the city, so that an hour after sunrise, you see all the streets of Paris swept clean, completely free of all dirt and garbage. This is first civic amenity I noticed in the city of Paris.

Now let us return to our narrative. After entering the city, we walked for half an hour until we came to the house of a friend of my master. We lodged with him, because my master's native town, called Rouen, is a four days' journey from Paris. We stayed with that man and were treated with great honour. They delivered our luggage and prepared a room for us with beds and everything we needed.

We entered the city of Paris in the month of February, 1709 [*recte* August-September 1708]. We stayed a number of days in the house of that man, waiting till my master arranged his affairs. He had an expensive suit of clothing made, in the height of fashion. He sent a volume of his travels to the press, which detailed everything he had seen and heard in every country he travelled in, for every day he used to write it all down. Finally, he ordered a fine cage to be made for the animals, previously mentioned, of which two had survived.

When everything my master required had been done, he asked me to don the costume which I had sent for from Aleppo. I put on a long shirt of a mixed silk and cotton weave from Syria, a pair of wide Turkish-style pantaloons and a handsome belt with a silver-plated knife and a turban wrap and a *kavuk* and similar items typical of Syrian costume. After donning my clothes, the turban wrap and *kavuk* didn't look right to me, so I put on a *qalpaq* like the beautiful sable *qalpaq*s my master purchased in Egypt at Manshan.

Then we rode in a carriage, making for the town of Versailles, where the palace of the king of France was located. It is about an hour and a half from Paris. When we drew near Versailles, I saw from afar something shining, which dazzled the eyes. I asked my master "What is that gleaming I see?" "Those are the king's stables" he answered. When we drew near, I saw it was a handsome, solidly built structure, roofed with that black stone used for writing on. The shafts of the chimneys of that building were gilded. When the sun shone on them, the intensity of the reflection was so great you couldn't believe your eyes. We walked the length of those stables and it took almost half an hour.

Then we arrived in Versailles and saw the king's palace. There is a very large, wide square in front of it and it is surrounded by iron railings the height of a man's outstretched hand, the points sharpened like spears. In the center is an iron gate through which one passes to enter the square. It is guarded as if by leopards. They allow no one to enter unless they recognize him, and know he is known to the court.

When we came to the gate they wanted to block our entry, but my master gave them a password, which they recognized, and they let us in. Then we crossed the square until we reached the door of the king's palace. Here, too, there were soldiers on guard, like the others, and there was a uniformed captain seated there, with a bunch of servants. He was terrifying and splendid. My master approached him and spoke with him, identifying himself. He was welcomed and nobly treated and given permission to enter.

We climbed a wide, long, stone staircase and when we reached the top, we went to the palace of the minister, who was named Pontchartrain.[131] He was Minister of the East. After obtaining permission, we accompanied the captain into his presence. When we stood before him, my master bowed to him, informed him of his safe return to Paris from his travels and gave him the inventory of the contents of the seven chests of items he had purchased during his travels on behalf of the king, as we have mentioned before. When the minister had read through the list, he welcomed him and complimented him on his safe return, after all the difficulties encountered on his travels.

I was standing behind everybody else, holding the cage with the animals. The minister turned and saw me standing there holding the cage and asked my master, "Who is that youth, and what is he holding?" He answered him, saying, "This youth was my interpreter on my journey, and when we were in Upper Egypt, I found some strange looking animals, which I had never seen anywhere else I had been. I took seven of them, although the hunters had great difficulty in capturing them. I put them in a cage and brought them with me, but along the way, five of them died and now only two remain. If Your Excellency so wishes, you may inspect them here in the cage".

The minister gave orders for me to be allowed to approach, and they took the cage from my hand and showed it to His Excellency. When he saw the animals' claws and its weird body, he said to my master "I want to show these animals to His Majesty tomorrow, because the hour of his entry to palace is past". He immediately gave orders that we be given chambers in his palace, and they took us to a furnished room. Then they brought us food and drink and everything else we could possibly require.

We stayed in that room until the next day until two hours before noon. Then the minister ordered us brought before him, and he accompanied us to the king's audience hall. When we arrived, he entered, while we waited outside until the king left his apartments and entered the audience hall. The minister informed him of my master's arrival and asked him to permit us to enter.

We went in and saw the king standing there, with on his left and right the grandees of the kingdom, lined up with becoming modesty and respect. He was tall, splendid in appearance, with a gaze so sharp it was impossible for a man to meet his eyes. Then my master stood before him and did him reverence, wishing the king long life and everything else that is customarily said on greeting kings. I overheard, on the part of the king, gentle and loving speech to my master, to the effect that he hoped he was recovered from the fatigues he had undergone in his service.

Then the minister approached and asked the king if he wished to see those animals. So the king ordered them to be brought before him. They took the cage from my hand and placed it in front of the king. When he saw the animals, he wondered at their form and asked my master in what country he had found them. He answered "In the country of Upper Egypt". Then he asked, "Do you know if they are male and female?" "My Lord", he replied, "there were originally seven, some male and female among them, but now I don't know whether these are male and female". He also asked what they were called in their country. My master hesitated, unable to remember, and said he had forgotten. Then he turned to me and said to His Majesty, "This young man with me knows what they are called".

Then the king and all the grandees of the kingdom turned towards me, and one of them asked, "What is the name of these animals?" I told him that in their homeland they are called *yarbūʿ*, jerboa. Then the king ordered them to bring me a pen and paper so that I could write their name in my language. When they brought the paper, I wrote their name in Arabic and also wrote it in French, because I knew how to read and write French. After I had written down the name as requested, they showed it to His Majesty the King.

The king looked at me and asked my master, "Who is this youth and what country does he come from?" My master answered, bowing to the ground, saying "My Lord, this youth comes from Syria, in the Holy Land. He belongs to the Maronite nation, which has been in communion with the Church of Peter since apostolic times, and has never split from it".

At that moment Monseigneur the Dauphin, the king's son, entered. He is corpulent and unpopular.[132] It is said of him, "His father is a king, his younger brother is King of Spain, but he is not a king". He approached and examined the animals, and was astonished at their appearance. He had an enormous painting, depicting all the animals in the world, except this one. He immediately commanded the presence of the king's physician, whose name was M. Fagon.[133]

This man was learned and a professor, and had no equal in the world in medicine or the natural sciences and related disciplines. When M. Fagon appeared, he studied the animals. The king's son asked him if he knew about them and if they were mentioned in books of natural history, but he answered that he had never seen them mentioned or depicted. Then he summoned the painter to add them to his painting of animals.

The king then commanded the minister to hide those animals away someplace, and not let anyone look at them until Madame de Bourgogne returned from the hunt. She was the daughter-in-law of the king and wife of his son, the Duc de Bourgogne, and the king loved her very much, and called her his daughter.[134]

Here, in his audience hall, was the first time I looked upon the face of the king, I mean the Sultan of France, Louis, the fourteenth of that name. Everything I have mentioned just now is exactly what happened, with no additions and no omissions. I have written it in summary form, lest the reader imagine that I am making it up. For I saw many things, but didn't write them down, and I haven't thought about them for fifty-four years, for I am writing this account of my travels in the year 1763, and I was in Paris in 1709. Do I recall everything I saw and heard in complete detail? By no means!

Now let us return to our story. We left the king's audience chamber, accompanied by the minister, and entered our apartment. The minister ordered the guards not to let any of the nobles, or anybody else, in to look at the animals before the daughter-in-law of the king, as the king had ordered. We waited until 10:00 PM, that is, two hours before midnight. Then the minister summoned us to his presence. When we arrived, he proceeded, led by four lantern-bearers, until we came to the palace of Madame de Bourgogne, the afore-mentioned daughter-in-law of the king.

The minister knocked and requested permission to enter. After a short wait, two handmaidens came out on her behalf and politely asked the minister to enter. The minister went in and told her about the animals, and how the king had ordered "That no one should see them before you!" She summoned us to her presence, and the handmaidens came out and ushered us in.

When we entered, I saw the princess seated on a chair, surrounded by the children of the nobles, also sitting on chairs, playing cards. In front of each was a heap of gold coins. Standing beside them were ladies-in-waiting, like moons, wearing precious gold brocade.

We stood before the princess, who was beautiful and dressed more splendidly that all the rest, while she walked around and examined the animals, and all the nobles did the same. Then they began to examine me and my costume and lift it up. One of them put their hand on my chest, another lifted off my *qalpaq,* exposing my head.[135] They left off staring at the animals and began staring at me and my costume and laughing.

Finally, the princess asked my master, "Who is this youth? And from what country does he come?" After he had told her, she said, "Why does he have whiskers, that is, a moustache?" He answered, "It is the custom of their country not to shave their moustaches".

We stayed with this princess for half an hour. Finally, we left her and went out with the minister. While we were walking along, a beautiful young girl appeared, dressed in a royal robe of brocade and wearing a crown studded with precious stones, like diamonds, rubies and emeralds, such that it dazzled the eyes. She was attended by four ladies-in-waiting, all beautiful, all wearing splendid dresses. It appeared to me that she was a daughter of the king.

When the minister saw her, he stopped and bowed, with great politeness and courtesy. Then she asked about us and he told her about the animals we had. She asked if she could see them, and he said "I hear and obey!" and immediately took the cage from the hands of the servant and put it in front of her. Then the minister removed the cover from the cage in order to show her. But when she looked at the animals she was frightened, and fled in terror. The minister ran after her to try to calm her and bring her back to look, but was unable to convince her to return. So he came back and told us to go to his palace.

We had barely taken a few steps when a demand came from His Highness the King, brought by two of the palace handmaidens, asking him to present himself before the king with the cage of animals and its bearer. He ordered us to return, and as we entered the king's palace. I saw some forty tall soldiers, like a troop standing guard. These were the king's special palace guards. We finally came to an inner room, that is, the king's bed chamber. The handmaidens escorted me in, leaving the minister and my master in the outer room. When I went in, I saw the king, seated on a chair flanked by two candles, reading a book. On the other side of the room, I saw a bed, covered with brocade and a princess reclining on it. The girl we had met on the path was standing beside the bed.

The ladies-in-waiting pushed me forward before the princess and placed the cage on a chair so she could examine the animals. At that moment, the king rose from his chair and came to my side, holding a golden candlestick so that the princess could see the animals. I was standing beside the king, and through my naivety, I took the candlestick from the king's hand. With great discernment, he gave it to me, realizing I had done so without knowing that what I had done was something unheard of, for no one has the insolence to stretch out his hand to the king and take something from his hand. My master used to tell people in Paris, "This is the young man who took the candelabra from the king's hand".

Finally, after the princess had looked her fill, the king returned to his apartments and they gave me back the cage. When I left, I found the minister and my master standing outside awaiting me. We went in the minister's company until we came to our quarters. There we met two ladies-in-waiting sent on behalf of Madame d'Orléans, who was one of the king's daughters. They asked the minister to send the cage with the animals and its bearer, so he told me to go with them.

When we came to their palace, I found a group of princesses gathered to see the animals and their bearer. When they had examined the animals, and me too, they sent me along to another princess, and from there to another. They kept taking me from place to place until it was two hours past midnight. At last they returned me to the place we were staying. My master was waiting for me, and we spent that night until dawn in the lap of luxury.

It chanced that Madame de Bourgogne, the king's daughter-in-law, formerly mentioned, woke indisposed because of the fatigues of the hunt she had been on the day before, as we have said. The womenfolk of the princes had gathered about her to distract her while she lay in her bed. Among them was one of the princesses who had heard of the animals, and she wanted to see them, and asked Madame, the daughter-in-law of the king, to ask them to be brought before her so she could examine them. She immediately sent a servant on her behalf to the minister, asking him to send the cage of animals and the Easterner who carried the cage.

When the messenger arrived, the minister gave the order, and immediately summoned us and told us to go with the servant. When we came to the palace of the princess, they bid me enter alone, and I carried the cage into the princess' apartment and bedchamber. When I entered, I saw that royal bed, and it was adorned with precious brocade. On it reclined the princess, unique in her age for beauty and grace.

Sitting around the bed were the womenfolk of the princes, like moons, dressed in garments I cannot begin to describe, they glittered so with the jewels and precious stones with which they were encrusted. They pushed me forward before the princess, who was lying in the bed. When I stood before her, I set down the cage and bowed to the ground, and did reverence to her, just as my master had taught me. When I bowed, one of the princesses noticed the silvered hilt of the knife I was carrying. She reached out her hand and grasped the knife and said to the others, "Come and see the sword of the Muslim!"

When I heard these words from her, I immediately adjusted my robe and said to her, "No, my lady, this is not a sword you see, this is a knife". When she heard the word 'knife', she immediately drew away from me and changed colour, but did nothing more. Meanwhile, the princesses continued examining the animals and my costume. Finally, they let me go, and I picked up the cage and left.

I found my master standing at a distance, monitoring the situation. When I came up to him, he looked at me, his eyes bulging with anger, and didn't want to speak to me, he was so furious. When we got back to our quarters, he reached his hand to my belt and took the knife and threw it to the ground and tried to break it.

Then he turned to me and began to rebuke me for what I had done, and for my ignorance, saying, "First, you insolently take the candelabra from the king's hand, an insolence never dared by anyone but you, but because the king is kindly, and exceedingly goodhearted, he let you take it from his hand. And now you commit a second insolent act, saying to the princess "This is not a sword, it is a knife!" Don't you realize that the governors have sternly decreed that anyone, even the king himself, found with a knife or dagger, will be sent to the prison ships, that is, the galleys, forever, and some of them condemned to death, if they are so suspected? They say the knife and the dagger are an enemy hiding behind the rapier, because the rapier is used to protect a man from someone similarly armed, but with a knife or a dagger you can draw close to your enemy and strike him without him knowing, and he would have no protection from you. This is why the governors have decreed that no one may carry a knife or a sharp dagger".

Then he said to me, "What would happen if what took place in the palace of the king of France should become known in Paris? That an insolent fellow like you had entered the king's bedchamber, carrying a sharpened knife? But God saved you, and saved me, from this disaster". And right then he took the knife and broke the blade and kept it with him.

I finally won his forgiveness by saying, "I didn't know!" Then he said to me, "Because you did this from ignorance, God saved you and the king didn't reprove you". Then I went on to ask him about the places we had entered and about the princess I had seen in the king's chambers, and the girl who was standing beside her and appeared to us on the path, was she perhaps the king's daughter? "No", he said, "but this is a long story. I want to tell it to you so you know, and can speak of what you have seen. If you ask me about the princess in the king's chambers and bedroom, she is called Madame de Maintenon, and she is the king's wife. The girl that I saw was raised by the aforementioned queen, in place of her daughter". Then I asked my master, "How can this woman be the wife of the king, when she is devoid of all beauty and attraction, and has no marks of nobility?" "That is a long and amazing tale", he replied.

> "The king took her to wife because of the beauty of her remarkable intelligence, which has no equal in his entire kingdom.[136] This is why the king fell in love with her. She was one of the ladies-in-waiting to Madame d'Orléans. This princess loved the king very much and he very often spent time in her company. There he noticed the aforesaid young woman, and was struck by her learned conversation, modesty, charming character and refined intelligence.

151

One day he sent a note to Madame d'Orléans, inviting her to visit him. When the letter in the king's own hand arrived, she had no idea how to respond. She wanted to excuse herself, because at the time she was very indisposed, and couldn't compose a reply herself. She therefore asked her lady-in-waiting, Madame de Maintenon, to reply on her behalf, and to apologize for the delay in coming to see him.

The lady-in-waiting gladly agreed to carry out her mistresses' request and quickly wrote a letter. She addressed it to His Highness the King, profusely apologizing in the sweetest way, with great delicacy, and such skill, that the king was astonished. When he read her elegant prose and admired the beauty of her style, his love for that lady-in-waiting increased, and he wanted to draw her near him and elevate her rank. The queen [137] was not amused at this plan, lest it cause a scandal, for she was a devout, God-fearing woman.

Some years later, the queen died, and was gathered up into God's mercy. A great funeral was held for her and all the bells in Paris were tolled, even the great bell whose sound could be heard a seven hours' journey from the city.[138] They placed her remains in the church of Saint Denis, where all the kings of France were interred. I visited her tomb and those of all the kings of France buried there.

Forty days after her death, the king's ministers took counsel and agreed the king should remarry. And because Christian kings are not allowed to marry twice, they sent seeking a dispensation from the Roman Pontiff to allow their king to remarry, in order to ensure the succession. After receiving the dispensation, they approached His Highness the King and beseeched him to marry. They had in mind a princess of striking beauty, descended from noble kings of ancient lineage, and told him of her.

He refused, and would not accept marriage with that princess. Instead, he said to them, "I will take Madame de Maintenon as my wife". When they heard these words, they were astonished, and throwing themselves at his feet, said to him, "How can our lord and king possibly think of marrying someone who is a servant, and a stranger in our country? Someone of whose lineage we are ignorant, because she comes from Savoy, a country that is your enemy? What will other kings say about you, when they hear you have married someone like this cast off?" Then the king, his face suffused with anger, answered them, saying "Let them say what they like!"

And for a second time they threw themselves at his feet and urged him to change his mind, but it was impossible, and he held to his decision. When they saw that the king's decision was final, they said to him, "O our king and master of our well-being, if Your Highness wishes to go through with this marriage, we will not accept her as our queen".

The king was furious, and threatened them with banishment if they did not do as he said. They withdrew from his presence in order to consult, and agree on what answer to give him. They decided that their only option was to beseech the dauphin, the king's son, to prevent his father from carrying out his plan and to reconcile them to the king. So monsignor the dauphin went to his father and began beseeching him to abandon this detestable plan. His father immediately turned on him, saying, "Go to your castle!", that is, he ordered him to be imprisoned there.

Next, the notables of Paris convened and wrote a petition to the king, saying they would never accept the foreigner as their queen. When the king saw that the people of the country and the leaders and powerful men of the state were all in agreement that they did not want the king to marry this foreign woman, he finally retracted his decision and told them he would not marry her. So things calmed down, the gossip died away and everything returned to normal.

The king remained unmarried for an entire year, and during that time threw himself into building Versailles. There he constructed a palace without equal in the world, providing it with gardens, groves, and vistas beyond description. Its fame is well-known among all the Christian kings. The strange thing is that the river Seine, a river as large as the Euphrates, flows just outside Versailles, on the other side of a mountain. The king wanted the river to flow through Versailles. He gathered together all the learned men and commanded them to make the river flow through the gardens he had planted around the royal palace in Versailles.

The learned men consulted with each other and saw no other solution but to cut through the mountain and let the river flow through it. When they explained this to the king, he answered them, "What is the point, if the river runs at ground level? I want the water to flow down from the summit, in order to irrigate the gardens and groves. The learned men were astonished at his answer, and replied to the king that this was impossible, thus revealing their inadequacy. The king was confounded by their saying it was impossible.

At that moment, a learned man approached and kissed the hem of the king's garment and said, "O my lord, I can bring the water down to you from the top of the mountain, but it will cost you a great deal of money".[139] When the king heard these words, he commanded them to write an authorization for all his expenses and signed it with his own hand. Then he said to him, "If you exhaust what I authorized for you, ask for whatever more you need". So he kissed the ground before the king and departed.

He immediately undertook that astonishing project.[140] First, he gave orders to cast long iron pumps, shaped like cannons and steel water wheels and steel plungers [for the pumps]. When everything had been completed according to the plans he had drawn for them, he summoned the builders, and ordered them to dig a deep reservoir beside the river and beside it another deep reservoir, and so on, until they reached the summit of the mountain. Then two walls were erected beside that reservoir and the first waterwheel was mounted. Beside it was a pump. The water flowed over the waterwheel and when it revolved, the water was lifted to the pump. When the pump was full, it released the water into the second reservoir, through a channel like a mill race, where it works the second waterwheel. When the wheel turns, it operates the plunger in the pump and raises the water to a third reservoir, and from there to a fourth, and so on, until the water reaches the summit of the mountain, and in this way abundant water reaches the king's gardens.

Then the king ordered large pools and ornamental fountains of stone, with step-like cascades for the water to flow over and reach the bottom. He arranged orange, lemon and citron trees and other fruits all made of tin, and they had tubes for the water to enter, so water issued forth from each leaf of those trees. Beneath those trees was a meadow, in which were two high jets from which water flowed. Over all they had made a walkway wide enough for four people to walk abreast and it is about two hundred cubits long. The water flows from its two sides, the water on the right flowing left, and the water on the left flowing right, the two cascades meeting and forming a sort of dome of water. Those that walk under it don't feel a single drop, and all this despite the fact that the water is falling from the top of the mountain. The overflow issues into a small river through the garden and flows out of Versailles and joins the river which flows on the other side of that mountain.

In addition to all this, there are the plantations of trees, all intertwined, forming a veritable forest. Hedges are planted on either side, of a kind of plant whose leaves weave foliage so dense an arrow cannot penetrate it. The forest is filled with hares and deer and other similar game, for the hunt and the chase. The forest takes more than a day to traverse, and these animals are born and grow up there. Meanwhile they are still at this time multiplying the number of waterwheels that make it possible to bring the water down from the summit of the mountain. If you should ask about the beauties of this place, they are so various as to be beyond description. I have only been able to describe a few of the many.[141]

Now let us return to our main subject. When all these works were finished — the beautifully constructed palaces, the gardens and the fountains which we have mentioned, and everything was exactly as it should be, the king commanded that everything in the palace in Paris be moved to the palace in Versailles, so that he could establish the throne in a place worthy of kings. He gathered all the great men of the kingdom, the ministers and courtiers, in Versailles, showing his resentment to the people of Paris for their refusal to accept Madame de Maintenon as their queen. For this reason he sent for her and brought her to his palace and married her with all the Christian rites. He stayed in Versailles until his death, never again entering Paris. This is what my master told me of the story of the queen that I saw reclining on her bed in the king's apartment.

I stayed in the king's palace eight days, until the cage the dauphin, the king's son, had ordered was finished, and the animals had been placed in it. During those eight days I roamed the palace, and no one obstructed me.

Afterwards, I returned to Paris, where my master had rented a house on the Pont St Michel, where we stayed. Many of the great men of Paris came to visit us, and he would return their visits, and take me with him so I could see their palaces and lovely dwellings and the beauty of their furnishings.

One day we went to the house of a nobleman and I noticed in the salon a portrait of a man holding a bird in his hand, but it appeared to the viewer as if his hand reached out of the picture, with the bird. I examined this picture and was certain his hand reached out. Those present told me, "This is just a picture!", but I couldn't believe it, until one of them came forward and touched it with his hand. Then I believed him, and praised the artist who had painted such a wonderful picture. Then they told me this was a work of the painter Nicolas [142] and had been purchased for five hundred piastres.

The story of this painter is very strange and wonderful.

> In his youth, this master painter had been a shoemaker and contemptible in appearance. One day he happened to see the daughter of one of the nobles. She was incredibly beautiful, unique in her time. When he first glimpsed her, she was walking along with the sons of the nobles. He stared at her and his heart was conquered by love, to such an extent that he followed her from place to place, until she reached her father's palace and disappeared from view. He started to lie in wait for her to leave the palace to go for a walk, as was the custom of that town. He would follow her, just looking at her.
>
> He did this a number of times, but the girl didn't notice him until her companions, who accompanied her on her walks, started teasing her about her elegant, handsome, incomparable lover. The girl was furious, and went to tell her father, the prince, what the youth was doing, and how whenever she went out, he followed her and stared at her, and how her companions teased her about him.
>
> The prince was furious, and had the youth brought before him and angrily asked him, "What's the matter with you? Following my daughter wherever she goes, what are you up to?" The youth immediately answered, "I love her".
>
> When he heard this, the prince laughed at his stupidity and began to question him further, saying, "Do you wish to marry her?" "Yes!" replied the youth. Then the prince said to him, "What will

you give as her bride price?" "Ask whatever you like", he answered. "I want you", said the prince, "to paint a picture of her with your own hand. If you do this, I will give her to you in marriage, but only on condition that if you follow her again I'll hang you".

The young man was content with this condition and left the prince's presence very happy. He began to sketch on walls to see if he could capture the girl's likeness, but was unable to achieve anything in this art. So he apprenticed himself to one of the painters, for whom he ground the colours. He stayed some time with that artist, and watched how he worked and how he drew and painted with oils. In his mind, he began to draw a picture of the girl, because she had been imprinted on his memory by the strength of his love for her.

At last he succeeded in capturing her likeness to perfection. When he had finished the picture, he went to the prince and gave it to him. When the prince examined it, he was astonished at its beauty and the skill of the artist. He couldn't believe the young man had painted it. "Are you the one who painted this picture?" he asked. "This picture is the work of my hand, as you stipulated", he answered.

The prince couldn't believe the youth had painted it, and wanted to know the truth of the matter. He summoned four master artists and showed them the picture, and asked them if they knew who had painted it. "There is no one in this country or even in India"[143], they replied "who could paint that picture. This is not a painting by a human; it is the work of angels or demons."

After the prince had made sure of the truth of the matter, and knew that that youth had actually painted the picture, he summoned him and asked him yet again if he were truly the painter of the portrait. The youth answered him, saying "Find out if there is another painter capable of producing anything like it; if so, I am a liar". "You're right, my son", said the prince, "but because I had so little faith that you could paint a picture of my daughter, I married her off. If you like, I will honour my oath by giving you her sister."

When the youth heard that the girl was married, he lost his mind. He went out like a madman, unable to think, from the depth of his passion and love for that girl. He wandered off into the wilderness and deserted places. Tormented by hunger and exposure, he went to a city to work for a painter, grinding colours for a morsel of bread. He stayed with the painter for some time. He saw that the artist was meticulously painting a beautiful, unique painting, with which he intended to establish his ascendency over the rest of the painters. When he finished it, he displayed it in a prominent place and went to invite the other painters to come and see it and witness his mastery.

When the painter went out to invite the other masters, his employee, Nicolas, painted a fly on the nose of the person in the portrait, then went and sat down once more to grind colours. A short time later, the artist returned with the other artists, and they all sat down on chairs. Then the artist presented the painting so the others could view it, and he noticed that fly on the picture and stretched out his hand and brushed it, but it didn't fly off. Then he examined it closely and realized that it was painted. He was chagrined that he had been fooled, and turned to his assistant and asked: "Who came here and painted this fly?" His assistant answered, "No one entered but Nicolas, the madman, your employee, and it is he who painted this fly".

When the artists heard his name, which was famous throughout the country, they all stood up and welcomed him with honour. They said to him, "Why do something like this, when you are so skilled in this art? Sit among us, and all of us will become your pupils". He refused, and paid them no heed, and tried to leave their presence. Then his master said to him, "Stay with me, so that you and I can compete in painting". Nicolas asked, "What do you want me to stay for?" The artist answered, "I will paint a picture, and then you paint one too, and the painter that astonishes the other painters the most will be the master painter". Nicolas agreed to this competition before the other artists, who then went their ways.

The master began to paint a picture, and when he finished it, he sent for the other artists and showed it to them. It was a picture of fruit and bunches of grapes, and he hung it in the courtyard. The birds gathered and started to peck the picture, convinced they were pecking real fruit and grapes. When the assembled painters saw that, they testified to his artistry, because he had fooled the birds.[144]

Then they turned to Nicolas and said to him, "Now it's your turn to paint a picture, so we can judge which is the better painting". "Give me a room", said Nicolas, "so that I can sit alone and paint the picture, and let no one enter until it is finished a month hence." The painters were pleased to do so, and gave him a room and painting materials, and left him alone. Nicolas began painting the picture, and finished in a single day, but he wanted the painters to think that he laboured long over it because of its technical difficulty. When the appointed time came, the painters hurried to that place to see the painting, knowing that it would be unique and wonderful.

Then they told Nicolas, "Open your room, so we can take a look at your picture!" So he gave the key to his master, and when he opened the room he saw a picture draped with a curtain on the wall of the room. His master reached out a hand and tried to lift the curtain from the painting, but his hand struck the wall, for that drapery was painted on the wall. The master was embarrassed, for he had been fooled for the second time. Then Nicolas turned to his master and said, "It isn't clever to fool the birds. What is clever is to fool the experts, like you". And he went out, leaving them astonished at that curtain, and the skill with which it had been painted.

This Nicolas, when he entered an inn, used to stay two or three days, eating and drinking. When the innkeeper asked him to pay the bill, he would ask for a piece of paper and draw on it, then say to the innkeeper, "Take this drawing to a master painter and ask him for five gold pieces. If he only offers four, bring it back to me". The fellow went off and gave the drawing to a master painter among the artists, asking a price of five gold pieces. He was offered three. So he returned to consult him, but Nicolas took the drawing from his hand and tore it up, then drew another, even nobler and finer, and said to him, "Don't take less than ten gold pieces!" The man went back, and asked ten gold pieces for it, and was immediately offered five. He returned to consult Nicolas, but found he had left the inn never to return, as if he were angry. He passed a good part of his life in this vagabond way, carrying a pack on his back dragging a dog along with him. And right up to the present time, his paintings and drawings sell for a great deal. This is an abridged version of the tale.

Now let us return to what we were saying of the beauties of Paris and the excellence of its institutions. First of all, more than eight hundred churches are to be found in this city, not counting monasteries and nunneries.

In every church there are a number of poor boxes, some for the destitute of the parish, some for the needy who had once been well-off, but had been reduced to poverty, and could not beg publicly or reveal how needy they had become. For their sake, in every church there is a box especially for them. Two priests are in charge of distributing funds to them, so that no one learns of their need. There are boxes for the poor of the parish, among them the blind and cripples, the aged men and women, and widows who have children. These poor boxes are supervised by two men of exemplary character from the parish, who distribute the funds according to need. The names of the recipients are written down in a ledger.

I never saw a beggar accost and ask for alms from anyone at all, but I saw a soldier who had lost a leg severely beaten by the governor's men, without pity. When I asked one of those present why they were beating that soldier, he answered that they had seen him begging. I was astonished, and said to him, "You mean in your country you kill someone who begs? Especially a cripple, who can't work? How can that be permitted?" "That man", he answered, "deserves the beating, because the king, may God preserve him, supplies everything they need and their food, and they lack for nothing that would drive them to beg. If they do, it is an insult to the king's person."

I questioned him further, saying "What is the story of these soldiers?" He said, "The king has built an enormous hospital for those soldiers returning wounded, or having lost arms or legs.[145] It is staffed by doctors and surgeons, and contains a church and confessors. Lunch and dinner are provided, and everyone has a bed to rest on and sleep in, and so on. They therefore have no excuse for begging, they only do so from greed. This is why anyone who sees them begging punishes them on the spot, and here in the hospital they throw him down over a saw horse and whip him with a bull whip to teach the others. There is another box dedicated to the hospital of that parish".

In addition to all the other churches in Paris, there is the cathedral of Notre-Dame. It is huge and spacious and has a big bell the size of a small dome. It is mounted at the top of a high steeple, supported by four columns. It is a small hand span thick and suspended in its middle is an iron clapper. There is a system of pulleys and ropes leading down into the church. When they want to ring it, it takes twelve men to pull the ropes and cause the clapper to strike the sides of the bell. When they ring the bell, the reverberation stuns the people of Paris with its noise. The sound can be heard a seven hour's journey from Paris. This bell is only rung on special occasions, such as the death of a king or prince or cardinal, or someone similar.

This cathedral contains eighty chapels, and each is the size of a small church. In the middle is a large chapel with two façades. It has seven doors, and each looks out on a different Parisian parish, and each parish is the size of Aleppo inside the walls. This is not an exaggeration, because it is the opinion of travelers that the city of Paris is seven times the size of Istanbul, for its streets take an hour to walk, at a brisk pace. The head of this church is a cardinal appointed by our lord the Pope, and his authority over the land of France is that of a second Pope [146]. In the service of the cardinal is a man named Christofle, brother of Paolo Čelebi in Aleppo. He is the most powerful of all the cardinal's retainers and is his secretary.

The festival of Corpus Christi fell during these days, and it was the custom of the people of Paris to walk in procession with the Corpus three times. The first is on the Friday of the festival itself, and the Sunday afterwards, and the following Friday as well. On the day of the procession they decorate the walls, doors and shops with fine cloths and set out their precious ornaments and strew the streets with flowers. At the end of each street they raise a dais like a chapel.[147] When they arrive at that chapel they venerate the Corpus and make vows and sing hymns, and perform similar devotions. That was the day of the procession of the church of Notre-Dame and it passed through the quarter I was living in.

I stood in the window to watch the great procession pass. It included more than five hundred priests and deacons, all dressed in costumes sprinkled with gold, and carrying candles of camphor and crosses of gold. The cardinal came after the priests and deacons had passed. They had raised a large, wide baldachin over him, held up by twelve poles carried by twelve men, holding the monstrance containing the Corpus. When I gazed on that monstrance it was like looking at the sun. A man could not fix his gaze on it, such were the jewels with which it was encrusted — diamonds, rubies, emeralds and other precious gems, which the eye could not take in.

While I was standing there, dazzled by the sight, my master came up to me and said to me, "Read what is written on top of the baldachin!" When I looked at the script, I saw a large square of dark red cloth on which was written in white letters 'There is no god but God', etc.[148] It startled me that such an inscription should be on that baldachin. My master asked me "What does it say?", so I told him what it said. He was astonished, and didn't believe me. Then he ordered me to go to the neighbour's house, because I could see the inscription better from his windows. So I did what he ordered and looked again at the inscription, and saw it was just the same as before. I returned and told him the truth of the matter. I said to him, "It is not possible that I could be mistaken, because the cloth is red and the letters are white. How could I be mistaken?"

When my master was certain of the meaning of the inscription, he ordered me to go tell the cardinal what I had noticed. He said to me, "The cardinal will thank you with a large tip". I waited until two o'clock in the afternoon, then went to the cardinal's palace. When I entered the palace, the guards at the door of the palace asked me, "What do you want?" I told them that I had something to say to His Eminence the cardinal. Then they asked me, "What do you want to tell him, and what do you want?" I told them, "I am under orders to tell no one but His Eminence the Cardinal".

Then they sent one of the guards with me, and he took me into the palace to the quarters of the cardinal. One of the servants immediately came and asked me to accompany him. I went with him and we climbed up to a high place and he bade me enter a room. When I went in, I saw an imposing looking man sitting on a chair. He stared at me and asked, "Who are you, and what country do you come from?" "I am from Syria", I replied, "from the city of Aleppo." Then he asked me in fluent Arabic, "What sect are you?" "I am of the Maronite sect", I answered. "Welcome to a son of my country!" he said, and received me with great politeness.

Then he asked me, "Do you recognize me?" and I told him "No, my lord". "I am from the Zamārīyā clan [149] and my elder brother is Paolo Čelebī. My other brother is Yūsuf, and the oldest of us all is named Zamārīyā and he is the Custodian of Jerusalem in Istanbul, lodging with the ambassador". I answered him, saying that I knew his brother *khoja* Paolo Čelebī and his brother Yūsuf in Aleppo, and their names were well-known to everyone and they were always spoken of with great respect.

At last he asked me, "What is the reason you have come here? I saw you from the window, entering the quarters of His Eminence the Cardinal with one of the guards. If you have need of him, tell me, and I will do anything you require". "May God prolong your life, My Lord! There is nothing I need from His Eminence, but I have something I wish to tell him." "What do you have to tell him?" he asked, "Tell me, because I am the cardinal's secretary, and no one can see him without permission."

When I heard these words, I decided to tell him what I had noticed about that calligraphy. When he heard what I had to say, he was astonished, and asked repeatedly whether it was true. I told him "Yes, it is, and could cause you great embarrassment". Then he said to me, "There's no need for you to see the cardinal. I will investigate the matter. Come and see me tomorrow afternoon, and I will tell you whether this is true or not and then let you enter to see the cardinal".

So that day passed, and the next day I went to him and he told me that everything I had said was true, and that he had told everything to our lord His Eminence the Cardinal, and that he had immediately summoned the sacristan and ordered him to bring the cloths that were over the baldachin of the Corpus. When they were brought to him, he saw that calligraphy and then the cardinal asked that man "What are these canopies?" The man replied, "My Lord, these canopies are old. They are the battle standards of the Barbary corsairs, kept in the treasury in the sacristy, and used to embellish the top of the float, to protect it from mud falling from roofs". Then the cardinal ordered them to be burned immediately.

The reason for the presence of these battle standards in the church of the Virgin is that when the French kings won a victory over the corsairs, they captured their battle standards and placed them as a memento in the church and gave a prayer of thanksgiving; that is the reason. When he finished speaking, he said to me, "Now you don't have to go see the cardinal", and let me go, after urging me to continue visiting him.

In the parish of this church is a large hospital called the *Hôtel de Dieu* [150], that is, 'The Temple of God', because it accepts anyone who wishes to enter it without question, whatever their religion, whether poor or rich or destitute. All are alike accepted. Now let us explain the excellent organization of this hospital, and great charity that is found in it. First of all, when a patient is received, he finds a man, clothed in dignity and authority, seated, surrounded by assistants, standing ready to serve. He asks the patient if he is a foreigner or native of the city, his age, and whether he has his baptismal certificate with him. Then he asks if he is Christian, or some other religion. After the patient has answered all these questions, he writes down his name and the date and these can be found in a register that records the names of all the patients. These number more than 1500, never less.

Then he sends him with one of the servants into the hospital, where there is a church with priests to give confession. One of the priests greets him and takes him to his cell, hears his confession and afterwards gives the patient a general absolution and sends him off with someone to the Chief Physician to diagnose his illness. After the Chief Physician has examined him, he is turned over to one of his understudies, and instructs him to take the patient to the ward where his particular illness is treated. For in that place there are various wards, that is, halls. Each hall is dedicated to a specific illness. It is divided into two rows of beds covered with red broadcloth. At the head of the bed is written a number, called *numéro*, in white paint, and nothing else. The two rows contain two hundred beds. In the middle of the ward is a chapel, dedicated to the name of a saint, and early every morning a mass is said in the names of the patients in that ward.

Now let us return to what we were saying. The doctor takes the patient to a large room in which are boxes, that is, cubicles, in which are hospital garments. The patient strips and puts on the garments and puts his clothing in the cubicle and they write his name on it so that after he is cured he can get dressed and go on his way. If someone wishes to visit him in the hospital, a family member or friend, it is not possible without searching in the Chief Physician's register. Then they direct him, saying, 'Go to ward 3, or 4, or 5, and look for so-and-so's number'. Otherwise, the visitor could spend three days searching without finding him. Every ward has a doctor who distributes medication, mornings and evenings.

Every day after mass, soup is served to them, and also at noon and in the evening. I saw how they served the soup. They place a pot on a wagon and one man pulls it. A second wagon follows, bearing a long box filled with tin bowls, and the servants distribute them to the patients until they reach the end of the ward. I also a saw a number of well-born ladies, sitting beside the patients, serving and cleaning them. When one of the patients asked for something, they would send their servants to get it for them. And I saw how when a patient needed to perform a natural function, the lady sitting with him passes him the chamber pot, even though she has four or five servants attending her. Not one of them would serve that patient, only her, with her own hand would do what was necessary, despite the filth and evil smell.

I also saw that when one of the patients was seized by his death throes and on the point of death, they immediately brought him a priest to administer extreme unction, and everyone who passed by that place stopped and said a prayer on his behalf. When he died, they placed him in a coffin right there and carried it to the graveyard, which was nearby.

Next to this hospital is another, for women. No one may enter but priests and physicians, no one else. It is the twin of the men's hospital already mentioned. Below this place is a nunnery with two or three hundred nuns, employed in washing and sewing the clothes of the patients and keeping them neat. They also knead dough and make bread for them. Beside the nunnery runs the big river that flows through the middle of the city of Paris. I saw them washing the garments of the patients and they told me of a hidden place within the hospital for the sake of girls who had grievously erred. Before their pregnancy becomes visible their families send them here to this place without anyone knowing, and they stay here until the girl gives birth. They raise the child until it is old enough to be put to a master to learn a craft. Many of these children become skilled craftsmen, and some reach the heights of their profession, some becoming managers, and some entering monasteries and taking holy orders, and some of them become heads of monasteries and saints.

This is the great good which is done by this blessed hospital. I have only told a small part of the things I saw and heard in this place, which is called the *Hôtel de Dieu* in French, that is, 'The Temple of God'. It has a number of endowments, among them villages and lands, houses and shops beyond counting, and they have poor boxes, which are placed in every church in Paris, and everyone throws an offering into the boxes. Many of the merchants and great men write wills leaving sums of money to the hospital, which provide a large income, greatly in excess of expenditure.

Also in the city of Paris is a hostel for delinquents.[151] It is in a monastery on the outskirts of the city. I went there and visited the area where the boys were imprisoned. It is a long hall, and stretching the length of the room is a long wooden bench. Above are iron tracks to which the boys are fastened by chains that hang from the track. The distance between them is just enough so they can't reach their companions. Each has a piece of matting beneath him and works at one of the crafts specialized in by the monastery. Their food is bread and water. Every day they are whipped twice, spread-eagled on a saw horse. Each of them stays in this place till the time when their father or mother wants to take them away. Otherwise they stay forever.

In the city of Paris there are schools for all the arts and sciences to be found in the rest of the world, because the Sultan of France has sent for and brought learned men from all the climes to teach the sciences found in their kingdoms in France.

At that time a very strange thing happened to the king. One night while he was lying asleep, he had a nightmare and became filled with foreboding. He couldn't stay in his bed, and got up, haunted and fearful. He went out of his bedroom and saw the guards keeping watch as usual outside the door, for he always had forty tall guards, all the same height, guarding his person night and day. This is an ancient practice of all kings.

He looked at them, scrutinizing them well, to see if there were an interloper among them, but saw none. Then he asked them if any unknown person had entered the palace, and they answered, saying "Our Lord, who could possibly enter this place?" Then he ordered them to light the lanterns and search the palace to see if they could find someone. They did as he commanded and searched everywhere. The king accompanied them but they found no one, and the king returned with them.

Finally, the king entered his apartment and lay down again on his bed. But his unease increased twice as strongly, and he got up and went out a second time and said to the guards standing outside, "Is there an enemy somewhere here? Tell me the truth!" They stood at attention and said, "We searched everywhere, and saw no one. The doors of the palace are locked, and guards are standing wherever a stranger or enemy could enter". The king was still very worried, and commanded them in God's name to go with him into the garden of the castle, I mean the pleasure gardens, and light their lanterns. So they went with the king through the palace and opened the door that led to the garden. They searched through the garden with their lanterns alight, they searched under the trees and in each corner of the garden, and saw no one.

They started to return to the palace, when one of the guards, searching under the trees carrying a lantern in his hand, saw a shape beneath a willow tree. He halted and raised the lantern and saw someone hiding in that tree. He told the king, and the king ordered him to come down from the tree. When he descended, and stood before the king, he saw he was an armed youth. The king told him to throw down his weapon, then asked him, "What are you doing in this place? What is your intention? Tell the truth, and God will have mercy on you".

The youth answered, "If you ask about me, O king of the age, I am your mortal enemy. I entered and hid in this place so that I could kill you in your bed, nothing else". The king replied, "What is it that drove you to want to kill me? What evil have I done you that you should want to murder me?" The youth answered, "My religion demands that I kill you because you are the enemy of our religion".

When the king heard these words, he replied, "If your filthy religion commands you to kill me, though I have done you no harm, my holy religion commands me to pardon you. Go, tell that to your comrades". Then the king ordered him to be freed, and they released him outside the palace. The king returned to his apartment and lay down on his bed, and that nightmare did not return. Our Lord had saved him from that peril by an undeniable miracle [152]

When this story spread in the city of Paris, the great men of the state and the leaders of the community came to the king and congratulated him on his deliverance from the peril that had threatened him. Then they asked him to convene a general council of bishops and heads of the monasteries. When the council had been formed, and everyone was in his place, the Duc of Orléans came forward and informed the king that there were many Huguenots to be found in the kingdom of France, that is, heretics, and that they were the enemies of the Catholic faith, and were leading many of the simpler members of the flock astray and continuing to sow corruption. 'It is to be feared, O king, that in time their heresy will spread throughout the country of France'.

When the king heard these words and realized they were true, he commanded that a royal decree be promulgated and read out throughout his kingdom, saying, "Six months from now, all the heretical Huguenots in my kingdom shall be killed and their wealth confiscated for the kingdom. Everyone who has a debt must collect it, and everyone who owes a debt must pay it. If he possesses houses, fields, gardens or similar property, he may sell it without compulsion. After this period, they will pay for their sin".

He also ordered the bishops and priests and heads of monasteries to write to all the cities of France, on the orders of the cardinal of Paris, that anyone who knows one of those Huguenots must report him to the governor of the town, and that anyone who disobeys shall be excommunicated and cut off from the church. In the same vein they wrote to the metropolitans of every province, so that every metropolitan could inform his bishops of this decree. The king also commanded that in every port of entry to France a captain appointed by the king should be stationed to prevent the heretics from entering his kingdom. They forbade entry to anyone unable to show his baptismal certificate. The Huguenots began to leave in droves right up to the end of the six month's grace. Some went to England, some went to Flanders, and some spread out in Italy, while others went to Austria and other cities, until the land of France was completely cleansed of them.

Sometime later, a shoemaker in Paris returning to his house one evening, noticed two strangers entering a door, and thought perhaps they were thieves. He went into his house and went to the window and began to keep watch on the place they had entered. He saw three more men enter, and after them, three more, and then four. More and more people arrived right up to midnight. The man was astonished at this sight, knowing that the house had been abandoned for a long time. He said to himself, "I'm going to keep an eye on this place, and try to find out who these people entering it are". He kept watch from the window until three hours after midnight. He saw nothing but people coming and going until finally no one was left inside, and they locked the door.

When dawn broke, the shoemaker went to the governor and told him that he had seen people entering and leaving throughout the night. When the governor heard this story, he told the man not to tell anyone what he had seen, but to come back in the evening. When he returned, he sent two of his men with him, ordering them to hide in the man's house and check if the man's story were true or not, and to say nothing about it to anyone. They hid in the man's house until the time came. People kept coming and entering that house, and the governor's agents monitored their exit, and saw that people kept leaving, and then locked the door, just as that man had told the governor.

Then the agents went and told the governor what they had seen, and he sent spies to watch those people. They soon understood from reliable informants that that house belonged to Huguenots dwelling in Paris, and that they met in that house once or twice a month to confer. After the governor had confirmed the facts and made a thorough investigation, he informed His Majesty the King. The king ordered him to wait until they had all entered, then lock them inside, go to the top of the house and bring it down upon their heads. If anyone escaped from the ruin, he was to be killed on the spot. Then the site was to be ploughed, with plough-share and yoke of oxen. It was to remain unpaved, so that it would be a warning for the ages to come. Five hundred were killed, and their wealth confiscated by the Crown. I was walking with a Parisian, and when I saw that place I was surprised that it was unpaved. I asked the man with me why, for all the streets in Paris are paved with black stones, and he told me the story. It was for this reason, as a memorial, that they left it unpaved.

During this time, an ambassador from Istanbul [153], sent by Sultan Ahmad to His Majesty the Sultan of France arrived, seeking eight anchors for the five warships he had built. They welcomed him with the greatest honour, and his entry to the city of Paris drew large crowds. They furnished one of the king's palaces in Paris for him, and supplied cooks, bakers and abundant provisions. He brought forty retainers with him, not counting servants. The king assigned one of the dragomans to him.

A few days later he was received by M. Pontchartrain, Minister for Eastern Affairs, who received him with exceptional honour and served him a splendid banquet. After he had attended the banquet, the king ordered them to show him the delights of Versailles and the royal garden. They showed him the water jets which shot up from the trees, pools and fountains, and especially that dome of water we have mentioned previously.

After seeing the sights, the ambassador returned to Paris and entered the palace that had been assigned to him. Then the leading men of the city came to visit him, and congratulate him on his safe arrival. The womenfolk of the grandees and princes also came to see him out of curiosity. I myself used to go to his palace every day and sit with the retainers. Many times, when the dragoman wasn't present,

I translated the conversations between the envoy and the well-born ladies. The envoy was amazed at the modesty of those women, the courtly elegance of their phrases and the quickness of their wit. He used to say that the womenfolk of the Franks had better manners and were more modest than the women of his country.

Finally, after the leading men of the city had all visited him, he returned their visits. He delighted in looking at everything, admiring the good order, organization and the ease of their lives. He saw a great difference between the governance of the country of the Franks and that of his own country, filled as it was with prisons, revolts, oppression, and the injustice of governors towards the people. He used to say so in confidence to his personal retainers, and they used to tell me what he said, because their opinion was the same as their master's.

After several days of this, the minister ordered the dragoman and several of the great men of the state to entertain the ambassador by taking him to the Opéra. This is a place where they produce strange, wondrous spectacles during the winter. They go to them twice a week. The dragoman invited the envoy on behalf of the minister to go that very night, and the envoy agreed. At the time, I was present in the envoy's palace and when the news reached me I went and told my master and he gave me permission to go with the entourage of the envoy to enjoy the spectacle.

After getting his permission, I returned to the envoy's palace to wait until the time came to go. When the time came, men arrived on behalf of the minister and accompanied the envoy to the place I have mentioned. The envoy left the palace in the company of his entourage and I went with them. They escorted him into a royal carriage and drove him to that place. We all joined him there, and I saw it was a large high hall with two loggias on each side, divided into boxes, each holding eight people, and no more. Each was like a room, and had a door.

Inside the box was a balustrade and benches of finely worked walnut wood. Each box had a price, I mean, the first row of boxes at the end of the loggia each cost one piastre. The second row, closer to the stage, cost each person two piastres. The third row, the closest to the stage, cost each spectator one gold coin.

171

People who want to watch a play, whether eight, five, three or just one person, send one of their number to the manager of the theatre the day before the performance, and pay for the number of spectators, depending on whether they wish the first, second or third row, as we have explained. After having paid, the manager gives him a signed receipt for the number of spectators paid for, which indicates the row they can enter. When they go to the performance, they give the ticket to the manager, who shows them to the box indicated on the ticket, and locks the door behind them, so no one else can enter.

They placed the envoy in the first box, the noblest place, with the best view of the stage. His entourage was placed in the second box and the door was left open to give them more room. When we sat down, all I could see was a curtain hanging down before the stage. After a short wait, a light began to glow behind the curtain, so brightly that I thought it was the sun shining from behind. In a little while I saw the curtain lift, to reveal a sight to astonish the mind.

First of all, I saw in the center of the stage what looked like a mountain, with many trees growing on it. Peasants were walking among the trees with their donkeys. At the base of the mountain was a village, and peasants were walking in and out of their houses with their wives. Near the town was a herd of cows, sheep and goats and other animals at pasture. After I had gazed at all these things, I realized that everything I saw — people and animals — were real! Not silhouettes, not spectres, but real people, with souls and bodies!

After a little, the stage grew dark and a large cloud descended from heaven and came to earth. Out of the cloud stepped a tall man with a white beard and wearing a royal crown and holding a curved staff in his hand. He was an imposing sight, and one couldn't take one's eyes off him. He began to intone incomprehensible phrases in a deep, resonant voice. Suddenly I saw twelve maidens and twelve youths dressed in regal, golden garments, and they appeared like full moons. They formed two lines, to the left and right. Then music began to play, and those youths and maidens sang along with it with voices like gold thread, matching their voices to the instruments in a way that astonished the mind, to such an extent that I swooned.

The orchestra played for half an hour. Finally, the instruments ceased, and that noble figure began to recite verses in a soft voice. The youths and maidens approached him, two by two, and replied in verse, in gentle tones that would gladden kings. When they finished reciting poetry, the orchestra struck up again as before for the rest of the hour. Finally, that noble figure mounted his cloud and was lifted up to heaven, not to return.

As he was lifted up, in the blink of an eye, everything on stage was lifted away as well. In its place appeared a great lofty palace, with towers and reception rooms and glass windows and similar beauties, just like the palace of the Sultan of France. It had an arched portal of white and black marble, and out of it came forth a crowned king, wearing the purple with royal mien and holding the staff of kingship in his hand. Around him were his ministers and leading statesmen and they proceeded to the appropriate space. Then those youths and maidens came out to meet him, kissing the ground before him, then returning to their lines as before. The orchestra began to play and those maidens and youths sang with sweet, angelic voices until the music stopped and the stage fell dark.

Then there appeared in the heavens a large cloud inside which was a beautiful youth and two little children with wings like angels, each with a bow and arrow in his hand. He began to converse with the king while those children shot him with arrows without harming him. He continued to talk to him and flatter him, while trying to flee the arrows. Finally, they began to quarrel, and he fled, apparently angry, and he and children, entered the cloud and were lifted up to heaven.

Simultaneously, the earth split asunder, and I saw a devil with a long scaly tail emerge and breathe fire and smoke into the face of that king, then vanish into the sky. At that moment the king began to babble and foam and act like a madman, and when his escort saw that devil and the king apparently mad, they all fled, lest what befell the king befall them. The king remained alone, reciting a poem about what had happened, saying 'Did this happen in a dream, or am I awake?' Then he fainted.

The next thing I saw was four supports of a bed rising from the ground, then the bed itself, with all its furnishings and a pillow placed upon it. When the king saw the bed, he lay down on it and fell asleep. While he slept, four trees sprouted from the four corners of the bed, and when they reached their full height, leafy branches grew until they became big trees and shaded the bed, and he lay sleeping, as if in a garden. At that moment I saw rise from beneath the bed beautiful girls holding flutes. They began to dance around the bed playing the flutes sweetly and softly, in a way that conduced to sleep and rest, and they spoke to the sleeper in their language.

After a short time, he woke from sleep and all these things vanished and the king began to recite poetry as before. Then the cloud descended for the second time, and a girl issued forth from it and began to flatter him and seduce him. At that moment the queen entered and saw this sorceress and grew angry and drove her away. She immediately turned, entered her cloud and fled to the sky. The queen then turned to the king and began to reproach him for his actions with harsh words. How could he have lowered himself by flirting with a sorceress who had caused him to be deranged?

When he heard these cutting words from her he was very angry, and drew his sword and stabbed her in the waist. The blade came out the other side and she fell dead. When her handmaidens saw the death of their queen, they ran to tell the authorities what had happened. They all gathered together and summoned the soldiers and went to the king and tied him up and deposed him from his throne. There was a great outcry in the palace, and everything on stage vanished, except a fountain of white marble. Water issued forth from the mouth of a marble lion and overflowed into a second basin, which in turn overflowed into a third. Musical instruments began to play, and the youths and maidens came out and started to dance, two by two, in a modest dance, without licentiousness.

When the dance came to an end, they bowed to the ambassador and the audience and left the stage. Then the fountain and the water rose up and vanished without leaving a trace. I was overcome with wonder. How this was possible, when from the moment the curtain opened, I had watched that fountain, and although the scenes changed, the fountain was always onstage. I thought the water flowed from a pipe or spring. In any event, after it was lifted up the stage went dark and nothing could be seen and the play was over.

What I have said about this place and this play is nothing to what I actually saw and heard, which is beyond description. At last the ambassador rose, and with him the dragoman and the high officials of the minister and proceeded to the door. All the women in the theatre were lined up in two lines, most of them the daughters of princes and the womenfolk of the great men of the city, and the daughters of nobles and the like. While we were passing, I heard one of the daughters of the nobles commenting disagreeably on the ambassador's beard. Because I understood French, I turned and said to her in French, "Why, my lady, do you insult the honour of our guest with this derogatory phrase?" When she realized that I had understood what she said, she hid among the other women, because of her great shame and embarrassment at the lack of manners she had shown in impugning the honour of the ambassador.

In any case, we passed through them and left the place and every one mounted their carriage and went on their way. The ambassador went to his palace and I went to my master's house. When I entered I saw many of my master's friends awaiting me, so they could question me and make fun of me. When I stood before them, they began to ask me about what I had seen and heard, and whether it had astonished me. I answered. "Everything I saw and heard was wonderful, but what astonished me most was the fountain, which from the beginning of the play to the end continued to play, with water issuing forth from the mouth of the lion, and then at the end they lifted the fountain and the water together! This is what amazed me more than the rest of the performance". They all began to laugh, and one of them said to me, "This was the simplest of all the things you saw!" I said to him, "By your life, my lord, tell me how it was done!" Then he told me, "The fountain was made of oiled papier-mâché to look like marble. Behind it is a waterproof cistern filled with water, raised by a waterwheel and fed through a tube so the water flows out of the lion's mouth. When it reaches the bottom of the fountain, it is returned to the cistern by the waterwheel, which is turned by a boy. The water amounts to no more than a water skin full, and none of it is lost, it just keeps circulating. Black cords, invisible in the darkness, run through pulleys, and when they are pulled, they easily lift everything out of sight. All the other special effects are of the same sort".

Then I asked him about the old man and the cloud, and he answered: "He is called the 'Sultan of the Sky', and the king is called 'Bacchus', and the play is entitled 'The Sleep of King Bacchus', and everything you saw was scenes from the life of Bacchus." Then he told me that this theatre is very expensive to run, and all the girls and boys and actors I saw were employed by it. One after another, he explained all the scene changes, till my brain spun.

This subject would require a long explanation. I will be concise, and say that everything works by a variety of machinery of wondrous construction, in such a way that what you see changes in the blink of an eye. Backstage is a large area, and out of sight, and this is why you see what is before you, but can't see the mechanisms that produce it.[154]

Another theatre called the *Comédie* produces something like the shadow plays one sees in our markets. They show knaves and fools beyond description, played by human actors. The leader of the revels is called 'Harlequin' like 'Abwāt or Qaragoz among us.[155] Each of their plays is based on contemporary events, and the characters are drunken scoundrels, stupid fools and others, like cowardly, useless soldiers, unreliable in war, and similar characters, especially immodest, frivolous women. All this is recited in elegant verse, so the listener may be admonished from being like this hateful and cursed gang.

On specified days, in some churches, they teach how to distinguish the True from the False. This is the noblest thing I found, a lesson of great benefit to every man and woman, learned or unlettered, young or old. It is useful for everyone, unmarried or married, priest or monk. A priest learned in philosophy takes the pulpit, and facing him, lower down, is a man learned in philosophy, familiar with everything the learned are saying and their groundless speculations. The preacher in the pulpit begins preaching the truth, to which his opponent opposes the false, citing the opinions of the learned, deceived by Satan, the enemy of the good. The sermon of the preacher on high disproves his words with citations from the

Holy Book and shows how he has been deceived by his belief in these erroneous opinions. The speaker below begins by confessing the most common sins of the people and the preacher of Truth replies and destroys his confession, filled as it is with evasions and intricate excuses which make his sin worse than before, and shows him how to truly confess, without prevarication or ambiguity, especially women, chattering as if they were telling a story to the confessor and so forth.

On Sundays and festivals in the rest of the churches, children are taught about Our Saviour by a learned man, from one o'clock in the afternoon until evening. The children of the parish are gathered in the church to learn, and the child who is learning his lesson stands in the middle and recites what he learned the previous Sunday. If he does so correctly, the teacher gives him an icon or picture, and raises him above the pupils who have not memorized their lessons, and this goes on until they have all done so during this period.

Similarly, on Sunday and festival days there is a debate in all the schools, that is, the teacher and his philosophy students sit debating philosophy with each other, and the teacher gives the student who excels a silver icon and sets him at the head of the class. The same is true of Logic, Divinity and Cosmology and the rest of the sciences.

I visited an art school with an artist who was teaching me how to draw. It was Maundy Thursday, Good Friday's eve. When I entered I saw four teachers; all were famous artists. They went into the studio, and I accompanied them, thanks to the intercession of the artist who was teaching me to draw. When I entered, I saw a large room, with tables on all sides. In the middle of the room was a high wooden cross, with three steps leading up to it. At that moment, a tall, well-formed young man about thirty came in. He was naked, wearing only a waist wrap held by a white belt.

The teachers asked him to ascend the cross, so he climbed up and grasped the cross-piece, which was pierced by holes for ropes, with his hands and planted his feet on the footrest which was nailed to the cross. The teachers consulted each other until they all agreed on his position. Then they said to him, "Relax, as if you were dead". When he relaxed, he kept his feet firmly on the foothold, bent his knees, and hung by his hands. They asked him to bend his body, and he did so, so that the he really looked like a dead man. This represented the Lord Messiah when He died on the cross. When all this was finished, and the four teachers had agreed on his posture, they told the students to come in and draw the crucifixion. After they came in, each student went to his place and set about drawing on paper with a lead pencil for an hour. Then the young man came down from the cross to rest a little while, then resumed the same posture for another hour, until the students had finished their drawings. Finally, the students handed their drawings to the teachers, who examined them and selected the best of all and gave the student a gold icon on a chain, so he could hang it around his neck, and appointed him head of the class.

They have other places where they teach fencing, that is, the use of swords, like our *la'ab al-hakam*.[156] In other places they teach musketry and marksmanship, and in others they teach cannonry and in others horsemanship. As a result, in the city of Paris are to be found schools for all the sciences and arts in the world. There are even places that teach dance, and others that teach music.

There are also to be found in this city many prostitutes. Their houses are known by the signs hung on their doors, which depict a large bunch of thorns.[157]

There are also a large number of confidence men and women. One of the latter operated a con which is worthy of record.

> She rented expensive garments, suitable for wealthy ladies, and a carriage drawn by four horses, with four footmen riding behind the carriage. She drove to a monastery which instructed unruly children who disobeyed their parents. When she got there, she summoned the head of the monastery and confided to him that she had a dissolute son, who had frittered away their money on debauchery and playing cards, and that her husband was dead. She told him she would bring him there by trickery, and that he should be taken, his feet put in the stocks, and whipped every day. He should be fed on bread and water, as was their custom, until he learned to behave. Then she would return and take him away with her. She then took out her purse and gave him payment for

a month and told him, "Don't let yourself be taken in by what the young man tells you, because he is a consummate liar. He will tell you, 'I am the son of such and such a merchant, and my father doesn't know where I am. Let me go, so I may go to my father! This woman is not my mother!' Don't believe him. I will leave him with you until I return at the end of the month, and see whether he has come to his senses or not, and will either take him or leave him". The head of the monastery answered, "Set your mind at rest. I know about these young rapscallions. Go in peace".

Then she got in the carriage and ordered the coachman to take her to a place called *Le Palais*, that is, 'The Palace'. This place is where the wealthy merchants of the India trade have their shops, and in them are to be found all the goods of India, particularly textiles and *barjāwāt* [158] fine, valuable calicoes and similar things. When she arrived, she headed for the shop of the leading merchant and had the horses halt in front of that wealthy man's shop. The merchant ordered his servants to bring out a chair so she could dismount from the carriage and they lifted her under the arms and took her into the shop.

The merchant made her welcome, treating her with the appropriate courtesy. She sat down and took out a letter and said, "My brother sent me this letter from Spain, asking me to send him some things. Are any of them to be found in your shop?" "What are they?" he answered. Then she began to name each of the items, and the merchant said to her, "Everything you have mentioned is to be found in my shop". What she had asked for were the finest Indian textiles, and the most expensive. He took things out, one after another, and from every ten pieces he showed her, she would select five or six, and reject the rest. She continued choosing and refusing until her order was filled.

Then she began to bargain with him over the price of each piece and write down the agreed amount until the bill was finished. They added up the amounts, and the sum totalled a bit more than five thousand *écus*.[159] Finally, they wrapped up her purchases and loaded the parcels in the carriage. Then the lady got up to leave, saying to the merchant, "Send one of your boys with me so that I can send him back with the money". The merchant turned and said to his only son, "Go with your aunt, my son, and collect this sum from her!"

He wanted to send his son in his own carriage, but she wouldn't hear of it, and instead let him ride in hers. She told the coachman to drive to a certain address in a certain parish, and on the way they passed the monastery devoted to the reform of delinquent children. When the carriage reached the entrance of the monastery, she pulled the cord that was attached to the reins of the horses and stopped them. She got out and said to the merchant's son, "I wish to speak to the head of the monastery about something personal. Why don't you come too, and have a look at the monastery and at the delinquent children shackled here?"

The boy got down and entered the monastery with the lady. When they came to the cloister, she sent for the prior. When he arrived, she said to him, "This is the boy I told you about". While they were talking, the boy went in to look at the children in chains. As soon as he did, she bade farewell to the prior, left the monastery, got into the carriage and told the coachman where to take her. When they arrived, she stopped the carriage at a crossroads. She told them to unload the packages and leave them there, and then paid them the hire of the coach and coachmen and told them to be gone. Then she went into her house with her packages and no one until now knew of the trick she played.

As for the boy, after he had looked around, he wanted to leave, but they grabbed him and shackled him like the others. He said to them, "Why have you shackled me? I was simply passing by with the lady, go ask her!" "Sit down, you scoundrel!" they told him, 'Squanderer of your father's wealth in card games!" The boy cried out at these words, and tried to tell them, "I am the son of so-and-so, the merchant, and this woman bought Indian textiles from my father, and I was going with her to get the money!"

When they heard these words, one of them went to tell the prior what the boy had said, but the prior, warned by his mother that he was a liar and deceiver, told them, "Don't believe him! Instead, increase his punishment!" So the boy spent three days on bread and water, and they whipped him twice a day, without pity, and paid no attention to what he said.

His father waited till the afternoon, but his son didn't return. "Perhaps the lady invited him to lunch" he said to himself. So he waited until it was almost dusk, without receiving any news, and wondered at his absence. The day ended and night fell, and still no one came. Then he ordered his servants to search, and visit the houses of the great men and the merchants and ask if perhaps they had seen or had news of him. The servants went off, each to a different parish and began to search and ask after him, but they didn't see him or find a trace of him all night long.

They returned to their master and told him they had scoured the city of Paris, without finding anything. The merchant was devastated, distraught at the loss of his son and his money. He went to the governor and told him of the disaster. The governor ordered handbills to be printed, with an account of what happened, and they were posted at crossroads and in all the neighbourhoods. These handbills stated that anyone who had news of the woman would receive a generous reward and that anyone who had knowledge of her, but did not come forth, would be hung. They were distributed as the governor ordered and the handbills were pasted at street corners as we have explained.

The first day passed, then the second, but on the third it happened that a servant in that monastery went out shopping in the city to buy various things for the monastery and came across those handbills. When he read one of them, he realized that what the boy had said was true. He immediately returned and informed the prior, telling him that the city was aflame because of the lost boy, and that the governor had ordered that anyone who had knowledge of him and didn't report it would be hung. The prior immediately went to the boy and asked him his story, and the boy told him exactly what was recounted in those handbills. Then the prior believed his story and freed him from his shackles and took him to his father and told him the story from beginning to end, as we have previously recounted. So the boy was returned to his father, and the money vanished with that vicious woman, and they were never able to trace her. And this is how the story of the fraud of that depraved woman ended.

Another day, I was walking down one of the streets and saw someone standing there shouting out '*Le Sentence!*' In his hand he held printed pages, and people were fighting to buy them from him, at two *sou* a page. I turned to an acquaintance, and asked,

"What are these papers, and what is a *sentence*?" He said, "These papers record the judgment on a criminal who is to be hung".

He went on to tell me the procedure. When the law condemns a man to death, the execution is carried out at ten o'clock in the morning. The man's crime is recorded in a document, and the reason he merits the horrible death of hanging or 'breaking' or decapitation and other similar fates to which criminals are condemned. After the sentence is issued by the judge, they take it and have it printed, and men circulate through the city selling these handbills for two *sou* apiece.

Then they take the criminal condemned to death to a chapel inside the law court so that he can be absolved of his sins by a general confession to a confessor, who stays with him, confessing him, for two hours, until noon. When his confession is finished, he begs forgiveness, and is granted absolution. Then they bring the priest lunch, and he lunches with the condemned man. When the meal is over, the priest leaves, and an Augustinian friar enters to comfort and console him and fortify him for the ordeal, remaining with him until evening.

Then the executioner arrives and knocks on the door. He enters and puts the anchor around his neck and leads him out of the chapel. They descend the staircase of the law court and get into the carriage, the friar, the condemned man, and the executioner. They proceed to the place designated by the governor, and there the executioner climbs a ladder onto the gallows. The condemned man follows, halting beneath the executioner's legs. The friar climbs up last, carrying a crucifix in his hand and holding it up before the eyes of the condemned so that he will repent and face his fate bravely. Then the friar turns to the crowd and leads them in the prayer for the dead. They recite it after him, with lamentations, and when it is ended, they begin a second prayer, while the priest keeps urging the condemned to make a full confession.

When the second prayer is over, the priest turns to the crowd and asks them to beseech the 'Virgin Mary, who forgives sins, to forgive this soul that is leaving us.' The people pray and weep, begging the Virgin Mary to intercede for his soul. After the prayer is over, the priest makes the sign of the Holy Cross, and climbs down the ladder. At that moment, the executioner pushes the condemned man, with the anchor around his neck, and straddles his shoulders with his legs, rocking back and forth three times, then gets off. They lower the hanged man and put him in the carriage and the doctors buy him from the executioner and take him to their school, in order to examine him and instruct their students.

When he had finished speaking, I asked my acquaintance, "What did he do in order to be sentenced to hang?" He answered me, "This poor fellow's story is strange and astonishing. This is what I have been told:

> There was a very rich merchant to whom in all his life no son had been given. One day he visited a hospital for illegitimate children. Among them he noticed a good-looking child with perfect, expressive features and long eyelashes, his speech revealing a refined intelligence. He far surpassed the rest of the children in beauty, grace and modesty. The merchant's heart spoke to him, and he asked the director of the hospital if he could take the child and raise him like his own son. There they used to distribute the children to masters of various skills and trades, that is, anyone who excelled and was chosen by a master craftsman, was encouraged to take one of these children and treat him like a son and teach him the trade until he grew old enough to have learned it well. Then he was free, either to stay with his master, choose to work for another master craftsman, or set up for himself. This is one of the many excellent practices found in this country.
>
> So a legal document was drawn up and the child turned over to the merchant, who took him home. When the merchant's wife saw that child, she fell completely in love with him, to such an extent, that she and her husband signed a will, leaving the boy everything they possessed in the event of their death.
>
> The merchant then began to raise him. He appointed a teacher to instruct him in reading and writing, and when he had mastered both, he took him to his office and taught him bookkeeping and accounting for some time, until he had learned both. He began to help his father in buying and selling, borrowing and lending, to the point where he surpassed his father in the profession of merchant.

Things went on this way until he was a little over twenty years old. His mother then suggested to his father that they find a wife for the apple of their eye. His father agreed, and found a lovely girl among the daughters of the merchants. He settled a portion of his wealth upon his son, and the girl's father gave her a dowry, and they signed the marriage contract at the law court. A short time later the wedding was celebrated and they were married.

The young man then left his father and opened his own shop, and began to buy and sell on his own account. This was exactly what his father wished, because he had seen that he was a clever merchant and that his business would prosper. Things went on like this for some time.

Then one day the young man went to his father's house to consult him on some matter. His father was not there, so he went into his father's office looking for him, but didn't find him. He was on the point of leaving, when he was overcome by curiosity. He noticed two promissory notes in one of the pigeonholes of the desk. These had been issued by the king. One was for 500, the other for 300 piastres. For when the king ran short of revenue, he used to issue promissory notes in order to pay the army. The army chiefs took these notes and sold them to the merchants at a slight discount, took the money and bought provisions for the army. This was during wartime. Later, when the treasury was full again, everyone turned in their promissory notes and received the sum stipulated in the note. When the Treasury was unable to redeem them, merchants would use the promissory notes as if they were currency. For example, a merchant might buy some goods for 1500 piastres and say to the seller 'I have a promissory note for 1500 piastres, discounted', and the purchase would be made in this fashion.

When the young man saw the two promissory notes, he was overcome with greed, and said to himself "My father is so successful in buying and selling, that he doesn't need them, and perhaps has just forgotten them". So he took them, and went to his shop, and no one had seen him enter and leave his father's office. A few days later he bought some goods from a merchant, and he used the two promissory notes as was the practice, and everyone went their way.

Time passed, and one day a broker went to his father and said "I have some inexpensive merchandise, gunny sacks. Listen and I'll tell you what a reasonable price you can pay for them". When the merchant heard the price, he was pleased, and said to the broker "I have two promissory notes for 800 piastres, and I'll pay you the rest in cash".

The broker was content with that, and they wrote out the bill of sale. The broker showed it to the owner of the goods, who accepted it, and sent the goods to the merchant with the broker. When the merchant received the goods, he opened his cashbox and took out the money and counted out what he needed in addition to the promissory notes. Then he went to his office to get the promissory notes, but couldn't find them. He was perplexed, and searched among his papers and ledgers, but found nothing. He began to be very worried and asked his wife and servants "Who has been in my office?" "No one but you!" they answered. His perplexity increased, and he was forced to pay cash instead of using the promissory notes.

The matter continued to obsess him and after a thorough search and investigation, he lost all hope of finding them. He nevertheless began to talk to the merchants and tell them about his loss of the promissory notes. One of the merchants told him "Don't worry about the promissory notes, they'll turn up soon. Just tell us their dates, and one of us will undoubtedly come across them". So he gave their dates of issue to everyone, and after little more than a month had passed, they came into the hands of one of the merchants, who had accepted them in lieu of cash. When he examined them, he recognized that they were the ones being sought. He went to the original owner and showed him the promissory notes. When the merchant saw them, he recognized them, but said "What's the use, without finding out who entered my office and stole them? It is impossible to believe that a merchant — a respectable and clever class of people — would do such a thing, that one of them would go into my office and take them". The other merchant answered him, saying "Go to the governor and tell him your story, and he will try to find whoever stole them".

So the merchant went to the governor and told him the story, and explained how the notes had ended up in the possession of a certain merchant. The governor then ordered two of his men to go with the merchant and find out exactly what had happened. They went with him to the merchant who had received them, and asked him, on the governor's orders, to tell them from whom he had obtained those promissory notes. He replied "From so-and-so the merchant". They went to him to and asked him where he got the notes, and he gave them the name of yet another merchant. They went on, going from one, who would point to another, until finally they ended up with the young man himself, the son of the merchant aforementioned. When they asked him, he was unable to say, indeed, he was tongue tied and fell silent, and they realized that he was the thief.

They took him to the governor, and when he stood before him, he was terrified. The governor asked "Where did you get those promissory notes?" He was unable to answer. He was ordered to be imprisoned and tortured until he told the truth. He finally confessed that it was he who had taken them from his father's office. So the governor sent him to the courts, and the law sentenced him to be hanged in front of the door of his house as an example to others who had betrayed their trust.

When the news reached his father, he regretted what he had done, but it was too late for regret to do him any good. He immediately went to the governor to ask him to intercede for his son, saying to him "This young man is my son by adoption, and my heir, and I have no quarrel with him or he with me, and all my wealth is his". "Is it not the case," answered the governor, "that he stole them from you without your knowledge? And you trusted him. That is why the law condemned him to be hanged."

His hopes in the courts dashed, he turned to the nobles of the city, pleading desperately that they save his son from death, but they were unable to defy the law. Then he went to the palace of the king and showered gifts on all the great men of the state, but they too were unable to oppose the law. He finally appealed to the king himself, by means of the princes, the king's sons. They, too, were unable to change the sentence imposed by the law. He lost all hope, and he and his wife went home, weeping and lamenting. No one could console them in their grief, until a long time had passed.

Here is how the affair ended. I passed by the law courts one evening and saw an empty, open carriage at the bottom of the staircase and an escort of soldiers, their commanding officers mounted on horseback. They were all waiting. A little while later, the executioner came down, then the condemned man, bent under the weight of the anchor, followed by the priest. They came down the stairs and got into the carriage and the priest placed one hand on the young man's shoulder, while he held the Holy Crucifix in front of his face with the other, at the same time encouraging and exhorting him as they proceeded down the street, until the moment they came to the scaffold.

When we got there, I saw a plank of wood mounted on a three-legged support. One end projected from the support, and placed against it was a ladder. The executioner climbed to the top of the ladder and the youth right behind him, the executioner pulling the anchor around his neck. Last of all came the priest, the crucifix in his hand. The youth, with the crucifix in front of his face, lifted his weeping eyes to the window of his house. After the prayers had ended, as we have said, the people began to weep for this young man, still on the threshold of youth, for he was good-looking, with a nice face, dressed in fine clothes, in fact, his wedding clothes. According to what they said, he was twenty-two years old, and this was what broke people's hearts. I heard the sound of their weeping and lamenting, as if every one of them had lost an only, beloved son.

When the preliminaries were over, the executioner pushed the condemned man, as we have described, then they dumped the body in the carriage and the physicians went off with it. As for the executioner, he was unable to descend the ladder until the soldiers surrounded him, for fear the people would kill him, for among them the executioner is thoroughly hated and despised.[160]

Another day, I was standing on the bridge of Saint Michel, where our house was located, when the men selling handbills of sentences, that is, *sijill* [161], passed by. Two highwaymen had been condemned for holding up, stripping and killing those they had robbed. Towards evening, I went to the courts to watch. I saw two carriages and the soldiers, as we have mentioned. They brought the two men down the stairs, their hands bound behind their backs, the soldiers holding on to them. Accompanying them were two priests and the executioner. They all got into a carriage, with the priest holding the holy cross. They took them to an open place, and when we arrived, I saw a platform raised to about half a man's height. In the middle was a rough wooden cross, shaped like the cross of St Peter.[162]

The soldiers hauled one of the condemned men up to the platform. Then they broke his shoulders and stretched him on the cross. He was naked. They lashed one of his forearms firmly to the cross, then the other. Then they lashed both legs to the cross, so that he remained hanging there supported by the two pieces of wood. When they had finished fastening him to the cross, the executioner stood and read out the sentence on the condemned man to the crowd: it was to break his four limbs. When he had finished reading, a man came forward with a long thick club. At that moment the priest began to lead the crowd in prayer, as usual. When the three prayers were finished, the executioner struck that highwayman bound to the cross three blows on one forearm with the club, until the bones were completely shattered. I could hear them splintering. Then he struck him on the other forearm, also with three blows, then three blows on each thigh, until not a sound bone was left. Finally, he struck a single blow on his cranium, saying "This is a favour from the king, so he will die quickly".

At last they freed him from the cross and laid him on a cart wheel, piling him up on it so that he looked like a heap of meat. Then they lifted that wheel and put it on a wooden axel tree next to the platform and left it revolving so the torso hung over the rim of the wheel. Then they brought the second criminal to the platform. When he saw the state his comrade was in, he fell to his knees and began to beseech the priest not let them give him such a horrible death, but to strangle him before breaking his bones.

The heart of the priest was moved, and he turned to the officer who represented the governor and interceded for him, asking that he be strangled before having his bones shattered. Reluctantly, the officer acceded to the priest's request, and ordered them to strangle him. Then, like his comrade, he was lashed to the cross, as was the custom, and they put a rope around his neck, suspended him over the hole in the platform and lifted him up and down, and he was instantly strangled. Then the executioner began to smash his bones, as he had done with the first, and dumped him on the cart wheel as they had done with his comrade and left them there until the first man died. This spectacle filled the hearts of everyone with fear and distress. Then they all went their way, despondent and saddened by what they had seen.

Another day I saw a crowd gathering and went to join it. I went with them until we came to a crossroad, where I saw a woman with her arms bound, walking behind the sort of wagon which they use to collect garbage. It is like a half-carriage, with sides that only come up to the waist. When they reached the crossroad, the wagon stopped. Then the executioner read out the sentence for her crime. It was that she had corrupted the minds of youths, marrying them to ignorant women, unaware that they were prostitutes. For this, the law demanded she be exposed to public humiliation throughout the streets of Paris.

When he finished reading the sentence, he gave her twelve lashes with a bull whip, so hard that you could see her flesh ripped and torn from those painful strokes. When the whipping was over, the wagon moved on, dragging her behind it. She was walking barefoot, and was at the end of her strength. The carriage continued to drag her violently along, until she looked on the point of death. What a terrible sight and shame for the feminine sex!

Another day they passed by with handbills of a sentence. I went to the law court to see what was going on, and when I got there I saw the executioner and the priest descending the staircase with a dignified woman in her seventies. They escorted her to the carriage, and the priest, the executioner and soldiers sent by the governor surrounded it. They moved on until the came to the place where the gallows had been erected. The three climbed up the ladder. Then the executioner read out the sentence.

This woman had been a servant in the house of one of the nobles for a number of years. The man and his wife loved her because of her faithful service and for having looked after their children. During the lifetime of that nobleman's father, some silver vessels had vanished. They couldn't be found, nor could whoever had taken them from his house. A number of years passed, and the father of that man died.

Now it happened that that nobleman traveled to Toulouse, and one of his friends invited him to dinner. When he sat down to table, he recognized among the silver vessels a platter, because it bore an ownership mark. When the meal was over he asked the master of the house, "From whom did you buy this platter?" He answered, "I asked one of my friends to have some silver vessels fashioned for me in Paris, and he sent me this platter along with a number of other silver vessels. If you would like to inquire about it, ask so-and-so, the merchant in Paris".

The man stayed a while, then returned to the city of Paris, taking the platter with him, along with a few other vessels that had gone missing from his house. A few days after he arrived at his palace, he sent for that merchant and asked him, "Where did you buy these silver vessels?" The merchant named a certain silversmith. He sent for him, and when he arrived, he mentioned another man, who wore foreign clothes. Then the nobleman went and informed the governor of what had happened. The governor sent two men to investigate on his behalf and find out the original seller of the vessels and bring whoever it was before him.

The governor's men proceeded to eliminate suspects until they came to the elderly serving woman already mentioned. When they saw she was unable to point to anyone else, they arrested her and brought her before the governor. They were able to establish that it was she who had stolen the silver vessels. The law condemned her to be hanged, but the executioner did not read out the whole story. Instead, he concentrated on her betrayal of her master, and because she had been in a position of trust, she was condemned to hanging. You should have seen how, standing on the ladder, she appealed to the crowd to pray and beseech forgiveness for her sake. Then they hanged her, like other criminals, as a warning to all servants in a position of trust.

During this time, an epidemic of plague broke out in Paris.[163] People without number died because of it. The victim suffered twenty-four hours, then died. The people of Paris prayed to be relieved from this affliction. Then they sought intercession from the patron saint of Paris, St Genevieve.[164] They decided to take her body in procession throughout Paris praying for her intercession, so that God Almighty might lift this affliction from them.

They went to the metropolitan of her cathedral to seek permission to carry the body of the saint in procession, but he refused. He did not want them to remove her body from her church, for fear, perhaps, that they might steal this blessed treasure. All the bishops of Paris reviled him, and so did the heads of monasteries and even the cardinal himself, but they couldn't get his permission to take out the body of the saint.

Then all the leading men of Paris and the judges gathered together and went in a body to the metropolitan of the church of the saint, and threw themselves upon the ground before him, imploring him to grant them permission. Perhaps because he feared the cardinal or that someone else might steal this treasure, they gave him signed statements, pledging that they would return the body of the saint to its resting place, which is in a silver casket resting on three marble pedestals. It performs many miracles. They even hang the shirt of an invalid from the end of a cane and touch it to the casket and he is cured, according to the strength of his belief.

This is how the affair ended. The metropolitan was content, and gave them permission to take out the saint's body. Then the cardinal — who is like a second Pope in the kingdom of France — ordered everyone to take part in the procession, all curates, priests, monks, and clergy found in all the churches of Paris and its monasteries in all seven parishes, which numbers 800 churches and monasteries. All were to be dressed in their finest clothes and carry candles and walk in procession. He also ordained that on that day no one should work, but that it should be a full holiday for everyone.

On the stipulated day the procession went out, composed of priests, monks, and deacons, dressed in the finest costumes and carrying lighted candles in their hands. Four metropolitan bishops carried the sarcophagus containing the body of the saint on their shoulders. They passed through the streets of the city, and you could see each group of priests, monks and deacons singing angelic hymns in soft voices set to wondrous melodies. They took two hours to pass by. It is possible that there were as many as ten thousand persons taking part. The people all stood in front of their shops, imploring Almighty God to accept the intercession of the saint and remove the plague from them. Our Lord answered their prayers, and the sickness ceased completely. I was in Paris at the time and witnessed the procession and the miracle that God performed for them through the intercession of St Genevieve.

I came across her story.

> The saint was a servant to a rich man, one of the grandees of Paris. In his household, she was like a devout nun. She loved the poor, and gave to them from her own provisions and what she earned by the labour of her hands, as well as leftovers from the household. When her master, a hard-hearted miser, realized that she was distributing alms to the poor and other needy people, he threatened this working woman, saying "The day I see you giving something to the poor, you may be certain I will kill you and throw you out of my house!" He warned the servants to keep an eye on her, and if she offended again, to tell him, so that he could punish her.
>
> She was grieved by his parsimony, and the fact that she was unable to give anything to the poor, for fear of her master. She still had, however, access to left-over crusts of bread, which she concealed until she had a chance of giving them to the poor. One day, after her master had left the house, she collected the crusts of bread and put them in her apron and left the house in order to distribute them to the poor. It happened that just as she went out the door of the house, her master entered, and saw her going out, with her apron bulging. He asked her, "What have you got in your apron?" She trembled with fear at his anger, and was unable to answer. But our merciful Lord spoke through her, and she told him, "These are roses". It was the depths of winter, when roses are never found.
>
> Her master was astonished, and said, "Show these roses to me!" She opened her apron and he saw fresh roses, out of season. He was amazed, and turned to her and said, "Tell me the truth, where did

you get these roses?" She was compelled to tell him the truth; that she had had bread crusts in her apron, "And I only said they were roses on the spur of the moment". He then realized the miracle that had been worked on her behalf. He told the metropolitan of this wonder, and the metropolitan investigated it and established its veracity.[165]

The rich man founded a nunnery and she entered it. He built a church beside the nunnery and endowed them both. Genevieve lived in the nunnery, and eventually they chose her as their Mother Superior because of her devotion and angelic saintliness. When she died, her body performed many miracles, and their narration would take a long time. Because her body was working wonders, they placed it in a silver coffin and raised in on three pillars, for the sake of the sick, who came from many countries to visit her body and seek cures for their illnesses. From that time on they have called her 'Genevieve, Patron Saint of Paris'.

Towards the End of 1708

On the 25th of December, there was a terrible cold spell [166], to such a degree that the trees dried out and the Seine, which flows through the centre of Paris, froze solid. The ice was a hand span thick, so that carriages could cross it as if they were driving across dry, stony ground. This freezing cold lasted fifteen days. During that time people from the seven parishes of Paris died. Each parish is the size of Aleppo. The death knells of the churches tolled eighty thousand times, not counting the deaths of little children, the poor and the immigrants. They found mothers and children dead in their beds, the man and wife dead in one another's arms, because they lived on the upper floors of buildings, where the rent was low. Parisian houses have five floors, and each flat is cheaper than the one below.

They found the children of peasants, who had come from the towns to work as servants, lying in heaps in the garbage, in the throes of death. The city was empty of people. Everyone had taken refuge indoors. No one left their room and stove. I took refuge in my room with my stove and stayed imprisoned there for fifteen days in front of the fire. The priests were constrained to put braziers on the altars lest the vessels of consecrated wine placed there freeze.

The urine of many people not only froze in the air when they urinated, but inside their urinary tract as well, causing their death. The brass chamber pots they keep in their rooms burst. They broke their bread into little bits and soaked it in hot water in order to eat it. And what shall I say of their gardens? All the trees were frost bitten, including the vines and olive trees, as well as the crops in the fields, which normally ripen two or three times a year. This calamity afflicted all France.

On the fifteenth day, I left my bedroom and went to the barber. When I came out of his shop, I went rigid as a statue and the hairs in my moustache froze and fell out. I was certain I would die. When I reached my bedroom, they saw the condition I was in and told my master. When my master came, he immediately ordered the servants to strip me, but they were unable to remove my outer garment because my arms were frozen. Then he ordered them to cut off my sleeves. After they had stripped me, leaving me as naked as the day I was born, they lit the fire. We had in our possession a vial of 'vulture oil' [167] we had bought in Tunis, and they rubbed my body with that oil from head to foot and placed me next to the fire so the oil would melt on my body.

Then they warmed a white blanket and wrapped me in it and two boys carried me and put me to bed. I was still like a statue, unable to move my hands or feet. They wrapped me in three or four sheets and left me. The heat was so intense that it was as if I had been in the inner room of a bathhouse. They left me in bed twenty-four hours. After this period, I came to myself. I began to move my hands and feet without pain. I finally got out of bed, completely restored. I put on my clothes and walked about in the courtyard of the house. After two days, my master ordered one of the boys to take me to walk about in the city streets for a couple of hours, and never let me stop, until the circulation was restored to my feet. This resulted in my full recovery.

Not long after this, the city was struck by serious famine and inflated prices, to such an extent that the civic authorities wrote down the names of the people in the houses, and the governor ordered that every person be given an ounce of bread, no more, so that they would not perish. The members of each family were registered with the baker, and seated in every bakery was a government official with a register of the names of the members of all the families. Because of this regulation, no one else could get any food, not even the weight of a dram.

A few days later the peasants, people from towns and villages, flocked into Paris to beg, so they wouldn't starve to death. I myself saw many people lying dead of hunger in the streets, for no one could give them alms, because everyone had only one ounce [168] of bread, and it was not possible to divide that ounce and give anything to the beggar. This was the reason so many died of hunger.

When the grandees of the city, and the metropolitans and officials saw this calamity, they thought of — or rather sought — help from Our Lord, who is merciful to His servants. They decided to employ these peasants, paying them from the city's charitable endowments, to build houses on the outskirts of Paris, where there was a hill. They wanted them to level the ground, and build houses. They brought wheat for them from other countries, but it was expensive. They set up a bakery there to make bread for those people, and gave every man, woman and child able to move earth a loaf of bread weighing two ounces and a wage of two *jarq*, that is, eight *'uthmānī*, which equals four *sous*. They kept on working and the citizens of Paris were given a respite from them, until times improved and wheat imported from the Levant and North Africa and other places brought down prices.

When I went to Marseille, I witnessed the arrival of four galleys sent by Our Lord the Pope, along with barges filled with wheat, because in Marseille the unrest was even greater than in Paris. People attacked the houses and took any food they could find. The governor was forced to erect a scaffold in every quarter and he stationed soldiers to stop the people looting the houses.

Then the ships that had been sent to the Levant to buy wheat from the villages and towns arrived, nearly three hundred ships and settees. Wheat became abundant, and was distributed throughout the provinces of France. Bread was now available, but their *ratl* of bread, is three fourths of our Aleppan measure.[169] Bread remained at this price until there was a new rise in prices, and everything returned to normal. This is what I saw of the inflation which occurred in France in 1709.

Antoine Galland

During this period I grew wearied and sick of living in that country. A gentleman used to visit us often. He was in charge of the collection of Arabic manuscripts and could read Arabic very well. He translated Arabic books into French. At the time, he was translating an Arabic book into French, and it was *The Book of the Stories of the Thousand and One Nights*. This man found me useful, because of certain passages he couldn't understand, which I was able to explain to him. The manuscript was lacking a number of nights, so I told him stories I knew, and he finished his book with these stories. He was very grateful to me, and promised me that if I had a problem, he would help me with all his heart.

One day when I was sitting chatting with him, he said to me, "If you can keep a secret, I will do you a great favour". I said to him "What is the favour you wish to do me?" He replied "I will tell you what it is tomorrow". After we had finished talking, he went off. The next day, he came and told me, "Rejoice in your good fortune! If everything works out, you will be very pleased!" Then I said to him, "Tell me the favour!" He responded by saying, "A certain prince, one of the great men of the state, has asked me to find a man to send on tour, like Paul Lucas. It occurred to me to tell him about you, for you are honest, and know what is required". Then he told me, "I will take you to him, so that he can see you and speak with you. I will wait for you tomorrow in such-and-such a place, so that we can go see him together. But be very, very careful not to let your master know anything about this, because he would stop you going". We agreed on this, and he left me.

The next day I went to the place agreed and found him waiting for me. I went with him until we came to the palace of the prince. He went in to him and a little while later, the servants asked me to come in too. I entered and stood before him. He bade me welcome with great kindness and asked me to be seated. I sat down, and he began to ask me about the countries I had visited, and the things that I had found there, which were old coins and idols and books of the history of ancient kings and similar antiquities. I answered him, "Yes, My Lord, I bought all these things, and know all about them, because my master has taught me about them".

Then the prince said to me, "Go, pack your things, leave your master, and come back to me. I will send you with an order from the king exactly like that given your master, appointing you ambassador and addressed to all the consuls in the Levant. I will also give you letters of recommendation, and whatever you ask of the consuls during your tour will be given you. The things you buy should be given to them so they can forward everything to the Customs House in Marseille. You will be given a salary of one *écu* a day, in addition to your expenses. When you return safely to me, I will promote you to a higher station, to a position with a considerable salary". When he had finished speaking, he said, "Go, do what I told you, then return to me".

I left his presence, uncertain what to do. On the one hand, I was upset by the things that had happened during my stay. On the other, I was fearful lest the arrangements I had made fall through, and I remained torn between fear and hope. What decided me was something serious and extremely frightening that happened soon after.

The Story of Joseph the Jeweller

One day I encountered an Armenian from Persia named Yūsuf al-Jawharjī, 'Joseph the Jeweller'. This man occupied himself in Paris selling valuable gems, like diamonds, rubies, emeralds and pearls, and similar precious stones. When he saw me, he greeted me in Turkish, without knowing who I was. When I returned his greeting, he proceeded to ask me, "What country do you come from?" I answered, "I am from the country of Syria, from the city of Aleppo". When he learned that I was from Aleppo, he greeted me again, extremely effusively. He asked me about everybody, how they were, he hoped they were well, and I replied to his queries, saying, so-and-so is fine, and such another is dead, and another has gone on a trip, and other such things. At last we walked on together, until I came to our house. I bade him goodbye and ascended the stairs.

But he followed me to the second floor, and asked me, "On what floor do you live?" "On the second", I told him, and he left me and went off.

I told my master about the man I had met, and how he had welcomed me and showed me such extreme love and affection, and how this man was known in Paris and received by all the grandees. My master said to me, "Why didn't you invite him to visit us? If you see him again, invite him to visit us, so he and I can talk about the properties of jewels, that is, precious stones. I want to find out whether he really knows about them". For my master was an unrivalled authority on gems, their properties and values. For this reason he wanted to meet him and find out whether he was worth talking to or not.

A few days later, in the afternoon, there was a knock at the door. My master and I were sitting relaxing in front of the stove, having just finished coffee. I quickly rose and opened the door and saw that it was Joseph the Jeweler. I welcomed him, and invited him to come in and drink coffee with us. "I can't come in at the moment" he answered, "because I have an appointment. I want you to come with me, to translate some words of a learned man, because I don't know how to explain my problem to him, for I don't speak French well. I speak to him in Italian, but he doesn't understand Italian. That is why I am asking you to generously translate between the two of us. Then I told him, "Wait a moment, till I ask permission of my master, then I will go with you".

I went in to my master and told him of the matter. He immediately rose and invited him in, insisting he enter, and refusing to take no for an answer. He came in, and we gave him breakfast and prepared coffee for him, receiving him as one must a guest so warmly invited by my master. Then they started to talk together about the properties of precious stones for almost an hour. My master then agreed to send me with him to translate for him in his serious emergency. "What is this emergency?" he asked, "tell me, I may be able to help." "This matter", he answered, "is secret. If you want me to tell your lordship about it, you must assure me that you will keep it secret." "Speak" answered my master, "and do not fear! Your secret is safe with me forever."

So he told him all about the difficulty and how it had come about. "I have asked for a girl's hand in marriage, and signed the marriage contract in the law court. But now people have approached me and said they want me to ask so-and-so's daughter in marriage, referring to a very rich merchant, one of the India traders. "He has been in India a number of years trading, and has no intention of returning to Paris", they told me. "The aunts and uncles of the girl want to marry you to the girl and send you to India to the girl's father, fearing lest he die there and his fortune dissipate, for the man is very old." They don't know I am already spoken for, and now I don't know what to do. I ask you, is it possible to retract my commitment to that girl, and switch to the other?"

My master answered, saying "I can see a way, but it is not legal for you to take it, and I wouldn't advise you to try". Then he kept asking and begging him to tell him what it was. My master answered him, saying "Can you assure me you won't do it?" He assured him that he wouldn't.

Then he said to him, "Because you are a foreigner, you can claim you have received a letter from your family, and that you must return to your country for a grave reason, either the death of your father, or of your partner, or whatever. Then you could tell the family of the girl that you really must go, you have no choice, because the matter is so very serious. For this reason, you could say to them, they should tear up the marriage contract, so the girl will be free to marry. And tell them, 'If I return, and she is still unmarried, I will take her.' Then they will be unable to prevent you from leaving, and will tear up the marriage contract and break the proposal. When the contract has been torn up, tell the news to the family of the new girl whom you want to marry, and say 'I have money in such and such a country, and I am going there to collect it. After a certain number of days, I will return and seek your daughter's hand.' If, after that period, you return and ask the second girl in marriage, the family of the first girl will have no case against you, and cannot prevent you from marrying".

When he heard all this, he was very grateful, and went on his way.

But his thirst for wealth did not stop there. He did what my master suggested, and disappeared for a time, then came back and asked for the hand of the girl, the daughter of the India merchant. This was during Lent. Because they wanted to marry him off quickly, and send him to India, they got permission from the cardinal for him to be married during Lent, during which time marriage was normally not permitted. When the cardinal gave them permission, they rushed to marry him off.

Now in that country, when a foreigner wishes to marry, the marriage is announced in the largest churches three times. The priest announces that a foreigner from such and such a country wants to get married, and anyone who knows that he is already married must inform the bishop. Anyone who knew, but didn't speak, was excommunicated. They announced the marriage on the first Sunday, then the second Sunday, and no one came forward.

On the third Sunday, however, a Chaldean priest was present during the announcement, and he went to the bishop and told him, "I know this man is married in Syria, in the city of Aleppo. This is the truth. He married a woman named Mariam, the daughter of Jabbār, and had a son by her. Then he left her and travelled, and this could well be him, because when I returned to Aleppo I asked the woman what her husband looked like, and she described exactly what I see. He is tall, dark and thin. God only knows if it is him or not".

When this priest had testified, and they had verified his testimony, they informed the governor of the city of the affair. The governor immediately ordered the culprit to be placed under arrest, his goods confiscated and that he be hanged. The man who brought the news to the bishop was right. The Armenian disappeared and no trace of him was ever found. They sought him everywhere, but could get no news of him. Three days later, they went to his house to confiscate his goods, but found nothing. He had taken many precious stones from the houses of the grandees, to sell them on their behalf and give them their price. They found nothing, except that he had taken the money and run.

The search for him intensified. They arrested his neighbours and associates and tortured them to find out if they knew his hiding place. I was among those arrested. I was on my way to work when two of the governor's men laid hold of me and ordered me to go with them. I was frightened, and asked them, "What do you want?" They answered, "You. You must come before the governor and he will tell you what he wants from you." My fear and trembling increased. I had no choice but to go along with them.

Steven the Coffee Maker

We passed by the coffee shop of *khoja* Istifān the Syrian. He was a good friend of mine, and there was great love and affection between us. The reason was that when I arrived in Paris, my master asked me to go say hello to him, since he was a son of our country. He told me his story.

When he came to Paris, he began to beg, but no one gave him alms. He decided to go to *Khoja* Christofle Zamārīyā and beseech him to get permission from His Excellency the Cardinal to stand at the door of the Church of the Virgin and beg. The *khoja*'s heart softened for him, and since he was the cardinal's secretary and very close to him, the cardinal gave him his permit, which asked people to take pity on him as a stranger, poor and in need.

He took the permit and stood in the door of the church begging. When people saw that he had a certificate from the cardinal, they began to give generously, until he had accumulated close to two hundred piasters.

The Festival of St Michael

Around that time the festival of St Michael took place. The city of Paris has seven parishes, and each parish is named after a saint. When the saint's day falls, a seven-day festival is held in an open space. During this period there is buying, selling, and spectacles. People come from other towns to buy and sell, because there is no duty levied on sales or purchases, and none of the usual expenses incurred at other times.

When they celebrated the festival of St Michael, I went to have a look. Of all the things I saw, the most striking was a black monkey in an iron cage. It was very ugly, as if it were Satan. There was also a two-headed serpent. Finally, I came to a place where someone was beating a drum. I asked what it was and they answered that in this place was an amazing spectacle. I wanted to see it, and the proprietor asked me for a quarter *sou*, and I saw that this was more expensive than the other sideshows. I didn't want to give him more than the price of the others. Then people intervened between us and we settled on four *šāhiyyāt*, and they let me enter. When I went in, I found a little camel sitting there, nothing else. I regretted going in, and said to the owner, "In our country, there are lots of these camels, and this is the smallest there could possibly be!" "Console yourself", he said to me, "I could have made you pay the quarter *sou*."

The Story of Steven the Coffee Maker *Continued*

Now let us return to our story. A number of people who loved the poor and strangers suggested to Istafān or Steven that he buy himself two coffee pots and some cups and everything else needed to make coffee and go to the festival. This was at the time of the festival of St Michael. The man did as they suggested, and sold coffee during the festival, and because he was a Levantine and a foreigner, he began to attract regular customers, for there was no other coffee seller. At that time, coffee shops had not spread in Paris, and everything new is sweet. He began to do very well selling coffee and took on employees to help him deal with the crowd that flocked to him.

The upshot was that during the seven days he earned the sum of two hundred piastres, and now had a total of four hundred. When the festival was over he returned to the city and opened a coffee shop. His clientele increased so much that in the space of a year he had accumulated a lot of money. He was known in the city of Paris, as 'Istafān al-Qahwājī, 'Steven the Coffee Maker'. People came to him from the seven parishes, grandees and merchants and others, the whole world. His name became known in Versailles, even in the king's palace. The minister sent and asked him to open a coffee shop in Versailles, and soon he was pouring coffee in the king's palace.

He became known to the great men of the state, and was soon

famous. He took to wife an extremely rich widow, mistress of wealth and property. She wanted to take him as her husband, and sent people to sound him out about the matter. He accepted and married her and they had a daughter. The girl developed an illness and became partially paralyzed.

Istafān sent a go-between to speak to me on his behalf. This is what he said: "*Khoja* Istafān has decided to open a coffee shop in Versailles, and stay there. He would like you to marry his daughter, and he will give you the coffee shop in Paris. Because you are a Levantine, the regular customers will patronize you more than they would a fellow countryman". When I heard these words from him — and I had met his daughter, who was pretty but crippled — I answered by asking that he give me a while to consult my master, and then I would give him my answer. The man went off, certain I would give him my answer in two or three days.

So I consulted my master. He was not pleased that I should ask the girl in marriage, because she was crippled. When the man came back to receive my response, I could not give him a straight answer, and said, "Leave this question until I have sorted out my affairs". My answer was still pending on the day the governor's men apprehended me, as we have mentioned. When we passed in front of his coffee shop, he saw me and quickly came out and asked the governor's agents, "What are you doing, arresting this youth? What is his crime?" They answered, saying: "The governor was told that he too was among the associates of Joseph the Jeweler, and that perhaps he knows where he is hiding. If they can't find him immediately, he will suffer greatly".

Khoja Istafan was unable to free me from the hands of the governor's agents. At that moment my master appeared, for the news of my arrest had reached him. When he saw me under arrest, and that I was as frightened as could be, he rebuked the men holding me and told me to go to the house, telling them, "Don't you know the youth is with me, and that I brought him from the East to work in the King's library of Arabic manuscripts? What do you want with him?"

They told him the story: how the governor was investigating the matter in order to find Joseph the Jeweler and the governor had been informed that this youth had been seen in conversation with the fugitive and that "This was the reason we arrested him, and we didn't know he was with you". He answered, "This youth is with me, and I am his guarantor, and I will answer to the governor if the affair warrants it". Then the governor's men left me and went off, but I was still frightened and very perplexed by this country. I determined to leave Paris and do what the prince had asked me, to travel and tour like my master. I made up my mind to do just that.

So I asked my master permission to return to my country. When he heard these words from me, he was astonished, and said, "Are you lacking something, or is it that you're unhappy with your life with me? I worked hard for you, to the extent of bringing you to this country, so that I could do you a great service by obtaining a noble position for you, under the patronage of the King of France, so that you might pass the rest of your life in comfort and happiness. Now you want to kick aside this happiness and return to being a prisoner of the Muslims, the way you were before!"

His words struck me forcibly, and I changed my mind about leaving. Especially because he always told me that the minister's mind was completely occupied with the events taking place at that time [170], but when peace was achieved, "I will fulfill my promise to you, and appoint you to the Library".

In that hope, I had put off going to see the aforementioned prince, and when three days had passed, he sent some of his retinue to summon me. When I came before him, he greeted me and said, "Why did you delay coming to see me? I've been expecting you!" "O My Lord', I answered, 'I couldn't get my master's permission to leave, because he has worked hard on my behalf and brought me to this country as a favour to me, and to free me from servitude to the barbarians. This is the reason I don't want to go against his wishes."

Then the prince said to me, "I want to do you a favour, and make you one of my suite. You will always be under the king's protection and mine. Go tell your master you have received a letter from your family and have to return to your country. Do what I tell you and hurry back to me so that I can equip you and send you off". When

I heard these words, I fell silent, and the only answer I could make was to leave. I went out, my head spinning, but this is how God, may He be praised, disposes.

I returned to my master, and said to him, "My lord, I have received a letter from my brothers, and cannot continue to stay here". When he heard these words from me, he was furious, and did everything he could to dissuade me, saying "You Levantines are faithless. Go where you want!" He was very angry. He then gave me one hundred thirds [of an *écu*], and said, "Go in peace! But you will regret it when regret no longer avails". Then he departed and left me alone.

I got my things together and left them with a neighbour, then went to the office of the *diligence*, that is, the place where carriages set off for the city of Lyon. There are two carriages, and they leave on scheduled days, for on the arrival of one of them in Lyon, the other sets off from Paris. These carriages are drawn by eight horses, and carry eight passengers. On the outside, between the two rear wheels, is a bench. This is for the servants accompanying their masters. Those on the inside pay two piastres a day, while those on the outside on the bench pay one. If someone should ask, 'Why is it so expensive?' I would answer, 'Because this carriage is like a little palace. It has four windows of gleaming glass, and is lined with leather. There are four seats upholstered with scarlet broadcloth, and only eight people may enter, no more. It is drawn by eight head of powerful horses. Each stage of the journey lasts two hours. You may see eight head of fresh horses standing waiting in the road to be exchanged for the exhausted ones, because they make a two day journey in just one.

At noon they stop at an inn used only by the carriages, no one else. The passengers alight and enter the inn. There you see the table, set with all things necessary. They serve a splendid lunch, better than that found in the houses of the grandees, with superb food, fine bread and delicious wine. Four or five servants hold cups in their hands to serve anyone who asks. After everyone has lunched, the passengers and their servants, who are served the same food at a separate table, get in the carriage and are handed a carafe of wine and a glass and a jug of water in case they want to drink along the way.

The same thing happens in the evening, around sundown. They come to an inn specially dedicated to these two carriages, and enter and dine, as we have said, on superb food. Then they stay up chatting until time for bed. They give each of the passengers a bed with a broadcloth coverlet if it is winter and in summer with fine white linen. Beside the bed is a *priedieu* and above it an icon and a cross, towards which to pray. The bed has three coverings, and each has two clean white sheets no one has slept in, and also a clean night cap.

When dawn breaks, everyone goes to the local church to attend holy mass. Then they return to the inn to find breakfast laid out, consisting of fine white bread and cheese and good wine. After finishing breakfast, they get in the carriage and travel on. As we have explained, they lunch and dine and sleep in another inn, and continue doing so until they reach Lyon. It is normally a journey of twenty days, but they arrive in ten.

When I reached that place, I signed my name and paid the fare, as was usual. This was on a Tuesday, and the coach was scheduled to leave on Thursday. They recommended that I sleep there the night before, because they set off early in the morning, before sunup. I wrote down my name as one of the departing passengers in the coach, as we have said. Then I returned to His Excellency the Prince and told him what I had done, and that I had left my master, and paid my fare in the *diligence* and he said to me, "What is your hurry? Why didn't you come to me before doing so? But no harm is done". Then he summoned his secretary and instructed him to write a letter to one of the dukes in the king's palace at Versailles, so that he could obtain royal orders in accordance with the summaries in the letter. After folding and sealing the letter, he told me to go to Versailles and enter the king's palace and deliver the letter to that duke.

I took the letter and waited until evening, lest my master hear that I had gone to Versailles. I rode in a coach to Versailles and entered the king's palace without being challenged, because the guards recognized me from the time I spent eight days in the king's palace exhibiting those wild animals of which we have spoken. For this reason, no one prevented me from entering.

When I entered the palace, I inquired about the duke, and they showed me in to him. He was pacing about in an inner hall of the palace. When I saw him, I bowed and gave him the letter. He took the letter from my hand, and drew near a lighted lamp and read the letter. Then he turned to me, addressing me politely, and asked me to follow him. I went with him to the place where they copied the *firmān*s and orders of the king. It is a large room, with many desks. Then he summoned the director of that place, that is, the chief secretary, and read the letter to him and instructed him to write a *firmān* in the noble style demanded by such a document. After having given his instructions, he left me and went off. As for me, I stood about waiting for the *firmān*. A long time passed, and I was still waiting. The aforementioned chief secretary came to me and asked, "What do you want?" "I'm waiting for the *firmān*", I answered. He smiled, and said, "What good will the *firmān* do you, when it hasn't been shown to the king, and he hasn't signed it?" "How long is this going to take?" I asked. "Until Monday", he answered, "when a council is held, and all the *firmān*s are shown to the king. He signs the ones that strike him, and tears up the others."

When I heard these words, I was astonished, and the world closed in on me, and I regretted that I had already paid the fare and had no option but to leave on Thursday. I left the palace and went to an inn, where I had dinner and slept. When morning came, I went to Paris, to His Excellency the Prince. When he saw me, he asked if I had gone to Versailles. "Yes, I went and gave the letter to the duke." Then I told him what had happened, and that the *firmān* would not be ready until Monday, and that on Thursday I must leave. "No problem", he said to me, "I will go to Versailles, and in a few days I will send you the *firmān* and the letters of recommendation."

Then he summoned the secretary, and instructed him to write a letter to the harbour master of Marseille, who is the person who deals with the Eastern trade which comes to this country. He told him to say in the letter, "Keep this youth with you until the official courier arrives with the *firmān*, and give him a letter in your own hand to all the consuls stationed in the Levant, stating that whatever funds he requests should be given him in exchange for a receipt and whatever he deposits with them should be sent to Marseille, care of the harbour master. He also instructed him to write a letter to His Excellency the Ambassador in Istanbul recommending me and requesting that he obtain from the Grand Vizier letters of recommendation for me to all the provincial governors. Then he bade me goodbye, and I left, taking the letters.

I went and collected my belongings from the neighbour and consigned them to the director of the *diligences*. Finally, I went to say goodbye to acquaintances and friends. Among them, I went and said farewell to *khoja* Christofle, secretary to His Eminence the Cardinal. When I said goodbye to him, he gave me a letter to his brother, *khoja* Zamārīyā, who is resident in Istanbul. His position is Custodian of Jerusalem, by royal decree. He is a man of high rank and standing. He asked him to keep an eye on me. This went on until I left Paris.

We headed for Lyon, and arrived in ten days in excellent health. From there I bought passage very cheaply with carters who going to Marseille. They had long wagons, and placed the bales on top. They were drawn by six horses. I sat on top of the bales, and was very comfortable, with none of the discomfort of the road. At noon we lunched at inns, and dined and slept at others. I envied them their life, and their journeys transporting bales, without fatigue, eating well and sleeping in beds. The servants of the inns looked after their animals and their feeding, and in the morning even took them out of the stable, and hitched them up to the wagons. Each of the wagons had one carter, no more. They had no fear of the road. I ate with them and they never charged me for the food. The result was that we arrived in Marseille in the best of spirits.

When I had arrived, safe and sound, I went to the inn in which my master and I had stayed, when we were on our way to Paris. The woman who ran the inn welcomed me, and gave me a place to sleep. An hour after my arrival, I went to the custom's house and asked to see the harbour master. When I stood before him, I handed him the prince's letter. He opened it and read it, then rose to his feet and welcomed me with great respect. Then he said, "His Excellency the Prince wrote me to have you stay with me until the *firmān* he is sending you arrives. I will give you a letter to the consuls, as he requests in this letter".

Now I had supposed that the *firmān* would have arrived before my own arrival in Marseille, because every week a courier arrives with correspondence for Marseille. At that moment I realized the hopelessness of my situation. It was because of this that I did not want to stay with the harbour master. Instead, I told him, "I am staying in an inn called *Le Petit Paris*. When the *firmān* arrives, send for me". "As you wish", he said.

I left him, feeling drunk without wine, regretting what I had done. But what good does regret do? I remembered how my master had told me I would regret it. Nevertheless, I was still torn between hope and fear, until the second week when the courier arrived. I went to the harbour master and asked him if any news had arrived from the prince. "No news has reached me, and no letter", he answered. Then I decided to send a letter and ask whether the *firmān* had been sent or not. He sent me a reply in his own hand, saying in it, "I am surprised the *firmān* I sent you hasn't arrived. I sent it with one of my friends to Marseille", and he gave me his name. I combed the city searching for him, hoping to see him, but found not a trace of him in Marseille. I waited three weeks, then four, and no one appeared. Then I was sure my situation was of little importance to the prince. When I had lost all hope in him, I wrote him a letter of rebuke, that is was disgraceful that a nobleman like him should separate me from my master, and cause me to be deceived on both sides. But this is how Divine Providence worked for my own good. I sent the letter, and put the situation from my mind.

During that time, a traveler from Paris came to stay in the inn where I was lodging. One day when we were talking, he asked me about my country, and how I had come to France. I told him how I had come with a man named Paul Lucas, one of the king's travellers, and how I had gone to Paris with him. I recounted the whole story of my situation, from beginning to end, and how so-and-so the prince tricked me and caused me to leave my master, and how he broke his promise to me.

He said to me, 'You are right, my brother, but the fault lies not with His Excellency the Prince, the fault lies with your master. I will tell you in detail how it all played out. The gentleman who used to visit you is the one who convinced the prince to send you touring. He had a hidden motive. For he had heard, nay, he knew for certain, that your master wanted to get you the position of Keeper of Arabic Manuscripts, and fearful that this position should slip through his hands, he set up this scenario, and convinced the prince to send you off.

When everything was settled, and the prince sent you to Versailles to get the *firmān* from the king that night, one of your master's friends saw you. He told him that you had given a letter to so-and-so the duke, and how the duke had sent you with the chief secretary to obtain a *firmān* from the king recommending you, to facilitate your travels. When your master heard this news, he went to Versailles to that duke, and learned the truth of the matter.

Your master felt threatened, since his position was that of the king's traveler. So he immediately went to His Excellency the Prince and slandered you, saying "Be careful, My Lord, of putting your affairs in the hands of someone like that. These Levantines are treacherous, and he could quite possibly, thanks to your orders, obtain money from the consuls and take refuge in his country, and you would have no recourse against him. For your sake, I will take his place, and perform this service for you, and whatever I collect, I will send you". When the Prince heard these words from my master, he changed his mind and sent him off to travel at his expense.

This is indeed how it happened, because some time after my arrival in Aleppo, my master came to Aleppo. I ran into him, and greeted him and invited him to stay with us. I catered to his every need and showed him every honour. He stayed the night with us, and I made up a bed for him on the roof terrace. After my brothers had left, he and I sat up talking. He began to rebuke me for not telling him of my agreement with the prince to go on tour, and he said to me, "This was a failure in your duty to me. I never thought you would do something like that to me. I intended to do you a great favour. Instead, you kicked it away". After talking a long time, with many reproaches, we finally slept.

The next day after breakfast, we went down to the town. I had opened a shop selling broadcloth. He would visit me every day, and

I would walk with him, as we used to do on our travels, looking for coins, medals and precious stones. One day we entered the Jewelry Market, and he saw a little stone, the colour of carnelian. He bought it for two *paras* and gave it to me, saying "Hang it around your mother's neck, and she will be cured of her illness".

For when he was staying with us, it had occurred to me to have him look at my mother. She had been ill for twenty years, and not one of the local doctors had been able to cure her of her illness. We showed her to him, and told him her symptoms — that she was unable to sleep or speak, didn't want to leave the house to get some fresh air, or go to mass, that she ate very little, and it was only with difficulty that she could be made to eat at all, to the point that her body looked like a stick of wood.

When he hung the stone around her neck, she slept well that night, as she used to do. The next day, she changed her clothes and asked to go to the bathhouse. She returned from the baths in perfect health. We were all amazed at the effect of this stone. It was like a miracle. Finally, I asked my master about the qualities of this stone, and its name. "Its name in Italian", he replied, 'is *calcedonio*, and it has this property: it attracts the vapours of black bile immediately, and your mother's illness was caused by black bile, nothing else.[171]

In the end, that man told me, "The prince sent the *firmān* to your master, so that he could travel about on his behalf and he dispensed with your services. There is no point hoping for anything more from him". I suspect this man had been sent by the prince to bring me this news. This is how the story of my departure from Paris ended.

Let us return to what we were saying. I stayed in that inn in Marseille until a ship was readied for Alexandretta, so that I could sail with it. Every day I went to the customs house where the merchants gather from ten in the morning to noon, and from two in the afternoon until dusk. All the buying and selling takes place here, and here can be found all the Levant merchants, and those that trade with the New World, Spain, North Africa and other places. When these merchants want to send a ship, they put up a notice giving the name of the ship and the name of the country it is sailing to.

One day I went to that place and saw a notice posted with the name of a ship going to the port of Alexandretta. I was overjoyed, and went to M. Samatan, the most powerful of my friends. He had been a merchant in Aleppo, and my older brother had been his treasurer. This man was very fond of me, and many times invited me to his house for dinner, treating me with great hospitality. I informed him that a ship was ready to depart for Alexandretta and that I wanted to go with it. "I know about it" he said, "and I will recommend you to the captain, and he will certainly agree to take you." I was very grateful for his kindness, and went to get my things together.

I was determined to leave, and went to say goodbye to the Aleppo merchants that I knew. A few days later, the ship owners changed their minds, and decided not to send it, fearing corsairs. When I heard this news, I was very downcast and the world closed in on me. I was miserable. I went to the customs house hoping to find a ship bound for the Levant.

Only two ships were ready to sail, one to Istanbul and the other to Smyrna. I asked for the captain planning to sail to Smyrna and they pointed him out to me. I asked him to take me with him to Smyrna. He was pleased, and immediately asked me to give him an advance payment of forty piastres for my fare, not including my food and drink. At that moment, all I had was ten piastres.

I was at a loss what to do, so I went to my friend *khoja* Samatan, and told him what had happened. He was not happy with my decision to go to Smyrna, and said to me, "Wait a little while, perhaps they will fit out a ship for Alexandretta, and I will send you there in it without fail". I answered, imploring him that I couldn't stay in this country. I was fed up, and had run out of patience. Above all, I wanted to leave, for every sort of reason.

Then he said to me, "I want to make a suggestion. Go up to the consul's house, which is above the Port Authority. Ask the consul to order the captain of the ship to take you with him. Say to him, "I am a poor stranger, with no way to earn my living here. There is no question that he will immediately order the captain to take you with him".

I did as he suggested, and went to the consul's house early, and by good luck found a priest preparing to celebrate mass before the consul. I entered just in time, and served the priest. After mass was over, the consul went out, surrounded by a group of merchants, and strolled in the courtyard of the palace. I went up to the consul and made the customary bow, addressing him in the French language with the respect due his position, as *khoja* Samatan had taught me.

When I finished speaking, the consul asked me, "What country do you come from?" I answered that I was from Syria. "What brought you here?" he asked. "I came here with a Frenchman", I replied "and went with him to Paris, where he abandoned me. I have returned from Paris and want to go back to my country, but what little I had, I spent getting here, and have hardly enough left to eat".

When I had finished speaking, he ordered one of his servants to go and summon that captain. Then he turned and said to me, "Wait here, don't go away!" After a short time, the captain turned up. The consul ordered him to take me with him, and said to him, "This youth is a stranger, and poor. We have an obligation to send him back to his country, as is our custom". "I hear and obey", said the captain, and turning to me said, "This evening load your things into the skiff, and come to the ship, for we leave early tomorrow morning".

Then I gratefully thanked the consul and the captain and went directly to *khoja* Samatan, told him everything that had happened, and thanked him for his generosity. Then he said to me, "One thing remains to be done. I will take you to the owner of the ship and get a letter from him to the captain recommending you, lest you be pestered along the way, because you have caused him to lose face. Then he took me with him to the owner of the ship, who was a friend of his. When we entered his house, he welcomed us warmly. Then *khoja* Samatan said to him, "I want to send this young man on your ship, and request that you kindly give him a letter in your hand recommending the captain to keep an eye on him on shipboard for your sake".

"On my head and eye!" he answered, and immediately wrote the letter. He told the captain that he was recommending me, and to look after me and not take anything at all from me. Indeed, that if I needed anything, to give it to me. He sealed the letter and gave it to me. Then we bade him goodbye and left. I took the letter and went to the inn where I was staying. I had scarcely arrived, when the aforementioned ship owner sent me abundant provisions, biscuit, cheese, a number of dried fish, a jar of olives and a little barrel of wine. He also came himself to bid me goodbye. I was very thankful for his charity and his generosity. Then he said to me, "Since the captain has not invited you to his table, take these provisions with you, so that you have no need of him".

I then gave him a letter to be sent to my brother in Aleppo along with the letters which were being sent to Istanbul overland. In it, I told him the date of the ship's departure for Smyrna. Sometime later, the letter reached my brother. Just after that, they heard that a ship leaving Smyrna for Alexandretta had sunk on the way, with the loss of all passengers. My brothers and family were very sad, because they knew that I was sailing from Marseille to Smyrna, and they assumed that I was in that ship, as they had had no further news of me, for after that one letter, I never wrote again. Their hopes for me were dashed, and they prayed for my soul in the service for the dead.

Now let us return to what we were saying. After I had bid goodbye to the ship owner, I carried my things to the port and got in the skiff, which took us to the ship that was anchored outside the channel. I climbed aboard ship, which was a large one, called *Le Galantan*, mounting twenty-four cannon and carrying eighty soldiers, not counting the sailors. The ship was only half laden, for fear of corsairs, and carrying equal numbers of soldiers and merchants. We slept onboard that night, and early the next day raised anchor, spread sails and set off. At midday I gave the letter to the captain, and when he read it, he smiled, and said to me, "You're safe!" But he didn't invite me to dine with him.

We sailed all the first day, but on the next, in the forenoon, what did I see, but the ship's officers assembling. They began to ready the weapons of war, that is, the cannons and muskets. They wrote on slips of paper, and hung one slip on each cannon. They bore the names of those who were stationed there to man the gun. They also wrote down the names of the soldiers who would fire the muskets.

When they came to me, they asked me, "What is your name?" and I said. "Why do you want my name?" "When the enemy attacks" they replied, "You must take a musket and fight like everyone else". I said to them, "Leave me alone. I am a foreigner, and know nothing about warfare, or how to fire a musket". Then the captain turned to me and said, "When you see us fighting the enemy, go hide in the hold, but I advise you in case of combat, not to hide your face, because if you do, the soldiers will kill you without fail". Finally, I agreed to inscribe my name, and enlisted like the others.

That day passed, and on the third day we sighted a large corsair ship in the distance. When it saw us, it made towards us, intent on fighting us and boarding us. Our ship too headed towards them. They opened the gun ports and the soldiers lined up holding their muskets, and I stood with them. When we drew near each other, we and the ship that had sailed with us, bound for Istanbul, both prepared for battle against the corsairs.

When the corsairs saw our two big ships closing on it, they feared that we were going to ram them. When we had them in range, they raised the French flag, knowing that we were French. Then the enemy ship announced through a megaphone that it was French too, turned and sailed off. At that point the fear that had gripped my heart vanished and I thanked Almighty God that it had not been an enemy, because I had been in despair and certain I was going to die.

One day I went down into the hold for lunch. Seated near me was a good-looking young man, with marks of good breeding, but dressed in rags. He was wearing a shift of old broadcloth, torn, exposing his flesh and no shirt and seemed despondent and depressed. My heart broke for him, and I invited him to lunch with me. So he came and had lunch with me, and I poured him wine from the pitcher and made friends with him. After we had finished lunch, I took a shirt, vest and robe from my basket, and told him to put them on. At first he refused, but at last he accepted gratefully, and put them on.

Then we sat down and talked. I asked about his condition, and what his story was. "Since you have asked," he answered "I am one of the chamberlains of the French ambassador in Istanbul.[172]

The ambassador sent me to Paris, and gave me letters of great importance for the minister. For when the ambassador went to be received by the king, that is, Sultan Ahmad, after presenting the gifts he had brought from the Sultan of France, he entered in the company of the Grand Vizier and the dragoman. They came to the third gateway, and the custom since ancient times has been that when an ambassador reaches the third gateway, the majordomo steps forward and removes the sword from the ambassador's side, out of respect for His Highness the King. Now when the majordomo approached to take the sword as usual, the ambassador pushed him back and wouldn't let him take the sword from his side.

The Grand Vizier was astonished at this action, and the dragoman departed from protocol and tried to urge the ambassador to let them take the sword, as required by ancient custom. But he wouldn't let them remove his sword. He said to the Grand Vizier, "I have been commanded to enter and present myself to His Majesty the King wearing my sword". The Grand Vizier refused, and said to him, "It is impossible for me to let you into the king's presence with a sword". So the ambassador left without having been received, and returned to his palace.

Then the Grand Vizier wrote a letter to the minister of the Sultan of France and told him what the ambassador, with no right, had done. The ambassador also wrote a letter to the minister on this matter and sent me with the letter so that I could deliver it to him. He warned me not to let anyone know that I had been sent by the ambassador.

I took the letter from him and with two companions, set sail on a French ship. As we were sailing, we were attacked by corsairs. They took our ship and stripped us and took everything we had, including our clothes, leaving us naked. One of the sailors took pity on me and gave me this torn robe. Finally, they dumped us in the port of Livorno. We had to go begging to eat. But I still had the letter, and in order to carry out my master's order, I proceeded from Livorno to Marseille. I was forced to spend many days in Marseille, naked and hungry, and I could find no way to get to Paris in that condition, and no one took pity on me, until you did, just now. So I decided to send the letter by post and return to my master lest I perish in this country.

When I heard these words from him, I felt sorry for him, and tried to comfort him. After that, our affection for each other grew, and we became close companions. I told him everything that had happened to me, from first to last.

We continued sailing until one night we were near the island of Sicily. This island was in the hands of the Hapsburgs, and the Hapsburgs were at war with France. As we were passing by that place, our ship prepared for battle, fearing lest a corsair ship should set out from the island. It was dark, because the moon was in its fourteenth night. The lookouts, saw a ship pulling out from the island, and warned the captain and crew. As soon as they sighted it, our ship set out after it, along with the ship that had accompanied us from Marseille, which had also seen it, and like us had set out so we could surround it. All we had to do was send out a longboat with a company of soldiers to capture it. When the ship saw that it would be caught between the two ships, and that flight was impossible, they furled their sails and came to a stop, lest they be sunk by our cannon. When they did so, we launched a longboat with a company of soldiers to take them and lead them away with us. When the longboat drew near them, they fended it off with grappling hooks, and prevented it from drawing close. At the same moment, they unfurled their sails and fled, by means of the wind that came up on their poop, that is, their stern.

When our two ships saw the other had fled, they gave chase, and trapped it between them, and it did the same thing, and again fled, and then a third time. They raked it with lead from both sides, fearing lest it escape yet again from their hands. While they were raking it with broadsides, they heard the captain telling his crew to descend to the hold lest they be struck by the lead that falling on them like rain. They realized from his voice that he was French, and stopped firing. They asked through the megaphone, "Who are you?" "I am Captain so-and-so", he answered. Then they knew who he was. He was the one who had left the port of Marseille to join them. When they had ascertained who he was, that he was in truth that captain, they regretted what they had done to him, and began to try to make amends.

The next day they sent him a sail, because all his sails had been shot to pieces. They advised him not to separate from them, and to accompany them until our ship was near the port of Smyrna. At that time a strong land breeze forced us back to the lands of the Morea. From there we returned, and on our return the wind and heavy seas drove us among the rocks located in that place, which faces Istanbul. We spent a day and a night among those rocks, and were sure our ship would break up and we would be lost. The next day, our Lord sent us a favourable wind and we were able get out from among those rocks safely. We thanked the Almighty Creator for his goodness and generosity to us.

Chapter IX

On Our Entry to the Lands of the East

We arrived safely in the port of Smyrna. After anchoring, I left the ship, along with the youth I have mentioned. When I disembarked from the skiff and planted my feet on land, and saw all the Muslims in the customs house, my heart trembled and I felt as if I were entering prison, and I regretted what I had done, leaving the land of the Christians and returning to Muslim captivity.

Then my companion turned to me and said, "Follow me wherever I go!" So I followed him until we arrived at the house of the French consul. It is an elegant house, with janissaries, dragomen and servants and so forth at the door. We went upstairs, and the youth asked permission to enter and speak to His Excellency the Consul. After obtaining permission, we stood before the consul. The youth began to tell him how the ambassador had sent him to France, how he had been stripped of everything by corsairs and was now returning to Istanbul to the ambassador. When he finished speaking, and the consul realized he was telling the truth, he immediately called for one of the dragomen, and commanded him to accompany us to the inn.

It was a charming place, where sea captains, merchants and travelers stayed. They gave us a place to sleep, with clean bedding and white sheets, like those in French inns, or even better. We stayed there for lunch and dinner, eating and drinking. The food was excellent, and the service as it should be. The next day that youth said to me, "Don't keep spending all your money on me. Get up, and follow me!"

I walked along with him and on our way looked at the sights of Smyrna. Near the harbour is a long, heavily populated quarter. All the houses are occupied by French merchants, and other Franks buy and sell there. Their womenfolk sit in the shops, just like in France. It is called 'the French quarter'. The main city is about a mile away, which is the town and city where the Muslim merchants live and the governors, as in the other provinces. Only Muslim merchants and other Ottoman subjects enter this quarter.

He took me to the Jesuit hospice.[173] When we entered, the head was surprised, for he had known that youth when he was in Istanbul, and they greeted one another. Then he took us into the refectory and entertained us and was very attentive to our needs. The head then asked what his situation was, and the reason for his destitution. So he told him what had befallen him, as has been previously related, and the head consoled and comforted him, for he knew the ambassador was very fond of him, and that he was chief of his household retainers.

Just as we were on the point of leaving, the youth asked the head how much money he could borrow, saying that he would return it to the head of their hospice in Istanbul.[174] "Help yourself", he answered, and immediately opened the hospice cash box and invited him to take whatever he needed. He took fifteen piastres and wrote out a receipt. Finally, we bade him goodbye and left.

When we were outside the Jesuit hospice, he gave me the money and said, "Keep it for travelling expenses". From there we went to the Capuchin monastery, and the prior entertained us too, and he borrowed ten piastres from him as well. After we left the monastery, he gave them to me, and said, "I was worried lest the money we took from the head of the Jesuits would not suffice, so I also borrowed these ten piastres in case we need them, and didn't have enough". So now I had twenty-five piastres, all of them in cash.

Then we walked about and looked at the sights and enjoyed ourselves. This is how we occupied ourselves for the next fifteen days, eating and drinking and sightseeing, until one day a large ship from Egypt arrived, laden with coffee, rice and textiles and making for Istanbul. The dragoman came to us and invited us to board that ship. That youth rose up and said to me, "Get up, my brother, let's go to the ship and sail!" I refused, and said to him, "I am going to Aleppo with the first caravan". "Don't think for a moment, my brother, that I am going to leave you anywhere, except in Istanbul."

In the end, I could do nothing but go with him. Accompanied by the dragoman, we came to the customs house in the port. There I saw the customs officer, and seated before him, the captain of the ship. The dragoman went up to the customs officer and spoke with him on behalf of the consul, asking him to take us in his ship and commending us to the captain's care. Then the dragoman turned and consigned us to the care of the customs officer, who in turn gave us into the hands of the captain, commending us to him, and the dragoman paid our *nūlīya*, that is, our fare.

Then the captain summoned the sailors who were manning the skiff, and ordered them to take us to the ship and give us a cabin all to ourselves and to look after us. We went with the sailors to the skiff, and found that the dragoman had sent us fifty ounces of biscuit, five ounces of hard cheese, fried fish and a bottle of wine. They even gave each of us five piastres for travelling expenses. We went to the ship and put our things in the cabin, that is, the little room.

We spent the day there, and early the next the sails were unfurled and off we went. We sailed in that sea until we sighted the long, wide strait of Istanbul. From there to the harbour of Istanbul is a voyage of four or five days. When we came to the mouth of the strait, the land breeze prevented us from entering. The captain decided to anchor in the port of Gallipoli, which is outside the strait. It is a little town. We went into town and walked around, returning to sleep on the ship. We stayed in that port for five days.

Then a sea wind rose and we set sail and entered the strait. Two days later another land breeze prevented us from going further. We anchored in a little port, waiting for a sea breeze. The wind came two days later, and we set sail and came to the harbour of Bujuk Jakmajā [175], and there we anchored.

That night we sighted two ships approaching us, and the captain thought they were corsairs from Malta. He sent immediately to inform the fort of the coming of these two ships. The fort began firing on them, and so did our ship, stopping them from entering the port. The two ships anchored out of gunshot of the fort and struck their sails, to show that they were not an enemy but it was impossible to stop the firing. Finally, they hung a lamp from the mainmast as a sign of peace, but even this did not stop the fighting. Everyone on our ship fled to the fort, while the people of the port took refuge in the mountains for fear of the corsairs.

When the people on the two ships saw that the men manning the fort did not trust the peace signals, they sent a skiff containing the ship's *yāzijī* and three officers. When the skiff reached the port, they fell upon them, arrested them and carried them up to the fort. Then they asked them, "Who are you? Why did you enter the strait?" "We are Flemings", they answered, "sailing about trying to buy wheat from the villages, but they won't sell us any without a *firmān* from the Grand Vizier, so we wanted to go to Istanbul to get a *firmān*, but on the way ran into French corsairs. We fled from them and came to this place to take refuge and be under the protection of the fort. And as for you, why are you making war on us and firing cannon at us as if we were your enemies?"

Their explanation satisfied no one, and they and the sailors who were with them in the skiff were imprisoned in the fort. Finally, the commander of the fort, along with several officers, came to our ship and consulted with our captain about what to do. He advised them, "You and I should go to their ship. I have two Franks in my ship, Frenchmen; we can take with us to translate, because one of them speaks Turkish".

They accepted his advice, and immediately prepared a skiff for us and we all boarded it. We headed for the largest ship and climbed onto it and entered the captain's cabin. We saw the captain and his companions sitting there. Before them were lighted candles and vessels of wine and cups and they were very merry and relaxed. The captain rose to his feet, as did those with him, and made us welcome. Then they entertained us with various kinds of sweets, refreshments and delicious drinks. We stayed there enjoying ourselves for two hours, then bade them goodbye and left, and sent them their companions from the fort. At that time, the Flemish captain asked our captain if he could kindly send his *yāzijī* with him so that he could accompany him to Istanbul to get the aforementioned *firmān* to buy wheat, as we have mentioned. Our captain agreed to that, and took the *yāzijī* with him to his ship.

A few days later, a sea breeze rose, and we sailed, along with the Fleming. We sailed until we came to the harbour of Buyuk Jakmajā and there we anchored. We went to look around the town, and everything we bought was paid for by that Fleming. Our stay at anchor lengthened, and the wait made that Fleming impatient, because the two ships were awaiting him.

He began to ask if it were possible to travel to Istanbul overland. They answered that it was, and that it was a trip of three days or less. Then he asked them to bring people to take him and travel with him. They immediately brought him a mount. Then he turned to us and invited us to travel with him. We refused, and told him we had already paid our passage on the ship, and the captain wouldn't let us go, because he had pledged to take us to Istanbul and deliver us to the house of the ambassador. He was extremely insistent, however, and said to us, "I will pay your passage. I can't travel alone, when I don't speak the language".

When we heard this, our hearts melted, and we went to the ship and left our things in the cabin and locked the door and asked permission from the captain to travel overland for the sake of that Fleming. "I pledged before the customs officer to take you to the house of the French ambassador", the captain answered. We said, "We have left our belongings in your ship, and when you have safely arrived, we will come to your ship and collect our things, and at that time give you a quittance from the dragoman, saying that we have arrived at the ambassador's house, and will collect our baggage". He was satisfied with our plan, so we said goodbye to him, and went to join the Fleming.

We found that two mounts had been readied for us and that he had procured ample provisions for the road. We all mounted and set off. We didn't stop travelling until we came to the city of Istanbul. We entered from the place called Topkapi, which is the beginning of the entry to the city. Here is a place called *Yedi Qillah*. [176] I noticed people digging very deep trenches in the ground there, and I asked, "What are these trenches for?" Our guide answered, "These trenches are dug in the search for pieces of marble, which are found in the earth here".

We rode on for about an hour until we came to a large harbour, where the custom house was located, and there we dismounted. We bought passage on a skiff, and crossed to Galata. There the

Fleming left us and went to Beg Oghlu.[177] I was uncertain what to do, or where to go, since I was a stranger. I asked the youth, my companion, to show me a place where I could stay, but he shook his head, and said, "Follow me to the house of my employer, the ambassador, that is your house!" I didn't want to go with him, but he insisted I do so.

So we went together, and climbed up to Beg Oghlu, where all the ambassadors lived. It is on an elevation. We were on the Kiz Kulasi [178], that is, 'The Maiden's Tower'. When Istanbul was under siege, this girl held out in the fortress, and bravely resisted for some time until they were able to take the fortress from her. It is a long story. We continued going up until we came to the main square, where the ambassadors' palaces are located.

At last, we came to the French ambassador's palace. It is larger and more beautiful than the others, and inside has a lovely garden. At the outer entrance to the palace was a group of terrifying-looking janissaries. When we came through the door, they all jumped up and greeted him. Then we entered the inner palace where the ambassador lived. When the ambassador's retainers saw him, they were astonished at his condition. Some of them went in and told the ambassador of his arrival. He summoned him into his presence and he entered, saying, "Follow me!" I did so, and we stood before the ambassador. When the ambassador saw the state he was in, he was astonished, and asked, "What on earth happened to you?"

The youth bowed to the ground, and said to him, "My lord, permit me to tell you what happened to me". Permission to speak was granted, and he bowed again, and told him what had befallen him since the time he left until his return, as we have previously related. The ambassador was very sorry for him, and consoled him. Then he asked about me, "Who is this young man?" "My Lord", he answered, "this young man saved my life, with help of the hand of God. He looked after me, comforted me, and dressed me in his clothes and accompanied me here." Then he told him everything that had happened.

By great good luck, I had the letter given me by the prince in Paris in my pocket, recommending me to the ambassador. I took out the letter and gave it to him, and after he read it, he welcomed me and said, "How can I be of service to you?" "My Lord", I answered, "if you like, you could accept me as one of your servants". "I've just received news from the Sultan of France," he answered, "that I must return to Paris, but stay here in my palace until the new ambassador arrives, and enter his service, for which I will recommend you." Then he turned to the youth, and ordered him to take care of me, and give me a room and a place to sleep, and that I should take my meals at the second table, with the chamberlains. I thanked him profusely for his generosity, and we left his presence.

The youth immediately summoned the majordomo and asked him on behalf of the ambassador to prepare a bedroom for me. He changed into costly garments, returning to his former self. When it was time to eat, they invited me to lunch with them, and I sat down with the chamberlains at the second table, which was near the ambassador's. When I entered, my companion seated me across from him, and said to his companions, "Treat this young man well, for my sake". Each of them took something from those delicious dishes and the roasted fowl and placed it before me. The ambassador's orchestra played from the moment the ambassador was seated until he was finished. The evening meal was the same, for it is the custom of ambassadors to have an orchestra play throughout lunch and dinner; they are always accompanied by lovely musical instruments, as I saw in Paris.

I continued for some time to eat, drink and indulge myself, until one day I told my companion that I wanted to go have a look at the city of Istanbul. "Willingly", he replied, and the next day he took me with him and we went down to Galata. On the way, he left me a moment to get a drink of water, and a drunken janissary jostled me and began to assault me in his drunkenness.

At that moment, my companion returned, and when he saw the janissary clutching me, and demanding the price of an arrack, he pulled him off me and kicked him in the leg and left him face down on the ground. I was afraid he would get us into terrible trouble because of this, for he seriously injured him. We walked away and left him there lying on the ground, and my companion didn't even look back. He said to me, "Come with me and don't worry!"

The Sights of Galata

Then we went down to Galata and I saw all the sights, which I enjoyed. There we boarded a skiff and crossed to Istanbul. First we went to the Valide Khan [179], a beautiful *khan* built of stone. Inside is another *khan*, and inside that, yet another. All the rooms are occupied by merchants, ship captains and money changers. It contains wealth beyond counting, because this *khan* is fire proof, and for this reason all the merchants and moneychangers dwell in it.

We strolled around the *khan* looking at everything. I saw people from Aleppo, but they didn't notice me. I recognized them, but didn't want them to recognize me. Among them were Ibn al-Qārī, and Shukrī ibn Shāhīn Čelebi and many others, not counting someone named *Khoja* Azāt, whose house is near my brother's. This man recognized me, and came up to me and greeted me, and identified himself. He invited me and my companion to his room, entertained us and gave us coffee, and was very attentive.

From there we went to the Sūq Tawīl, 'The Long Market'. This market contains every sort of craft. From it, we entered the Sūq al-Bālistān, also built of stone, because many valuable treasures are to be found in it. You can find anything you want here, every sort of merchandise, including weapons, and other precious things. Inside this market are storage chests for protecting valuables, fine clothing, and martin and ermine furs, from fire. Many people deposit chests full of money in that market for the same reason. No one locks their shop, because at night they lock the two outer gates with strong chains. Guards are stationed outside the gates, and stay awake all night. The result is a place as secure as the Sultan's treasury.

The Sublime Porte

From there we went to Bāb al-Humāyūn [180], that is, the king's palace. Then that youth said to me, 'Come in with me, so I can show you the mint'. We went in, and I saw a large open area with three streets. The first of these was on the left, and the gate led to the Qazrār Palace, which housed the king's harem. Anyone who entered it unwittingly was beaten with a club. The second street is in the middle, and leads to the king's inner palace. It is used only by the Grand Vizier and the great men of the state. The third street is on the left, and leads to the mint. Anyone can visit it, without harm or fear.

We reached the place that housed the mint, and went in. I saw a wide room, with two furnaces burning, into which they put the silver and gold ingots. On one side I saw a large pile of silver ingots, and on the other a similar pile of gold. In another place people were sitting pounding the ingots into slugs and heating them. On the other side they were sitting and forming those ingots by means of a compass into discs the size of piastres, half-piastres and quarter piastres. One of them would put the slug on the anvil while the other would twist the die and cut out the piastre, which would fall below. Others would stamp the coins with a die which inscribed the name, *tughra* [181] and date on both sides.

We left the mint and went to the church of Aya Sofia, which has now become the king's mosque because it is near his palace. The king prays there every Friday. We looked at it from the outside, because they do not allow Christians to enter it. I nevertheless saw that even from the outside its architecture is beyond description. It was built by the Christians kings of old.

From there we went to the Valide Mosque, a mosque with no rival in the city of Istanbul. Anyone may enter it, except for the domed area marking the direction of Mecca.[182] We left and passed on to the palace of the *Sāhib al-Hithām*, that is, the Grand Vizier.[183] The street that led there was crowded with people entering and leaving, making complaints or obtaining documents and so forth. I saw one of the pashas walking with only two bodyguards, and no one paid the least attention to him or stopped him, as if he were just anybody. We saw so many sights that we didn't return to our place until it was almost evening.

Arrival of the Venetian Ambassador

A few days later, news reached the ambassador that in three days the Venetian ambassador was to be received by the king, as he had recently arrived in Istanbul, and had already sent his gifts to the king. In three days he was going to be received by the king, as is the custom. Then the ambassador instructed the majordomo to prepare the costumes and the chamberlains to ready their regiment. By tradition, when a new ambassador was received, all the others would send their retinues to walk before him when he went to his reception. The French ambassador was in the habit of sending forty chamberlains, dressed in costumes of scarlet broadcloth, sent them by the Sultana [184], with embroidered sleeves, the front worked in gold-washed wire, wearing caps wrapped with gold turbans, their fair hair curled. According to what they told me, the price of each costume was more than five hundred piastres.

After the majordomo had readied everything, he found that three of the forty chamberlains were missing. He sent for two more, and I was chosen as the third. On the third day everyone donned their costume, as I have said, and I was one of them. We went to the house of the ambassador and the regiment formed up. The procession began at the house of the ambassador and reached all the way to Galata. The king's galley had arrived, and the ambassador boarded the royal galley and his retinue the others. They rowed to the *qarši*, I mean, to the port of Istanbul. There the janissaries and the chamberlains sent by the commander of the janissaries walked before them, along with others sent by the Grand Vizier, until they came to the king's inner palace. Only the Grand Vizier, the ambassador and the chief dragoman entered and proceeded to the king's chamber.

Three stairs led to it. They ascended the first and second, but before they ascended the third, the king entered a second chamber. On his entry, they draped the caftan bestowed by the king on the shoulders of the ambassador, and placed caftans on the shoulders of his retinue as well.[185] These were a sign of pleasure and peace loving on the part of the king. They left that place and entered the palace of the council, where they seated the ambassador on a chair especially for him in the council. Then they served him with drinks and dates and coffee and censed him with aromatics.

The ambassador then took his departure, the king's officials walking before him, along with the palace guard, confectioners, gardeners and beveragers and many others. They accompanied him to the jetty and the ambassador boarded the royal galley while the rest descended from the king's gate and were each taken to their palace with a retinue of chamberlains and janissaries, together with the chamberlains of the ambassador. When we came to the ambassador's palace, I saw a feast laid out for the janissaries and the others. It was a hundred cubits long, and was laid with every sort of sweet and refreshing drink, all in receptacles of bamboo. When they arrived at the feast, it was like the sack of a city. In a moment they devoured the sweets and cleared the plates and nothing at all was left of the feast.

A second feast was held inside the ambassador's palace for his chamberlains. Every sort of food was served, meat pies, *sanbūsik* [186], roast lamb and many other things. On every corner of the table was a barrel of wine, surrounded by many glass cups. Then they served us the food and drink, and we ate the food and drank that excellent wine. We toasted the ambassador's table and all cried out '*Viva!*' so loudly that they could hear us in the street. Then we left, and everyone went home. This is what I saw of the reception of the ambassador, except for his entry and exit from the king's palace, of which I saw nothing, but heard about from someone who had accompanied him inside. God knows best!

A few days later, a gentleman of high rank sent by the Sultan of France arrived with an order for the dismissal of the ambassador, and the demand that the palace and its contents be sealed for the next incumbent. From that moment the authority of the ambassador was undermined, and things would remain unsettled until the arrival of the new ambassador. The world closed in around me and it was no longer possible for me to stay in the palace, because most of the chamberlains had been laid off and their allowances cut. The dinners with musical accompaniment came to an end.

Hannā enters the service of a Venetian merchant

Not knowing what to do, I decided to move my things to an inn in Beg Oghlu. The head of the Jesuits, whose monastery was in Galata, and whom I had befriended, came and when he saw me, greeted me, just as I was on the point of leaving the palace. "Where are you going?" he asked. "To the inn", I replied. This didn't please him. "Why do you want to stay at an inn?" he said. "Then where, my Father, should I go?" I answered. He thought for a moment then asked, "Would you like to be a servant, my son?" "Yes, Father", I answered, "but with whom do you want me to enter service?" "Near our house in Galata", he said, "lives a Venetian merchant. He is a good man, and rich. If you wish, I can speak with him on your behalf." "Do just as you say, Father", I replied, "I am under your orders." Then he said to me, "Stay the night in the palace, and tomorrow I will take you to see him". Then he bade me goodbye and went off.

The next day he sent for me and said, "I spoke with the gentleman, and he agreed to take you on trial. Come". We left and went to the house of that gentleman. When we stood before him, he rose to his feet and welcomed the Father. Then the Jesuit said to him, "This is the young man I told you about. You can put your trust in him and in his service". This pleased the gentleman, and he set my wage at fifty piastres a year, plus half the commission at the gate from the purveyors of provisions, the other half being divided between the cook and another servant.

Then the Padre left and the gentleman gave me access to all the household vessels and the silver and brass, and gave me a key to the cellar and so forth. Then I went and moved my things from the ambassador's house to the merchant's. He gave me the key to my bedroom, and I put my belongings there. Then I inspected the room, and noticed that it was extremely dirty. I immediately began to sweep the floor and the rest of the house and put everything in order. I tidied the gentleman's bedroom, and that of his secretary and the dining room. I cleaned the brass and polished the silver and the knives. I went down to the cellar and filled the wine vessels and polished the cups. I took what was needed from the cellar, things like cheese and olives, and I knew how to do all this because I had learned to in Aleppo when I was in the service of M. Rambaut the elder, and then with M. Ramuset for twelve years, until the time I left Aleppo seeking to become a monk.

When the gentleman and his secretary came for dinner and saw how clean and orderly everything was, they were very pleased. So I stayed with him the first month, and he asked me, "Did you neglect to fill the jug with wine?" "It is still half full," I answered. Then he turned to the secretary and said to him, "During the time of his predecessor, a jug of wine never lasted a month". The cook and the *khizmatkār* [187] overheard what the gentleman said, and were not pleased. From that day onwards they hated me, because their treachery was revealed, but I didn't realize they wished me ill. I noticed the anger in their eyes, but paid no attention, and did not accuse them of anything.

The cook especially was implacably against me. I informed the gentleman of that and he immediately fired him, and started to look for a new cook. When I saw how concerned he was at being unable to find one he liked, I said to him, "Don't despair, I will cook for you until you find a cook you like". "Do you know how to cook?" he asked. "I do", I replied. "Thanks be to God!" he said.

I had learned how to cook from a cook who used to work for my master, M. Rambaut. So he decided to fire the new cook, and I cooked in his place, and he was well-pleased. Since at the time I was just a child [188], they were amazed at me. The upshot was that I became the cook, and the *khizmatkār* was under my orders. Envy and hatred of me grew in him, because the gentleman was so very happy with my cooking, and stopped looking for a cook. Soon the whole house was completely under my authority. I could command and forbid and do whatever I wished.

One night the gentleman had a dinner party and asked me for more food. I told the *khizmatkār* "Go and get such and such, do such and such", but he wouldn't do it, such was his hatred of me. I turned to him and scolded and abused him. Suddenly he drew a knife and fell upon me with satanic fury, trying to kill me. I put my trust in my guardian angel, and grabbed him, took hold of his hand and wrenched the knife away, flung him down and with all my strength tried to kill him.

The gentleman heard our cries, and came to the kitchen. He saw us struggling and hitting each other and yelled at us and we released each other. He turned to me and said, "Is this the place to fight? When we have guests? Get up, and get to work!" He didn't let me tell him what had been going on in his house. The fact was that I had shamed that devil, and I got up and prepared the dinner and service as usual. In the end, when the guests had left, I told the gentleman everything that had happened. He reassured me, and said, "Tomorrow I will get rid of him. You have my fullest trust. I know these Greeks well. They are malicious and without shame". He did not let me retire until my fears were put at rest.

At last I left and went to my room and locked the door from the inside for fear of being attacked in my sleep. I lay on my bed that night thinking. It occurred to me that if the gentleman fired that scoundrel, he might attack me one night in the street with his knife and kill me, because for the Greeks in that city, it is a small thing to kill someone, because they can immediately turn Turk and enroll in the corps of janissaries. For this reason my fears increased, and I couldn't sleep all night. I was in a quandary about what to do.

Then I remembered that I had run across a Maronite from Aleppo named Hannā ibn al-Zaghbī in the Jesuit church. This man had been an acquaintance of mine in Aleppo. After we had greeted one another, I had invited him to go with me to the house of the Venetian merchant where I was staying. There I entertained him, and then asked his reason for coming to Istanbul. He told me, "The reason I came to this country was in order to learn the craft of polishing cloth [189], because it is unknown in Aleppo. Now God has eased my way, and I have found a skilled craftsman who will teach me, and return with me to Aleppo. He will bring with him the folding polisher which is made of steel with all its moving parts. And this is what I wished. I am now awaiting the first caravan heading for Aleppo, which I will accompany".

After I had told him what had happened to me, and how I came to this country, he said that I should return with him to my homeland, and not waste my time in this exile. "Go to your family; don't imperil yourself in this affair." He said many other things besides this. I refused, and had no intention of following his advice. He repeated it many times, urging me to go with them, but I kept refusing. But that night, when his words came to mind, I decided to return to Aleppo in his company.

The next day I went to the gentleman and asked his permission to leave his employ. He began to flatter me, and comfort me by saying, "Have no fear, I will this moment drive him from my house, set your mind at rest". These words of his did not reassure me. On the contrary, I held to my decision and asked to be allowed to leave him. When he saw that I was resolved to go, he reckoned up the wages he owed me and the half-share of the gate receipts as we had agreed, and gave me all of it. Then I bade him farewell, and gathered up my things, returning to him everything in my possession that belonged to him, the silver and the brass utensils and other things, and left his house and went to the Jesuit hospice which was near the house of that gentleman.

I went in to the head of the monastery and told him what had happened, and how it had all ended, and asked if I could lodge with him in the monastery until the caravan departed for Aleppo. The head answered me, saying "My son, we can't accept anyone from the laity in our monastery. I will give you a key to the guest house in which the French captains and other travelers stay. At the moment, a Father is staying there, awaiting a bishop from Christian lands, in order to travel to Persia". [190]

I thanked him for his generosity and took the key. He sent one of the servants of the monastery with me to show me the place, which was near the jetty. I went into the house, which had two floors. Inside were small rooms, and inside each one was a dais with two sleeping places, made up with clean sheets and blankets. I put my belongings in one of the ground floor rooms and went out to the market and bought a clay casserole and two clay plates, so I could cook anything I wanted for myself.

That evening the Father came to visit me. He was staying in the room above mine. I chatted to him for a while then went to bed. Around midnight I heard a knocking noise, which kept me awake all night. The next night was the same. On the third night, I got out of bed to find out what the noise was. I went up to the door of the Father's room and I saw through the cracks in his door that he was prostrating himself before the crucifix and praying and beating his breast. From time to time he bent forward and struck his forehead on the floor. Having seen this, I went back downstairs and slept in my bed without fear.

On the fourth night I said to him, "Father, you aren't getting any sleep! What are you doing?" He sighed and groaned from a grieving heart and said, "O my son, when I look at all these people in the city, all of them Muslims with their souls bound for perdition, I feel so sorry for these souls who have lost the way to salvation, for whom Satan is their leader. I have been beseeching my Lord Jesus the Messiah to enlighten the mind of the Muslim leader, I mean the king, so that he might believe in Him and guide this flock whose only shepherd now is the Wolf of Hell". He turned to me and said, "You too must pray with me, perhaps God will accept your prayer".

When I heard these words from him I was astonished, and said to him, "This is something beyond comprehension". 'Everything that is impossible for man", he answered, "is possible for God." The zeal of this Father amazed me. I left him and went to my room, while he continued to pray and lament all night.

This Father taught me how to make an ointment to cure every affliction of the eye. He placed it before me and said, "Have no fear, put it on any disease of the eye. You can earn your bread with this ointment for the rest of your life". He showed me other things useful for bodily health. In those days I was not interested in learning. On the contrary, I was careless, and governed by the impetuousness of youth and ignorance.

Launching five new warships

I used to go out and walk through the streets of Istanbul and look at the sights and the markets and the streets. I heard that Sultan Ahmad had ordered the construction of five large warships, each with four decks and 72 guns. I heard from someone that the ships had been finished and that the king had ordered that they be launched on Thursday. This was a terrific spectacle. I and some friends from Aleppo decided to rent a boat so we could go out and watch.

When the day came, everyone in Istanbul went down to the seaside. You would have seen the harbour so full of boats, so crammed together that you could walk from one to another. They told me on good authority that there were to be found in Istanbul harbour twelve thousand boats paying license fees, not counting those belonging to the *agha*s, each of whom had two or three for transport and pleasure.

They launched the first ship into the water with a tremendous splash and everyone yelled *Allah! Allah!* and embraced his companions. Then they launched the second, then the third, and finally the fifth, all in the presence of the king and the ministers and all the great men of the state. What a day it was! And this is what I saw of the launching of the ships in Istanbul, but hearing about it is not the same as seeing it, which was something unique.

Arrival of Eight French men warships

A few days later eight warships sent by the Sultan of France arrived. One after another they entered the harbour, and when they reached the King's palace, which is on the left hand as you enter the harbour from the sea, they began to fire their guns in salute. The smallest of the ships had seventy guns and carried some seven hundred soldiers, not counting the crew. When the first finished firing, the second entered and began firing broadsides from both sides, then came the third and did the same as the first and second. The outskirts of Istanbul were terrified, and thought the French had taken the city. Many people fled to the interior. You could see the smoke filling the harbour. No one could see his companion, or hear a word he was saying.

Then the Grand Vizier sent a *bash agha*[191] to the captain on his behalf to ask him to stop the cannonade, because His Highness the King was getting a headache. At that moment the rest of the ships entered, without saluting, and anchored in the harbour, as is customary. Then the ambassador's interpreters went to greet the admiral with all respect. They then went formally to inform the Grand Vizier of the arrival of the eight galleons sent by the Sultan of France, and that he had come to deliver to His Highness the

King, Sultan Ahmad, eight anchors for his new ships, which he had presented as a gift, and that he had dismissed the ambassador because he had failed to do what he had asked. Then he ordered the Grand Vizier to bring the admiral to him the following day, and to immediately allot the ships abundant provisions.

The Grand Vizier presented the admiral with valuable gifts and honoured him greatly on behalf of the king. At the same time, he warned him saying "Make sure you don't neglect to ask for anything we can do for you". The admiral answered, "Tell your Lord that at this time prices are high in our country because of a lack of wheat, and what we want from His Highness the King and from Your Eminence is to issue us with a *firmān* authorizing us to make the rounds of the villages and buy grain, and that no one should oppose us. The vizier answered, "I will immediately grant you what you wish", and bade him farewell. When the vizier told the king of the admiral's request, the king issued a document in his own hand, ordering the eight galleons to be filled with good wheat and not to accept payment. The galleons stayed twenty days, while the vizier sent galleys to the estates and brought the required wheat.

During those days he released almost two hundred captives. They had jumped in the sea and climbed aboard the galleons, thus escaping capture. Because whenever a captive succeeds in grasping the side of a ship, he is free, and no one may remove him from that galleon. On the contrary, they pardoned them for the sake of the Sultan of France.

A Swedish Prince arrives in Istanbul

During this time, one of the princes of the Sultan of Sweden arrived in Istanbul.[192] He wished to tour the area, and his retainers were searching the inhabitants to find people who spoke Italian and Turkish. One of my friends came to me and he was that chamberlain of the ambassador that had accompanied me from Marseille and he wanted to introduce me to the prince as an interpreter. I was pleased with the idea, and I gave him my word and assured him I would travel with him. It was my firm intention to go with that prince, because I had heard that after his tour, he would be returning to his country overland.

My friend wanted to take me and introduce me to the prince. On the day I was going to see the prince, the aforementioned Hannā ibn al-Zaghbī came to me. When he heard that I was going to that prince, he was not at all pleased, and began to dissuade me, doing everything he could to prevent me from going. He said, "The caravan is leaving for Aleppo in two days, and I have rented an animal for you, from Ahmad of Aleppo, the guide, and I already gave him a deposit". He went on nagging me until I changed my mind about travelling with the prince.

Departure from Istanbul

When I had changed my mind, I gave him my word that I would go with him to Aleppo. Then he said to me, "We have to get our things ready for the journey. We need to take with us some things that will be useful on the road. We need an *oka* [193] of coffee, several *dirham*s of cloves and ginger and other spices, as well as some sheets of pretty *ebru* [194] marbled paper, and a little soap, because these things are much more in demand on the road than cash. The people in the country will give us whatever we need to eat, and for us it will be sufficient". I accepted what he said and took out one gold coin and gave it to him, and said, "Buy whatever you want".

He went off, and I settled my affairs and went to say goodbye to the head of the Jesuits and my friend the chamberlain. Then I awaited the arrival of the aforementioned Hannā. He arrived in the afternoon two days later, saying, "Get up, we're leaving!" I left Istanbul in the middle of June in the year 1710. I picked up my belongings and went with him to the harbour. He had rented a boat to take us to Eskidar. I met that gentleman, the master polisher, with all his equipment. I put my luggage in the boat and we went to the Eskidar landing. I lifted my things from the boat, and we went to rent a room in the *khan*, where we stayed while awaiting the guide and the caravan.

Soon the *awādlaq* pasha of Afiyun Qara Hisar [195] arrived with our caravan leader, along with other caravan leaders. We asked the reason for his delay, and he answered that they had been searching for mounts, and that he and the other caravan leaders had been politely constrained to agree to take the pasha. "We were told to leave your baggage and load that of the pasha. But if you want, I still have three horses at your disposal, and seven for myself. I am now going to travel with the pasha to Afiyun Qara Hisar. If you want to travel with me, you may; if not, you can hire someone else. It's up to you."

When we had absorbed this news, we were downcast, and couldn't decide what to do. We made the rounds of the other caravan leaders, but couldn't find anyone to take us. So we decided to travel with our caravan leader to Afiyun Qara Hisar. We stayed there the rest of that day, and on the next, the pasha came to Eskidar. They immediately set off with the *awādlaq* pasha, and we followed their track until we came to the place where our road began. We had crossed over in the boat with our animals to that place and now rode with the awādlaq until we came to Kawarkoy.[196]

When we arrived, the caravan camped a mile from the town in a barren, hot place. I and my friends dismounted near the village in a meadow with trees and springs, flowing as in a garden. When the caravan had made camp, the caravan leader came and ordered us to camp where the rest of the caravan had alighted. He told us the people of the village were villainous and bandits. "They will come at you during the night and strip you of everything." Neither I nor my companions wanted to leave, and we told him, "We have nothing worth stealing!" He couldn't make us leave.

So we spent the night in that place, and the caravan leader sent his brother to spend the night there with us. He told him to yell when the caravan was about to leave, so that he could come and get us so we could travel with the caravan. Because we feared that the people of that village would attack us at night, and steal our things, we each tied up our packs and then went to sleep. In the middle of the night the caravan set off, and the caravan leader yelled to his brother to bring us. His brother replied, but then fell asleep again and didn't wake us, for we were all sleeping and didn't hear.

An hour later the boy woke up and listened for the caravan, but saw nothing and didn't hear the sound of the animal's bells and realized that the caravan had departed. He started to yell and abuse us, saying, "This time they are going to rob you and steal all your things and animals too!" We jumped up and loaded our packs on the animals and rode away. When we came to the place where the caravan had camped we didn't see a soul, only the traces of a campfire. We stopped there and noticed that there were two tracks. We asked the boy which we should take, but he didn't know which the caravan had followed. We were confused and frightened lest the inhabitants of the village attack us.

We were still in those straits and confusion when, Praise be to God, I noticed that my mount was setting off and seemed to know the way. So I dismounted and loosened his halter, and he took the upper path, and we followed on horseback. We reached the highest place, and saw beneath us a deep canyon. From its depths we could hear the jangle of horses' bells, and were certain that our road lay there. We were overcome with grief at the thought of having to retrace our steps. The boy who was guiding us called out to his brother, then lay flat on the ground to see if he could hear his brother reply, which he did, saying "How did you know to take the upper road?" Then we rejoiced that they, not we, were the ones that were lost.

We waited for them until they arrived, then we all followed the true path until dawn. Two hours later the pasha passed by us, and we followed him. Heavy rain fell all day, so hard that all our baggage was soaked. The downpour continued until evening without let-up.

When the pasha saw that the rain was not going to stop, he took refuge in a village near the road. He and his retinue entered it and drove the owners out of their houses and moved in. His soldiers pitched their tents outside the village and took refuge from the rain. As for us, we remained standing in the village square in the rain. We asked the peasants if they could give us shelter, even just a stable, so we could get out of the downpour. They told us their wives and families were already hiding between the legs and feet of the horses and cows.

We had no idea what to do. We were standing there trying to decide what to do, when, May the Lord be Praised! a good looking young man suddenly appeared before us, and asked my companions about me, for he had realized I was in disguise. I was dressed as a

Frank, my hair was long and I was wearing a stone-marten fur *qalpaq* on my head. I told my friends "Tell him I am a doctor".

When he heard that I was a doctor, he was delighted and beseeched them to ask me to go with him, because he had a sick man for me to look at. At this point, I spoke to him in Turkish, saying, "If you can give us refuge with you this night, I will examine your invalid". He invoked blessings upon me, but said, "I am afraid someone in the pasha's retinue will discover where I live, and force me and my womenfolk out of the house and take it over. But I will walk some distance in front of you, and you can follow me so that I can bring you into my home".

I agreed, and said to him, "Go, and we will follow at a distance". So he walked in front of us and we followed through a grove of trees beyond the village and stopped at the mouth of a cave. He bent down and vanished into the interior before our eyes. When we reached the place, we saw that he was there waiting for us. We entered the cave and saw before us a door. He knocked on the door, giving those inside a signal to open. They opened it, and inside we saw three youths standing. I and my companions jumped back, fearing the place belonged to a gang of robbers. But what could we do if we had fallen among thieves?

We stood there mulling this over, when suddenly the young man came out with the others, and they took the reins of our horses from our hands and led them inside. Then they invited us to enter. We went in with them. The place was spread with carpets, and in the center was a stove. Then they fetched our baggage and clothes. Seeing that we were soaked, they immediately lit a fire in the stove in order to dry them. Then the youth who had brought us there made us welcome.

Evening had fallen, and we dried our clothes and rested a little. The youth asked the men standing around to bring us the evening meal, and one of them went off and prepared a feast, laying out food and napkins on our laps. They brought drinking water and a bowl to drink from. All this time we were astounded at what had happened to us, and how Our Lord, May He be Praised! had sent that youth to us to give us shelter, and extend his hospitality to us.

Next, they served dinner. There was a big plate of rice with lamb, a large serving dish of mutton stew, and roasted pullets on skewers. Everything was delicious. The youth joined us for dinner, and when we were done, he brought a bowl and pitcher of water to wash our hands. Then he served a large pot of coffee, and filled all our cups twice over.

Then he prepared our water pipes, and we all talked for a little, and I said, "Where is the patient you mentioned. I'd like to take a look at him, and do what I can for him, for you have overwhelmed us with your generosity". "Finish your pipe, then set my mind at rest about him." When we had finished our pipes, the youth got up and invited me to go with him. We entered a corridor which ended in a door. He knocked, and it was the harem. He told them to get out of sight. Then we entered, and found ourselves in a pretty courtyard. He took us to a room, beautifully furnished and decorated.

An elderly gentleman was lying in the bed. He was the youth's father, and owner of the village. I sat down beside him and took his pulse. It was uneven and very weak and he was unable to catch his breath. His sickness came from the amount of phlegm in his lungs. I consoled and encouraged him by telling him, "It's nothing serious. Don't worry, this phlegm is the culprit, and I will quickly remove it, and you will find relief and be able to get up from your bed". I told his son to order them to pluck two chickens tonight, because the cure requires that he drink their broth. I told him not to salt it and advised him to make a deep bowl of broth.

At last I bid him goodbye and left them and went to join my companions. I had brought with me some tablets which my master had brought along for the journey. He had given them to several people, and I had seen their remarkable effect when added to various broths, because their composition was beneficial to the four humours of man, that is, black bile, phlegm, yellow bile and blood. If someone takes a single tablet, it acts on all four humours. It takes effect within two hours, and then the patient will be fine and able to return to his work as if he had never drunk a potion. I saw this for myself, and in others as well. I still had ten or twelve of these tablets which he had given to me to take and had forgotten.

At last, when I had returned from visiting that patient, I opened the packet and took one of the tablets, ground it up and wrapped it in paper so it would be ready. Then I and my companions lay down to sleep until morning, when the youth came to wake me. I quickly got up and took the paper with the medicine with me, and we went to the patient and found him sleeping. I asked them for a cup of broth, and poured the medicine into it and gave it to the patient, ordering him to drink it to the last drop. After he had done so, and rested for a quarter of an hour, he began to choke violently and cough, until he almost fainted. Then I told them to give him another bowl of broth. A little while after he had drunk it, he asked for a bowl and vomited, filling it half full, all black and yellow bile and other horrible stuff. When he had finished vomiting, I asked them to give him another bowl of broth. When he had drained it, he asked to go outside. When he came back, I gave him another bowl of broth, and continued to do so, while his stomach heaved until his body was cleansed of all the phlegm and humours which were lodged inside. The result was that after two hours had gone by, he was able to sit up and relax, asking for his water pipe.

At that point I told them to add a little rice to the broth and make a chicken soup, to give him strength to get out of bed and go wherever he wanted. At last I bade him goodbye and started to return to my companions. The patient said, "Wait a moment, doctor!" and pulled a purse from under his pillow and took out a handful of *dirham*s and tried to give them to me. "God forbid that I should take anything from you!" I said, "You are the generous person who took us into your house and fed us from your provisions. Your son treated us with great courtesy. Because of this, there is no way I can repay you for your kindness".

Thereupon he gave the coins to his son, for him to give to me, but I refused to accept them, and went to my companions. And what did I see, but they had brought us breakfast and coffee! Afterwards, they gave us four boiled chickens, forty hard-boiled eggs, cheese and bread and placed them on the tablecloth we had brought with us. At that moment the first whistle of the pasha sounded, and they fetched our horses from the stable, after they had strapped on their barley, that is, their fodder. They loaded on our baggage and we put on our boots and readied ourselves to ride. Then the second whistle sounded, and we mounted and bade farewell to that youth, thanking him profusely. The third whistle blew, and the pasha mounted, and we followed him until we were out of the village.

We saw that our caravan leader was acting as if he were crazy, for he had been looking for us, and when he saw us, he was astounded, saying "Where were you? Where did you spend the night? I have spent all night looking for you!" Then we told him everything that had happened. He hadn't noticed how they had brought the animals and loaded them and given them feed early in the morning. At that he smiled, and said, "How I wish you had taken me with you! If you had, I wouldn't have had to spend all night in the rain".

At that moment I told my companions, "If anyone asks about me, tell them I am a doctor, so that I can travel this road in comfort". From that day forth, news spread throughout the land, that I was a doctor. Many men in the pasha's retinue summoned me to treat them. I wrote them prescriptions and sometimes gave them purgatives.[197] The result was that we travelled in the company of the pasha, receiving great courtesy from his retainers. They cosseted me and honoured me and even did me the courtesy of allowing me to stay in their tents.

And so we journeyed on until we arrived at Eski Shahr [198], a small but densely populated town. There is a *qablūja*, that is, a spring with very hot, suphurous water in the town. Built above the sulphurous water was a sort of bathhouse. All the inhabitants of the city used to go there to take the waters. When we arrived, the pasha pitched his tent about three miles outside the city. The news spread that he was going to stay there three days. We decided to stay in the city, till the time came for the pasha to leave. We rented a room in the market, and slept there. A Christian who was staying in that market came to visit us. He was from Afiyun Qara Hisar. He began to question my companions about me. They answered that I was a doctor. He came to me and showed me his eye. It was swollen, and covered with a white film. He begged me to cure him. My heart softened for him, and I took out a pot of the ointment

I have mentioned before and put some in his eye and told him to come back the next morning so that I could apply more.

On the third day we left the city and went to the campground on the outskirts. It was almost evening, because we knew that the next day the pasha was setting forth. I and my companions were sitting there talking when a thought occurred to me. I said to my companion from Aleppo, Hannā ibn al-Zaghbī, that all the retainers of the pasha knew that I was a doctor. If the pasha happened to fall ill, what was I going to do, since I knew very little of medicine? "Don't worry", he said, "when the time comes, God will guide you." We were still discussing this, when suddenly two chamberlains of the pasha appeared, asking some of the people, "Where is the doctor?" They pointed us out to them. When they came over to us, they asked, "Which of you is the doctor?" "I am" I said. "Get up!" he ordered, "Orders of the keeper of the pasha's harem!"

I got up, my heart in my mouth, and went with them. The pasha, when he fell ill and feverish, went with his womenfolk to the house of the *agha* of the village, and ordered them to go to the city and fetch a surgeon to bleed him. They answered, "There is a very skilled French physician right here among the janissary corps". "Bring him!" commanded the pasha. This was the reason I had been summoned.

When I came to the dwelling in which the pasha was staying, I saw a man of distinction standing at the door. He was the keeper of the harem. When I stood before him, he said "Greetings. Come with me and take a look at His Excellency, our Efendi, because he is ill, and can't get relief". Then I excused myself, saying that I didn't have my medicine chest with me, because I had sent it by ship to Aleppo, while I went overland in order to see something of the country. "Our pasha is not ill," he answered, "but has had some sort of attack. Yesterday evening he went to the hot spring at night. When he came out, still sweating, the cold wind hit him, and his face swelled up and got hot".

He ordered me to enter, and I accompanied him to the pasha, who was in his bedroom asleep. I knelt beside him and felt his wrist and found it very hot, as if he had a high fever. His face was swollen and painful, and he was gasping like a bull. I told the keeper of the harem that I needed some oil of roses, and he said, "I will send a man right now to the city to bring us some". When the pasha heard that I wanted oil of roses, he ordered him to go to the treasurer and get a little bottle of French oil of roses that a French doctor had sent him. He had two bottles, and he brought one of them. When I got the bottle of oil, I had the idea of adding something else to it, so that it would appear that it contained some ingredient other than just oil.

I went back to my companions and consulted Hannā, whom I have mentioned before, and he said, "There is nothing better than *jādbūn* ointment [199], because it reduces swelling'. I had some of that ointment, so I took a little and returned to the pasha. I said to that gentleman, the keeper, "Bring me a brass pan". I poured in the oil and heated it over the fire and then threw in a dollop of ointment, until it was completely melted. Then I anointed the head of the pasha, which he had rested on my knees, rubbing the oil on his cheeks and chin and under his chin as well. Then I asked the gentleman to heat two towels for me, and after I had finished anointing him, I wrapped him in one of the towels, and tied the other on his forehead. Then I lifted his head back onto his pillow.

The pasha turned to me and said that his head ached very much. I replied, "I will give you something that will make your head feel better". I had in my possession a kind of herb, like anise, from Egypt, that was good for headaches. I immediately went and brought that herb and placed it in the pasha's palm and invited him to sniff it. I then asked the keeper to bring His Excellency a cup of coffee. When he had finished the coffee, they brought him the water pipe, and when he had finished smoking, his headache receded, and he became comfortable. Then I kissed the hem of his garment and left, cautioning the Keeper not to give him anything at all to eat until I returned to examine him.

Then I returned to my companions. Scarcely an hour had passed when he sent someone to get me. When I got there, the keeper met me, saying "The pasha asked for food, and you told me not to give him anything. What do you think?" "Make him soup and lemon juice" I answered, "and now I will go in and examine him. When I return, I will tell you whether you can feed him or not". So I went in and took his pulse. I saw that he was still feverish, but less so than before. Then I said to the pasha, "O My Lord, I cannot permit you to eat while your fever continues. Be patient a little while longer, till the fever passes. Then you can have soup, but nothing else". He accepted my advice, and continued to fast, while I returned to my companions.

They had prepared our evening meal, and we dined and were having coffee. It was after sunset, and the pasha was hungry and demanding something to eat. The keeper sent for me, and I went into his presence. He told me, "The pasha can bear it no longer. He wants to eat". I went in, and saw that he was thwarted and that they had prevented him from having food brought to him. I knelt down and took his pulse, and saw that the fever had receded. Then I told the gentleman to bring the soup and the lemon juice, and they immediately brought in a large porcelain bowl of chicken soup and another containing a chicken. I poured a little of the lemon juice in the soup, and invited him to eat. He ate the soup until almost nothing was left in the bowl. Then he asked us to joint the chicken so he could eat it. I said to him, "Slowly, My Lord, I fear lest your fever return". He listened to what I said, but I could see how much he longed to eat. I cut off a single chicken wing and gave it to him. He turned to the Keeper and said, "Do you see how French doctors treat their patients?"

In the end, he ate that chicken wing and washed his hands and they brought him a cup of coffee. When he finished it, they brought out his water pipe. He was visibly refreshed, and the fever had subsided. This was because of the help of Almighty God, May He be Praised, and not my skill. I was inspired by Almighty God, and His generosity, which guided me through this crisis. Then I got up and unfastened the towel on the Pasha's face, and saw that the swelling was much less, only a little was apparent. Once more I heated some oil, and bathed his cheeks and chin, and replaced the towels as they were. Then I kissed the hem of his garment and requested permission to return to my quarters. The pasha then said to me, "I want to travel tomorrow". I answered, "My Lord, I will come early tomorrow to examine you, and tell you whether or not you can travel". Then I left for my quarters.

When morning came, he summoned me to his presence. I went and entered and asked the keeper how the pasha was feeling, and he answered that he was fine, and had slept well. Then he asked me to go in with him to see the pasha. When we entered, I saw the pasha sitting up smoking, and he looked very well, with no trace at all of swelling. Then the pasha asked me, "Do you want me to travel?" "My Lord", I answered, "it is up to you. But if you do, make sure your stages are as short as possible, because I am afraid the sun's heat will exacerbate your condition." "Fine", he said. He told the keeper to notify them to pitch the tents at a place two hours distant. Then he gave the order to sound the first trumpet. This was the signal to march. So I went up and kissed the hem of the pasha's garment and returned to my companions.

I was very happy, and gave them the good news about the recovery of His Excellency the Pasha, and how he was now in excellent health. We all thanked God, then loaded our packs on the horses and got ready to travel. Then the third trumpet sounded and the pasha mounted and the band started playing. We rode on until we came to where the tents had been pitched, no more than two hours away. The pasha dismounted and went in to his pavilion; then the cavalry dismounted and went to their tents. My companions and I dismounted near the tent of the treasurer, because we were acquaintances of His Excellency the Pasha.

Scarcely had I alighted, when the pasha's chamberlain-in-chief came and summoned me, saying 'His Excellency the Pasha wants you!' I went with him, and we entered the pavilion and I saw the keeper waiting for us. Together we appeared before His Excellency the Pasha, who was reclining on two cushions. I went up to him and took his pulse, and found him to be in perfect health. He said, "I want you to give me some of the stuff you put in that oil of roses, because I saw how quickly and effectively it reduced the swelling". "I hear and I obey", I replied, and immediately went and cut a large chunk of the ointment and brought it to His Excellency wrapped in a piece of clean paper. I kissed his hem, and gave it to him and he was pleased. After requesting permission, I left the pavilion.

I had hardly taken one step when one of the chamberlains ordered me to return to the Keeper. When I stood before him, he said to me, 'His Excellency, our Efendi, has ordered a housing allowance for you. He sent for the *qonaqjī*, the quartermaster [200], and ordered him to assign the Doctor *Bashi* quarters and fodder for his animals. The quartermaster asked me, "How many in your party?" "Three", I answered. From that time onwards, whenever we arrived at a castle or village, he gave us a sealed order directed to the headman of the village, and he would lodge us in a house. The owners of the house undertook to feed us, serve us an evening meal and give us fodder for our horses.

After a number of days, we arrived near the city of Afiyun Qara Hisar, which was the head-quarters of the pasha. The pasha alighted in a place a day's journey from the city, and sent to tell us that he was planning to stay there five or six days in order to collect taxes from the peasants and landowners who lived there and were under his authority. He dismissed the caravan leaders who had come with him from Eskidar [201] and paid them the rent of their animals and their expenses.

Our caravan leader came to us and suggested we go to the aforementioned city that night. When I heard what the caravan leader had to say, I wanted to go back and ask permission from the pasha to leave. Hannā stopped me from doing so, by saying, "What if the pasha doesn't want you to go, and says 'Stay here with me!' You are in his power. What kind of answer can you give? Let's just go, and get out of this mess". I realized he was right, and I changed my mind about going to the pasha, fearing lest he prevent me from leaving.

In the end, we stayed there until midnight and then travelled until the afternoon of the following day, when we arrived at the city. When we entered, and were walking along, the man whose sore eyes I had treated in Eski Shahr chanced upon me. When he recognized me, he embraced me, kissed me and welcomed me with joy. He invited me to stay in his house. I refused, saying "There are three of us. But I would ask you to show us a nice place where I and my companions can stay". He took us to a *qaysarīyya* ²⁰² and asked the door keeper to give us a nice room. Then we went upstairs with him and he opened a room for us. The man who had taken us there brought us a mat and rug, and bedding from his house, told us not to cook dinner, and went off.

That evening he brought us the evening meal and he brought with him a jug of arrack and a jug of wine and sat down to dine with us until nightfall. He told me, "I can't thank you enough for the wonderful thing you have done for me by treating my eye, which was damaged and I couldn't see a thing". "Thank God, my brother, this was the work of Our Lord, and it was He who cured your eye, because I don't believe that it was my drops that cured you." Finally, he thanked me again, profusely, and went home.

We stayed there that night in the greatest comfort until dawn when the sun came out. After we had breakfasted and had our coffee and were sitting around chatting, a good-looking, well set up Christian youth appeared. He asked me to go with him to his house to examine someone's eyes. "No, my brother", I answered, "I won't go to visit anyone. Bring the man to me, so that I can examine his eyes." The reason the youth had come to me was that he had heard from that man that I had cured his eye after it had become damaged, and he had told him where I was.

Then he began pleading that I go with him to his house. I refused, as I did not want to go with him. When I assumed he had lost all hope of my going with him, he took me aside and told me, "The person I was speaking about to you is my wife, to whom I have been married a year. It is not possible that she should enter the *qaysarīyya*". He took both my hands in his and said, "For God's sake, come with me! Have no fear, we are Christian folk". When I heard this, I decided to go with him. My companion, the aforementioned Hannā, did not want me to go, lest word of the presence of a renowned physician spread in the town, because there was no doctor there. This was the reason why he did not want me to listen to him.

In the end, I took my box of eye drops and went with him to his house. When we entered, he immediately placed a table before me and invited me to lunch with him. After we had eaten, and drunk our coffee, they brought in the young lady. She was very beautiful. I examined her eyes, and saw that they appeared healthy and clear, with nothing obvious the matter with them. I asked her husband, "What does she complain of about her vision? As far as I can tell, there is nothing wrong with it". The young man answered that she could see nothing. So I asked her how she saw the world, and she said that all she saw was darkness, and couldn't distinguish light from dark, man from woman. I was sure there must be water trapped in the pupils of her eyes, and as far as I knew, this was incurable according to the best physicians. I was therefore very sad for her, but in order to comfort her husband, I put drops in her eyes, and gave her husband some more so that he could continue treating her. Afterwards, I said goodbye and went back to join my companions, feeling very sorry for the girl.

I saw that there were people waiting for me, some sick, some with eye diseases, and some wanting to take me to their homes to examine invalids. I had no idea what to do. I gave some of them eye drops, and prescribed things for the sick. The news that there was a very learned French doctor staying in such-and-such a *qaysariyya* spread in the city, and people came and went and I did what I could for them, till the third day after our arrival.

Then what did I see, but the door keeper approaching, with two chamberlains of the governor of the town. They summoned me to his presence. The reason was that a *qabījī* [203] had appeared along with forty horsemen. He had been sent by the Grand Vizier, with in his care a young man who was the nephew of Nasīf Pasha, who at that time was the pasha of the *hajj*. He was held in high esteem in the state because he had led the pilgrimage for a number of years, and always brought the pilgrims safely back to Syria. He had reduced the Arab tribes to obedience and opened the pilgrimage route, and for this reason won renown and a high position.

It happened that he was angry with his sister's son, the aforementioned nephew, and wanted to kill him, because he had stolen from the funds he had collected in taxes from the provinces and for which he was responsible. When the nephew heard that his uncle had ordered his death, he fled at night and went into hiding. Then he travelled in disguise to Istanbul and took refuge with the Grand Vizier, telling him the whole story. The Vizier took pity on him, and protected him. After a time, his uncle heard he was being protected by the state, and realized how he had managed to escape his vengeance. Because of this, he laid hold of the Egyptian tax receipts for two years. Then he sent a message to the Vizier, saying "I won't send the treasure unless you send me my nephew, because I have an account to settle with him".

So the Grand Vizier decided to send him his nephew in the custody of a captain, a *qabījī* , so that he could bring him face to face with his uncle, and then return him safely to Istanbul. A specific number of days was imposed for the journey, which was to take place without impediment, by means of a royal order from the king. Now this youth was terrified that when he arrived, his uncle would kill him, for Nasīf Pasha feared neither the Grand Vizier nor the state. His forebodings and fears increased on the road, and he fell ill, and could no longer ride. The *qabījī* didn't know what to do with him, and sent someone on his behalf to the governor of Afiyun Qara Hisar to request that a surgeon be sent to bleed the sick man he had with him. When the *bostānjī* [204], the janissary who had been sent as a messenger arrived, he went in to the governor and asked him to send a surgeon with him, explaining the young man's condition. Then the governor ordered them to bring a skilled practitioner from among the surgeons.

By chance there was present in the place a Chief Imām, who had preceded the others to the city, and been lodged in the pasha's palace in a room specially prepared for him. At this point, the Imām said to the governor, "A skilled French doctor accompanied us from Istanbul. He's the one who cured the pasha when he fell ill on the way".

When the *bostānjī* heard this, he said to the governor, "I will go to His Excellency the Pasha and look for him". People from the entourage of the governor who were sitting there said to the governor, "The French doctor who came with the pasha is right here, staying in such-and-such a *qaysarīyya*". So the governor ordered them to go and bring me before him.

This was why those two came looking for me and ordered me to go with them to the governor. When I heard what they had to say, I was very frightened. I thought the pasha had looked for me, and not finding me, had sent orders to the governor to arrest me because I had left without his permission. Then I got up and went with them, my mind awash with foreboding, my fear and worry increased at the thought that he might order me to be beaten with a cudgel or thrown into chains, and similar black imaginings.

When we came to the palace, I with my back bent and trembling, and stood before the governor, I saw that the pasha's Imām was standing there too, and I was certain what would happen to me. Seated on the same side was a *bostānjī*. Then the governor asked the Imām, "Is this the doctor?" "Yes", he answered. Then the governor turned to me and told me, "The *qabījī* is camped outside the town. With him is a man of noble descent who has fallen ill along the way, and he has sent this *bostānjī* to us to look for a doctor. I order you to go with him to examine the patient".

When I heard these words from him, my soul returned to my body, because I had been half-dead with fear. I tried to excuse myself to the governor, saying, "I don't have my medicine chest with me to cure him. What's the use of my going, when he is somewhere in the desert, in a place where there is nothing to be found with which to treat and cure the patient?" The governor replied, "Go for the sake of the *qabījī* and do what you can. This would be a good deed". The *bostānjī* too urged me to go, and promised me a good recompense. I answered them, saying "I can't go". Then the Chief Imām turned and told the governor that he couldn't compel me to go, because His Excellency the Pasha was keeping an eye on me.

So the governor ordered them to bring one of the surgeons and send him off with the *bostānjī*, and they let me go. I returned to my companions, happy at how I had been able to escape from that mess. I told them everything that had happened, and how it had ended. Then my companion, Hannā, went to the caravan leader and said to him, "If you are not going to depart, then we are going to hire someone else". He answered, "There is a caravan ready to leave for Konya, and I have hired mounts. We are setting off the day after tomorrow, without fail. So get your things ready".

We waited two days, fearing the pasha would send for us. When the two days were up, the caravan set out, and we travelled with it until we were close to Konya. While we were still on the road, we saw the *qabījī* and forty cavalrymen passing at a distance. One of the horsemen broke away from the rest and rode up to the caravan and asked, "Who's the leader of the caravan?" They pointed towards our guide. He went up to him and said, "The *qabījī* wants the French doctor who is with the caravan to come to him in Konya. And watch him! Don't let him out of your sight! If you do, you will suffer a terrible fate at the hands of the *qabījī*". The guide answered, "I hear and I obey!"

That *bostānjī* then returned to his commanding officer, and they preceded us into the city, because they were riding post-horses. The reason for all this was that the *bostānjī* who had come to the governor to ask for a surgeon had seen me and recognized me and told the *qabījī* about me, "He's the one who didn't want to come with me!" Then the *qabījī* ordered him to notify the leader of the caravan to make sure he didn't lose sight of me until he sent for me.

When the caravan leader told me this, I was seized with the fear, that having escaped from one, I was falling into another disaster. I relied on God and consigned my fate to Him. We continued on our way until we came to the city of Konya. The caravan leader ordered me to go with him to where he was going to dismount, telling me that he was under orders from the captain to do so. We entered the stable where they tied up the animals, and we had barely arrived when a sergeant sent by the governor appeared, accompanied by a *bostānjī* from the captain's retinue. They ordered me to come with them to the captain.

I went with them and we arrived at the captain's quarters. They took me up a staircase and we entered his presence. When I was standing before him, he gave me a furious look and said, "Why didn't you want to accompany my suite from Afiyun Qara Hisar?" I immediately threw myself on the ground and kissed the hem of his garment and said to him, "Pardon me, My Lord, what prevented me from examining your patient was the fact that I don't have my medicine chest with me, and without it I can't prescribe medication to anyone. That is the reason, may your life be noble!"

Then he softened, and told me to sit down and gave me a cup of coffee. He began to tell me about the condition of the sick man he had with him, much as he had the first time. He spoke to me soothingly, and tried to coax me to visit the patient, and treat him and do everything I could to get him better as quickly as possible, because time was short. I answered him, "It is in God's hands, My Lord". Then he ordered one of his servants to take me to the patient.

When I entered, I found the youth reclining on the bed, breathing stertorously, like a sea monster. When I examined him, I found that he was burning with fever, as if he had been thrown in a furnace. I wondered what on earth to do to bring down his fever. And at that moment Almighty God, May He be Praised, inspired me with an idea I would never have thought of. I asked one of the servants attending him to bring me a bezoar stone [205] and some rose water. "I don't have any", he replied. Then he took out a purse full of money and gave it to me. "Go and buy what you need in the city." I did not accept the purse, but said to him, "Give it to one of your mates to go with me to the market place so that I may buy what we need".

So he sent two men with me from his entourage of chamberlains, and we went to the market. I began to ask the merchants about the bezoar stone, but it was not to be found among them. So I thought about what I could treat him with in place of the bezoar, and bought a selection of spices and tamarind and plums, and rose water and started back to the camp.

Just before I left the market, a native of the place came up to me said, "Did you want a bezoar stone?" "I do", I replied. Then he told me someone had some, but because of the men accompanying me, he feared we would take them without paying their price. When I heard what he had to say, I gave one of the chamberlains the spices and told him to go to the camp and have them crush the spices and steep them with the tamarind and plums. I ordered the other man, who carried the purse, to wait for me.

They both did what I said. I turned to that fellow and said, "Show me where this stone may be found". "Come with me", he said, so I followed him until he pointed out a dignified man sitting in front of his shop. "That man has what you want," he told me and went off. I went up to the gentleman and asked him about the aforementioned stone. "I have it", he replied, "but you must pay me what it is worth". "I will," I answered. Then he opened a chest and took out a purse in which were five stones. I picked the best of them, which was olive coloured. He asked a price of fifteen piastres. After bargaining, I got it for twelve, and went back to the waiting chamberlain and ordered him to give him that amount. So we took the stone and returned to the camp. I immediately pulverized the stone into a large cup of water and gave it to the patient to drink. Then I squeezed a small cup full of the juice of those spices, and gave it to him to drink. Then I mixed vinegar and rose water in a vessel and told them to rub his extremities with it. After that, I steeped some tamarind and *mārdānī* plums and first made him drink the concoction of spices, and then the tamarind water again, then the bezoar water once more.

I continued administering these infusions till evening, when I noticed that he had improved and that his fever had broken. He opened his eyes and sat up in bed and asked for his water pipe and a cup of coffee. I asked him how he was feeling, and he said "Thanks be to God for curing me, I feel better!" At this, I said goodbye and advised his servants not to give him anything at all to eat, but to continue to administer those infusions. Then I left, intending to rejoin my companions, but before I could leave the house, one of the *qabījī*'s entourage summoned me. I returned with him, ascending the staircase once more and went in to the *qabījī*. He asked how the patient was, and I told him that, Praise be to God, he was better. "Can he travel tomorrow?" he asked. "I will be able to tell you early tomorrow. If he maintains his present condition, he can travel."

Then I asked his permission to return to my quarters. He was displeased, and ordered me to sit down and told them to bring me coffee and a water pipe. When I had finished my coffee, he asked. "Where are you from?" "I'm from Aleppo", I answered "and my father was an Aleppan physician named Baydāw. My father died when I was still a child and they sent me to stay with my uncle, who lived in the city of Marseille in France. After having studied medicine there, I determined to return to my country, and took ship to Smyrna. From there I went to Istanbul to see the sights then decided to travel overland to Aleppo to see something of the country, sending my medicine chest to Aleppo by sea. Now I am on my way back to Aleppo."

"I was a custom's officer in Aleppo," he answered, "and many French merchants were my friends. Among them were *khojas* Sauron, Bazan, Banfay, Roux and Simon. My best friend among them was called *khoja* Rambaut, who spoke Turkish. I visited him many times, and used to drink his liqueurs. He had a treasurer named Anton who used to fetch the liqueur from the cellar."

When I heard these words I went white, fearing he had recognized me and knew I was lying, because *khoja* Rambaut was my master, and the master of my brother Anton. I was the one who used to bring him the liqueur and serve him. Yet he apparently didn't recognize me because at that time I was only a boy, a little over twelve years old. I thanked Almighty God that he didn't recognize me.

At last I requested permission to return to my quarters. "Go!" he replied, "but make sure you get up early and come here to take a look at the patient and see if he can travel. "On my head and eyes!" I replied, and left his presence and returned to my companions, who were impatiently awaiting me. I told them everything that had happened, from beginning to end. All of us thanked Almighty God for aiding us.

After we had slept in peace for half the night or a little more, two chamberlains of the sick man came for me and woke me. They were worried, and said "Come quickly, the youth is near death!" I left my room and went with them, almost out of my mind with worry. I kept asking them and urging them to tell me what had happened to cause his fever to return, but they couldn't seem to tell me the truth. Finally, one of them came to me in secret and said, "After you left him, he ordered them to bring him ice. He ate about an *oka* of it, and put what was left of it on his chest and on his belly".

So now I knew what had caused his relapse! I had in my hands a good excuse to save myself from the *qabījī*. When I came to the room, I went in to the patient. He was in a pitiable condition. His fever had come back, twice as bad as before. He was on the point of death. It was apparent from my expression that I was very astonished. I questioned them about what they had given him to eat, and how he had reacted, saying "Tell me the truth!" They all denied it, saying "We didn't give him anything to eat". Then I said to the one who was in charge, "If you don't tell me the truth, and that man dies, the punishment will be on your necks".

When he heard these words, he took me aside and spoke to me in secret, because the patient had implored them to say nothing. He told me that he ate ice, and placed some of it on his chest, and this was the cause, "But, by your life, don't tell this to the *qabījī*, or he will take vengeance on us. Finally, I ordered them to crush some more seeds and give him a big cup of bezoar water. I went on treating him as before until dawn broke, and the *qabījī* heard that his illness had returned. He sent for me and they brought me before him. He was furious. He looked at me narrowly and said "Did you lie to me yesterday when you told me that he was better? Now I hear that his illness is worse than before! Were you making fun of me?"

When I saw how angry he was and that he wanted to punish me, I decided to tell him what had happened during the night, how he had eaten snow and placed some on his chest, as they had told me. When he heard this, he was even angrier, and said to me "I'm going to travel with him, and if he dies, I'll tie a rope to his feet and drag him along like a dog, I don't care if I lose my head for it".

Then I threw myself on his mercy and beseeched him to be patient for a day to see if he improved a little, and was able to travel. Then I went back to the patient and continued treating him with infusions until evening and he improved a bit. The *qabījī* had ordered a litter prepared for him, so that he could be carried in it the next day. Then he summoned me, and told me that I must go with him to Syria in order to treat the patient along the way. "I hear and I obey" I said. Then he said to me, "Come tonight with everything ready to travel with us tomorrow!"

I returned to my companions and told them I was accompanying the *qabījī* to Syria. My friend Hannā was not pleased. He tried to prevent my going, saying to me, "I fear lest something happen to the patient along the way, or that he die, and his uncle is Nasīf Pasha! They will say that the physician is to blame for his death, and how on earth do you plan to save yourself from the hands of Nasīf Pasha? There is no doubt that all you can hope for is death. Even if you arrive safely, aren't you worried that the doctors in Aleppo will question you, and find out you don't really know a thing about medicine? What will you do then? Your fate would be even worse!"

He continued to admonish and warn me, and I grew increasingly worried. I was completely perplexed, because I had given the *qabījī* my word that I would go with him. I spent the night completely at sea about how and what to say to the *qabījī*, who had the status of vizier.[206]

When dawn broke, our caravan leader and those who had rented mounts, heard that the *qabījī* was on the march, pulling the litter, and everyone got ready to travel with him, saying "We are going to split off at Antioch, and from there make our way to Aleppo". They began to load their horses with provisions and prepare for the journey. At that time the *qabījī* sent someone to bring me to his presence. When I entered his quarters I saw the litter and a saddled horse and everyone dressed for the journey. When he saw me, he said, "Where is your baggage? I ordered a fine horse for you. Go immediately and bring your baggage and other stuff and come right back, I am waiting for you!"

So I went to get my things ready and return to set off, when I saw that those who had been all ready to travel with us were just sitting around. I asked what was going on, and one of them answered, saying to me, "At first we knew that we were going to travel with the litter, but a certain gentleman advised us that the *qabījī* was going to change horses every two hours. He was going to change mounts in every place he came to. That way, he can make two days journey in one. Your horses could not possibly keep up with him. This is the reason we have decided not to travel with him".

When I heard him say these words, I changed my mind about the journey, because I hoped I could part with the captain in Antioch and conceal myself. When I realized that only I would be travelling with him, I again changed my plan, seeing a pretext that might satisfy him. I went to the camp and saw that the patient was already in the litter, with his entourage gathered around him, waiting for me. Then I climbed the stairs to see the *qabījī*. I kissed the hem of his garment, and excused myself, telling him, "I don't have the strength to ride with the post horses. If I do, I will die along the way". I implored him to forgive me, but I was completely unable to make this journey. Almighty God had mercy upon me, and he said to me, "You don't have to go. Do what you please". And he immediately mounted his steed and rode off.

The patient and his entourage, meanwhile, tried to ingratiate themselves with me by saying, "We will all look after you on the road, don't worry". Their *agha*, the patient, assured me that when he arrived in Syria, he would give me a horse and send me to Jerusalem with my expenses paid, and give me a generous recompense. However, I was alarmed by what Hannā had told me, and afraid lest I get in terrible trouble, so I refused to go. When he realized I wasn't going with him, he was absolutely furious, and ordered the official in charge of the litter to depart. Then his chamberlain turned to him and told him to give me a tip. He reached into his pouch, grabbed a handful of coins and angrily flung them on the ground. They gathered them up and gave them to me. They amounted to twelve thirds of a *thaler*.[207] Then they went their way, and I returned to my companions.

We spent five days in Konya after the *qabījī*'s departure. Afterwards, we joined a caravan bound for Aleppo and accompanied it until we were near Adana. Here there was a narrow pass, so narrow that it could only be negotiated single file. In that place sat the *agha* of the *sibinj* [208] in order to collect the poll tax from arrivals. This amounted to one and two-thirds piastres, levied only on Christians [209] passing through.

When we came to the pass, the retainers of that *agha* stopped us going any further until we had paid the poll tax. After my companions and the others had paid, he turned to me and demanded that I pay and accept a receipt in return, as everyone else had done. I immediately answered him, saying "When I start paying taxes to your sultan, I will pay you the poll tax". He looked at me closely, and asked those with me "Who is this man?" "This is a French doctor," they answered, and he believed them, because he had noticed that I differed in my clothing and my hair and that I was clean shaven. He welcomed me, and told me to sit down, saying, "I didn't know who you were, you don't have to pay".

In the end, he made everyone else pay, and let us go and we mounted our horses and journeyed on. We kept on until we reached the bridge of Missis [210]. I rode at the head of the caravan, and when we drew near the bridge I saw two chamberlains barring my way. They asked me politely to visit their *agha*, who was the *agha* of Missis. I thought someone had reported that I wasn't a Frenchman, and was worried. I didn't want to go in with them to see their *agha* until my companions arrived and I could give them my mount, that is, my horse. They waited patiently and didn't use force on me. The reason was that their *agha* was ill, and had heard that there was a French doctor with the caravan. He sent these two so that if I arrived, they could bring me to him. His house was near the bridge.

When my companions arrived, I gave them my horse and entered with those two men to see that *agha*, who was the governor of the city. When I stood before him, he ordered a servant to take off my boots. Then he invited me to sit down in front of him and ordered them to bring me coffee and a water pipe. I was surprised and began to wonder what the reason was for the honour and friendship a man of his high rank, the governor of a city, was showing me. I was still puzzling over this when he said, "Come closer to me!" I did so, and he said to me, "You are safe, O Learned One. Cure me of this ailment and I will give you whatever you want". "What is your ailment?" I replied. Then he exposed his forearm and I saw that the flesh was swollen and ulcerated, and that that swelling and ulceration affected his whole body and insides and skin.

When I saw the condition he was in, I examined him thoroughly. I told him that I understood the ailment, but didn't have its cure with me. He beseeched me even more, and I answered, "Don't worry, I will describe to you how to make something to apply to your body externally that will alleviate your ulcers. To treat you internally requires the preparation of a special compound for the treatment of this disease. At the moment, I do not have it, but I can make it for you in Aleppo, for the ingredients are not to be found in this country. If you have someone you can send to me in Aleppo, I will give him a jar of that medicine, and if you use it before elimination, you will be cured of this ailment. This is well-tested. Then he asked me, "Where are you to be found in Aleppo?" "My shop", I replied, "is in Khan Abrak.[211] If your messenger asks for me, he will find me there." Then he asked, "What is the prescription you told me about?" I replied, "Take fifty drams of copper sulphate, which in Turkish is called *kuzdāšī*, and soak it in water inside a glass vessel. Let it steep for twenty-four hours until it dissolves. Then take some of that water in a cup and wet your sash and then wipe your ulcers. This will eliminate the pus. Send a man on your behalf to the caravan tonight so that I can send you some pills, of which you should take three before sleep. I will also send a little *darūr* [212], which you should squeeze on your ulcers". Then I arose and asked his permission to leave, and returned to my companions where the caravan had camped, which was by the bridge on the riverbank.

At nightfall, we began to think what to do about dinner, and at that very moment a large tray arrived from the *agha* with three different dishes. The servant called for us, inviting us to come and eat. We sat down on that meadow by the river and had a very satisfying dinner. Finally, we got up and washed our hands and gave thanks to Almighty God for the benefits He had bestowed upon us. Then they brought us a jug of coffee, also sent by the *agha*. When we had finished our coffee, the chamberlain who had brought it said to me, "The *agha* sends his compliments, and asked me to ask you to give me what you had promised him". "On my head and eyes!" I answered. I immediately opened my pack and took out fifteen fresh pastilles. I also had some 'burned alum' that was specific for ulcers. I wrapped a little in paper and gave it that chamberlain, and told him how to apply it. The procedure was to apply it after he had anointed himself with that water, applying that *darūr* to his ulcers and squeezing them to dry them out, so they absorbed the pus. He was to swallow five of the pastilles every night before sleep.

We spent the night in that place, and at midnight set off, without learning how the *agha* was faring. We travelled on until we came to the province of Adana called 'Ramadan Province'. It lies at the base of a mountain covered with trees and springs of water. It was like the Earthly Paradise. Before arriving at the mountain we passed a fortress called Arkalī.[213] This castle also resembled its surroundings, for it was like a garden, because of all the trees and the water found there. When we entered that province, we dismounted and made camp. You could see that it was inhabited, because the head of every family had hung curtains between the trees and marked off an area for his womenfolk and children. Because of the summer heat and dust in the city of Adana, they send their families to this place to spend the summer. Everyone employed in buying and selling, tailors and carpenters and other similar crafts moves here. There is even a market which has everything found in the city itself.

We stayed there that night, and at midnight set off for Adana. Along the way we passed men, women and children heading at night to the province, carrying torches and lanterns as if going on a family picnic. When day broke we entered Adana. We camped under the bridge in one of the arches. This bridge has forty arches, and in all my travels I have seen nothing to match it.[214.] The smallest stone used in its construction is the size of a Frenchman's tomb. It is something beyond description. Queen Helena, the wife of King Constantine, was responsible for its construction. She also built other bridges and a paved road from the outskirts of Istanbul to the city of Jerusalem the Noble, as well as watch towers. The stories about her are long, and we will leave them.

A short while after we had alighted under that arch, a Christian man accompanied by a chamberlain in uniform, came to check if any of us had neglected to pay the poll tax at the aforementioned pass. They began to ask, "Show us your receipts!" Everyone showed him their piece of paper. Then he came up to me where I was reclining and asked me to show him my receipt. The other people in the caravan said to him, "Leave him alone, he's a French physician, and doesn't have to pay the poll tax. Not even the *agha* of Missis could make him pay. On the contrary, he treated him as he deserved and honoured him". They turned away, and bothered me no more.

We spent the day in that place, and at sunset the caravan leaders wanted to us to go. We asked him, "Why do you want us to move on before time?" He answered that we were approaching a dark pass called Qarāniq Qabī [215], and that this was a place bandits laid ambushes. "We want to get through it tonight, lest one of them spots us." We obeyed his order, and all mounted our horses and rode through the night until we came to the aforementioned pass. It was of black stone and extremely dark inside. Anyone who entered was terrified. God made it easy for us, and we got through the pass and started to descend. On our right was a towering mountain, covered with trees; while on our left was a huge thicket. Beyond lay the sea.

We continued to walk, terrified, until close to midnight. It got cold and damp because of the moisture of the sea, to the point that you could actually see the dew dripping on you like honey. We could scarcely open our eyes because of that unhealthy air, so that the riders dismounted from their horses. As for me, I was so exhausted by the fatigue that had overcome me that I stayed on my mount and rode ahead of the caravan for about a mile.

There I dismounted and went a little way off the trail and went in to the bush, wrapped the reins around my forearm and collapsed in a deep slumber, without a thought, because I was so tired. The caravan passed by while I slept, and I dreamed I heard the horse whinnying for its companions, although I was sound asleep. When the sound of the caravan ceased, it was far away from me. The horse wanted to join his companions, and pulled at his reins so that he could set off, and when he pulled them, he woke me.

I listened to see if I could hear the bells of the horses, but heard nothing. Instead, the horse, with all its strength dragged me along, trying to join its companions. I was bound tightly to the reins, but in that place there was nothing high enough for me to stand on to climb onto his back. Meanwhile, he was still pulling me. I was afraid in that place because I had heard them saying that there were thieves there, who stripped and killed their victims. In the end I appealed to the Virgin Mary and the Saints. I didn't have the strength left to run with this horse, and it occurred to me to put my foot on his girth and mount. I stood in front of him in order to calm him down and mount, but I was unable to do so because he began to run and drag me along with him. My strength was failing, and I resolved to loosen the reins from my hand and walk at my own pace, but how was I to do this in my condition? Suddenly, what should I see, but the horse calm down and slacken his pace to a walk! This was a miracle by the Virgin Mary to whom I had appealed and my Guardian Angel. When I saw that the horse had slackened its pace, I placed my foot on the front girth, jumped on and rode off. The horse no longer held back, but began to gallop, straining the reins. In a short while we reached the caravan. No one had had news of me. Then I cried out, and everyone ran over. I gave thanks to Almighty God for his mercy to me.

We went on travelling until we came to Bayas.[216] We entered in the afternoon through the gate of the Bayas market, since it was from that market that one enters and leaves the town. When we reached the middle of the market, what did I see but a man rushing from his shop! He embraced me, and began to welcome me lovingly. I was astonished at that, and the affection he was showing me, when I didn't know him. I asked him, "Who are you? How do you know me?" "Don't you recognize me, O brother Hannā?" he responded. "I am none other than Hannā ibn Mīkhāyīl Mīrū, your friend in Aleppo!"

When I heard these words, I recognized him. Then I embraced him and excused myself for not knowing who he was. He used to come to Aleppo with his father and stay in the Khan al-'Alābīyya [217] where we lived. His father was in partnership with my brother Anton. They used to correspond with each other. We had them as guests in our house many times, him and his son. We had great affection for each other, and this was the reason he recognized me. The result of all this was that he took my hand after he had handed over my horse to someone to take to my friends in the caravan, which was camped outside the market.

He held on to my hand until we came to his house, where he led me up a staircase to a reception room. Below the reception room was a garden stretching as far as you could see, planted with citrons, lemons and oranges. It was beyond description. We sat down and he immediately ordered his servant to prepare lunch for us. Then I requested that they not prepare any greasy food, because I had resolved not to eat anything heavy from my entry into Adana until I reached Aleppo, lest I get indigestion. When he heard these words, he ordered them to cook rice, sea fish and *bottarga* and similar tasty food. Then he told them to bring arrack, aged arrack. When they brought it, he poured it out and handed me a cup. When I started to drink it, the scent was so overpowering that I fell on my face for a little while. When I came to, I said to him, "O my brother, what kind of arrack is this?" He answered me, saying "This arrack will prevent your indigestion, and keep you from falling ill". We waited patiently a while, then they brought the table and placed those various light dishes upon it. He then wanted to pour me another cup of arrack, but I didn't drink it. Instead, I drank an excellent wine with lunch.

When we had finished lunch, we drank coffee. Then we went and walked in the gardens fit for kings, and he began to pick citrons and sweet lemons for me, as well as some fruits, like pomegranates and cucumbers and the like. I stayed with him almost until evening, then said goodbye and went to join my companions.

We spent the night on the sea shore, and around midnight mounted our horses and rode on until we came to Alexandretta. We by-passed Alexandretta and camped near al-'Ayn and spent the day there. After they had cut fodder for the animals, we went on and passed by Baylān during the night. We continued travelling until we reached Khan Jadīd, and from there Qurt Qulāq and from there to Jasr Jadīd. From there we reached Antioch and made camp on the banks of the Dog River, where we spent the night.

The next day we travelled on, and came to Sūq Antakīyya and dismounted. I went to the Sūs'ānī bakery to buy bread. After he had weighed out the bread for me I gave him the price in official *paras*. He refused to accept them. Instead, he said "I want *jarqāt*", but I didn't have any. I rebuked him, and grabbed him by the collar and pulled him down and told him, "I'm not going to release you anywhere but in front of the governor, because you refuse to accept the sultan's coins from me! No, you will only accept the coins of the

Franks!" People gathered around us, and with difficulty prized my hands off his collar. They took the *para*s from me and gave me the bread and let me go in peace.

So I mounted my horse and rode out of Paul's Gate to rejoin the caravan. But I strayed from the trail and went by another. All I could see were gardens. I left the trail and strayed among mulberry trees and irrigation channels, unable to find the road by which I had come. I was confused, and for almost an hour twisted among the trees, while the caravan eluded me and drew farther away from me. The world closed in on me, and I was very irritated. Then, God delivered me from this difficult situation. I saw a peasant walking by and asked him if he would show me the road. He very kindly said "Follow me!"

I followed him until he had led me out of those gardens to Paul's Gate and showed me the road the caravan had followed. Then he went off, leaving me alone. I began to worry lest a robber chance upon me and steal my clothes and horse. I waited patiently for a while, hoping to meet companions, but no one passed by. I oscillated between fear and hope, and then decided to travel alone, and trust in God. I drove my horse along as quickly as possible.

Then I noticed a man coming up alongside me. It was the brother of the caravan leader. They had noticed that I wasn't in the caravan and couldn't find me, so the caravan leader halted the caravan and sent his brother back to Antioch to find out what had happened to me. When he drew near me and recognized me, he was relieved, and asked me the how I had missed the caravan. I told him what had happened. Then my heart was full, and I rejoiced that I was safe. I went with him until we came to the caravan, and I explained my absence.

We went on travelling until we came to a valley called 'The Valley of the Djinn'. In truth, it was the Valley of the Djinn, because we underwent great difficulties and dangers in passing through it. These roads are hard to negotiate. In fact, it took all day for us to pass through that valley. We came to Hayram, and stayed the night there until dawn broke. Then we journeyed on from there through villages and scattered fields and two days later arrived at Khan al-

'Asal.[218] We spent the night there, and the next day entered Aleppo. Just before we entered Aleppo, there was a violent earthquake, the like of which had never been told. It lasted more than five minutes, but we didn't feel it because we were riding on horseback. When I entered [Aleppo] I headed for my sister's house in Zuqāq al-Khall, lest I become a public spectacle.[219] This was towards the end of July, 1710.

In the end, my brothers and sisters heard, and came to find me, and welcomed me and brought me my things. I went from there to my brother 'Abd Allah's house, and family and relations came to visit me, and welcome me, because news had reached them that I had drowned at sea, because I had written a letter to my brother Anton (Antūn) from Marseille, informing him that I was boarding a ship bound for Smyrna, and from Smyrna to Aleppo. Later they received news that a ship out of Smyrna bound for Alexandretta had broken up and all aboard had been drowned. My brother was certain that I had drowned along with everyone else, and they had said a mass for my soul, because they had had no news of me, for when I travelled from Smyrna to Istanbul in the company of the ambassador's chamberlain, I didn't dare write to my brother that I was going to Istanbul.

This is the reason they were so happy at my safe arrival in Aleppo. I spent three or four days with my brother, until they had brought me things to wear and I had had my head shaved. I donned a sash and loose trousers, and they sent out to get me a resident permit. Afterwards, I left the house to return greetings to my family, loved ones and neighbours.

Finally, I went down to the city to visit my brother in his shop. A few days later, my brother 'Abd Allah provided me with a shop selling broadcloth [220] and my uncle Shāhīn appointed a manager to assist me until I had learned the art of selling broadcloth. I was a seller of broadcloth for the next twenty-two years. The reason my brother did this, was because he feared I would set off travelling once more.

All of this was the plan of Almighty God, for during this time they betrothed me and I married and had children. It is perfectly clear that it was the Almighty, Praise be to Him, who summoned me to marry, because when I left Aleppo secretly, my intention had been to return to being a monk. But then the aforementioned tourist encountered me, and I changed my mind from leading the life of a monk in the village of Kaftīn. My destiny was to travel with him to those countries which I have mentioned.

Let's return to our story. I continued working in the broadcloth shop, and a year later my master, Paul Lucas, with whom I had formerly travelled, came to Aleppo. He lodged in the French consul's house. When I learned of his arrival, I went to him and greeted him. When he saw me, he embraced me, then severely reproached me for the way I had abandoned him, without telling him the reason. At that moment, a number of foreign merchants entered and interrupted us, so we agreed to meet another day.

I later learned the reason why he returned to travelling. When he heard that the prince had sent me to travel about as he had done, then changed his mind, he gave the prince assurances that he would travel instead of me. And this was the reason he had come to Aleppo, to fulfill his contract with that prince.

A few days later, I invited him to visit us and dine with us. He accepted, and so I invited my brothers to dine with him. In those days I was still unmarried, and they had fitted out a room especially for me. I prepared a nice dinner for him, and then went and picked him up and took him with me through the city to the house. My brothers were there and welcomed him very warmly. When the time came, we sat down at the table. When we had finished, we sat chatting with him.

It then occurred to me that I had spoken to him about my mother's illness, and the physicians had been unable to do anything for her. At the very moment, I mentioned her to him, he told me to bring her before him so he could diagnose her ailment. So we brought her before him. When he saw her, he knew immediately what was wrong with her. He sent her away; then said to me, "Let me think a bit about what to give you that will give her relief from her illness".

In the end, we spent the evening chatting with him until the first hour of evening. I had prepared a comfortable bed for him, and he slept until dawn broke. After we had drunk our coffee, we went out into the city together. He visited me frequently at my broadcloth shop, and I would go with him sometimes to tour the city, as was his practice, because he wanted to look for antiquities, like old coins and books and rare precious gems, and similar things.

One day when he visited me, he said, "Today, take me to the Gold Market". When we arrived, he began to look in the display cases in the goldsmith's shops. In one of them he saw a *mabkhūsa* stone, [221] which is like carnelian. He bought it from the goldsmith for two *para*s.

I was astonished at him, and after we had looked at the shop, I asked him, "What do you want with that ordinary little stone?" "I wanted to buy it," he replied, "in order to cure your mother." Then he asked me to put a thread through it and hang it on my mother's neck, so that it touched her skin, and that it would cure her ailment. I laughed, and said to myself, "If so many doctors have treated her without success, what good can this stone do?" The truth was, however, that I didn't want to challenge him, so I took the stone from him and did what he asked. I didn't think about it again until later that week. When I returned from the city, they told me, "Today your mother asked to be taken to the baths after she had changed her clothes".

It had been three years since my mother had visited the baths, or sat with us at table. She had been unable to sleep, or talk to anyone. But that day she sat down with them at table and talked with them in her usual way. They were amazed at how she appeared to be completely cured. When she came back from the bath, she sat with us at table and ate as she used to, as if she had never been ill. We were all astonished at this. So I told them, "Don't be so astonished, this is the result of the properties of the stone which I hanged about her neck". They didn't believe me until I asked my master, and told him that she was all better. He said, "Advise her to be careful, and not remove the stone from around her neck, lest her melancholy return, and she relapse to the condition she was in before, for this stone has the property of dispelling the feeling of melancholy". It all happened just as he had said. A year later she removed the stone from her neck in the bathhouse, and had a relapse. I went out searching to see if I could find the like of that stone, but couldn't find it. She remained like that until her death.

Another time he came to me and started to reprove me, saying, "How can you have a place called *Kanākiya*, and not tell me about it?" I couldn't understand what he was saying, and asked him, "What is this place, and how did you learn about it?" He told me that it was a tunnel that led to the city of 'Antāb. Then I understood that he meant the *Khanāqīyya* [222], I mean, the 'Cave of the Slave'. I said to him, 'What do you want in that dangerous, haunted place? No one who goes in it ever comes out. It is a cavern, huge and dark, and no one goes in or out. Many people have entered, none have come out'.

Then he said to me, "Have you ever gone to this place, and found out if were true or not?" I answered him that everyone would confirm what I said, but that I didn't know whether it was true or not. Then he said to me, "I want to examine it thoroughly until I have discovered the truth. I want you to find some old man who might know this place and guide us there. I will pay him well. I'm going there on Thursday, so bring that man with you without fail!" "On my head and eyes!" I answered, and he left me.

I didn't pay much attention to what he had said, saying to myself, "On Thursday I'll go to him, and he will have forgotten all about it". Early on Thursday morning, I went into town as usual. I saw a venerable old Christian gentleman called Abu Zayt. This man was very old, and had lived all his life in the wild, sometimes selling grapes to the Christians to press, and when the grape harvest was over, he became a wood cutter, bringing firewood long distances by camel to Aleppo for sale. When I came across him, he was standing on a hill waiting for the camel loads of firewood. It occurred to me that this man would know the truth about that place.

I went up to him and greeted him, and asked him if he knew anything about the 'Cave of the Slave', that is, the Khanāqīyya. He at once answered, "I have entered it many times, and know the place well, but I have never gone all the way to the end". When I heard these words from him, I was overjoyed, and told him there was a certain Frank who wanted to go there and examine it. "Come with me, and he will give you a generous tip if you guide him through that cavern." "Most willingly!" he replied. So we went together, along with another man who was with him.

A short time after we reached the Khanāqīyya, the *khoja* arrived with a group of Franks and servants, all of them armed and carrying provisions and a sack of straw. When they came up to us, my master asked me, "Have you found anyone who knows the place?" "Yes", I answered, and pointed to the man. He was very pleased, and congratulated me. We asked that old man to show us the place, and he told us, "Follow me!" We followed him until we entered a high, wide cavern cut out of chalk called 'The Palace of al-Tamātīn', the place of the slave who revolted. We penetrated it until we reached the end of the cavern. There we saw a small door cut into the living rock. Inside was the Cave of the Slave, which the old man had told us about.

When we saw it, we were frightened and refused to enter it. The *khoja* tried to encourage us, and ordered the servants to get out the lanterns, for he had brought six lanterns with beeswax candles. Then we sat down in that place and they unpacked food and drink for us.

After we had eaten and drunk, he ordered the servants to light two lanterns, and get a sack of straw from the bundle. When they had finished doing as he asked, he went up to the entrance and fired his pistol, loaded with lead, and it made a tremendous noise. He waited about three minutes, but then we all decided not to go in. When the *khoja* saw that we didn't want to enter, he went in with two servants, one holding a lantern, the other carrying a sack of straw in order to strew it on the ground while he walked, lest he lose the way. When he went in all alone, our courage returned to us and we all entered except for two servants who stayed outside to guard our things, so no one would steal them.

When we were all inside the cave, extremely frightened, with two men walking in front of us with lighted lanterns and another scattering straw on our path so we wouldn't lose our way, we realized that everything they had told us was a lie, because there wasn't a single curve in the path! On the contrary, it was straight and easy and high and its width was two hundred feet. The only thing we saw besides the bones of animals were cuttings in the stone. We continued walking for about a quarter of an hour.

Suddenly the lanterns went out and it was difficult to breath. We couldn't catch our breath because the place was so oppressive and there was no ventilation. At that moment we were scared and wanted to return lest we all perish. Then the *khoja* encouraged us, and said to us, "Don't be frightened, the place is wide, and won't stifle us. Wait until we have taken a few more steps, then we will go back".

We followed his advice and walked another hundred feet with him and saw that the way before us was blocked, although at the top, cut out of the mountain, was a sort of bench. Then the *khoja* asked that old man, "Why did you tell us that this tunnel reached all the way to 'Antāb [223]? For here we have reached the end". The old man said that the door of the tunnel was on top, but they had blocked it off with earth lest anyone enter and perish.

When the *khoja* heard what he had said, he got on the shoulders of one of the servants and climbed up to that ledge. He took out his poignard and scraped out some earth and saw that it was blocked, and cut out of the mountain. Then he was certain we had reached the end of the cave, and what they had told us about it was a lie. He reproved and insulted that old man, and exposed the lie of those that said it reached all the way to 'Antāb.

At last we turned back until we had gone out of that door. We began to explore the Khanāqīyya, place by place. We asked those around who were cutting stone, and told them what we were looking for. They showed us to an old man, whose age must have been ninety. They told us, "This old man will show you the entrance to the tunnel which leads to 'Antāb, because he is very old and is familiar with all these places. We asked them to bring us the old man.

When he came before us, the *khoja* gave him a third of a piastre and said to him, "Show me the entrance to the tunnel which leads to 'Antāb". "Follow me!" he said. We followed him until we reached one of the caverns found around there. He showed us a place that was very deep, but filled with rubble to the brim. "When I was a boy", he told us, "I came to this place with my father and saw the entrance to this tunnel, but afterward the governor of the city gave an order to fill in the entrance lest someone go in and perish. Everyone used to say that a group of youths, a bride and groom among them, came to celebrate in this place. Some of them dared the others to enter the tunnel and not one returned. They all perished, because they lost their way because they hadn't thought to bring a long rope and tie one end to the door of the tunnel so the others in the party could pull them back with it."

When he finished his story, the *khoja* asked him about the place we had entered, and what it was. He said, "When they were beginning to build the city of Aleppo, this is where they cut the stone it was built with. The evidence of that are the shafts every hundred feet, through which the cut stone was taken out".

This is true, because when we entered the tunnel, we saw that the shafts had been blocked. The *khoja* now credited the statement that the entire place was a quarry, and they entered through these narrow passageways in order to cut stone. The old man said there were two reasons for this. The first was that the stone here was hard, and as good for building as ordinary stone. The second, and better, reason was that the early kings used these subterranean chambers to move armies underground without anyone realizing it. To the casual observer, they appeared to be cutting stone for building purposes, but actually it was for moving armies underground. The *khoja* was forced to agree with what the old man said, as well as that the blocked up tunnel reached all the way to 'Antāb.

Then we departed and returned, climbing up to a vineyard called 'The Vineyard of the Little Fort'. There we had lunch, and stayed till evening. Then everyone went their way. Thus ends our story and travels. We seek forgiveness from God both for saying too much and saying too little.

Completed on March 3rd, 1764.
Completed on December 22, 2015, Seville

Taşköprü, the Great Bridge at Adana. View from *Life in Asiatic Turkey* by Edwin John Davis, 1879.

Notes

PL's ms of Hannā had numerous asterisks, indicating points which he intended to annotate. Some of these would have been to clarify references for the general reader, while others would have referred to the vocabulary of Christian Arabic in which he was particularly interested. His very detailed research would also have enabled him to identify all, or almost all, the people and places mentioned and provide background information about them. It was not possible to retrieve his proposed notes from his computer files, and I did not have the courage — or knowledge, since many of his notes are written in Arabic — to go through the dozens, perhaps as many as a hundred, notebooks dealing with this and other Christian Arabic texts. I have, therefore, tried to annotate points to help the non-specialist reader and have included some things that PL related which seem of particular interest. I cannot stress too strongly that all mistakes, or misinterpretations, are mine not his.

1. Deir Qannubin (modern spelling) is the oldest of the Maronite monasteries, with claims to have been founded by the Emperor Theodosius in 375 A.D. It is rock-cut and was once the seat of the Maronite Patriarch.
2. *Kavuk*: the word has several meanings but here, presumably, the cap, often quilted, round which the turban is wound. Under the Ottomans, the shape varied among different groups and ranks and there was a strict code of who could wear which form.
3. Bsharri (modern spelling). The town is a center of Maronite Christianity — "the city of churches" — and the neighbouring Qadish Valley is the site of some of the most ancient monasteries and hermitages. The last remaining Cedars of Lebanon are to be found there.
4. Bsharri to Zgharta (modern spelling) is c.40km/25 miles.
5. Ra's al-Nahr — Head of the River, also a name for the Mar Sarkis Monastery.
6. Hamidīyya Shadhiliyya — Sufi order with a center at the village of al-Hamidīyya. Hannā clearly had doubts about their honesty.

7. M.Ramuset — a prominent member of the French merchant or consular community — see Introduction.
8. Khan al-Zayt — the khan of the oil merchants, perhaps in the Souq al-Saboun, the soap market, since soap-making was an important industry in Aleppo.
9. On the King's travelers, see Introduction. Hannā often uses the term *sultan* for the French king and *malik* (king) for the Ottoman ruler. PL retained this, as part of the distinctive flavour of the account.
10. This refers to the Church of St Simon Stylites, founded in 475 A.D. and the column on top of which he said to have lived for decades, fleeing the world.
11. See Introduction on clothing and sumptuary laws.
12. Kaftīn — a predominantly Druze village near Idlib c.50km/31 miles from Aleppo.
13. *Khoja* — a polite honorific, regularly used by Hannā for Paul Lucas and others.
14. Hannā mentions a very large number of different coinages in the course of his narrative. Numismatics being a highly technical field, I have not attempted to give values to most of the coins. It is usually clear whether a large or small sum is intended. This probably refers to a *leeuwendaalder*, or lion *thaler*, very widely circulated in the Ottoman Empire at this date, where it was known as *aslanti qurush*, or lion coin. It would therefore have been familiar and acceptable to the shepherd and his share would have been c.10gr silver.
15. Jisr al-Shughur (modern spelling) — an important stopping point on the trade route since classical times.
16. Khan al- Ghamīdā — Khan of the Mystery; a suitable name for a Christian monastic community.
17. Joshua? Isaac/Yeshaq has also been suggested.
18. Hannā was not always accurate about dates — hardly surprising after 50 years — but PL preferred to leave the dating as it appeared in the ms, rather than correcting it.
19. Mount Lebanon district, modern Keserwan. The area is predominantly Maronite Christian.
20. Zouk Mikael (modern spelling), is again largely Maronite.
21. See Introduction.
22. *Agha* — Lord or master — honorific title in the Ottoman Empire, particularly, although not exclusively for military officers.

23. Turkish: *kalpak* — a common head covering across the Turkic-influenced world, either cylindrical, or tapering to a point, usually made of felt or sheepskin.
24. Now an Aleppan name, but presumably originally from Persia.
25. Jebel Druze — the rugged mountainous region c.230km/142 miles inland and south of Beirut. Earlier, however, the term was also used for the mountainous area closer to the city.
26. PL put an asterisk against this, presumably indicating that Hannā had once again misremembered the date.
27. A standard type of single-decked Mediterranean cargo vessel, usually double-masted. The settee sail is a lateen with the front corner cut off, like the sail of an Arab *dhow*.
28. *Kalimera* is "Good morning" in Greek. Was it really his name?
29. Maronites migrated from Lebanon to Cyprus in the Middle Ages. Under the Venetians, when the island was very prosperous, the community was estimated to number about 50,000. Numbers declined under the Ottomans and still further after the Turkish invasion of Cyprus, with some 6,000 remaining on the island today.
30. This is still a very surprising feature of the building — the Cathedral of St Sophia (c.1209) was converted into the Selimiye Mosque in 1570.
31. See note 26
32. Extortionate tax collecting by the local *aghas* had led to serious revolt in the late 17th century, with the result that Cyprus was placed under the direct control of the Grand Vizier in 1703. Rivalry between the Orthodox and Catholic communities, as Hannā describes, going back to the sack of Constantinople in 1204, during the ill-fated 4th Crusade, did nothing to increase prosperity.
33. Logically, one would expect this to be Pompey's Pillar (in fact commissioned by Diocletian in 297 AD), which is a monolith of red granite from Aswan, more than 20m high and with a metallic look. However, it is not decorated in the way Hannā describes, so he may have conflated two memories.
34. There are a number of caves along the coast at Alexandria, but I have not managed to find PL's note identifying it.
35. *Bottarga* — salt-cured and sun-dried roe, typically of grey mullet — a delicacy, widely exported from the region since classical, and possibly Pharaonic, times. Similarly, linen has been a major

Egyptian production for at least 4000 years and Asyut, a heavily Coptic city was (and is) an important textile center.
36. One of the many types of sailing boat in use on the Nile. A classic work on sailing boats reports that: "the *Maash* or *Rahleh* is the largest, and has the most lofty and commodious cabins" — Henry Coleman Folkard, *Sailing Boats from Around the World*, 1906, p.368. Another Englishman writing in 1847 adds, however, that "unless a traveller has plenty of time to spare, a *Dahabeeh* is far preferable".
37. Fresh water springs in the ocean are a phenomenon recorded across the globe, notably at Bahrein, where diving for fresh water was recorded from the 15th century
38. The old Jewish quarter.
39. Oghuz Turks, originally from Central Asia, who were the military basis of power in Ottoman Egypt.
40. It is not clear which of the numerous palaces extant at this date in Old Cairo is meant, but none of them would have been Pharaonic.
41. *Sanjak* — administrative division of an Ottoman province, but the term was also used for the *sanjakbeys* who ruled them.
42. Historically, the term chrysolite was used for a number of greenish stones, primarily peridot. It was believed to have healing properties and, indeed, a modern website claims that it is a remedy for — among other things — cardiovascular disturbances, insomnia, nervous problems and eye disease.
43. Haret Zuweila in Old Cairo, originally built in 10th-12th centuries A.D. The travels of the Holy Family in Egypt are of the greatest importance in the Coptic Church and common places of pilgrimage.
44. Joseph's Granaries, as in Genesis 41. By the Middle Ages, it had been largely forgotten that the Pyramids were the burial places of kings and they were believed to have been Joseph's Granaries. By the 10th century, al-Muqaddasi was mulling the various identifications. By the 16th century, a Dominican friar could comment that the idea of their being granaries was the "mistaken opinion of the ignorant common people" — but the idea lingered on in Egypt.
45. The text would have been in Hebrew and the commentary, probably written in the margin, in Estrangelo, the oldest form of written Syriac, a cursive script, descended from Aramaic.
46. *Qaysāriyya* — the name comes from Caesar — and is found all around the Mediterranean. The precise meaning varies with time and place, but it was often used for a building or a section of a

market, specializing in valuables: gold, jewels, money changing, luxury textiles, etc. Unlike *khan*, the term was not usually a synonym for caravanserai.

47. For mummies and *mummia* — see Introduction.
48. This was identified by PL, but I have not managed to find the reference. It has been plausibly suggested that it was a *lapsus calami* for *maqāmāt* — tombs, places of burial.
49. Now known as Bahr Yussef (lit. the Sea of Joseph), a canal originally built at the time of Amenenhat III, c.1850 B.C., joining the Nile with the Fayyum.
50. *Jadid* — a copper coin, widely circulated and very variable in value. *Fals* — another small copper coin — hence *fulus* a common term for money. See also the note on coinage in the Introduction.
51. *Kamis* — the long wide sleeved shirt worn by the peasantry, as opposed to the slightly more upmarket *galabeya*. Hannā is apparently shocked that he cannot tell Copts and Muslims apart.
52. Reed mats, presumably here a local specialty, rather than from Simān in Kermanshah, were important articles of trade. Al-Idrisi, writing in the first half of the 12th c., mentions the ones from Baisan, saying:….."the reed is not found anywhere else except here and nowhere…. is there any reed to equal it".
53. Obviously, both men would have seen the significance of this particular sum.
54. Paul Lucas published his *Travels*, based on his diaries. I do not know whether the original mss. survive, together with this entry, but it is interesting that Hannā apparently had access to his papers, given that Paul Lucas was clearly secretive — with reason — about a good number of things.
55. Unidentified.
56. A classic dish, originally from Central Asia, cooked in a Balti-type iron pot. Lucas would have been still used to the medieval pattern of leaving all the dishes on the table (c.p.Mrs Beeton), rather than the modern habit of separate courses, credited with being a Russian introduction, roughly at the end of the century.
57. Again unidentified.
58. Interesting that cauterization was still being used in such a general way. Hannā was clearly shocked, as was Usāma ibn Munqidh in the 12th c., when faced with the Crusaders ideas on medicine.
59. A pink — small, flat-bottomed cargo boat.

60. *Kūn* in Arabic generally means manifesting, existing or coming into being.
61. PL put an asterisk against this and the heading, presumably indicating that Hannā had once again misremembered the date.
62. The Gulf of Sidre or Sidra, also known as Sirte, was notorious in Classical times for its dangerous sandbanks and unpredictable tides. Strabo describes them and the burning and inhospitable shore in some detail. The crew of the ship carrying the Apostle Paul refused to take the Sirte route, because of the storms and risk of shipwreck. They ended up wrecked on Malta instead.
63. *Dil* — (Turkish) tongue, here inlet of the sea.
64. Usual meaning, clerk or scribe, here perhaps record keeper.
65. Foresail. It is interesting the number of different languages represented in *the lingua franca* of the Mediterranean as regards ships.
66. PL had written "gunnel" and I am not sure whether this is what Hannā had put, or whether it was a mistake in naval terminology.
67. A very variable unit of weight, usually between 0.750/1.65lbs and 1.5 kg/3.3lbs, but at an earlier date as much as 3.5kg/7.7lbs.
68. Bilad as-Sudan — the Land of the Blacks — was the Arabic term for Sub-Saharan Africa, especially West and Central Africa, roughly above the equator.
69. This was identified by PL, but I have not managed to find the reference.
70. See note 69. M. Le Maire was presumably part of the Le Maire family, members of which served as consuls in numerous posts across N. Africa and the Levant.
71. In July 1711, Ahmad Karamanli, a local nobleman of Turkish origin, seized Tripoli, executed the Ottoman Pasha and took the title of Bey.
72. In fact, the new Karamanli dynasty was hereditary.
73. Unidentified.
74. Members of the Ottoman Turkish cavalry, essentially a military aristocracy and rivals of the janissaries.
75. For pirates and slaving — see Introduction.
76. Literally "proof" or "evidence", often in a theological context.
77. The 17th century saw a great expansion of the Jesuit presence across the Middle East and even North Africa, and the church of Sta Maria degli Angeli in the medina of Tripoli was built in 1645 with the permission of the Ottoman Sultan.

78. See note 2.
79. The janissaries were in fact the real power in Libya and the ruler was largely obliged to do as they demanded; the fear of revolt was therefore a very genuine one. By this date, discipline was weakening and the janissaries across the empire were a major source of disorder and anti-social behaviour.
80. A janissary's *orta* or battalion and, within that, his unit was the center of his life and his commander had ultimate power over him.
81. *Berat* — Turkish, a formal authorization or permit granting certain privileges; *firmān* — the Arabic/Persian equivalent. Hannā was, of course, familiar with both languages.
82. Jerba (Djerba) off the coast of Tunisia in the Gulf of Gabès was intermittently controlled by the Kingdom of Sicily and later by Spanish forces, who were decisively defeated by the Ottoman navy in 1560. The island was an important center for trade (and piracy) with a substantial Jewish community.
83. A *mithqāl* is c.4.5gr/0.15 oz.
84. Interesting that Paul Lucas had with him Chinese ceramics, especially the martaban jar. This would presumably have been one of the brown glazed storage jars, exported from China and S.E. Asia in large numbers. The term comes from the Arabic name given to a port in Burma (Myanmar) and the jars were first mentioned outside Asia by Ibn Battuta. Martaban jars are generally thought of as very large, but the type in fact comes in a range of sizes, including quite small.
85. A very variable measure, sometimes given as 1/16th of an ounce, but sometimes as much as 35gr — c.1.25 ounces.
86. Sugar was sold in cone-shaped blocks from medieval times in the Arab world and was standard in Europe until the 19th c.
87. Borj er-Rous, the Tower of Skulls — see Introduction
88. The decline of the Fatimid Caliphate in the 12th century meant that, by the date under discussion, Ismā'īlīs were more or less non-existent as a power in North Africa.
89. The region known as Ifriqiya, hence Africa — modern Libya, Tunisia and Eastern Algeria — was originally home to many more than eighteen bishoprics.
90. There was no considerable Circassian community in North Africa, with the possible exception of Egypt. The significance of this seems to have been identified by PL, but I have not managed to find the reference.

91. Again, I do not know what PL's comments (indicated by asterisks) on this would have been. Fossils are found at numerous sites in Libya, including Cyrenaica, as well as Gafsa and Chenini. Dinosaurs and other fossil vertebrates occur in southern Tunisia. Could this have been a village engulfed by sand and preserved by drying out in the *khamsin*?
92. Unforgivable insults, especially from a Christian.
93. Tunisia was a major source of wild animals for the games under the Roman Empire and at this date still had abundant populations of lions, leopards, cheetahs, bears, wolves, hyaenas, jackals, wild boar, etc. most of which are now extinct in the region.
94. Tunisia has numerous hot springs in use since Classical times, Korbous being especially famous. Hannā could be referring to Zaghouan, which would have been on their way, although rather further from Tunis than he implies. Leo Africanus, writing in the mid-16th, described the springs near Gabès in some detail and shared Paul Lucas' reservations about the heat.
95. Generally, diseases, infirmities.
96. The beauty of the place has been praised by travellers back to the mid 15th century and the name is thought to come from the Spanish *prado* — a garden — suggesting links with the Andalusians who relocated at the time of the *Reconquista*.
97. A space or hall, walled on three sides, leaving one open, often with a ceremonial intention, a very typical element in Islamic architecture, of Iranian origin.
98. See Introduction re slavery.
99. The Bey, al-Husayn ibn Ali, was the son of a Turk from majority Christian Crete and a Tunisian mother. His first councillor at this time was a Frenchman, which may explain his liberal attitude.
100. Perhaps the Greater Egyptian Jerboa, although it is much smaller than the size given. PL points out that a jerboa was described and illustrated by Corneille le Brun, *Voyage au Levant*, Delft: Henri de Kroonvelt, MDCC, who saw it in Venice in 1686.
101. A shortened version of the classic Spiritual Exercises of St Ignatius Loyola.
102. Born in 1664, Paul Lucas would have been in his mid-40s.
103. Interestingly, jerboas are normally solitary and do prefer individual burrows.
104. Hannā seems to use the term fairly generally to refer to the Eastern soldiery used as government troops throughout the

Ottoman Empire and its dependencies. In fact, in Tunisia, these seem to have been mostly Mamluk rather than Circassian.
105. PL put an asterisk against this and the heading, presumably indicating that Hannā had once again misremembered the date.
106. Feast of the Eucharist, celebrated roughly two months after Easter.
107. Old Damascus, famous for its swords made from Indian steel.
108. He seems to have been identified by PL, but I have not managed to find the reference.
109. To avoid infection. Plague was raging in Russia and the Baltic and had reached the Ottoman Empire.
110. For Paul Lucas' version of this episode, described in dramatic and highly coloured terms and in which he plays a far-more heroic role, see Introduction.
111. Syria at this date still had a large Christian population and it is probably the non-Catholic Christians — Orthodox, Nestorian, Jacobite, etc. who are being referred to rather than the Muslims.
112. Indian chintzes and other printed fabrics were very much in fashion and similar materials were imported from Iran. By *kharīsāna*, Hannā might possibly be referring to goods from Khurasan, again famous for its textiles, especially its carpets, as well as numerous other exports.
113. The War of the Spanish Succession was in progress — the Battle of Malplaquet was on September 11th, 1709. See also Introduction.
114. These sorts of figures are often given colloquially to mean 'a lot', rather than literally.
115. See Introduction.
116. Venetian ducats were highly prized for their high quality and stability and contained roughly 3.5gr of very pure gold. The value of each coin today (2019) would be very approximately £119/133€.
117. There were many who felt the Doge of Genoa, was a tyrant, but historically events did not develop exactly as Hannā tells them — see Introduction.
118. Between May 18th and 28th, 1684, the French fleet, commanded by Abraham Duquesne bombarded Genoa with an estimated 13,000 cannon balls, explosive bombs being used, apparently, for the first time.
119. Presumably Mme de Maintenon.
120. A cubit = c.45cm/18"

121. *Shahbandar* (Persian) was originally the Port Master in charge of the traders, collecting taxes and settling disputes. Later, as the term spread abroad, it evolved to mean an official overseeing particular communities of traders.
122. Louis XIV and his finance minister set up the *Compagnie Française des Indes Orientales* to compete with the Dutch; it was not a great success. Colbert also heavily encouraged the Levant trade and this, on the whole, worked better.
123. Sainte-Baume — the cave where Mary Magdalen, fleeing after the Crucifixion, is said to have retired, after landing at Saintes-Maries-de-la-Mer. It is still a major pilgrimage site, as is Notre-Dame de la Garde.
124. I have not managed to locate PL's identification; perhaps transliteration of a French name?
125. The Basilica of Notre-Dame de La Garde. Hannā would have seen the chapel dating from 1214, enlarged in 1477, with the 16thc. fortifications. Almost everything vanished at the French Revolution, including the statues, perhaps from a Via Crucis, which would have been very shocking to an Eastern Christian, unaccustomed to this kind of three-dimensional art.
126. I have not managed to locate PL's identification, nor of the other merchants mentioned below.
127. The clock is very much as Hannā describes it. See Introduction.
128. Interestingly, Don Juan of Persia, the royal convert to Catholicism, was also much impressed with European inns in the late 16th c. and describes them in similar terms.
129. I have not managed to locate PL's identification. Possibly from the Bteghrine district.
130. The first public lamp in Paris was a candle lantern installed in 1318 at the Grand Chatelet. In 1667, an ordinance of Louis XIV increased the number of lamps, which were to be lit from November 1 until March 1. A commemorative medal was struck in 1669 recording the improved urban safety.
131. Jérôme, Comte de Pontchartrain (1674-1747) Secretary of State *et al.* under Louis XIV.
132. Louis XIV was probably have agreed, but Le Grand Dauphin, although fat, lazy and rather dull, was not unpopular with the people, being affable and open-handed, however, clearly this is what Hannā would have heard at court.

133. Guy-Crescent Fagon (1638-1718) was physician to Louis XIV and an eminent botanist. He commissioned his friend, the painter Jean-Baptiste Oudry (1686-1755), to paint the ground floor rooms at his estate with numerous plants and animals. It is possible he was responsible for the work Hannā mentions.
134. Marie Adélaïde of Savoy (1685-1712), first brought to court aged 11 and largely raised by Madame de Maintenon. She was indeed said to be one of the very few people whom Louis XIV really loved and she had great influence over him. She, her husband, the Dauphin, and one of their children died of measles.
135. All of which would have seemed particularly ill-bred to someone from the Levant.
136. Hannā is surprisingly accurate in his report. The marriage was, inevitably, morganatic, but seems to have actually taken place.
137. Maria Theresa of Spain, died 30th July 1683.
138. Emmanuel, the great 13-ton bell of Notre Dame, dating from the 15th c., was recast in 1681 on the orders of Louis XIV. The other bells were melted down at the French Revolution. It also survived the fire of April 15th, 2019. See also below.
139. The problems connected with the water supply were enormously discussed at the time and numerous solutions were proposed. There is a considerable literature on the subject.
140. Hannā is attempting to describe the giant Machine de Marly, designed and built by Rennequin Sualem and Arnold de Ville with fourteen paddlewheels and two hundred pumps.
141. Hannā's description of the gardens by André Le Nôtre is good and elements that he mentions that are not there today may have been destroyed by Louis XVI, or at the French Revolution.
142. PL spent a lot of time trying to identify "Nicholas" but, as far as I know, never came to a conclusion.
143. India's fame in producing and copying works of art was legendary in the Arab world, as in the West.
144. A version of the classical story, popular in the 18th c., of Zeuxis (born c.464 B.C.) and Parrhasius, told in the *Naturalis Historia* of Pliny the Elder. A version of the story also crops up in China.
145. Les Invalides, a project initiated by Louis XIV in 1670 for the care and housing of wounded and disabled veterans, housing at some periods more than 4,000. The Hôtel National des Invalides continues this function.

146. It is not clear which cardinal is intended, but he would certainly have been flattered by this estimate of his power — perhaps Hannā is recording a memory of Richelieu or Mazarin. It seems that PL had identified him and had material on the Čelebi brothers (see below), but I have been unable to trace the note.
147. The feast is still celebrated almost identically in Seville and a few other places today (2019), although with fewer clergy and more of the laity.
148. The first part of the Muslim profession of faith, the *shahada*.
149. The Zamārīyā family — a famous and powerful Aleppan clan with a notably beautiful house, the Dar Zamārīyā, in the Jedaideh Quarter, which dates from about this period and was still extant, much as Hannā might have known it, until the civil war (2011—). *Čelebi* is simply a Turkish title, roughly the equivalent of "gentleman".
150. The Hôtel-Dieu de Paris was founded by St Landry in 651 AD and is still partially functioning. By the time Hannā visited it, it was underfunded and suffering from serious overcrowding, even by the standards of the time, and hence had a very high mortality rate. It was revived later in the century by Joseph Necker, the Finance Minister, and his wife. For noble women performing menial tasks for the poor c.p. La Caridad in Seville still today.
151. Possibly La Salpêtrière, built by Libéral Bruant for Louis XIV in 1656, as a hospice for women, but enlarged with the addition of prisons, an insane asylum, etc. c.1684. At one stage it had some 10 000 inmates and is still one of the largest hospitals in Europe.
152. This presumably happened in reaction to the Edict of Nantes in 1685, which made Protestantism illegal in France, causing enormous ill-feeling and disruption, and with serious economic consequences, the benefits of which were felt in particular by England and Holland.
153. The ambassador from Istanbul — see Introduction.
154. Analyses of official attendance at theatres in London in the 17th-18th century, indicate that many visitors from the Levant, the Ottoman empire and North Africa had a passion for plays and masques, often going to the same one several times, although they could not have understood a word. This was no doubt in part for the elaborate special effects being developed at the time, which would have been completely unfamiliar and very exotic, as Hannā indicates.

155. Hannā's spelling differs from the normal Turkish: *Karagöz*, the traditional shadow play, popular across Asia and an entertainment in the Ottoman Empire from at least the 16th c, if not earlier. He is quite correct in suggesting that it has considerable similarities to *Commedia dell'Arte* although, for obvious cultural reasons, with much less emphasis on love. Both use a range of stock characters, to which are added jokes, improvisation and even veiled political criticism; both were very popular.
156. *la'ab al-hakam* — Play/referee — exact meaning uncertain.
157. A bush has been used as an inn sign since Roman times, while the sign for a brothel was more often a lantern, in later periods red, but Hannā was very observant and may well be right.
158. I have not managed to locate PL's identification.
159. The *écu* has a very complicated history and was minted in both gold and silver. It is value here may have approximated to a purchasing power of c $30/23€/£23 (2019) — so a very large sum was involved.
160. Interesting that Hannā was so shocked (as on other occasions), but also that similar stories of the absolute intransigence of the law are told of the Ottoman Empire; "All equal from the Vizier down to the shepherd on the mountain…" However, both should be taken *cum grano salis*.
161. Arabic from the Latin *sigillum*, a seal — the decree of a judge, or record from a court of justice.
162. The standard Latin cross, but upside-down, as it is said St Peter was crucified.
163. The plague epidemic from c.1709 particularly affected Northern Europe and the Baltic, causing hundreds of thousands of deaths. It spread south and from c.1720 the Great Plague of Marseille (the last major plague outbreak in Europe) left some 100 000 dead.
164. St Genevieve (c.419/422-503/512 A.D.), patron of Paris, was associated from the earliest times with saving the city in times of plague, besides driving away Attila and the Huns in 451 and negotiating with the besieging Chilperic in 464. For the purposes of comparison, Madame de Sévigné describes this procession.
165. Another classic story — c.p. Sta Casilda in Spain.
166. This winter is considered, on modern evidence, to have been the coldest in 500 years and Hannā in no way exaggerates. France was especially hard hit and it is reckoned that cold and the subsequent

famine caused some 600,000 deaths, as the result of *Le Grand Hiver*. See also Introduction.
167. PL's text indicates that he had found out something about this but, unfortunately, I have not been able to track it down.
168. Attempts were made to distribute bread, as Hannā says, in order to stop or prevent rioting, and there were many complaints that the relief was inadequate, but it must have been more than a modern ounce. Efforts were made to buy wheat from anywhere that would sell it, to relieve the famine, possibly what the Flemings were doing — see below.
169. See n.67.
170. The War of the Spanish Succession was raging — see Introduction.
171. c.p. n. 42.
172. Charles de Ferriol (1652-1722) — see Introduction and Appendix.
173. Thanks to their tolerant and far-sighted policies, the Jesuits came close to healing the rift between the Catholic and Orthodox communities and were an important religious presence in the Levant during the 17thc. As always, they were much concerned with providing education and medical care, and in Smyrna (modern Izmir) seem to have had their own church dedicated to the Jesuit saint, San Luigi Gonzaga. All trace of their presence was destroyed in the events of 1922.
174. At this date, probably Saint Benoît in Galata, still a Catholic church in use today, in spite of having burned down several times, through carelessness rather than fanaticism. Evliya Çelebi, writing in the 17th c., described it as "a French church with an organ".
175. I have not managed to locate PL's identification here or below, with different spelling. Possibly Büyükade, the largest of the "Princes' Islands" in the Sea of Marmara.
176. Perhaps the Yedikule fortress, which included a formidable prison. It was built on the site of the main gate of the city, the Porta Aurea, and incorporated parts of the Byzantine city walls. It would have been an excellent place to look for marble.
177. i.e. Beyoğlu (Pera), the European quarter, on the North Bank of the Golden Horn.
178. Various romantic stories are told about Kiz Kulesi (also Leander's Tower); Hannā's is one of the less common ones.
179. Büyük Valide Han, famous in more recent times for the beautiful views from the roof, was built by the powerful and influential Kösem Sultan. Of Greek Christian origin, she was wife, mother

and grandmother of sultans. This vast complex was, at one time, the *khan* of the Persian merchants, but is now (2019) basically in ruins.
180. The Imperial High Gate — the main entrance to Topkapi Serai. The term "The Sublime Porte" was used in the West as a metaphor for the Ottoman Empire.
181. The elaborate calligraphic signature of an Ottoman sultan.
182. The *mihrab* — possibly Hannā had never been in a mosque before.
183. Here, as elsewhere, Hannā uses the Arabic rather than the Turkish term — *Vezir-i Azam*.
184. Hannā's habit of reversing the European and Ottoman titles makes this mildly confusing. Logically, one would expect the clothes to come from the French court, but, if he does mean the Ottoman Sultana, he is probably referring to the mother of Ahmed III, the Valide Sultan, who was originally a Greek Christian. Scarlet from *kermes* was traditionally extremely expensive. The word is thought to derive from the Arabic *siklāt* and entered the Romance languages via Almeria, where the insect was intensively cultivated.
185. Giving robes of honour was a very old and deeply symbolic tradition across Eurasia and especially in the Muslim world.
186. Pastries stuffed with roast lamb or chicken.
187. From the Hindi — a combination of the Arabic *khidmah* (service) and the Persian *–gar* suffix, indicating possession or agency, thus (male) waiter or house servant waiting at table, or butler.
188. If Hannā is referring to his current posting, he was hardly a child — he must have been at least in his mid-twenties.
189. Presumably calendering with rollers to produce a glossy or watered effect.
190. Possibly one of the Carmelites, who were very active in Persia at that date. It may have been Fr. Joseph of St Mary or Fr. Maurice of St Teresa, titular bishop of Anasiopolis. They were, incidentally, robbed and imprisoned at Erzurum later that year.
191. Chief of the Admiralty Guard.
192. King Karl XII of Sweden stayed in the Ottoman Empire from July 1709-October 1714, hoping to persuade the Ottomans to attack Russia. The Turkish reaction apparently was: "A guest stays for five days, not for five years!" It is hard not to regret that Hannā did not travel with him and record his experiences.
193. A very variable measure, often about 1.2kg/2.5lbs.

194. Marbled paper — the origin of the art is contested among various countries. Flower patterned *ebru* became very fashionable in the 18th c and is often particularly associated with the Ottoman Empire.
195. *awādlaq* — PL's gloss not found — probably a proper name. Afiyun Qara Hisar — (modern) Afyonkarahisar — the Black Castle of Opium.
196. Perhaps Karaköy — Black Village — the name for the port side area of Galata/ Beyoğlu, but also the name of numerous villages across what is now Turkey.
197. The medieval cure-all was still in fashion at this date.
198. Present-day Eskişehir.
199. *jādbūn* ointment — PL's gloss missing; perhaps transliterated from some other language.
200. Or, by extension, steward in charge of guests.
201. Üsküdar/ Scutari — more of less where they started out.
202. See note 46
203. Arabization of the Turkish *kapiji* — the janissaries who guarded the main gate of the sultan's palace and were entrusted with carrying his orders to the provincial governors.
204. *bostānjī* — literally, gardener, but actually one of the sultan's corps of Imperial Guards, guarding the *seraglio*, etc. Their chief had the rank of pasha and at some periods were united with the janissaries.
205. A mass trapped in the intestine of a human or animal — gall-stones of oxen, et al. — believed to have powerful medicinal properties, especially as antidotes to poison. The name comes from the Persian for antidote *pādzahr* and, according to modern research, might actually be of some use in the case of arsenic.
206. High-ranking minister.
207. Almost impossible to calculate. A *thaler* varied, but often c.25gr silver, so possibly in the order of 100gr (c.£65 in 2019). See also note 14.
208. *sibinj* — ford or crossing place.
209. Many of the taxes in the Ottoman Empire — and the Muslim world in general — were only levied on non-Muslims.
210. Misis Bridge (modern spelling) is a Roman bridge over the Ceyhan River on one of the major trade routes East of the classical world. It is still in use.
211. Khan Abrak or Khan al-Qassabiyya was largely a silk and cloth market.

212. *Darūr* — PL's gloss missing.
213. There are some 40 castles in the Adana region and it is not clear which this is. It is tempting to think of Gülek Kalesi, already very old when the Crusaders passed that way.
214. This is presumably the Roman bridge at Adana. It was, in fact, built at the time of the Emperor Hadrian in the 2nd c. A.D. It originally had 21 arches and was in use for traffic until c.2007. St Helena was the mother of the Emperor Constantine, and both saints were much revered, especially in the Eastern churches, Latin and Orthodox.
215. A pass in the Taurus Mountains, possibly the famous Cilician Gates, a trade route since remote antiquity and notorious for its bandits and robbers, as St Paul noted.
216. Unidentified. Many Turkish place names of non-Turkish origin were changed as part of the Turkification programme in the early 20th c.
217. Unidentified.
218. A district c.12 km/7.5 miles WSW of central Aleppo, now notorious for the chemical attack of 2013.
219. Perhaps because he was more or less clean-shaven and in European dress or simply because he was a returning traveller.
220. This would have been English broadcloth, a major export to the Levant and the Ottoman Empire at this time. It was in great demand for ordinary clothing and for military uniforms.
221. *mabkhūša* — see note 42
222. *Khanāqīyya* — unidentified — possibly somewhere in the Afrin Valley?
223. One of several variants of the name of Gaziantep, 185 km/115 m east of Adana and 97 km/60m north of Aleppo.

Appendix (PL)

Charles de Ferriol, French Ambassador to the Porte, 1699-1709/10
Of the few of PL's notes that I managed to retrieve, the following quotes from de Ferriol's correspondence relating to his time in Constantinople and his contacts with Paul Lucas seemed worth reproducing just as they were found. See Bibliography and also www.francearchives.fr — Affaires étrangères. Correspondance reçue du consulat de Constantinople — Ambassade de Charles de Ferriol à Constantinople (1699-1709).

1707
11 June 1707. "Je crois que M. Lucas sera en France au mois d'août, on l'avoit dit mort, mais la nouvelle n'est pas trouvée veritable". II/175
[Note: the editor says in a note "…il mit largement en pratique le proverbe 'A beau mentir qui vient de loin".]
*20 Dec 1707- de Ferriol writes to his brother: M. Paul Lucas étoit au Caire, il y a deux mois, il n'est pas été tué par les Arabes comme on l'avoit dit. (Correspondance II/247).

1708
2 Feb 1708- de Ferriol to Blondel de Jouvancourt. Mentions that the Capitan Pacha (kapudan bashi, admiral of the fleet) has sent a 'chaioux' [çavuş, 'doorkeeper'] to the king to have de Ferriol recalled. [This must be Bahri Mehmet Pacha].
*Same letter: 'Je crois que le Sr Paul Lucas se rendra incessament à Marseille; je vous prie de ne remettre qu'à luy seul des boëttes que je vous ay addressé'. Correspondance II/259.
16 Feb 1708. Letter to his brother, mentions that he is also enclosing an account of the 'no less curious than extraordinary' new volcano near Santorin. Correspondance II/265.
Same letter, page 267: Je joins icy un mémoire de ce que ma musique demande; je vous prie de me l'envoyer; je vous avoi demandé deux trompettes, une d'argent, la meilleure qu'il se poura, et qui soit forte et une autre ordinaire, vous l'avés négligé.
12 June 1708. Letter to brother. "les Turcs ont fait beaucoup de bruit de leur armament naval, il sembloit qu'il dussent conqueror tout le monde entier avec sept vaisseau, quinze galères et quelques galiottes." II/303.

*6 Aug 1708. To Blondel de Jouvancourt. "Vous verrés un jour M. Lucas lorsque vous vous y attendrés de moins, ses dangers l'ont fait mettre dans la Gazette de France; si ce qu'on dit est vray il pourroit arriver un jour nud a Marseille, ce ne seroit pas je pense la 20e fois qu'il a été pris par les corsaires ou par les voleurs." II/310.

*16 Oct 1708. To Blondel de Jouvancourt. "Je ne scay ou M. Paul Lucas peut s'etre arresté, lui qui avoit coutume de faire le tour du monde dans un an; il paroître lorsqu'on s'y attendra le moins, et je le verray peut-être à Constantinople quand je n'auray pas encore appris son arrive en France." II/325

"Le vaisseau du Roy est arrive ici le 22 de ce mois; (Sic!) le Grand-Seigneur m'envoye d'abord demander le nom du vaisseau et du capitain, la force de son armament, le manifeste de ses merchandises, on n'avoit jamais vue icy un vaisseau si riche." II/326.

[Same page: The Ottoman attempt to manufacture woolen cloth in order to compete with French, setting up a workshop in the serail, is a miserable failure. Previous letters give more details of this attempt, which I have not copied.]

*A Turkish envoy, apparently passing through Livorno, is mentioned in the same letter, also page 326. [This might be the mysterious envoy mentioned by Hannā Diyāb].

*At the end of the letter, de Ferriol says: "Je vous recommende l'ambassadeur turc; c'est un grand fripon aussi bien que son maitre." II/328. [See below; both these refs may be to Bahri Mehmet Pacha.]

26 Nov 1708. To Blondel de Jouvancourt. Reports on his very bad health; he is in great pain, feels as if his bones are dislocated, his eyesight very weak, can't write at night, can only dictate; his chest very weak. II/331-2

Reports on terrible fire in Constantinople; 2000 houses destroyed, including most of the beautiful palaces. II/332.

"Je plains M. Lemaire, qui a été dépouillé par les corsaires qui n'ont pas même voulu mettre à rançon les hardes de ses filles; je le crois arrive à Alep depuis près d'un mois; cet échelle avoit encore besoin de sa presence.." II/333

12 Nov 1708* Letter to his sister:
*[The date of this, or preceding letter, must be wrong].
Has received many requests from the Grand Duke and Cardinal de

Medici to demand release of unjustly enslaved Livornois. Why didn't they arrest the Turkish ambassador when he passed through Livorno on a Venetian ship and without my passport?? II/335 [Yes, this is Bahri]]

7 April 1708. To Blondel de Jouvancourt.

"Vous aurès sans doutte remis au Sr Lucas ce que je vous avois envoyé pour luy; il est certain qu'il a perdu beaucoup sur un batiment que les corsaires ont pris. M. de Roye en peut render témoignage." II/383

His health still bad; I am good some days, bad on others. II/383

"L'abondance est icy si grande que le bled qui valoit ces derniers années 20 paras le *___n'en vaut plus que huit; je travaille à vous envoyer quelques vaisseaux chargées". II/385. [* blank in text. The missing word is probably 'charge'].

19 Dec 1708. To Blondel de Jouvancourt.

"Toute ce que Bahry Mehemet Aga vous a dit n'est que mensonge; il étoit parti d'icy avec le Capitan Pacha son maître qui l'a expédié de Candia où le Visir avoit envoyé par Rhodes la letter qu'il a écrit à M. le compte de Pontchartrain.

Quand Bahri dit qu'il n'a pas eu le tems de me voir avant son depart de Constantinople, qu'est-ce cela signifie? il va en France, et il n'a pas une heure à me donner pour prendre un passeport et une letter qui le fasse reconnoiter.

Comment ne l'a-t-on pas fait esclave à Malthe et à Livourne, et comment ne l'avés-vous pas traitté d'importun?

Les letters du Visir et du Capitan Pacha ont-elles un caractère particulier pour être connues parmy-nous, et les orders du Visir passent-ils chez les ennemis de cet empire?

Le passeport du vice-consul de Canée donné sans pouvoir et contre toutte sorte de raison suffisoit-il et M. le Bailly de Tincourt étoit-il dans un assez grand commerce avec les Turcs pour scavoir que Bahry étoit l'homme de confiance du Grand-Visir envoyé à de nos ministres? pour M. de Riancourt par quel motif l'a-t-il défrayé à Livourne et pris tant de soins pour assurer son passage en France?

A quoi sert un ambassadeur de la Porte, si un Turc, partant et traité avec les derniers honneurs? Il ne manquoit plus que de luy faire tirer le canon à Toulon et à Marseille.

[This long complaint continues — The following passage, from page 338, is important:]

J'admire l'imprudence de Bahry, petit aga du capitan pacha, d'écrire à M. le comte de Pontchartrain "mon cher amy", c'est un peu trop de licence, et il est faux de dire que ce soit l'usage des Turcs, hors parmy égaux.

[There follows a long, complicated account of the Sultan's charges against the French.]

Je ne doute pas qu'il ne se soit passé de nouvelles scènes à l'arrivée de l'envoyé turc; on vouloit icy le rappeler sur ses letters, voyant la faute qu'on faite de le faire passer en France sans une lettre ou un passeport de ma part; mais l'accueil qu'on luy a fait à Marseille a donner de bonnes espérances du succes de sa mission ; j'envoye à la cour la traduction de ses lettres que j'ay touttes interceptées, jusqu'à la chanson qu'il a faite sur son épouse, et que j'ay mis tres-fidèlement en françois; j'ay ensuite fait rendre les lettres à leur addresse ; il y avoit pour Djianum Hodgia, commandant des vaisseaux du Grand-Seigneur et pour le kiaia du capitan pacha ; il n'a point eu la hardiesse d'écrire au capitan-pacha, encore moins au Grand-Visir. [342]

[In 1709, Charles de Ferriol, the French Ambassador in Constantinople, fell ill and became unable to perform his function].

4 Jan 1709. Letter to sister :

[Describing Bahri]

C'est un homme qui parle peu et qui veut imposer par son silence ; il espére rapporter de France de quoy entretenir icy sa famille le reste de ses jours… [344]

[de Ferriol mentions just before this, same page, that he has sent « mon fils de Pontdeveille » the burlesque song, apparently in Latin, that he composed for one of his comedians to recite. He adds : « j'ay intercepté touttes les lettres de Bahry qu'il a écrit dans sa route ; je ne sçay si je pourray en faire de même de celles qu'il écrira en France ; car il paroit qu'il y a ses partisans ; c'est un homme… [continues as above].

[Note : Pontchartrain clearly fired de Ferriol on the basis of the report by Bahri, and he is thus replaced by des Alleurs. It is clear from this letter that Bahri is still in Paris, so it must have been around this time that Hannā Diyāb met him. But see below!]

5 Jan 1709. To M. Sissonne [unidentified].

[Thanks him warmly for defending him, having heard of his support in a letter from his brother dated 23 Oct 1708. This means Bahri had reached Paris around the beginning of October 1708, which coincides closely with my assumed date for the arrival of Hannā Diyāb and PL in Paris.]

Je vous diray seulement qu'ayant fait plaisir à tout le monde à Constantinople et dans les Echelles, je ne puis imaginer qu'on ayt écrit des lettres de plaintes contre moy à M. le comte de Pontchartrain ny sur quel sujet ; ce seroit une grande curiosité pour moy d'en voir une pour sçavoir ce qu'on peut dire. [345]

Pour le Visir, je mourrois plutôt que de me rendre son esclave ; il est le seul avec le capitan pacha avec qui je suis icy brouillé. [346]

10 Jan 1709. To Blondel de Jouvancourt

Il y a deux jours, Monsieur, que j'ay fait passer pour l'Italie un des mes courriers pour me justifier sur plusieurs fausses accusations que mes ennemys avoient fait au Roy, pour prévenir d'une part Sa Majesté contre moy, et de l'autre pour appuyer la mission informe de Bahry Mehemet Aga.[347-348]

[This must be Hannā Diyāb's mysterious messenger! He was therefore sent 8 Jan 1709. In the same letter, de Ferriol says he has been resident in this city 17 years! What was he doing before he became ambassador ?]

7 Feb 1709. To his sister.

Je vous diray que ma conduitte est irréprochable en tous points, et qu'on ne peut avrir aucune prise sur moy de quelque côté qu'on puisse tourner les choses…

Après cela, Bahry est un chevalier d'industrie, qui parle peu et pense beaucoup ; il est pauvre, avide, et il a reconnu que sa mission étoit défectuese, mal digérée, entreprise légèrement et hâtive sur le faible fondement de la haine. Ce sont la ses propres paroles ; il ne voulait pas revenir à Constantinople vuide comme il en étoit party ; que faire ? il falloit d'une mauvaise commission en faire une bonne, et exécuter en même tems les ordres de ses maîtres ; voicy comment-il s'y est pris, il a refusé constamment de remettre à Marseille les lettres dont il étoit porteur afin d'être conduit a la cour, et présenté au ministre ; quand il a esté en sa présence, il luy a donné ses lettres, et en cela il a accompli ses ordres, il a ensuite fait entendre qu'il ne me seroit pas difficile de regagner le Visir et qu'alors la Porte ne s'é loigneroit pas de prendre des liaissons agréables au Roy pour la renouvellement de la guerre ; comme on croit aisément ce qu'on désire, on a écouté Bahry, on l'a estimé, et peut-être l'a-t-on traitté libéralement ; c'est tout ce que le pauvre diable demandoit ; cependant comme il a craint qu'on ne touchat

26 June 1709 — His secretary and chancellor, M. Belin, assembled the French nation to inform them that, according to an examination on 24 June by four doctors, he was suffering 'd'un alienation d'esprit'. For the next two months, Belin, together with the deputies, took his place. Then de Ferriol recovered.

27 Aug. 1709 — De Ferriol writes to his brother, telling him how angry he was at being replaced by Belin, which he regarded as an attempt to replace him permanently. Before the end of 1709, de Ferriol was recalled to France.

14 Nov 1709 — De Ferriol informs Pontchartrain that the Capitan Pacha [*kapudan bashi* — admiral of the fleet] has been deposed and appointed pacha of Cairo and replaced by the Tersana Kaya [kahya-lieutenant governor], an old friend of de Ferriol.

24 Dec 1709 — De Ferriol writes to Pontchartrain, expressing his surprise, and attributing his recall to the machinations of Belin. He asks permission to remain in Constantinople until early July to complete negotiations for grain. Pontchartrain answers, thanking him for his conduct during his term of office, and regretting that he cannot keep him in his post.

1 Jan 1710 — Pierre Puchot des Alleurs, comte de Clinchamps is appointed ambassador to Constantinople.

12 Feb 1710/11. *[sic-CS]* Sutton to Dartmouth

"The French have no men of war in these Seas except the Eclatant at Smyrna bound hither with a rich Lading and Monsr. Desalleurs Equipage, but there are many French Imbarcations lading corn and oil in the archipelago for that king's service."

24 April 1710 — des Alleurs arrives, but de Ferriol continues his function until des Alleurs receives and presents his credentials.

16 June 1710 — des Alleurs informs Pontchartrain of the deposition of the Grand Vizier Aly Pacha, to the joy of all. He is replaced by Numan Köprölü Pacha.

[Çorlulu Damat Ali Pasha 3 May 1706-15 June 1710]

17 Aug 1710 — Numan Pacha deposed (see below).

26 Aug 1710 — des Alleurs informs Pontchartrain the de Ferriol was still performing his duties. The same day de Ferriol informs the

minister that Numan Pacha has been deposed on 17 August after only 62 days in office. Sent back to Negropont the same day by the Sultan.

[Köprölü Numan Pasha 16 June 1710-17 Aug 1710]

9 Sept 1710 — des Alleurs informs Pontchartrain that there is not yet a new Grand Visir, no one knows who has been chosen, but ships have been sent to get him.

17 Sept. 1710 — Pontchartrain informs des Alleurs that Dorgnon de Terras, commander of the man o'war L'Esclatant is bringing gifts for the Sultan, along with the personal effects and domestics of des Alleurs. He will bring de Ferriol back to France.

1 Oct 1710 — des Alleurs informs the minister that the new Grand Visir, Mehemet Pacha arrived in Constantinople 26 Sept. He had previously been governor of Aleppo, and had once before served as Grand-Visir. De Ferriol is thrilled with the appointment, and had met Mehemet Pacha on 29 Sept.

[Baltaci Mehmed Pacha 18 Aug 1710-20 Nov 1711]

22 Oct 1710 — de Ferriol informs the minister that Mehemet Pacha has deposed the aga of the Janissaries, something his predecessors, Aly and Numan Pacha had been unable to do.

2 Nov 1710 — des Alleurs finally receives his credentials.

5 Nov 1710 — des Alleurs informs the minister that he has still not been received by de Ferriol, even though he has been in Constantinople six months.

22 Nov 1710 — Pontchartrain writes to deputies in Constantinople that 30 anchors have been loaded on the warships L'Escalant (built 1688; 68-70 guns) and La Perle (built 1690; 50-52 guns).

6 April 1711 — Sutton to Dartmouth

"The Fleet designed for the Black Sea hath been much hastened, and is in a readiness, except two new ships, which will be finished in a few days". p. 45

[These must be the two ships Hannā Diyāb saw being launched]

Glossary

Hannā Diyāb wrote in the form of Arabic used by the Christian community, which had its own expressions and vocabulary. PL had made a study of this, but I not been able to retrieve all of his notes. There are also a number of Turkish terms, since Hannā Diyāb, living in the Ottoman Empire, spoke Turkish as well as Arabic.

agha — (Turkish) lord or master — honorific title in the Ottoman Empire, particularly, although not exclusively for military officers
asqām — generally sickness, disease
barjāwāt — it has been suggested that this could refer to Barjāwā in the East Indies
bash agha — (Turkish) Chief of the Admiralty Guard
bashi — (Turkish) chief, head of
basīsa — dough made with barley flour
bawāšī — a kind of eye-salve brought to Egypt/ the Levant from Derbend, N. of Tehran
berat — (Turkish), formal authorization or permit granting certain privileges, c.p. *firmān* — the Arabic/Persian equivalent
bīrū fīlūsūfa — the Philosopher's Stone, elixir of life
bostānjī — (Turkish) literally, gardener, but actually one of the sultan's corps of Imperial Guards, guarding the *seraglio*, etc.
bottarga — (Italian) salt-cured and sun-dried roe, typically of grey mullet
darūr — some kind of medicine (?)
dil — (Turkish) inlet of the sea
dirham — silver coin with many variants across the Muslim world, generally slightly over 3 gr silver
ducat — see n.116
ebru — (Turkish) marbled paper, sometimes with an elegant flower design; an Ottoman specialty
écu — (French) a coin with a very complex history, existing in both gold and silver versions
efendi — (Turkish) courtesy title: gentleman, comparable to English esq.
escudo — (Spanish) at this date, a Spanish gold coin with a wide circulation
fals — coin (see Introduction)

firmān — formal authorization or permit
galabeya — somewhat more formal coat often worn in towns
hijāb — Muslim veil, now usually refers to a head covering, but here clearly covers the face
hujja — proof or evidence, often in a theological context
jādbūn — a kind of ointment. Name perhaps transliterated from some other language?
jadīd — coin (see Introduction)
jarq — low value coin; see Introduction
jarqāt — coin (see Introduction)
kabak — (Turkish) dog
kalb — dog
kamis — the long wide sleeved shirt worn by the peasantry
kavuk — (Turkish) the cap, often quilted, round which the turban is wound; in the Ottoman Empire, different ranks and classes used different shapes.
khan — (Persian/Turkish) caravanserai or a large building with a courtyard, used as inn, warehouse or centre for a for a particular trade or group of merchants
kharīsāna — goods from Khurasan (?)
khizmatkār — (Persian) waiter or house servant waiting at table, or butler
khoja — (Turkish) a polite honorific
körek (Turkish) — oars
kūn — (?)
kuzdāšī — (Turkish) copper sulphate
la'ab al-hakam — play/referee — exact meaning uncertain
ma'āsh — a large Nile boat
mabkhūša — a stone similar to carnelian
Maghribi — from the Maghreb — North Africa.
malik — king
mārāmat — perhaps intended for *maqāmāt* — tombs, places of burial
mithqāl — a unit of weight c.4.5gr/0.15 oz
mu'as irānī — unidentified
nūlīya — fare
odabashi — (Turkish) gate-keeper, or concierge
oka — *a* very variable measure, often about 1.2kg/2.5lbs
orta — (Turkish) battalion of janissaries
para — a low value coin of the Ottoman Empire
pinque — (French) pink — small, flat-bottomed cargo boat
qablūja — hot spring

qalbaq (Ar.) *kalpak* (Turkish) — a common head covering across the Turkic-influenced world, either cylindrical, or tapering to a point, usually made of felt or sheepskin

qāqūn — a kind of wood (unidentified)

qaysarīyya — generally building or a section of a market, specializing in valuables. See also n.46

qaz'an kebab — (Turkic) a Central Asian dish

qonaqjī — (Turkish) quartermaster or steward in charge of guests

raàl — very variable unit of weight, usually between 0.750/1.65lbs and 1.5 kg/3.3lbs, see also n.67

real — Spanish coinage — calculating the value in modern terms is extremely complicated

šāhiyyāt — low value coin; see Introduction

sanbūsik — pastries stuffed with roast lamb or chicken

sanjaq — (Turkish) administrative division of an Ottoman province, but the term was also used for the *sanjaqbeys* who ruled them

settee — A standard type of single-decked Mediterranean cargo vessel, usually double-masted

shahbandar (Persian) — originally the Port Master in charge of the traders, collecting taxes and settling disputes. Later, as the term spread abroad, it evolved to mean an official overseeing particular communities of traders

shāsh — the scarf of a turban

sibinj — ford or crossing place

sijill — the decree of a judge, or record from a court of justice

sipāhī — (Turkish) members of the Ottoman Turkish cavalry, essentially a military aristocracy

sou — (French) low value coin

tarbush — (Persian/Arabic) or *fez*, a stiff low cylindrical headdress, generally red, at this date used as a turban base and great quantities were exported from N.Africa to the Ottoman Empire

Tarīsī — from Tarīsī, a town in SE Anatolia

trinchetta — (Italian) foresail

tughra — (Turkish) elaborate calligraphic signature of an Ottoman Sultan

'ulama — body of religious scholars learned in religious law and responsible for maintaining Islamic orthodoxy

uthmānī — coin (see Introduction)

yarbū' — jerboa

yāzijī — (Turkish/Arabic) clerk or scribe, perhaps here record keeper

Hannā Diyāb Bibliography (PL)

Abdel-Halim, Muhammad. *Antoine Galland. sa vie et son oeuvre.* (Paris: A.G. Nizet, 1964)

Ambraseys, N. N. , C.P. Melville and R.D. Adams. The Seismicity of Egypt, Arabia and the Red Sea. A Historical Review. (Cambridge: Cambridge University Press, 1994).

Bamford, Paul W. *Fighting Ships and Prisons. The Mediterranean Galleys of France in the Age of Louis XIV.* (Minneapolis: The University of Minnesota Press, 1973).

Berger, Robert W. and Thomas F. Hedin. *Diplomatic Tours in the Gardens of Versailles Under Louis XIV.* (Philadelphia: University of Pennsylvania Press, 2008). [Useful illustrations]

Bluche, François. *Louis XIV.* Trans. Mark Greengrass. (Oxford: Blackwell, 1990). [for le Grand Froid, etc]

Boogert, Maurits H. van den. *Aleppo Observed: Ottoman Syria Through the Eyes of Two Scottish Doctors, Alexander and Patrick Russell.* (Oxford: Oxford University Press, 2010).

Cornette, Joël. *Chronique du Règne de Louis XIV.* (Sedes, 1997).

Dew, Nicholas. *Orientalism in Louis XIV's France.* (Oxford: Oxford University Press, 2009).

Eldem, Edhem. *French Trade in Istanbul in the Eighteenth Century.* (Leiden: Brill, 1999).

Eldem, Edhem, Daniel Goffman and Bruce Masters. *The Ottoman City between East and West. Aleppo, Izmir, and Istanbul.* (Cambridge: Cambridge University Press, 1999).

Elger, Ralf. "Herschaftskritik, Karrierestreben, Djihâd, Das Osmanische Reich und Istanbul in arabischen Reiseberichten des 16. bis 18. Jahrhunderts". In: *Istanbul: vom imperialen Herrschersitz zur Megapolis. Historiographische Betrachtungen zu Gesellschaft, Institutionen und Räumen,* hrsg. von Yavuz Köze. (München 2006, 71-82.)

Elger, Ralf and Yavuz Köze (eds). *Many Ways of Speaking About the Self. Middle Eastern Ego-Documents in Arabic, Persian, and Turkish (14th-20th Century.* (Wiesbaden: Harrassowitz Verlag:2010*).*

Elger, Ralf. *Glaube, Skepsis, Poedsie. Arabische Istanbul-Reisende im 16. und 17. Jahrhundert.* (Beirut /Ergon Verlag Würzburg, 2011).

Gacek, Adam. *Arabic Manuscripts. A Vademecum for Readers.* (Leiden: Brill, 2009)

Gorce, Jérôme de la, *L'Opéra à Paris au temps de Louis XIV. Histoire d'un Théatre.* (Paris, Éditions Desjonquères, 1992).
Greenhalgh, Michael. *Marble Past, Monument Present. Building with Antiquities in the Medieval Mediterranean.* (Leiden/Boston: Brill, 2009.
Greenhalgh, Michael. *Constantinople to Córdoba. Dismantling Ancient Architecture in the East, North Africa and Islamic Spain.* (Leiden: Brill, 2012). [Lemaire, etc]
Khater, Akram Fouad. *Embracing the Divine. Passion and Politics in the Christian Middle East.* (Syracuse, Syracuse University Press, 2011) [Useful background; Abd Allah Qara'ali, Jirmanus Farhat, consuls, dragomans]
Kurat, Akdes Nimet. *The Despatches of Sir Robert Sutton, Ambassador in Constantinople (1710-1714).* (London: Offices of the Royal Historical Society, 1953).
Leeuwen, Richard van. *Notables and Clergy in Mount Lebanon. The Khāzin Sheikhs and the Maronite Church (1736-1840)* (Leiden: E.J.Brill,1994).
Levi, Anthony. *Louis XIV.* (London: Constable, 2004).
Lough, John. *An Introduction to Seventeenth Century France.* (London: Longmans, 1954).
Lough, John. *Locke's Travels in France, 1675-1679.* (New York & London: Garland, 1984).
[Itinerary; great clock at Lyon; Marseille; canal du midi, etc]
____ *France Observed in the Seventeenth Century by British Travellers.* (Stocksfield: Oriel Press, 1985). [very useful for comparison]
Loyau, Marcel.(ed). *Lettres de Madame de Maintenon.* Vol. IV: 1707-1710. (Paris: Honoré Champion, 2011).
____. *Voyage du Sieur paul Lucas au Levant. On y trouvera entr'autre une description de la haute Egypte, suivant le cours du Nil, depuis le Caire jusques aux Cataractes, avec une Carte exacte de ce fleuve, que personne n'avoit donné.* Paris, Guillaume Vandive, 1704; 2 vol.
____ *Voyage du Sieur paul Lucas, fait par ordre du Roi dans la Grèce, l'Asie Mineure, la Macédoine et l'Afrique.* Nicolas Simart, Paris, 1712; 2 vol.
____ *Voyage du Sieur Paul Lucas, fait en 1714... dans la Turquie, l'Asie, la Syrie, la Palestine, la Haute et la Basse-Égypte, etc...,* Rouen, R. Machuel le jeune, 1719; 3 vol.
MacDonald, D.B. "Ali Baba and the Forty Thieves in Arabic from a Bodleian MS." JRAS 64 (1910), pp. 327-386.

____ Further Notes on "Ali Baba and the Forty Thieves". JRAS 67 (1913), pp.41-53.

Maintenon, Madame de. *Lettres de Madame de Maintenon.* Ed. Marcel Loyau, Vol. 1707-1710. (Paris: Honoré Champion, 2011).

Monahan, W. Gregory. *Year of Sorrows: The Great Famine of 1709 in Lyon.* (Columbus, Ohio: Ohio State University Press, 1993).

Omont, Henri Auguste. *Journal parisien d'Antoine Galland (1705-1715).* Précédé de son autobiographie (1646-1715). Mémoires de la société de l'Histoire de Paris et de l'Isle-de-France, tome XLVI. (Paris, 1919).

Peter, Jean. *L'Artillerie et les Fonderies de la Marine sous Louis XIV.* (Paris: Economica, 1995).

Pouradier Duteil-Loizidou. Anna. *Consulat de France à Larnaca. Documents inédits pour servir à l'histoire de Chyrpre.* Tome IV (1703-1705). (Nicosie: Centre de Recherche Scientifiques, 2002). Tome V (1706-1708), (2006).

____ "Un antiquaire français à Chypre malgré lui". *Epetiris tou Kentron Epistimonikon Ereinon,* Tome XXV (1999), pp. 171-181.

Princess Palatine (Elisabeth-Charlotte of Bavaria, duchesse d'Orléans). *Lettres de Madame, duchesse d'Orleans.* Ed. Olivier Amiel. (Paris: Mercure de France, 1982).

Rado, Sevket. *Paris'te bir osmanli seferi. Yirmiswekiz çelebi'nin Fransa seyahatnamesi.* (Istanbul: Türkiye Bankası kültür yayiniari, 2008).

Revault, Jacques. *Le Fondouk des François et les Consuls de France (1660-1860).* (Tunis: Éditions Récherches sur les Civilisations, 1984)

Rowlands, Guy. *The Financial Decline of a Great Power. War, Influence, and Money in Louis XIV's France.* (Oxford: Oxford University Press, 2012).

Saint-Simon, duc de. Ed. and trans. Lucy Norton. *Historical Memoirs of the Duc de Saint-Simon. Vol. 1: 1691-1709.* (London: Hamish Hamilton, 1967)

Schwab, Raymond. *L'auteur des milles et une nuit.* (Paris: Mercure de France, 1983).

Sheehan, J.H. *Philippe, Duke of Orleans, Regemt of France 1715-1723.* (London: Thames and Hudson, 1979).

Venture de Paradis, Jean-Michel. *Tunis et Alger au XVIIIe siècle. Mémoires et observations rassemblés et présentés oar Jacques Cuoq.* (Paris: Sindbad, 1983). [Bardo; Beys and Deys; military organisation]

Weiss, Gillian. *Captives and Corsairs. France and Slavery in the Early Modern Mediterranean.* Stanford: Stanford University Press, 2011).

Yirmisekiz Çelebi Mehmed effendi. *Le Paradis des Infidèles. Relation de Yirmisekiz Çelebi Mehmed effendi, ambassadeur ottoman en France sous le Régence.* Traduit de l'ottoman par Julien-Claude Galland. Introduction, notes, textes annexes par Gilles Veinstein. (Paris: François Maspero.1981).

Additional Bibliography (CS)

Adahl, Karin, *The Sultan's Procession: The Swedish Embassy to Sultan Mehmed IV in 1657-1658 and the Rålamb Paintings*, Swedish Research Institute in Istanbul. (Istanbul, 2006).

Aïssé, Charlotte, *Lettres*, ed. Voltaire. (Paris, 1787).

Anderson, Sonia, P. *An English consul in Turkey: Paul Rycaut at Smyrna, 1667-1678*. (Oxford University Press, 1989).

Belon, Pierre, trans. James Hogarth, *Travels in the Levant: The Observations of Pierre Belon of Le Mans on Many Singularities and Memorable Things Found in Greece, Turkey, Judaea* (Hardinge Simpole, 2012)

Burton, Robert, *The Anatomy of Melancholy*. Vol. II. Ed. Nicolas K. Kiessling, Thomas C. Falkner and Rhonda Blair. (Oxford: Clarendon Press, 1990).

Caruso, Carlo, *The Life of Texts: Evidence in Textual Production, Transmission and Reception*. (Bloomsbury, London, 2018).

Chick, H., ed. and tr. *A Chronicle of the Carmelites in Persia: The Safavids and the Papal Mission of the 17th and 18th Centuries*. (I.B.Tauris, London, 2012).

Davis, R., *Aleppo and Devonshire Square*. (London, 1967).

Dew, Nicholas, *Orientalism in Louis XIV's France*. (McGill University, 2009). On-line at www.academia.edu

Fournier, Joseph, *La Chambre de Commerce de Marseille et ses représentants permanents à Paris, 1599-1875 : étude historique et documents inédits*. (Barlatier, Marseille, 1920).

Frangakis-Syrett Elena, *Trade practices in Aleppo in the middle of the 18th century : the case of a British merchant* in: Revue du monde musulman et de la Méditerranée, n°62, 1991, pp. 123-132. On-line at www.persee.fr

Garritt Van Dyk, *The Embassy of Soliman Aga to Louis XIV: Diplomacy, Dress, and Diamonds*. On-line at www.emajartjournal.files.wordpress.com

Göçek, Fatma Müge, *East Encounters West: France and the Ottoman Empire in the Eighteenth century*. (Oxford University Press, 1987).

Goyau, Georges, *Un précurseur: François Picquet, Consul de Louis XIV en Alep et Evêque de Babylone*, Bibliothèque Orientale — Tome II, Institut Français de Damas. (Paris, 1942).

'Hanna Dyâb, D'Alep à Paris: *Les pérégrinations d'un jeune syrien au*

temps de Louis XIV, ed. and trans. by Paule Fahmé-Thiéry, Bernard Heyberger, and Jérôme Lentin. (Paris: Sindbad, 2015).
Irwin, Robert, *The Arabian Nights: A Companion*. (Penguin, London, 1995).
Lachiver, Marcel, *Les Années de misère : la famine au temps du Grand Roi, 1680-1720*. (Fayard, Paris, 1991).
Lamprakos, Michele, *Life in the Khans: the Venetians in Early Ottoman Aleppo* in Muqarnas, (Brill, Leiden 2017). On-line at www.academia.edu
Lemos Horta, Paulo, *Marvellous Thieves*. (Harvard University Press, 2017)
Locke, John, *John Locke's Travels in France 1675-1679*. (New York & London: Garland Publishing, 1984)
Lunde, Paul, *Arabic and the Art of Printing* (ARAMCO World, March/April, 1981). On-line at www.aramcoworld.com
____. *A Turk at Versailles*. (ARAMCO World, Nov/Dec, 1993). On-line at www.aramcoworld.com
Mehmed efendi, *Le paradis des infidèles*, [1720-21], tr. Julienne-Claude Galland [1757]. (FM, Paris, 1981)
Rycaut, Paul, *The Present State of the Ottoman Empire*. (Printed for C. Brome, London, 1665)
Sint Nicolaas, Eveline et al, *Jean-Baptiste Vanmour: an Eyewitness to the Tulip Era*. (KoçBank, Istanbul, no date)
Stone, Caroline, *An "Extreamly Civile" Diplomacy*. (ARAMCO World, Jan/Feb, 2012). On-line at www.aramcoworld.com
ter Meetelen, Maria, *The Curious and Amazing Adventures of Maria ter Meetelen, Twelve Years a Slave (1731-43)*, tr. Caroline Stone with Karen Johnson. (Hardinge Simpole, 2010). [On corsairs and white slavery in North Africa]
Tsiptsios, Lukas, *Les consuls français au Levant*. On-line at www.lesclesdumoyenorient.com
www.thejanissaryarchives.wordpress.com

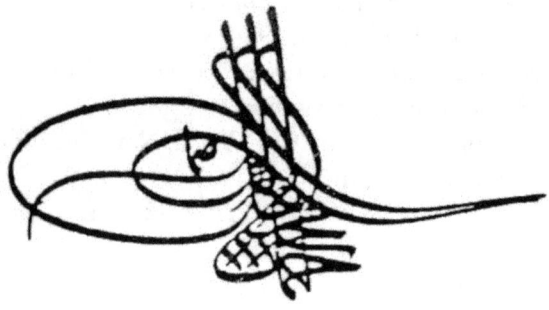

The Tughra. or official signature, of Sultan Ahmed III

Index

A

'Abd Allah 11, 267
Abu Zayt 270
Abyssinia 43
Adana 259, 262, 265, 291
Adonis xxix
Afiyun Qara Hisar 237, 238, 243, 248, 251, 253, 290
Africa xxxi, 60, 64, 76, 84, 102, 195, 211, 280, 281, 286, 300, 301, 303, 307
agha 18, 30, 31, 235, 244, 259, 260, 261, 262, 277, 299
Ahmed III xxxvii, 289
Aissé, Charlotte xxxvii
Aix 139
Aladdin i, iii, ix, xliii, 1
al-'Ayn 265
Aleppo passim
Alexandretta 211, 212, 214, 265, 267
Alexandria 29, 30, 31, 32, 36, 49, 52, 61, 277
Algiers xxvii, xxxii
al-Halabī 18
Ali Baba and the Forty Thieves xliii, 303, 304
Ali Cogia Merchant of Baghdad xliii
al-Jawharjī, Yūsuf 197
al-Khāzin, Hannā 17, 18
alKhidr xxix
al-Mabūdī, Yūsuf 3
al-Mukāhil, Yūsuf 18
al-Zaghbī, Hannā 232, 237, 244
'Antāb 270, 272, 273
Antioch 258, 265, 266
Anton (Antūn) 256, 264, 267
Arab vii, xv, xx, xxvii, 250, 277, 281, 285
Aragon xvii
Aramaic xiii, 278
Arkalī 262

Armenia xxiv, 12
armoury 114
arrack 225, 249, 265
Arsaniyus 8
Arsenal xxxii
asqām 81, 299
Asyūtī cloth 44
Asyūtī linen 33
awādlaq 237, 238, 290
Azāt 226

B

Baalbec xxiv
Bāb al-Humāyūn 226
Badr al-Budur xliii
Baghdad xxiv, xliii
bagnios xxxi
Balan 15
baldachin 162, 163
Balkans xxix, xxxvii
Banfay, M. xx, 137, 256
Barbary xxxi, 53, 163
Barbary pirates xxxi
Bardo 83, 304
barjāwāt 179, 299
bash agha 235, 299
Bashi 248
basīsa 57, 299
bawāsī 80, 299
Bayas 264
Baydāw. 255
Bazan, M. xx, 137, 256
Bedouin 14, 42, 56, 63
Beg Oghlu 224, 229
Beirut xxix, 18, 20, 277, 302
Belon, Pierre xxvii
ben Aisha, Abdallah xxxii
berat 73, 299
Berbers 52, 53

bīrū fīlūsūfa 90, 299
bitumen xxvii, 30
Blind Baba Abdalla, The xliii
Borj er-Rous xxix, 281
bostānjī 251, 252, 253, 290, 299
bottarga 265, 299
Bourbons xl
Bourgogne 142, 147, 149
Bremond, Captain xxiv, xxxi, 98, 99, 100, 105
Britain xl
broadcloth xxv, 93, 164, 205, 206, 210, 215, 228, 267, 268, 269, 291
Bsharra 8, 11
Bulaq 36
Burton, Richard xlv, 306
Buyuk Jakmajā 221, 222

C

Cairo 30, 33, 34, 36, 37, 38, 41, 42, 43, 51, 278, 297
capitana 131
Capuchin 18, 85, 105, 220
Carmelite 16
Catholic xiii, xv, xvii, xxxi, 12, 23, 26, 27, 107, 168, 277, 283, 288
cavalier 17, 62
Cave of the Slave 32, 270, 271
Čelebi 286
Čelebi, Paolo 161, 163, 286
Čelebi, Shukrī ibn Shāhīn 226
Cervantes, Miguel de xxxi
Chalkis xxiii
Charles XII xxix, xxxix
Chillon, M xx, 123
Christina of Sweden xxvii
Christofle 161, 201, 208
chrysolite 36, 38, 278
Church of Rome xiii
Church of the Holy Sepulchre xxxvii
Circassians 76, 93
City of Gold, The xliii
Clothing ix, xxv
cloth merchant xxv

Cogia Hassan Alhabbal xliii
Colbert, Jean-Baptiste xvii, xlv, 284
Comédie 176
Constantinople xxix, 277, 292, 293, 294, 295, 296, 297, 298, 303
Copts 37, 44, 51, 279
Corpus Domini 97
Corsica 94, 96
Crusades xxix
Cyprus 22, 23, 24, 30, 277

D

Damascus xxii, xxiv, 107, 283
Damietta 34
darūr 261, 299
de Bonnac, Marquis xxxvii
de Bourgogne, Duc 147, 149
de Ferriol, Charles xxiv, xxxv, xxxix, 288, 292, 293, 295, 296, 297, 298
Deir Qannoubine xv
de Maintenon, Madame 151, 152, 155, 283, 285, 303, 304
dil 53, 299
dirhams xxv, 98, 107, 116, 237, 242, 299
Djerba xxix, 281
doge xxxii, xxxiv
dollar xxvii
dragoman, dragomans 28, 39, 67, 70, 71, 72, 73, 84, 170, 171, 175, 216, 220, 221, 223, 228, 303
Dragut (Turgut Reis) xxxi
Druse xv
ducat xxv, 299
Duquesne, Abraham xxxii, 283
Duran, M xx, 34
Durasso xxxiv
d'Usson, Jean-Louis xxxvii

E

ebru 237, 290, 299
écu xxv, 197, 205, 287, 299
Edward III xxix

Egypt ix, xxiv, xxvii, 29, 30, 35, 40,
    42, 43, 44, 48, 50, 86, 143, 145, 146,
    220, 245, 278, 281, 299, 302
Egyptian xxvii, 15, 19, 41, 52, 251,
    278, 282
Elias, Father 16
Empress Helena xxix
Encircling Sea 33
Enchanted Horse, the xliii
escudo xxv, 299
Eskidar 237, 238, 248
Eski Shahr 243, 248
Eski Sham 97
Estrangelo 37, 45, 278
Ethiopia xxix

F

Fagon, M. 146, 285
fals xxv, 44, 299
Farhat, Germanus xv, 303
Fayoum 43, 44, 48, 51
Festival of St Michael x, 201
firmān 73, 98, 99, 100, 106, 116, 117,
    118, 207, 209, 210, 211, 222, 236,
    281, 299, 300
fish 17, 32, 33, 44, 53, 77, 120, 214,
    221, 265
Flanders 169
flea 51
Flemings 222, 223, 224, 288
Florence 115, 119
Flushing xxiv
Fondouk des Français xvii
Fournier, Joseph xx, 306
Foy-Vaillant, Jean xxvii
France passim
Franciscan Fathers 23

G

Galata x, 223, 225, 226, 228, 229,
    230, 288, 290
Galland, Antoine ix, x, xxiv, xxxix, xl,
    xliii, 196, 302, 304, 307
Gallipoli 221

Genoa ix, xvii, xxxii, xxxiv, 125, 126,
    127, 128, 129, 283
Germanus, Abbot xv, 6
Ghuzz 36, 37
gold 15, 20, 47, 49, 74, 78, 80, 108, 123,
    131, 139, 147, 159, 162, 171, 178,
    227, 228, 237, 279, 283, 287, 299
Gold Market 269
Grand Vizier xxxv, xxxix, 208, 216, 222,
    227, 228, 235, 236, 250, 251, 277, 297
Greek xv, xlv, 23, 25, 26, 27, 29, 31,
    32, 49, 90, 232, 277, 288, 289

H

hajj 250
hakawātī xxii, xliii
Hammamet 80
Hannā passim
Hapsburgs xxxii, xl, 217
harem 26, 28, 47, 67, 68, 226, 241,
    244, 245
Harun al-Rachid xliii
Hassan, seller of Ptisane xliii
Hayram 266
Hebrew 45, 278
hijāb 109, 300
Hisar 237, 238, 243, 248, 251, 253, 290
Hôtel de Dieu 164, 166
Huguenots 168, 169, 170
hujja 70, 300

I

Ibn al-Qārī 226
ibn Qara'alī, 'Abd Allah 11
icon 120, 124, 125, 141, 177, 178, 206
Indian Ocean 33
inflation 196
Invrea, Luca Maria xxxiv
Isfahan xxiv, 107
ISIS xxix
Islam 72
Ismā'īlī 75
Italian xvii, xxxvii, xlv, 14, 23, 26, 95,
    198, 211, 236, 299, 301

311

Italy xv, 94, 169
iwān 83

J

Jabal Druze 20
Jacob 44
jadīd xxv, 44, 300
Janissaries' Gate 42
janissary 72, 73, 225, 244, 251, 281
jarq xxv, 195, 300
jarqāt 265, 300
Jasr al-Shughl 15
Jerba (Djerba) 74, 76, 281
jerboa xiii, 146, 282, 301
Jerusalem 12, 20, 21, 22, 107, 135, 163, 208, 259, 262
Joseph's Canal 44, 51
Joseph the Jeweller x, 197, 198, 203
Jurudī wine 142

K

kabak 78, 300
Kaftīn 12, 15, 268, 276
Kālīmīra 24
Kanākiya 270
kavuk 70, 71, 72, 73, 143, 300
Kawarkoy 238
Kerala xxix
khan 16, 20, 21, 35, 38, 42, 82, 85, 226, 237, 276, 279, 289, 300
Khan al-'Asal 266
Khan al-Banadiq xvii
Khan al-Ghamīdā 15
Khan al-Zayt 276
Khanāqīyya 270, 271, 272, 291
kharīsāna 107, 108, 283, 300
khizmatkār 231, 300
khoja passim
Kisruwān 18
Kiz Kulasi 224
Konya 252, 253, 259
körek 95, 300
kūn 52, 300
kuzdāšī 261, 300

L

la'ab al-hakam 178, 287, 300
Larnaca 23, 24, 28, 29, 30, 304
Latin xiii, xv, 76, 287, 291, 295
lazaretto 99, 100, 101, 103, 108
Lebanese 3
Lebanon xiii, xv, 142, 275, 276, 277, 303
Le Grand Hiver ix, xl, 288
Leigh-Fermor, Patrick xxii
Lemaire, Consul xx, xxiv, 61, 62, 63, 64, 70, 73, 293, 303
Lercari Imperiale, Francesco Maria xxxiv
Levant and Levantine passim
Libya xvii, xxiv, 281, 282
Limassol 30
Livorno xvii, xxiii, 93, 94, 98, 105, 108, 115, 116, 117, 123, 126, 216, 293, 294
Locke, John xxxii, xxxiv, xxxv, 303, 307
Louis XIV xiii, xxiv, xxvii, xxix, xxxii, xxxiv, xlv, 128, 284, 285, 286, 302, 303, 304, 306, 307
Lyons ix, xxxiv

M

ma'āsh 33, 34, 36, 43, 300
mabkhūša 269, 291, 300
Maghrib ix, 52, 53, 62, 75
Maghribi 52, 54, 55, 56, 57, 60, 300
Malplaquet xl, 283
Malta xxxii, xxxvii, 62, 108, 221, 280
Manshan 143
Marāmāt 40
Margarita, daughter of Consul Lemaire 71
marlūs 135
Maronite vii, xiii, xv, xxiii, 13, 25, 106, 146, 163, 232, 275, 276, 303
Maronites ix, xiii, xv, xx, 18, 21, 25, 277
Marseille passim
Martaban 75, 76, 281
Mehmed Efendi xxix
Messina 67, 125

Milan xxxii
Mīrū, Hannā 264
Missis 260, 262
mithqāl 75, 281, 300
Molière xxxix
Monardes, Nicolas xlv
Montague xxix
Montenero ix, xxii, xxxv, 119, 120, 121, 122, 123, 124, 125
Morea 218
Morocco xxxii
mosque xxix, 27, 227, 289
Mosul vii, xxix
moustaches 31, 105, 148, 194
Mt Sinai 42
mummia xxvii, 279
mummies xxvii, 40, 41, 42, 279
Muski quarter 36, 40, 51
Muslim vii, xx, xxv, xxxi, xxxii, xxxix, 13, 19, 20, 27, 150, 219, 234, 286, 289, 290, 299, 300
Muslims xxix, xxxii, 27, 28, 52, 77, 204, 219, 234, 279, 283, 290

N

Nabi Jurjis xxix
Nasīf Pasha 250, 251, 258
Negroponte xxiii
Netherlands xl
Nicolas, son of Consul Lemaire 69, 70, 71, 73
Nicolas the painter 158, 159
Nicosia 23
Nile 33, 34, 35, 36, 43, 44, 51, 278, 279, 300
Niš xxxi
North Africa xxxi, 60, 64, 84, 102, 195, 211, 280, 281, 286, 300, 303, 307
Notre-Dame 161, 284
nūlīya 221, 300
numismatics ix, xxv, xxvii, 276

O

odabashi 16, 300
oka 237, 256, 300
Opéra 171, 303
Orléans, duc de xxxvii, 149, 168, 304
Orléans, duchesse de xl, 149, 151
Ottoman passim

P

Palace of Pharoah 36
Paphos 30
paras xxv, 28, 44, 39, 46, 211, 265, 266, 269, 294, 300
pasha 26, 28, 71, 237, 238, 239, 240, 242, 243, 244, 245, 246, 247, 248, 250, 251, 252, 253, 290
Paul's Gate 266
Persia xxvii, 197, 277, 284, 289, 306
Philip II xxxvii
Philip V xxiv
Philosopher's Stone, The 90
Pidou de Saint-Olon xxxii
pigs 24, 30
pinque 52, 300
piracy xxiv, 281
Pontchartrain, Jérôme, Comte de xvii, 137, 144, 170, 284, 294, 295, 296, 297, 298
Pont St Michel 155
Pouqueville, François xxix
Prince Ahmad and the Fairy xliii
Prior Germanus xv
Prophet George xxix
Prophet Muhammad xxii, xxv
Protestant xxxi, xl
Provence x, xxxii, 139, 142
Prussia xl

Q

qabījī 250, 251, 252, 253, 255, 256, 257, 258, 259
qablūja 243, 300

Qadisha xv
qalpaq 19, 72, 73, 143, 148, 240, 301
Qamr al-Din xliii
Qannoubine xv
qāqūn 47, 301
Qarāniq Qabī Pass 263
qaysarīyya 249, 250, 251, 301
qaz'an kebab 47, 301
qonaqjī 248, 301
Qozhaya xv
quintal 30
Qur'an xxix

R

Rambaut, M. 136, 137, 230, 231, 256
Ramla 36
Ramuset, M. xx, 16, 21, 230, 276
Ra's al-Nahr 275
ratl 56, 104, 195
reals vii, xxv, xxxvii, xxxix, 38, 39, 95, 96, 98, 136, 140, 158, 172, 281, 301
Rhodes xxxii, 294
rhubarb 107
Rimbaud, M. xx
Rome xiii, xv, 70, 107, 108, 134
Rosetta 34, 35, 41, 52
Roux, M. xx, 137, 256
Ruman, M. 16

S

Sāhib al-Hithām 227
šāhiyyāt xxv, 202, 301
Sa'īd, Upper Egypt 44
Sâi'd Efendi xxxix
St Catherine xv
Saint Denis 152
St George ix, xxix, 18
St Michael x, 201, 202
St Paul 27, 291
St Peter 27, 188, 287
St Yash 16
Samānī 44

Samatan xx, 212, 213
sanjaq 36, 39, 42, 43, 44, 45, 46, 47, 48, 50, 51, 301
sash xxv, 3, 4, 12, 13, 18, 70, 71, 72, 98, 261, 267
Sauron, M xx, 12, 13, 256
Sayyida Zghrata 8
Sbath ms collection xxii
Scotland iv, 20
Sentence (punishment) 113, 114, 119, 133, 182, 186, 188, 189
Sephardim xvii
Serbia xxxi
settee 23, 52, 277, 301
Sfax 76
shahbandar 135, 301
Sharif, xxv
shāsh 73, 301
Sicily 217, 281
Sidi Nu'man xliii
Sidon 16, 20, 21, 22, 23, 107
Sidre 53, 280
silk xxv, 139, 143, 290
Simon xiii, xx, 137, 256, 276, 304
Sindbad the Sailor xl
sipāhī 65, 301
skulls xxxi, 4, 15, 75
slave xxxi, xxxvii, 271
slaving xxxi, xxxii, 280
Smyrna 107, 108, 212, 214, 218, 219, 256, 267, 288, 297, 306
sou xxv, 181, 182, 202, 301
Souq Marcopoli xvii
Sousse 77, 80
Spain xxiv, xxxii, xl, 146, 179, 211, 285, 287, 303
Steven the Coffee Maker x, 201, 202
Sublime Porte x, xxv, xxxvii, xxxix, 226, 289
Sudan 43, 280
Süleyman Ağa xxxix
Sultan of France 13, 16, 66, 93, 98, 99, 100, 125, 127, 128, 129, 137, 147, 166, 170, 173, 216, 225, 229, 235, 236
Sultan of Samarkand xliii

sumptuary laws xxv, 276
Sunni 77
Sūq al-Bālistān 226
Sūq Antakīyya 265
Sūq Tawīl 226
Sūs'ānī 265
Sweden xxvii, xxix, xxxix, 236, 289
Syria xvii, xliii, 107, 143, 146, 163, 197, 200, 213, 250, 257, 259, 283, 302
Syriac xiii, xv, 37, 278
Syrian xiii, xl, 107, 115, 143, 201

T

Taliban xxv
tarbushes 98, 101
Ten Wazirs, The xliii
ter Meetelen, Maria xxxi, 307
thaler xxv, xxvii, 15, 259, 276, 290
Thévenot, Melchisédech xlv
Thousand and One Nights ix, xx, xl, xliii, 196
Timur xxix, xxxi
tobacco 34, 47, 104
Topkapi 223, 289
Torah 37, 38
Tower of Skulls xxix, 281
trinchetta 53, 301
tughra 227, 301
Tully, Miss xvii
Tunis xvii, xxiv, 73, 74, 77, 79, 80, 82, 83, 84, 85, 92, 93, 94, 97, 102, 104, 194, 282, 304
turban xxv, 3, 18, 70, 71, 72, 73, 143, 275, 300, 301
Turgut Reis xxxi
Turks xxiii, 18, 36, 39, 278
Two Jealous Sisters xliii

U

'Ulama xxxix
uthmānī xxv, 28, 81, 195, 301

V

Valide Khan 226
Valide Mosque 227
Valley of the Djinn 266
Vanmour, Jean Baptiste, painter xxxv, xxxvii, 307
veil 106, 108, 109, 120, 300
Venetian x, 25, 63, 64, 65, 66, 108, 123, 227, 229, 230, 232, 283, 294
Venetians xvii, xxiii, 64, 277, 307
Venice xvii, xxxiv, 63, 64, 65, 66, 282
Versailles xiii, xxxiv, 143, 144, 153, 155, 170, 202, 203, 206, 207, 210, 302, 307
Vienna xxxvii
Virgin Mary 37, 119, 120, 121, 122, 123, 124, 125, 126, 140, 182, 263, 264
Voltaire xxxvii, 306

W

Wādī al-Sibā' 79
War of the Spanish Succession ix, xl, 283, 288
Western Gate 42

Y

yarbū' 146, 301
yāzijī 53, 54, 56, 95, 96, 222, 301
Yedi Qillah 223

Z

Zamārīyā 163, 201, 208, 286
Zuqāq al-Khall 267

www.ingramcontent.com/pod-product-compliance
Lightning Source LLC
Chambersburg PA
CBHW052044220426
43663CB00012B/2437